LYING IN STATE

To my wife, Janet
– who stuck with it

LYING IN STATE

HOW WHITEHALL DENIES, DISSEMBLES AND DECEIVES

TIM SLESSOR

This revised and enlarged paperback edition
first published 2004 by Aurum Press

Originally published in Great Britain as *Ministries of Deception*
2002 by Aurum Press Ltd
25 Bedford Avenue, London WC1B 3AT

A catalogue record for this book is available from the British Library.

ISBN 1 84513 030 8

1 3 5 7 9 10 8 6 4 2
2004 2006 2008 2007 2005

Designed and typeset by M Rules
Printed and bound in Great Britain by Bookmarque Ltd, Croydon

CONTENTS

PREFACE

I will put some cards face up on the table. First, as will become apparent, I have a thesis. An agenda even. So, while I will try to be fair and reasonably dispassionate, I have no doubt that personal bias will intrude – not always unwittingly. Readers can judge for themselves where I stray, but, given that the signals will be obvious, it should not be difficult.

Second, this book has at least part of its beginnings in frustration. While that is hardly a commendable motive, it can provide a powerful spark. In my case, ignition grew out of the apparent impossibility, over a period of several years, of persuading the authorities in Whitehall with whom I was disputing a small aspect of naval history – the loss in 1940 of the aircraft carrier HMS *Glorious* and her destroyer escorts – that their long-standing account might not be the firmly anchored certainty that has always been claimed. My interest grew from the fact that my father was lost in the incident. Yes, 1940 is a long time ago, but the official version of what happened seems revealing of the way official minds work, even decades later, when they think it necessary to continue smoke-screening an ancient embarrassment. The sinking of those three ships resulted in what was probably the Royal Navy's biggest single loss of life in World War II. Yet everything that went wrong (which was plenty) has always been given an all-too-easy rationale. Further, it seemed to me that if they could continue to deny the possibility of getting things even slightly wrong in that narrative, they could deny it in much more recent ones. So I looked for later, sometimes contemporary, examples of unwarranted Whitehall certainties. And found them. They form the body of this book.

Perhaps, in the wider scheme of things, some of my stories are not so important. But that misses the point. In showing how bureaucratic minds can misinform, sometimes even lie, a small example can be just as illuminating as a big one. In their detail we shall know them. Furthermore, while some of the stories may seem familiar in their outline, in an analysis of their accompanying cover-ups I think they will be much less so.

Third, I am more interested in trying to peel back and pick apart the anatomy of cover-ups (especially those I have chosen for this book) than in getting into a philosophic discussion of just why departments of government dissemble. Much of the time, once they have been found out, it is obvious anyway. So, except for a first, rather discursive chapter about what I call the Whitehall Loop, I have focused on hard cases rather than abstractions, on the exemplary and the anecdotal rather than the theory. But if a general dictum (or two) is needed, it seems that too many inhabitants of Whitehall – both permanent and transitory, mandarins and ministers – will bend the truth where they think it is expedient to do so, and (most important this) where they think they can get away with it. Further, it is almost always the case that a cover-up is more corrupt than the blunder it is trying to hide. The latter may have been due to unthinking incompetence – bad enough. But the cover-up, by definition, is knowingly constructed to deceive. The calculated foul is more deserving of a red card than the merely stupid one.

Beyond that, a deep discussion about fictions in high places – whether, for example, official deceptions are more likely to be before-the-event conspiracies rather than cobbled-together *post hoc* cover-ups – is better left to those best qualified: Westminster journalists and political scientists. Anyway, Machiavelli and others got there a long time ago.

Fourth, I am not much interested (not here anyway) in the more obviously 'political' aspects of dissembling. The spin (and worse) flowing out of party headquarters or certain offices at 10 Downing Street is rather different from that coming out of Whitehall. For starters, one expects it and therefore allows for it. All the same, the difference between political fantasy and official falsehood is becoming increasingly confused as more and more party activists – 'special advisors' – take their places in ministerial outer offices. But, as the civil service remains the same from one election to the next, the misinformation coming out of that side of Whitehall is not particular to a government of either party. As the stories in this book will show, it makes no difference who is in power. The truth is still bent.

Fifth, the fact that most of the stories I have chosen come out of the Ministry of Defence does not mean that compared with other parts of Whitehall (and I use that term in its broad, generic sense) it is more prone to the sins of which I accuse it. But it is one of the biggest of all government departments and therefore probably presents a greater number of examples. Besides, it is where I started, and one thing led to another. But the business of obfuscation and worse is in no way limited to the MOD.

Sixth, our civil servants pride themselves on being as politically impartial and financially incorrupt as any in the world. They are probably right to do so. The rest of us should be grateful. However, in practice neither of those important honesties seems to guarantee a watertight morality in every other direction as well. Civil servants make mistakes they do not want the rest of us to know about. Consequently, too often, they cover up. The cement of departmental loyalty then helps to keep those cover-ups in place. And while one understands the pressures of families, jobs, promotions, pensions and mortgages on would-be whistle-blowers, it seems too easy to blame these pressures. What about the Whitehall system?

Lastly, I am sometimes asked if I have been in direct touch with any of the public servants with whom I have been in dispute. Have I given them a fair chance to reply to the comments and criticisms in this book? Yes and no. I started off that way. I really tried – and have files of correspondence, answered and unanswered, to prove it. Often we did not seem able to agree on what we disagreed about. They accused me of concentrating on irrelevancies; I accused them of avoiding the issues and not answering my questions. At times our exchanges became edgy, even bad-tempered. Neither side found it useful. So, since then, I have not bothered them too often. Digging seemed a better way to spend my time. In any case, my targets are quite big enough to look after themselves. And, whatever *they* think, I am happy to let the reader decide where, in the stories that follow, the balance of fairness lies.

So, enough of the preliminaries.

THE WHITEHALL LOOP

'Unsubstantiated rumour . . . unsupported by the facts'

Investigations into the allegations have revealed them to be a mixture of unsubstantiated rumour, incorrect information or repetition of earlier allegations which have been fully investigated and found to be unsupported by the facts.

A QUESTION: WAS THE OFFICIAL statement above aimed at refuting public disquiet about (1) the efficacy of measures taken against Foot and Mouth, (2) the reliability of the army's SA80 rifle and radio sets in Kosovo and Sierra Leone, (3) a government order that police should keep protesters out of sight during the state visit of the President of China, (4) the possibility that BSE can cross the species barrier to humans, (5) the loss of an RAF Chinook helicopter and twenty-five security personnel on the Mull of Kintyre, (6) the existence of illnesses collectively known as Gulf War Syndrome, (7) the 1970s export to Iraq of machine tools capable of arms manufacture, (8) the circumstances surrounding the torpedoing of the *Belgrano*, (9) the radiation sickness claimed by some participants in the British atomic tests of the 1950s, (10) experiments carried out at Porton Down during the same period (11) the denial of full pensions to thousands of disabled ex-servicemen (and their widows) for over fifty years, or, going even further back, (12) the loss of the carrier HMS *Glorious* and her two escorts in 1940? Or what about, most famously of all, (13) the BBC's assertion that Downing Street had been much less than honest in claiming that Saddam Hussein had the undoubted ability to make ready and launch weapons of mass destruction within forty-five minutes?

The answer is that the statement was made by the Ministry of Defence in December 1994 to refute a body of opinion that there might, indeed, be a condition commonly referred to as Gulf War Syndrome. But it could just as well have been the official answer to those who have suggested that there might be problems with the SA80 rifle, or those others intimating that the crash of the RAF Chinook may not have been due to the 'gross negligence' of the two pilots, as in the official verdict. Indeed, with only minor alterations to the basic message – that Whitehall knows best and everyone else is either ill-informed or making mischief – the denying sentiments above have been applied to all the random examples just listed. And many more. Yet in almost every case, usually as a result of whistle-blowing, media investigation or inconvenient MPs asking the right questions, Whitehall's scorn – 'unsubstantiated rumour . . . unsupported by the facts' – poured on so many conclusions that contradict its own official certainties has turned out to be ill-advised.

In fact, one can go further: in some cases one is looking at deliberate dissembling. It is not just that deceptions, even lies, are knowingly told that is shocking; it is the realization that our system *allows*, sometimes encourages them to be told. Fundamental to that system is what might be called the Whitehall Loop. At its simplest, this is the closed-circuit procedure where, in reply to questions asked of a government department or minister, the answers are put together by the very same civil servants whose earlier judgement is both the subject and the cause of the inquiry in the first place. It is an arrangement by which, in too many controversies, the inhabitants of Whitehall decide the rules and which cards they will then allow into play. They decide what is relevant and what is not. They advise the minister accordingly. Too frequently, they seem not to be accountable for these decisions to anyone but themselves. We will come to the details later.

Clearly, there is a problem. Hardly a week goes by without another spin being given to the public's accelerating cynicism about almost *any* response made by *any* government department to *any* controversy, even if it turns out – as it sometimes does – to have been right. Indeed, the credibility gap is now so large that almost any denying statement from Whitehall merely serves to widen that gap even further. The claim that MMR involves no risk to small children, though probably true, has caused a reflex spasm of suspicion across a large section of the public. In short, dissembling or, at the least, manipulation is now perceived to be very close to the norm. In a democracy such scepticism must be highly corrosive. Distrust begets a dysfunctional society – which is what, in the view of many, we are becoming. Or have already become. Perhaps that is one reason why, in Britain, anything approaching a 60 per cent vote at a General Election is now reckoned to be a good turnout. We are not just bored; we are disillusioned. And it is not only the politicians who are to blame. Whitehall is also deeply involved.

Of course, one can be cynical (and plenty of people are) in holding the view that a tendency to deceive is born in all of us, that it is part of our hard wiring. 'So what do you expect? It comes in our genes – particularly in the genes of the would-be governing elite. It's to do with Darwin and All That.' Certainly, subterfuge is inbuilt in nature. Each new generation of cuckoos depends on it. Fireflies are fraudsters. So are lyrebirds. Why do some butterflies have 'eyes' on their wings? What is a tiger's camouflage but disguise, a form of clever cheating? But those are deceptions over which the hosts have no control. Indeed, they are there to perpetuate the species. But what about *Homo sapiens*? His deceits seem to be on a different level; they are knowing and deliberate. Intriguingly, it is said that the inability to lie is a frequent characteristic of autism. Maybe that is what makes some autistic children so lovable; what you see is what you get. But what does that say about the rest of us? Surely dissembling, from mere spin all the way to the barefaced lie, is something we can all do very easily. But it requires a conscious decision. Where things get really interesting is when someone tells himself, or a whole group of someones all tell each other, the same half-truth or 'misinformation' or lie so frequently that they eventually come to think of it as the truth. They believe their own propaganda. The self-delusion becomes so hardened that if they were wired up to a lie detector, the needle would not even flicker. The phenomenon is an aspect of what has been called 'groupthink'. Not surprisingly, these people get bad-tempered when the rest of us refuse to believe their confident assurances. Examples of this occur in every story in this book. Besides, to suppose that there is no real difference between deceiving and the mere ability to do so is to be either deeply cynical or very deterministic indeed.

Official dissembling has been around for a very long time. Furthermore, bureaucratic deception is not confined to central government in Whitehall and Westminster. One thinks of the occasions when a senior executive of a social services department or an NHS trust reassures enquirers with a 'nothing-wrong-here' explanation – until public disquiet raises a sufficient head of steam to provoke a public inquiry. And then, as like as not, it is found that, yes indeed, there is cause for concern. Too many babies *were* dying, and had been for some time. Further, it often turns out that the problem had long been quietly recognized – in-house. Maybe it was hoped that if no one talked too loudly, the 'complication' would sort itself out. That example illustrates an interesting facet of this whole subject. Obviously, there never was a plot to kill babies. Or even to let them die. But once it is realized by the hospital that too high a proportion has not been surviving, and that therefore reputations and even jobs may be involved, the official reflex is to look for an alibi. Too often, that will entail coming up with an explanation to which everyone on 'the inside' is expected to sign up. It will entail both finding a justification for what went wrong in the first place, and also a rationale for why nothing was then done about it. All this presumes a degree of co-ordination. To some this is merely 'harmonizing a response'. To others it is somewhere near a conspiracy. So first, the cock-up. Then the cover-up.

But sitting-round-a-table conspiracies are often not necessary because, most of the time, there is no need for them. The culture of the place is enough. Bureaucrats know what is expected of them without being told. 'Mustn't let the side down.' It is much better that way because it allows all involved to claim that there was no overt (or covert) co-ordination. So there was no conspiracy. And if there was no conspiracy, *ergo*, there cannot have been a cover-up. At least that is the way the argument often seems to go.

There are many motives for dissembling. One of the most obvious rests in human nature: none of us likes to admit that we might be wrong, least of all our rulers – whether they are elected politicians or non-elected officials. In admitting a deceit (let alone acknowledging an initial cock-up, blunder or whatever) both groups have too much to lose: self-esteem, prestige, authority, and even, though rarely, their jobs. Further, the stronger and more unequivocal a 'denying' announcement becomes, the more difficult it is for the administration that made it in the first place to climb down later. If pressed, authority will almost always prefer to pump out an even thicker smoke screen. In Whitehall the bureaucrats are not set much of an example by their nominal masters, the ministers. How often does one hear a member of the government (any government) admitting that he or she was wrong? In the West we persuade ourselves that it is only the mandarins east of Suez who are concerned about 'face'.

So how have spin, obfuscation, half-truths and even lies become such a part of the nation's administration? Is it that the mandarins and ministers have a natural and particular propensity for deception? Is it really in their genes? Probably not. But, given that the system – the Whitehall Loop – gives them good protection from outside scrutiny, they certainly have a greater range of opportunities for dissembling than exist in most other large organizations. And opportunity tends to breed aptitude. It may even be habit-forming, and then it becomes part of the culture. Certainly, there are not many disincentives. As the stories in this book will show, Whitehall falls back on 'economies of the truth' to a greater or lesser extent for all kinds of reasons: to hide a future plan of action, to disguise the implementation of an existing one, to give the impression that things are better than they really are, to get out of a compromising impasse (often caused by an earlier cover-up), and, most frequently of all, to hide the embarrassment of some fiasco or incompetence – damage limitation. There is no shortage of reasons. There is no shortage of implementing techniques either. In this book I have identified them as Whitehall's SODEMs (Standard Offensive/Defensive/Evasive Measures). It seems an appropriate label. Interestingly, the whole business of official deception has now become so well recognized that its formal study made up a strand in the syllabus of undergraduates reading for a degree in politics. The University of Leeds offered a third-year course with the uncompromising title of 'The Politics of Lying'. Most of the case studies were drawn from contemporary Britain. Despite the fact that the course was always oversubscribed, it has recently been suspended due to 'lack of funds'. One wonders.

The activities of Whitehall are well fortified against inquisitive outsiders – and thereby, indirectly, against the electorate. To find out what is really going on in cases where the inmates would prefer otherwise (except in special situations like the Hutton Inquiry) one must burrow, sapper-like, under the ramparts of secrecy and obfuscation. The penalties if one is caught are not in the category of boiling oil, but they can still be severe.

A wall of secrecy, or confidentiality at the least, is obviously necessary in some parts of almost any effective administration – government or commercial. But even where it is quite inessential, much of the business of Whitehall is still conducted on a defined basis of only-those-who-need-to-know. And 'they' decide who needs to know. The fewer the better. In some areas the policy is reinforced by the Official Secrets Act under which a minister (probably on the advice of senior civil servants) can declare almost anything to be a secret if he so wishes – even his department's blunders and misdemeanours. Indeed, *especially* its blunders and misdemeanours. There is not much a civil servant with a troubled conscience (and many certainly exist) can do about that kind of cover-up. Whistle-blowing can lead to the sack. In fact, it is one of the few things that can. Constitutionally, civil servants owe no loyalty other than to their minister, and, non-constitutionally but even more powerfully, to their departmental colleagues. They are certainly not accountable to the allegedly sovereign body of Parliament. Indeed, for a civil servant to let MPs know that they are being fed less than the truth, even when nothing more serious than ministerial embarrassment might be involved, can be a criminal offence – as Clive Ponting famously found out.

After an Old Bailey jury had 'wrongly and perversely' acquitted Clive Ponting (the adverbs belong to Michael Heseltine, a minister directly involved) of leaking to an MP some non-classified truths about the sinking of the *Belgrano* that the MP had consistently been denied – because they were an embarrassment to the government – the already draconian Official Secrets Act was further tightened.[1] A jury would not be allowed to get things so wrong again. Today, Ponting's defence, that his action had 'not been contrary to the national interest' (the jury evidently agreed with him), would be a non-starter. In effect, the national interest and the government's interest have now become, constitutionally

1. Michael Heseltine's comments are found in his book *Life in the Jungle* (Hodder & Stoughton, 2000).

and *de jure*, the same thing. Had he lived, there is no doubt that Dr David Kelly would have been very forcibly reminded of this by his MOD bosses.

Whitehall has other 'safeguards' it can use to prevent unwelcome exposures. D Notices can be invoked. In the area of national security, they are usually, but not always, warranted. 'Commercial confidentiality' is another device – sometimes more convenient than justified. Another tactic lies in the Public Interest Immunity Certificate. This was originally intended to prevent the disclosure of information to an open court when, for example, intelligence methods might be compromised. In the Matrix Churchill affair (where the Department of Trade and Industry and MOD had earlier turned a blind eye to machine-tool exports to Iraq because, for reasons of intelligence gathering, it was reasonable to do so) an attempt to use PIICs was made in order to hide a number of subsequent Whitehall blunders and embarrassments.[2] Four of the most relevant ministers (at the Home Office, the MOD, the Foreign and Commonwealth Office and the DTI) were urged by senior civil servants – who had at least as much to lose as the ministers if the truth got out – to sign Public Interest Immunity Certificates. The PIICs would have denied key information to the defence of the accused businessmen in the forthcoming trial. But Michael Heseltine, newly arrived at the DTI and perhaps not fully up to speed on the background, jibbed at signing the PIICs put on his desk by his staff. Indeed, it was the very strength with which those senior advisors insisted he should sign that aroused his suspicion. As Heseltine puts it in his book *Life in the Jungle*, 'The more they argued, the more concerned I became that here was an example of Whitehall protecting its own.' Evidently, even a minister can come up against the Loop.

The inescapable fact was that there were those in Whitehall who were prepared to see the directors of Matrix Churchill go to jail rather than have their own misjudgements (and, just as important, the covering-up of those misjudgements) embarrassingly revealed. Had it not been for some stupid mistakes on the one side and some sharp legal probing by

2. *Report of the Inquiry into the Export of Defence Equipment and Dual-use Goods to Iraq and related prosecutions*, Scott Inquiry (HMSO, 1996).

the other, the deceits might have held. The trial collapsed – not least because Heseltine informed the judge of his disquiet, and because of a forced admíssion by Alan Clark (an ex-minister at the DTI) that previously he had been 'economical with the *actualité*'.

After the Gulf War, such was the parliamentary and public row about the whole business of our exports to Iraq that John Major was forced to authorize a full-blown inquiry by Lord Justice Scott. The sceptics claimed that this threw a convenient flak jacket of *sub judice* over the whole affair; it meant that ministers and their advisors were saved from (or prevented from) answering all inquiries in Parliament and from the media for the next two years. It took Lord Scott that long to complete his inquiries and then to write his report. From the mass of Whitehall files to which he demanded access, it is apparent that simple embarrassment was one of the strongest motives for the attempted cover-up. Here, in a memo disclosed by the inquiry, is a senior DTI official advising his superiors:

> Are Ministers willing to have the 1987 and subsequent decisions made the subject of court-room argument? The dirty washing liable to emerge will add to the problems . . . For the DTI, the timing is extraordinarily embarrassing . . .

And here is a sentence from the Scott Report itself. One suspects that it is at least partly consequent on the thinking demonstrated in the quotation above:

> The answers to Parliamentary Questions . . . failed to inform Parliament of the state of Government policy on non-lethal arms sales to Iraq. This failure was deliberate.

When Whitehall reckons that the lowered safety curtain of 'national security' may not turn out to be completely fireproof, it uses another device to douse down evidence that might be 'unhelpful'. It simply decides (to its own satisfaction – the Loop again) that such evidence is 'not relevant' to the debate, and therefore need not (should not) be brought to wider attention. Thus the other side in the argument is often denied all knowledge that such evidence even exists. The Scott Report pinpointed a number of instances in which items of 'obvious relevance' had been 'denied'. There are examples of this favourite device in every chapter of this book. In short, expediency rules. Or, put at rather greater length, integrity is all very well, but there is no need to take it too far.

BRITAIN HAS NO EFFECTIVE FREEDOM of Information Act. True, an Act was passed in 2000, but it now seems that proper implementation will have to wait for at least another three or four years. Even then, the opportunities for 'discovery' will be tightly circumscribed and the list of official exemptions will be almost endless. In practice, ministers and their advisors will be under no obligation to release any information they want to hold back. Yet back in 1996, while still in opposition, no politician spoke more zealously in favour of the Act than Tony Blair:

> Freedom of Information is absolutely fundamental to how we see politics developing in this country. It will signal a new relationship which sees the public as legitimate stakeholders in the running of the country.[3]

Even allowing for the usual up-for-election guff, one would not have guessed that the Act would give no one the right to know anything much until six or seven years after Labour had come into office. So why has the Prime Minister's enthusiasm cooled? Has he been nobbled by nervous mandarins?

Those mandarins have always been twitchy about too much openness. Perhaps they feel that sharing their secrets would erode their self-esteem. In this sense – that of a regard for their own importance – they have some justification. After all, top civil servants, and even those a little lower down, exercise very considerable power, at least as much as all but the front bench of the actual government. Most permanent secretaries are paid more than the ministers they serve. No one at those levels of authority likes to be bothered by interfering outsiders who accuse them or their staff of being cavalier with the truth. One can put it more strongly than that: the thought that they might be proved wrong – caught out by some uppity tabloid scribbler or a too-persistent MP or, who knows, a pushy Hartlepool housewife – is enough to make

3. From a speech at the Campaign for Freedom of Information's annual awards, 25 March 1996.

most mandarins come within a heave or two of being physically sick. To senior civil servants the implication that they are anything but 100 per cent straight is not only impertinent, it seriously calls into question the very basis of their authority, the mandate of their power. So to protect that power, a first line of defence is to be tight-lipped with outside inquirers. Another is to respond to almost any serious criticism with a salvo of denying counter-accusations: 'unsubstantiated rumour', 'a misreading of the facts', 'unwarranted innuendo', 'journalistic mischief-making', 'misinformed and ill-conceived conjecture' and (a favourite) 'speculative irrelevancies'. No doubt, if they bother to read it, they will say some or all of those things about this book. But they forget that, as often as not, such accusations are counter-productive; the outsider, smelling a rat (because Whitehall protests too much?), becomes even more terrier-like in his digging.

As has been observed, avoiding embarrassment is always a powerful reason to disguise the truth – in any of us. And, in the workings of government, there is another closely related motive. Within Whitehall, fear for one's reputation can generate a cover-up because, of course, if your actions are an embarrassment either to the government or to your colleagues, you will not be judged to have 'a safe pair of hands'. You may even be thought to lack 'bottom' – a sure way to dent your dignity and your prospects. It follows that the more senior the politicians and/or the public servants involved, the more energetic the cover-up – because they will have further to fall if found out. Which is why, more than two years after the sinking of *Belgrano*, the civil servant who eventually leaked some of the truths (which could have been told the day the conflict was over) wound up at the Old Bailey. After all, besides senior public servants, there were ministers, including the Prime Minister, who had an interest in preventing the disclosure of the fact that they had been involved in a prolonged and quite unnecessary obfuscation. Some dared to call it a cover-up.

IN THE WORLD OUTSIDE WHITEHALL – sometimes called the 'real world' – there are sanctions that can kick in when deceits are advanced, half-truths peddled, facts twisted out of true or pertinent data rejected as 'irrelevant'. One thinks of the inquiries of ombudsmen, the scrutiny of one's peers or colleagues, the reaction of shareholders or the operation of the law – not least the process of legal 'discovery' or the laws of libel, fraud or the Trade Descriptions Act. And there are certain 'natural' laws that operate: if someone makes too many cock-ups, they eventually get the sack. If a company insists on getting things wrong too often, the senior executives are replaced or it goes bust. Moreover, where it can be shown that a company's directors have deliberately fiddled their books, they can even be sent to jail. But, in the normal course of events, none of these possibilities (or their consequences) seems to intrude too heavily on the consciousness of the executive directors of Whitehall. True, journalists can dig, MPs can ask questions and Select Committees can be a thorough nuisance. But there are ways around these problems. One of the ways (small in itself but indicative of Whitehall cynicism) peeped out some years ago in a civil service training film. Here is Sir Brian Hayes, then top dog at the DTI, advising that if questioned by a Select Committee, an appropriate tactic is to stall or to spin out one's answers to the point of irrelevance. It is a way of wasting time and thus frustrating further questions:

> I don't think it is a good idea just to answer 'yes' – because then they go straight on to another question and you are foxed again. It also, of course, fills in a certain amount of time, and one remembers that all these Committees have, as it were, a finishing time.

No one doubts that senior civil servants believe themselves to be professional and disinterested – that they Get It Right. They are strongly supported in that leaky confidence by a system where, in any argument with the awkward world outside Whitehall, they not only act as their own counsel but often enough also as their own judge, jury and clerk to the court. All this has a multiplying effect on the very considerable power they already 'enjoy'. The closed circuit of the Loop works at all levels, from answering an individual question up to a parliamentary debate or a full-blown public inquiry.

It is obviously impossible for a minister to be familiar with the details of all the many subjects on which he (or she) may have to answer to Parliament or directly to the public. So, he is reliant on his advisors; they decide what to tell him: 'Yes, Minister' or, as the case may be, 'No, Minister'. By controlling his information, they keep him within the

Loop – their Loop. So, for example, when Sir Malcolm Rifkind was Minister for Defence in 1994, he announced that the Chinook crash on the Mull of Kintyre was due to the 'gross negligence' of the two pilots – because that is what his advisors in the RAF and the MOD had told him to say. Yet six years later, Sir Malcolm, now out of office, was of a different mind. In an interview on ITN, he made the following comment:

> Although we did have several meetings after the Inquiry had reached its conclusion of gross negligence, neither then or at any time since was I given any general indication that there had been serious problems with that type of aircraft.

Clearly Sir Malcolm Rifkind's advisors had decided what to tell him. And, more important, what not to tell him. On an obviously serious issue, *they* decided what was relevant, not the minister about to make an announcement to the House. Civil servants both run their departments and, on all but the broadest issues of policy, they evidently run their ministers as well.

People in Whitehall know that, as long as things don't get away from them – as long as they keep things within their Loop – they are safe. To whom, in practice, are they accountable? Certainly not, as any number of cases have shown, to Parliament. Further, in practice there is usually no disinterested in-house judge or referee. Whitehall's response to this subversive observation is that there is no need for an umpire. One is told that the conclusions reached on controversial matters are the result of careful and impartial analysis; they are free from the preconceptions of the media and outside investigators, who, of course, are working to their own disruptive agendas and prejudices. Yes, they probably are, but that does not necessarily mean that they are wrong. Even when a controversy builds to bursting point and there has to be a public inquiry, it is almost invariably the relevant minister who decides, on the advice of a Permanent Secretary or the Cabinet Office, who will conduct the proceedings (often it is a senior retired civil servant), what the brief and the all-important limits of the inquiry will be, and to whom the eventual report will first be made. In short, one of the parties to a controversy (usually the party with the most to gain) appoints the judge and defines the limits of the judgement. It is the Loop again.

Most of the time, members of the Whitehall Establishment remain in control. But, just occasionally, things get away from them and go wrong – sometimes quite spectacularly. One such occasion has been uncovered by the testimony and e-mails revealed at the Hutton Inquiry. Although originally limited to an investigation into the circumstances surrounding Dr Kelly's death, it quickly became a much broader (and more damaging) inquest than Downing Street had in mind. Perhaps it never could have been anything else. Very seldom before have the inner machinery (and machinations) of Whitehall and Downing Street been so exposed to public view.

Another time when things got away from the bureaucrats was the now almost forgotten affair of Crichel Down. The original owner of some windswept acres of Dorset was administratively deprived of her legal right to buy them back after the RAF had finished using them as a wartime bombing range. Although it happened over fifty years ago, it serves as a benchmark of Whitehall mismanagement. The story should be compulsory reading for every public servant. Maybe it is. (Though *if* it is, it has not had that much effect.) Fallacy was promoted to fact, conjecture became authoritative conclusion, cock-up became hush-up, which then became cover-up. It is a recurring pattern. But, in the end, a sufficient head of public steam resulted in a Public Inquiry. The truth got out. It occasionally does. The Minister resigned. Those were the days when they sometimes did.

One more example: things went wrong in 2000 when the legal process of 'discovery' caused the Foreign Office to open its files of years before on its decisions about what to do with the Ilois people. We will come to it in its own chapter; Whitehall's lies – no mere spin or mild dissembling here – are eye-popping. 'We are being asked to cook the books,' wrote one worried civil servant. That was a considerable understatement.

Then again, but this time at an individual level, things came famously unstuck for the Cabinet Secretary, Sir Robert Armstrong. The story, though broadly familiar, is (like a good joke?) worth repeating. Anyway, given that Sir Robert was the most senior civil servant in the land, the tale is directly relevant to this discussion. Sir Robert had gone to Sydney to put a legal stopper on Peter Wright, an embittered ex-member of

MI5 living in Tasmania. He was spilling a load of security beans in an indifferent book called *Spycatcher*. The book had already been banned in the United Kingdom. But Australia was different.

Sir Robert arrived expecting the same deference that he would have been given back home. But he misjudged the Australians and misplayed his hand. Under cross-examination by Malcolm Turnbull, a whipper-snapper of just thirty-two, he allowed himself to be pushed into a corner. Despite earlier denials and fudge, he was forced to acknowledge that the Government had dissembled about several other, security-sensitive books it had *not* opposed – because, at the time, it had not been expedient to do so. Yes, he supposed that earlier he had been 'economical with the truth'. Like Winston Churchill's 'terminological inexactitude', the euphemism has passed into the language. Outside Whitehall, it is what Sir Robert will be remembered for. The Government and Sir Robert lost the case. 'TOP POM BOMBS' ran one Sydney headline. The action cost the British taxpayer more than £2 million. The publisher and the author made about as much. Sir Robert went on to become Lord Armstrong and, on retirement, a director of RTZ, Shell, Lucas, Rothschilds, Inchcape and a whole bunch more.

The most obvious message coming out of the *Spycatcher* debacle seems to be that, when it comes to propping up the edifice of its own infallibility, Whitehall has no problem persuading itself that the end justifies the means – even when that involves being less than wholly truthful under oath. So, if a Top Pom – and, in civil service terms, they did not come any topper – can be thrifty with the detail, why should anyone lower down various Whitehall ladders be too squeamish? Again, integrity is all very well, but one has to be realistic.

EVERY NOW AND THEN A Whitehall controversy reaches Parliament. The relevant minister will have been briefed by his staff. Indeed, if appearing before a Select Committee, where the questioning may be much more sustained than in the Commons, he will probably be flanked by several members of his staff, Adam's apples all anxiously a go-go. These are not popular occasions in Whitehall because there is always the possibility that departmental certainties will be torpedoed by an MP on the Committee who knows at least as much about the subject as the

Minister's advisors. But at other times, and failing other, often fallible Parliamentary safeguards, there operates the mechanism whereby a denying explanation, sometimes mouthed by the minister, is put together by the same Whitehall staff who then sit in judgement on the worth of any research or conclusions which differ from their own. It is the Loop again.

When questioned about these closed-circuit procedures, Whitehall's answer can follow certain well-worn lines – whether the subject is Foot and Mouth, the Chinook, Gulf War Syndrome, nuclear testing in the 1950s or HMS *Glorious*. A key sentence in a letter from the MOD is typical: 'Our obligation is to portray an unbiased account . . . the only caveat being that the sources should be credible, relevant and as near contemporary as possible.'[4] Yes, indeed. But is that credo as entirely reasonable as it sounds? Is any of us best placed to be the sole judge of our own lack of bias, or to be the only arbiter of what, in any given debate, is 'credible and relevant'? It probably never occurred to the civil servant who wrote that letter that he and his colleagues were anything but uniquely qualified to make such judgements. Perhaps one should refer back to Sir Malcolm Rifkind's observations above.

So, given the Whitehall Loop, *quis custodiet ipsos custodes*? Where is the accountability? Can anything be done about situations where a government department, having made up its mind and then sifted (not always subconsciously) the data to fit, remains impervious to argument and contrary evidence? And if that is not how it works, it is certainly a widespread perception. The short answer to 'What can be done?' is probably 'Not much'. Nothing fundamental anyway. At one level the Parliamentary Question, though better than nothing, is not a reliable solution; too often it fails to penetrate – time is limited and notice must be given beforehand, which allows, if need be, a minister's advisors to work out an evasive reply. Far better, as just noted, is the forum of a Select Committee where a witness (perhaps the minister himself if he is willing) has to answer a string of questions from members who, if they have done their homework, can go on pushing until the truth has a sporting chance of emerging. An effective Freedom of Information Act,

4. Letter to the author from MOD's Naval Historical Branch, 30 December 1999.

if it ever comes, might help. But it will still allow the authorities to withhold information if, in their opinion, disclosure would 'prejudice the effective conduct of public affairs' (Clause 32–2). That can mean almost anything that they want it to mean. The Bookers, the Paxmans and the Humphrys must just keep asking questions for the rest of us.

The prospect is depressing. It is obviously quite unrealistic to hope that Whitehall itself might suggest a solution to these problems; its inhabitants are happy with the way things are. Indeed, most of them don't even recognize that there are any problems. To get them to do so would require a sea change in the culture of the place – something that is never going to be self-generated. But, whether it is Foot and Mouth or arms to Iraq, is it wholly unreasonable to look for the occasional Whitehall statement that might say, 'We can't be absolutely sure we got it right'? Or, 'While we cannot agree with them, we have to acknowledge that other qualified investigators have reached different conclusions'? That might be reasonable, but it is impossible. In fact, it is absurd. It is absolutely not the way administrations work. For starters, any 'reasonable' solution is, too often, neither black nor white; it is too much like life itself – grey, unspecific and administratively untidy. These are qualities which are not meant to have a place in Whitehall. So, the answer to the question just posed must be, 'Yes, it is wholly unreasonable – well, unrealistic – to expect anything along those lines.' All of which makes a solution most unlikely.

But maybe, if nothing else, our public servants might occasionally recognize, from examples in their recent history, that they have not always been the infallible and disinterested custodians of the truth they invariably claim to be. They deceive themselves, as we all do at times, if they think that they are not almost as biased, with as many axes to grind, positions to defend and agendas to promote, as the rest of us. The difference is that the rest of us usually know it. Some of us even admit it. Besides which, we don't run the country.

HUTTON, KELLY, GILLIGAN AND ALL THAT

Weapons of Mass Deception

There can be few subjects of greater public interest than the reasons presented by a government to its own people as grounds for going to war.

Andrew Caldecott QC, the BBC's barrister at the Hutton Inquiry

I was very disappointed to read that Alastair Campbell had no part in inserting the 'forty-five-minute claim' into the September dossier. Mr Campbell is paid as the government's chief propagandist. If he is not prepared to sex up boring old intelligence dossiers, I want my money back.

A letter in the *Guardian* from Harry Beresford of Southampton

This is an attempt to get the BBC to admit that the fundamental attack on the integrity of the government, the Prime Minister, the intelligence services – let them just accept for once that they have just got it wrong.

Alastair Campbell on *Channel 4 News*

When you have done a fault, be always pert and insolent, and behave yourself as though you were the injured person.

Jonathan Swift

TO BEGIN JUST BEFORE THE beginning: when Aurum Press said that they wanted to publish an expanded version of this book, including an additional chapter about Hutton, Kelly and All That, I replied that I couldn't do it. Other people, much closer to the action, would get there well before me. Then I had an idea. In following the whole long story, I had been particularly interested to see that Whitehall (or, more specifically, Downing Street and the MOD) had, in their argument with the BBC, Andrew Gilligan and almost everyone else, fallen back on a sequence of tactics drawn from what I easily identified as the Whitehall manual of Standard

Offensive/Defensive/Evasive Measures (SODEMs). I recognized the pattern from my own earlier research. As the reader will find out, individual examples of these manoeuvres and obfuscations occur in every chapter of this book. But now, as Lord Hutton's Inquiry unrolled day by day, I realized that almost all the different techniques used in official deception were coming together within this one single narrative. This was special. It doubled my interest. And it provided an incentive spark.

In this connection – and most importantly – it is surely the case that without the Hutton Inquiry, many, if not most, of the bureaucratic half-truths and deceits involved in our going to war might still be smoke-screened from public view. In other words, had it not been for the single act of Dr Kelly's suicide, we might still not know many of the things that were done in our name – rightly or wrongly – to justify our participation in the second Gulf War.

It seems to be the case that when Whitehall (whichever party is in power) smells trouble – whether it comes from an MP asking awkward questions about an obscure atoll on the other side of the world, or a researcher enquiring too persistently about a crashed Chinook, or an early-morning journalist getting too close to almost any hidden truth – the bureaucrats reach for their SODEM manual. It seems worth examining the contents of this much-used handbook. So, after a few broad-brush paragraphs at the start, that is what this chapter tries to do – among other things.

Lastly, two personal points. In reading this chapter, please do not assume that I was against the war. Although I had some doubts – as explained at the very end of the chapter – I was certainly balanced more for 'forcible regime change' than against it. Secondly, I deliberately finished this chapter before Lord Hutton's report was published. So, rightly or wrongly, my opinions and conclusions are just that – entirely mine. As I write, I have no idea how Lord Hutton will find. In short, I have not hedged my bets.

HE HAD SPENT THE LAST few days thinking about it. Now, waiting in his flat at just after 6 o'clock on the morning of 29 May 2003, Andrew Gilligan, the defence correspondent of the *Today Programme*, knew that he had a worthwhile story on his hands, maybe even something of a scoop. But listening on the phone for John Humphrys to lead into the interview from a BBC studio on the far side of London, he could have had little idea of the almost immediate furore he was about to cause, or, thereafter, the enormous consequences. But then neither did his anonymous source – who, ironically, was overseas and would not even hear the piece.

> What we've been told by one of the senior officials in charge of drawing up that dossier was that actually the government probably knew that that forty-five-minute figure was wrong even before it decided to put it in . . . Downing Street, our source says, ordered a week before publication [for the dossier] to be 'sexed up', to be made more exciting and ordered more facts to be discovered. Our source says that the dossier, as it was finally published, made the intelligence services unhappy because it didn't reflect the considered view they were putting forward – that's a quote from our source . . . and, essentially, the forty-five-minute point was probably the most important thing that was added.

Gilligan got a number of things wrong. He elevated the status of his source (to enhance the story or to disguise the source's identity?). Nor was his informant 'one of the senior officials in charge of drawing up that dossier'. Gilligan would also have been wiser – though, as it was eventually to turn out (see below), not necessarily much more accurate – not to have attributed to his source the claim that the government 'probably knew that the forty-five-minute figure was wrong'. This may have been what his source told him, but without specific corroboration (as Gilligan himself was later to acknowledge), the word 'wrong' was, at that stage, too strong. 'Dubious' would have been better – though only slightly less damaging to the official version of events. Again, the claim that 'the dossier . . . made the intelligence services unhappy' was too sweeping. It would have been more accurate to have said something like, 'a number of intelligence personnel were unhappy . . . '. Lastly, it was at least theoretically arguable at that stage that it had been not so much Downing Street that had incorporated that 'forty-five-minute figure' into the dossier as it had been the Joint Intelligence Committee – the body which claimed actual 'ownership' of the dossier. So Gilligan got some of the detail wrong. And some of the theory too. Nevertheless, knowing what we know now (and what his informant seems to have known then) about Downing Street's involvement in the editorial process of the dossier (most importantly, its 'sexing-up'), it seems Gilligan got the general practice of what happened about right. So, at the important end of what he reported (the 'sexing-up'; the unhappiness within the intelligence services; the doubts about the 'forty-five minutes' claim) he was very close to the mark. But it was a pity that his wording was loose on some of the less important details; he thereby debased the validity of those parts of his story that really mattered, and thus put into the hands of his enemies a diversionary stick with which to beat him. And, more importantly, with which to attack the BBC.

IN TAKING THE COUNTRY TOWARDS war, Tony Blair had faced an almost insurmountable problem: too many people were none too sure that they wanted to go with him.

To be fair to the Prime Minister, he seems to have had a number of perfectly honourable motives. He was undoubtedly appalled at the sheer evil of Saddam Hussein; he saw him as a menace to any fragile hopes for Middle Eastern stability, and as a future source of chemical, biological and even nuclear threats – threats which, in time, might extend far beyond the Middle East. At the same time he was obviously anxious to preserve the Atlantic Alliance and, if possible, to restrain George W. Bush. But neither separately nor even all bundled together were any of these motives strong enough to persuade a deeply sceptical public that war was the only solution.

In the United States, it was different. Over there, 'regime change' and revenge for 9/11, plus an alleged Iraqi link with al-Qaeda, were seen as reasons enough. But in Britain, after a series of 'shoulder-to-shoulder' declarations to George Bush (in effect, promises without any get-out clause), Tony Blair desperately needed to find a cause much stronger than mere regime change or even an al-Qaeda connection. So, co-operating closely with the intelligence services, his Downing Street crew went to work. Through the summer, a succession of papers – each one 'stronger' than the last – were drafted which set out the reasons why, given his probable arsenal of chemical and biological weapons, Saddam Hussein had to be removed. By force if necessary.

As new intelligence arrived and was appraised, the current paper was re-edited to accommodate it. Presently, late information came in that Iraq might have some chemical or biological weapons which 'could be ready within forty-five minutes'. The news was seized on by Downing Street. It was ideal – just what was needed to further strengthen the government's case. Such weapons were cited as 'a serious and current threat', and the subjunctive '*could* be ready' was changed to the unequivocal and indicative 'are deployable'. And, as the Hutton hearings were to reveal, that was far from the only 'improvement' (sexing-up?) made to the document being put together to persuade Parliament and, thereby, the nation that we should join the Americans in a war against Iraq.

In fact, the 'ready in forty-five minutes' claim became one of the two most chilling items in what was now known as 'the dossier'. Along with the unambiguous assertion that 'Iraq possesses extended-range versions of the Scud missile', one must assume that the public was meant to imagine that those 'extended-range' missiles (quickly loaded with anthrax spores, the smallpox virus, nerve gas, or whatever) could soon be arching out towards Israel, Turkey, our bases in Cyprus, and who knew where on earth beyond. When it became apparent that the public's imagination was doing exactly what was expected of it, the government must have been well pleased. Certainly, it did nothing to rectify the misconception – which would have involved telling the public that what it really meant was that Saddam might have some short-range *battlefield* weapons that could be loaded with chemical or biological agents within the hour.

The dossier – with four separate mentions of the forty-five-minute claim – was published on the same day as a Commons debate, so there was little time for MPs or anyone else to question its contents too closely. The Prime Minister, in a loose paraphrase of the dossier, set out his case for war. But he also emphasized that he intended to follow what he called 'the United Nations route'. No doubt he did. But the problem was that he had already nailed the nation's colours to George Bush's mast. And the President, unlike the Prime Minister, had never rated approval by the UN as having any significant priority. Indeed, involvement with the UN was likely to bring with it complications that Bush and his country did not need. It is very difficult to believe that Tony Blair did not realize this. Maybe he did – but hoped against hope that the UN could, in the few months remaining, be won over.

But the Americans were not going to wait for the UN or anyone else. Their build-up of troops in the Gulf had already begun. Rather late in the day, we Brits followed – in an equipment-short scramble. Over the few remaining months of winter, there continued to be much frustrating and inconclusive to-ing and fro-ing at the UN, in the hope that the Security Council would give its support. But by the time 'coalition' troops and armour were in position, the imperative of the oncoming Iraqi summer with its impossible temperatures became the most important element in the calculations. The generals were saying that, UN support or not, very soon it would be too late. If we were 'going in', it had to be now. So the Americans, British and Australians 'went it alone' – which was almost certainly the American plan from the start.

In the event, victory was quickly won – 'mission accomplished'. Then, after a brief period of relief and triumph, the questions began. So what about those weapons of mass destruction? Where were they? Where were the manufacturing laboratories? Where were all the scientists and technicians? Where were the extended-range Scuds? Patience – 'just be patient' – seemed to be the answer. After all, Iraq is a very big country.

The weeks went by, and still nothing. Then, early one morning, up sprang a BBC defence correspondent who claimed that someone on the inside had told him that the government probably knew right from the start that 'that the forty-five-minute figure was wrong'. To an already sceptical media, the implication was all too obvious: if one of the strongest items in the dossier might have been 'wrong', what else might be?[1]

1. In this connection, one should not forget the scepticism generated by the so-called 'dodgy dossier' – parts of which turned out to be based on a plagiarized version of a ten-year-old PhD thesis, complete with its original mistakes of grammar and punctuation. One looks in vain for any record of official apology (from Alastair Campbell or anyone else at Number 10) for that charade. The 'dodgy dossier' was published in February 2003 – more than four months after the 'WMD in forty-five minutes' dossier. Little wonder then that the distrust generated by the 'dodgy dossier' (when its origins became known) should give an extra impetus to the doubts long expressed by most of the media about the earlier (September) dossier. In short, by the time Gilligan made his BBC report (29 May), published doubts about the September dossier were already widespread. Gilligan's report and, even more so, his *Mail on Sunday* article (1 June), seem to have acted as a spark to an already highly inflammable media mix.

Furthermore, there was the allegation that people in the intelligence services had also been 'unhappy' about other aspects of the official argument. To a government and a Prime Minister already under deep and accelerating embarrassment to find a trace, any trace, of the WMD on which they had staked their reputation and justified the war, that single accusatory phrase – 'the government probably knew that the forty-five-minute figure was wrong' was a detonator to dynamite. It touched off an explosion from which the dust and debris, not least of careers and reputations, have not yet settled. The secondary detonations will go on rumbling around Whitehall, Downing Street and the BBC for years.

True, Gilligan had already ruffled feathers right at the top of the MOD when he reported that the Minister, Geoff Hoon, had taken off for a ski-ing holiday just as troops were being recalled from leave in order to make ready for war. And later, more seriously, he got right up the nose (both nostrils) of Alastair Campbell and others when he broadcast a report from post-liberation Baghdad saying that, in the chaos and the looting, some inhabitants said that they felt safer under Saddam than under the Americans. They probably did. In the immediate aftermath of most conquests, civilian populations are always likely to suffer great hardship. But the report was quickly cited as yet another example of the BBC's allegedly 'negative' attitude to the war. In short, the government's explosive charges, stacked up against the walls of the BBC, had been ready to blow – primed and fused – for some time. The detonator was that early-morning item on *Today*.[2]

Now, it was certainly true that Gilligan had been inaccurate in his claim that Dr Kelly had been 'one of the senior officials in charge of drawing up the dossier'. Nevertheless, Kelly was the next best thing: a world expert on biological weaponry who had not only contributed to successive dossiers but, as someone who had often been co-opted by the MOD's Defence Intelligence Staff, had virtually proofread the things. And he had expressed his doubts. Having been to Iraq thirty-seven times as a UN weapons inspector, he knew what he was talking

2. In fact, across the whole of the BBC, Gilligan contributed to at least a dozen other programmes that day; his phrasing was certainly more tightly judged in those later reports.

about. In short, he had had intelligence 'input' – both positive and negative. Now, if Gilligan was to be believed, this still-anonymous mole was unhappy, angry even, at the way critical aspects of his own input and, most certainly, that of some of his colleagues had been manipulated or, as idiom has it, 'sexed up' to make a more dramatic case. More specifically, where the forty-five-minute claim was concerned, the implication was that Dr Kelly had accused the government (or its immediate servants) not just of 'sexing up', but of something halfway to invention.

But what if Kelly had never suggested any such thing? What if, as in the government's counter-accusation, Gilligan was himself guilty of 'sexing up' his reports? (Across the BBC, he made more than a dozen other broadly similar broadcasts that day.) Where was his supporting evidence?[3] Two points arise. First, it is in the nature of whistleblowers (of which Kelly seems to have been one) that their tip-offs are often difficult to corroborate immediately in exact terms; that is a risk that journalists sometimes have to take. Second, in this case, we now know (though we did not at the time) that Dr Kelly had spoken about his concerns in broadly similar terms some time before to Gavin Hewitt, a BBC news reporter, and, more specifically, to Susan Watts, science editor for the BBC's *Newsnight*. She had taped one of her phone conversations with Dr Kelly and made shorthand notes of at least two others – though, curiously, she did not make known the fact that she had a tape until after Kelly's death. Once again, on tape, Kelly was more than merely sceptical about the forty-five-minute claim.

3. Apparently, in the week that expired between meeting Kelly and making his broadcast report, Gilligan had worked to find support for his story. It seems he had raised it with two government contacts. One had refused to comment; the other had apparently suggested to Gilligan that he should 'keep digging', which to any journalist is a strong hint that he is not far from the truth. Gilligan had also spoken to an American expert on WMD who confirmed that similar doubts about 'WMD in forty-five minutes' were current in Washington. None of this comes near to being full-blown corroboration – which was always most unlikely. But it does indicate some support for the story. Furthermore, it is known that Kevin Marsh, the overall editor of *Today*, had heard Clare Short, recently resigned from the cabinet, expressing the gravest doubts about the reliability of the 'WMD in forty-five minutes' claim.

> It was a statement that . . . just got out of all proportion . . . They were desperate for information; they were pushing hard for information which could be released. That was one that popped up and it was seized on. And it was unfortunate that it was. Which is why there is the argument between the intelligence services and [the] Cabinet Office – Number 10, because things were picked up on, and once they've picked up on it, you can't pull it back. That's the problem.

Now, a question which surely goes to the heart of the dispute between Number 10 (and chiefly Alastair Campbell) and the BBC: how 'out of proportion' does something have to be before it becomes so distorted as to be 'wrong'? To many people, that passage ('. . . out of all proportion . . . once picked up on . . . you can't pull back') would seem to come close to supporting Gilligan in his claim that Kelly had told him that the government 'probably knew that the forty-five-minute figure was wrong'. Yet it is precisely on this element that Gilligan has been most frequently attacked – not least from within the BBC itself. Elsewhere on the same tape, Watts asked Kelly if it was true that other people, particularly those in the intelligence services, were advising that the dossier's forty-five-minute/WMD claim was too unequivocal. Again, his reply would seem to confirm what Gilligan claimed Kelly had told him.

> There were lots of people saying that . . . People were saying 'We're not so sure about that' . . . the real concern that everyone had, it was not so much what they [the Iraqis] have now but what they would have in the future. But that unfortunately wasn't expressed strongly in the dossier because that takes away the case for war to a certain extent.

On another occasion, when Watts took shorthand notes of her phone conversation with Dr Kelly, he again commented on the forty-five-minute claim. Watts noted Kelly thus: 'A mistake to put it in – Alastair Campbell seeing something in there – single source – but not corroborated – sounded good'. Assuming that Watts's notes were made contemporaneously with the conversation, they would seem to support Gilligan's claim (in his *Mail on Sunday* article of 1 June 2003) that, rightly or wrongly, Alastair Campbell had indeed been named by Kelly in connection with the forty-five-minute claim. Watts never used this apparent Campbell 'connection' in any of her own reports. She was to say later that this was because she regarded Kelly's comment as merely a 'gossipy aside'. Is it possible that, as a science correspondent, she just did not spot the much wider political implications of that 'aside'? Certainly it seems strange that, given the hint, she did not press Kelly on what was potentially such a newsworthy story.[4] But, putting that aside, her careful records were later to lend invaluable support to Gilligan's version of events.[5]

In the long run, perhaps it did not matter that Kelly was not pressed by Watts, because later, from another direction entirely, there came even more convincing evidence that the government had, at the least, been duplicitous ('wrong'?) with its forty-five-minute claim. The 'revelation' (that the claim that 'WMD could be readied in forty-five minutes' was nothing less than a calculated half-truth) derives from none other than the Minister of Defence himself. It happened like this: back in September 2002, when the dossier was being put together, Downing Street, the Joint Intelligence Committee and the MOD may have genuinely thought that Saddam Hussein had the ability (as he almost certainly had in the 1991 Gulf War) to load and quickly make ready some of his short-range shells and 122-millimetre rockets with biological or chemical cargoes. After all, he had actually used such

4. Curiously, Susan Watts was to claim that neither her shorthand notes nor her tape recording could be held to be corroborative of Gilligan's reporting. Perhaps this 'denial' was part of a strategy to protect her source. She was unresponsive to my much later inquiries on this point.
5. One of the minor mysteries of the whole Kelly story is how and why Gilligan, a BBC staff reporter, was allowed to write an article for the *Mail on Sunday*. For many years there was a rule which specifically prevented (where potentially contentious subjects were concerned) such 'outside' work. Just occasionally an exception would be made, but only after the article had first been vetted by a departmental head. The reason was rather obvious: too often, the BBC (rather than the newspaper) had to take the flak from anyone who found fault with the article. The rule was relaxed by John Birt when he became Director General; he judged that allowing reporters to write for other organizations would raise their public profile – to the BBC's advantage. Gilligan's article, with its specific accusation that Alastair Campbell was directly involved in 'sexing up' the dossier (a claim that, though apparently true, he had not made in his BBC reportage) raised the stakes very considerably. It personalized the whole affair and, as Tony Blair told the Hutton Inquiry, gave it 'rocket boosters'.

weapons against the Iranians twenty years before. But the government also knew that these weapons (if they still existed in 2002) would, because of their limited range and small payload, only be effective on the battlefield. And such short-range weapons, while horrific enough, do not fit the generally accepted description of Weapons of *Mass* Destruction – as the term is sometimes used by, for example, NATO, and, for that matter, the MOD itself. At the Hutton Inquiry, Dr Brian Jones, a senior MOD intelligence official, suggested that such battlefield weapons, when or if they are loaded with chemical or biological 'cargoes' (or with nuclear warheads), are not usually regarded as WMD. In other words, while the term 'WMD' has no formal dictionary definition, it is normally taken – sometimes officially and almost always in the public imagination – to mean weapons (chemical, biological and, above all, nuclear), carried in long-range rockets, that might be aimed at large urban targets where the '*mass* destruction' of populations would be likely to run to many thousands. So there is a strong argument that the government's 'WMD' were not WMD at all; they were short-range battlefield weapons – horrendous, but not WMD.

Admittedly, it is just possible that when the term 'WMD' first came to be bracketed with the forty-five-minute claim (thus immeasurably 'sexing up' the dossier), Downing Street may not have appreciated the distinction between long- and short-range weapons; the difference has its grey areas – like the similar 'boundary' between tactical and strategic nuclear weapons. But the MOD across the road would certainly have known the difference. Indeed, as has been touched on above, Geoff Hoon, Minister of Defence, was forced to admit as much when pressed at the Hutton Inquiry. He said that he thought there was not much point in trying to correct newspapers – 'a time-consuming and frustrating process' – when they jumped to the wrong conclusions. So he 'was not horrified' to see that the media had got things wrong in assuming that the 'forty-five minutes' referred to long-range WMD missiles rather than, as was really the case, short-range battlefield weapons. But, of course, with the dossier's emphasis on 'extended-range Scuds' and weapons of *mass* destruction, that was surely just what the media and, thereby, the public were meant to assume. It was cynical sleight-of-hand – spin. In terms of going to war, it was frightening enough to be very persuasive – which, of course, is exactly what it was meant to be. Interestingly, the head of MI6, Sir Richard Dearlove, was later to cite this all-too-knowing 'mistake' as 'unhelpful' at the Hutton Inquiry and to agree that criticism of it was 'valid'. There are similar deeply misleading half-truths from Whitehall scattered throughout this book.

This episode alone seems to show that Gilligan was almost certainly justified in reporting that his informant had told him that the dossier had been 'sexed up'. Further, and more importantly, in claiming in his original *Today* report that 'the government probably knew that the forty-five-minute figure was wrong', Gilligan was only mistaken in the most theoretical sense: those around the Prime Minister almost certainly knew – before they even put the item into the dossier – that the forty-five-minute figure was likely to be *wrongly* interpreted by the media to mean long-range WMD. When this happened, they deliberately held off from trying to put things right. Even if one does not accept that the term WMD excludes battlefield weapons, the deliberate fostering of the public's misinterpretation that what was meant was long-range WMD is, at the least, dishonest – morally wrong.

Obviously, Downing Street, the Joint Intelligence Committee and the top echelons of the MOD were very happy to let the public assume the worst – that Iraq had 'extended-range Scuds' which could be on their way within less than an hour of Saddam Hussein's giving the command. Which must be why, when newspapers ran news items (referring to the British bases and holidaymakers in Cyprus) under headlines like 'BRITS 45 MINUTES FROM DOOM' (*Sun*), '45 MINUTES FROM ATTACK' (*Evening Standard*) and 'EUROPE WITHIN RANGE OF BLITZ BY SCUDS' (*Daily Express*), no one from the MOD, Downing Street or anywhere else attempted to put them right. To have done so would have spoilt the story. Indeed, it would have knocked the bottom out of it. One can appreciate Dr Kelly's concerns. And who is to say that Andrew Gilligan was wrong to report them?

Finally, it is surely worth noting the 180-degree turn-around in official response when (a) a wrong conclusion by the media inadvertently *supports* the government's aims and (b) those other occasions when, equally wrong (in the government's eyes), a media 'mistake' runs *counter* to the government's aims. So, when the press assumed that the dossier's talk of weapons of mass destruction referred to long-range rockets, the government looked the other way and did absolutely nothing to correct the mistake. But when the BBC, in the particular form of Andrew Gilligan, made some mistakes of detail, Downing Street's official spokesman, Alastair Campbell, became wholly obsessive in his demands for a whole series of corrections and apologies. Why the difference? Silly question.

IT NOW SEEMS APPROPRIATE TO examine, within the narrative of the Kelly story, the sequence of SODEMs employed by Downing Street and Whitehall to deny or, at the least, to obfuscate the real issues.

From Whitehall's point of view, there are too many uncomfortable occasions when an expert like Kelly makes a statement which does not fit (or is even contrary to) the official version of events. In such embarrassing situations, if the research for the rest of this book is any indication (and one thinks particularly of the Chinook affair, Gulf War Syndrome, and HMS *Glorious*), officialdom's first SODEM will simply be to deny the validity of the dissenting judgement – and hope that the problem will then go away. If that tactic does not work (and it stood no chance in the developing Kelly saga) the next step is to try to discredit the author of the contradicting judgement by downgrading the level of his authority and, thereby, the worth of his expertise. It may also be put about that he is an eccentric, a malcontent, a maverick 'working to his own agenda', or even a 'Walter Mitty figure' – and therefore, by implication, not to be taken seriously. One can see elements of these well-practised SODEMs being applied to Dr Kelly – as soon as he had 'owned up' to his MOD bosses that he had talked to Gilligan.

In a formal letter to his boss, Kelly wrote that in his 'private conversation' with Gilligan he had 'most certainly never attempted to undermine government policy in any way'. If true, this could be taken to mean (as had been asserted from the beginning by Alastair Campbell on behalf of the government) that Gilligan had invented his story about what Kelly had told him. But, intriguingly, the MOD must have been uncertain that Kelly was being entirely truthful in his denial because there was no significant change in its attempts to downgrade the still-anonymous source.

So, at an early stage, as part of the SODEM to discredit him, and well before the public knew his identity, Dr David Kelly CMG was categorized as a 'middle-ranking defence official' or, in one instance, as a 'middle-level technician'. It was true that, in terms of his civil service salary, he was indeed only 'middle-level'. Ironically, that was one of his complaints – he thought his work was important enough to merit a markedly higher level of pay. Maybe that was why, later, it was quietly hinted that he was a bit of a malcontent. Maybe he was. Maybe with reason: he had not had a pay increase in over three years. This would affect his final pension; he was just a year away from retirement. It is also true that he was employed for his technical expertise and microbiological knowledge rather than for executive or managerial skills. So, while it was certainly stretching things, it was not totally fallacious to say he was a 'technician'. But in that case, so is a brain surgeon. At that early stage, there could be no rush to tell the world any more about Kelly. The muddle over his 'outing' was to come later. Incidentally, the detail of discrediting Kelly is an example of another SODEM: statements are made which are literally true ('a middle-level technician'), but which are often seriously misleading. Sometimes wholly so. Examples occur in almost all the chapters of this book.

In fact, Kelly was one of the foremost experts on the very subject – Iraq's capabilities in biological and chemical weaponry – that was central to the whole 'going-to-war' dispute. In his time, he had been a chief scientific officer at Porton Down and then a key member of the UN's Iraq inspection team (1991–98). The leader of that team had even thought of Kelly as a possible nominee for the Nobel Peace Prize. Most relevantly of all, he had been a source of items of intelligence that had gone into earlier drafts of the dossier. Indeed, an internal MOD report (revealed at the Hutton Inquiry) described Kelly as being 'a recognized authority on all aspects of Iraq's WMD' who had given 'excellent, authoritative and timely advice'. For officialdom later repeatedly to claim that the BBC was wrong to refer to Kelly as 'an intelligence source' is ridiculous; that is precisely what he was: a source of intelligence. In short, for someone who was only a 'middle-ranking official', he had obviously done rather well.

One sees in all this, beside the attempt to downgrade the seriousness of the still-anonymous Kelly's concerns, another SODEM being applied. Whitehall will sometimes focus on a relatively minor error and then, by portraying it as a mistake of the greatest magnitude, attempt to discredit the whole of the opposition's case. An example: it would be officially emphasized (in pointing up a mistake by both Gilligan and Watts) that Kelly was *not* a member of any of the three main intelligence services. Again, this was undoubtedly true. But, as has already been pointed out, he had contributed valuable, first-hand intelligence about Iraq's microbiological 'capabilities' to all those services. In short, he may not have been *in* any of the intelligence services, but they had no hesitation in drawing on his expertise. Perhaps in his *Today* report Gilligan should, more accurately, have stated that where Iraq was concerned, his informant was a useful member of the 'intelligence-*gathering* community'.

Another Whitehall SODEM is to claim that almost anything which looks awkward is 'irrelevant'. Thus, a day or two after Kelly died, when 'security personnel' in the MOD found a stray bag of documents (in an unlocked office) which was evidently meant for the incinerator or the shredder, they noticed some papers which related to the Kelly affair – minutes of the MOD's Information Co-ordination Group whose task is evidently to ensure 'consistency and strategic direction' of MOD stories and press releases. The papers were almost certainly instructions to the press office and others as to how to cope with media questions about Kelly. (A fairly common instruction in such circumstances is: 'Rebut, play down or ignore'.) Somehow the story leaked out; the media were, of course, much interested. But the MOD's answer to inquiries was not that the papers were confidential and would be turned over to Lord Hutton, but that they were 'irrelevant'. Maybe they were. But that particular SODEM card is played so often that it is bound to be distrusted. One can never know the truth about alleged 'irrelevancies' because the sole arbiters are usually the very officials who have the most to gain by keeping such papers to themselves; it is the Whitehall Loop. One learns very early on that one of the first rules when asking awkward questions of Whitehall is not to expect a useful reply. You will almost certainly be told (with cool but correct courtesy) that the questions you raise are 'irrelevant' or 'not germane', and therefore, by implication, they do not merit a serious answer.

One does not know if the next practice is listed in that SODEM manual, but, when it comes to the coaching of witnesses ahead of their appearances before Parliamentary Select Committees or other investigating bodies, Whitehall has no qualms. Indeed, in one story detailed in this book (the Chinook affair), it seems that not only was a senior witness, a minister no less, primed ('briefed' would be the preferred Whitehall term) to tell a tale that was the opposite of the truth, but even the Committee's chairman was offered prior 'advice' about which area of questioning should be avoided. In the Kelly affair (for such it had now become) the government was desperate to torpedo Gilligan and thus to win its battle against its corporate enemy: the BBC. One way of doing this would be to put Kelly before the Select Committee for Foreign Affairs, where, in response to the right questions, he would cast doubts on Gilligan's reporting – as he had already done in his 'owning-up' letter, in which he said he had 'never attempted to undermine government policy in any way'. But discussion of Kelly's appearance before that Committee inevitably brought up the difficult question of whether or not Kelly should be officially 'outed'. And, if he were, how it might best be handled.

Even more important, it brought up the dangerous possibility that members of the Committee (who were just about to question both Gilligan and Campbell) might want to question Kelly on what an MOD memo had already called 'tricky areas'. Kelly had recently had meetings with his bosses at which he had talked of his own doubts about the same 'tricky areas', which included the forty-five-minute point and the more recent discovery of two mobile laboratories – laboratories which the government was anxious to portray as 'evidence' in support of its WMD claims. We can reasonably surmise that, to his bosses, he had expressed his doubts in much milder and less specific terms than the ones Gilligan had reported him using. Nevertheless, could those same bosses take the risk of letting him loose in front of MPs who would be trying to get to the truth? Yet, if Kelly were kept away from the Committee (and his anonymity thus maintained), accusations of a cover-up would follow immediately. A tricky dilemma. Perhaps the best tactic would be to make Kelly appear before the Committee, but to try, through 'advice' to the Committee chairman, to move the area of questioning away from anything that might jeopardize the official case.

They were worried over in Downing Street too. We know from disclosures at the Hutton Inquiry that there was concern at a meeting chaired by Tony Blair that Kelly should be given 'guidance' and that he should be 'properly prepared' before his questioning by the Select Committee. And John Scarlett, chairman of the JIC, also warned that 'he will need careful briefing in advance'. We know that a little later Kelly was summoned to the MOD to receive this guidance. We know too that the day before his appearance before the Select Committee, he was handed a letter from the MOD's Head of Personnel in which he was warned that he would be subject to disciplinary action 'if any facts come to light that appeared to call into question the account and assurances you gave to me'. In other words, if it became apparent during his appearance before the Committee (or anywhere else) that Kelly's account to his bosses of what he had told Gilligan was less than the whole truth, the consequences would be severe.

At the same time, Geoff Hoon, the MOD minister, in a letter to the Committee chairman, was trying to limit the area of questions that might be put to Kelly: he was to be 'questioned only on the evidence that you were given by Mr Gilligan and not on the wider issue of Iraq's weapons of mass destruction'. In passing, it is worth pointing out that such directions (another SODEM?) from ministers to Select Committees are not uncommon, even though some claim that this practice is in contempt both of parliamentary procedures and the terms of reference under which the Select Committee system was set up in 1979. It is something that has never been tested. Anyway, a Labour Committee member quickly rebuked Mr Hoon for his 'monumental cheek'. Interestingly, when, for his part, Gilligan e-mailed two members of the Committee, David Chidgey and Richard Ottaway, with some questions that he thought might usefully be put to Dr Kelly, Whitehall officials (and others) were later to complain that such 'guidance' was quite improper – because it sought to influence the Committee's lines of inquiry. Clearly, what was sauce for the privileged ministerial gander was not reckoned to be equally available for the lowly reportorial goose.

In the event, in his early replies to that Committee, Kelly came very close to denying (as his masters obviously hoped) key elements of what Gilligan claimed he had told him. So either there must be another mole somewhere (doubtful), or Gilligan must be exaggerating, or even making it all up. It looked as if the government case against the BBC was almost proven – that it was Gilligan who was guilty of invention and 'sexing-up'. (And the BBC governors would be equally to blame for supporting him.) Further, when Kelly was asked if he was the author of comments critical of the dossier which Chidgey and Ottaway now read to him ('. . . the forty-five minutes was a statement that was made and it got out of all proportion – they were desperate for information . . .'), he answered that he did not recognize the words as his. Chidgey now revealed that those words (and more) were drawn from Susan Watts's record of what Kelly had said to her. Kelly seemed taken aback. 'It doesn't sound like my expression of words,' he said, and added: 'I don't recognize those comments.' Question: 'So you deny that those are your words?' Answer: 'Yes.' The impression Kelly gave was that the words must have been invented and then put in his mouth. Who was to be believed? For a few minutes things hung in the balance for Andrew Gilligan and the BBC.

The fact is that even if Kelly did not recognize the exact words, he almost certainly *did* recognize the sentiments as his own. Suddenly, he must have wondered if a tape had been running during his phone conversation several weeks earlier with Susan Watts. If so, it would soon become obvious to everyone that he had been much less than straightforward in his evidence to the Committee.

For the government, Kelly's appearance before the Committee was a calamity – as Alastair Campbell noted in his diary.

> 15 July 2003. Looking forward to Kelly giving evidence, but I predicted it would be a disaster and so it proved – despite MOD assurances [that] he was well schooled . . .

Whether Kelly's dissembling had been entirely on his own initiative or whether it owed more to the MOD's 'schooling' and the threat in that letter we will probably never know. But, to be fair to his managers at the MOD, he had only been telling the Committee what he had told those bosses earlier. Yes, he had met Gilligan. No, he had not talked about the forty-five minutes or the doubts of some in the ranks of the intelligence services.

To a distinguished and honourable man, to someone widely recognized for his integrity, the realization of what he had done must have come as a terrible shock. He had been caught lying – once to his bosses, and now to MPs. Kelly must have left the committee room a very worried man: had there been a tape running? One wonders if a build-up of remorse, overwhelming shame even, were not key factors in what happened just two days later in a Chilterns wood.

For putting those two Committee members up to that (tape-based?) line of questioning, Gilligan has been much criticized, vilified even, ever since. Suggestions have even been made that this was a betrayal which directly caused Kelly's death. True, when Gilligan suggested in his e-mail that those Committee members might want to confront Kelly with certain lines from Watts's tape and/or notes, he was coming very close to confirming what most people already suspected: that Kelly was the sole and only possible source of his and Watts's stories. But betraying a confidential source in that way is something that an investigative journalist would normally never do because, quite apart from the ethics involved, once a secret source has been so exposed, no other potential informant is ever going to trust that journalist. His reputation is gone and, maybe, his livelihood. But, by the same token, he will be in a very similar hole if he is shown to have been inventing or faking key aspects of his stories. Again, as far as fellow journalists and his employer are concerned, he is finished.

So what was Gilligan to do? He had a real problem. He seems to have calculated that the most effective way (the only way?) in which he could come near to proving that he had reported what Kelly had told him with reasonable accuracy was to point the Foreign Affairs Committee towards the records made by Susan Watts. In so doing, it was axiomatic that he would reveal Kelly as both his and Watts's source. That was deeply regrettable. Yet not to have done so would have left *him* the liar. So, presumably in some desperation, he sent his e-mail. Perhaps his sin lay rather less in what he did, more in his not telling his bosses that he was doing it. If one finds oneself at the sharp end of a mega-row, it is surely prudent to keep one's bosses fully informed. Their support is likely to diminish if they feel that they have been left out of the loop. Had Gilligan sought their advice, they might have come up with another way of achieving the same end – though it is hard to see what that might have been. One further point: Gilligan's 'sin' was said to have been compounded by the fact that he himself had been a witness before the Select

Committee; there was therefore something improper about his trying to alert the Committee to what he saw as evidence which supported his testimony – evidence which the Committee might otherwise have missed. With Gilligan, it seems that he was damned if he sent his e-mail, and damned if he didn't.

In any case, there are at least three more Whitehall SODEMs that were brought into play. The first is the concealment of some highly compromising detail. A classic example lies behind one of Tony Blair's more emphatic assertions to the Commons (4 June 2003).

> The allegation that the forty-five-minute claim provoked disquiet among the intelligence community is completely and totally untrue.

How could the Prime Minister have been so emphatically sure? Answer: because that is what he was told by those immediately around him. The truth (as Kelly seems to have told Gilligan earlier) is that there *was* quite considerable 'disquiet among the intelligence community'. Confirming this is the testimony of Dr Brian Jones of the MOD's intelligence staff – the man who told the Hutton Inquiry that WMD was not a term usually used of battlefield weapons. Now recently retired and therefore no longer subject to the discipline of his MOD bosses, he told the Inquiry of his colleagues' doubts about the forty-five-minute claim. 'The way in which the information was reported did not give us any confidence that the primary source [i.e. the senior Iraqi officer] knew very much about the subject'. Jones and several others tried, both formally and informally, to bring their unease to official notice. But the truth was carefully smoke-screened – otherwise who knows where the embarrassment might have ended? At the Hutton Inquiry, Martin Howard, the Deputy Chief of Defence Intelligence (a senior MOD civil servant) was asked why he had suppressed written complaints from a number of his intelligence staff – complaints that language used in the dossier was too strong to be justified. His reply was that such doubts were 'an internal matter' and 'were dealt with in the line-management chain and not pursued further'. This seems close to saying: 'We decided to cover up.' One can reasonably guess that if the complainants had wished to make a major fuss they would have risked putting promotion and, thereby, final pensions in jeopardy – always a powerful disincentive.

The truth had to wait until Dr Jones had retired. In the event, both the Prime Minister and Geoff Hoon, the Minister for Defence, were allowed to make public statements emphatically denying that there was any 'disquiet'. Presumably, they did not know that they were lying. But a number of their advisory civil servants knew. Examples of this SODEM – wherein ministers are fed misleading or incomplete information – play a significant role in at least three other chapters in this book.

Onward – towards two more Whitehall SODEMs which were used in this affair. The first is the habit of raising conjecture to the level of official certainty. The second is what could be called 'the decoy gambit'. The latter is not that common, but there are examples of the first on almost every second page of this book. Indeed, the Chinook travesty is based on little else. In the matter of Iraq, almost everything in the dossier became an all-encompassing and heavy-duty exercise in elevating surmise to assured fact. No subjunctives, ifs, buts or maybes here. And if there had been any such equivocations in earlier drafts, they were removed. Authorship and 'ownership' of the dossier were claimed by the John Scarlett, the chairman of the Joint Intelligence Committee (JIC). But the 'advising' hand of Number 10 is clearly all over the thing. The dossier was, of course, specifically commissioned by Number 10 to set out the reasons why we should go to war. Given that he who pays the piper usually calls the tune, it is not surprising that e-mails and other testimony disclosed at the Hutton Inquiry show that Alastair Campbell and the rest of the Downing Street crew were constantly suggesting that John Scarlett and his JIC crew should go back and look again at their homework. In one instance, Campbell asked that a sentence in the dossier which read 'The Iraqi military *may* be able to deploy CBW [chemical and biological weapons] within forty-five minutes . . .' should be changed to '*are* able to deploy within forty-five minutes . . .'. A small point – until one remembers how adamant Campbell was in his denials that he had had input of any kind into the forty-five-minute claim or indeed into the dossier as a whole. It is also difficult to square his protestations of innocence with his memo to Scarlett (revealed at the Hutton Inquiry) in which he acknowledged that, while Scarlett would be in charge of the factual contents of the dossier, he (Campbell) 'will chair a team that will go through the document from a presentational point of view and make recommendations to you'.

Making 'presentational changes' is what they called it. Once upon a time it was known as propaganda; nowadays it is often called 'spin'. John Scarlett told the Hutton Inquiry that he had no difficulty with any of this advice; indeed, he welcomed Number 10's help on 'the presentational aspects' of his work. One wonders if he was ever likely to say anything else.

In fact, several of the changes made to the dossier before publication were much more than matters of mere presentation. Consider this example: in an early draft it was written that 'Saddam is prepared to use chemical and biological weapons if he believes his regime is under threat'. One of the Downing Street crew, Jonathan Powell, Tony Blair's chief of staff, did not think that this was good enough. He wrote to John Scarlett:

> I think the statement . . . that 'Saddam is prepared to use CBW if he believes his regime is under threat' is a bit of a problem. It backs up . . . the argument that there is no CBW threat and we will only create one if we attack him. I think you should redraft the para.

One can see Mr Powell's point. The original phrasing came close to making a case for *not* going to war. In the final version of the dossier, the implication that Saddam would only resort to CBW if attacked was entirely removed, and in its place the following sentence appeared: 'Intelligence indicates that as part of Iraq's military planning Saddam is willing to use chemical and biological weapons.' Some might think that the change involved rather more than cosmetics or presentation – that it was, in fact, a pre-emptive version of the 'literally-true-but-misleading' SODEM. It seems that when incoming intelligence pointed away from the official thesis, it was deleted; when it pointed towards the thesis, it was quickly stitched in – with, maybe, a little presentational help. This would seem to come well within the category of 'sexing-up'.

In the business of gathering intelligence, a great deal can be learnt by surveying 'the other side' from satellites and high-flying photographic aircraft, or with electronic eavesdropping on radio and telephone traffic.

But because it is difficult to see through the roof of a pharmaceutical factory or the walls of a warehouse or, even more important, inside the minds of a regime's leaders, there will still be gaps and uncertainties. In the end, there is no real substitute for spies, moles or defectors (though the latter are rather too likely to tell their new hosts what they think they want to hear). This human intelligence, or 'humint', is much sought after. The difficulty with Iraq was that, such was the dictator's grip, it was almost impossible to recruit or infiltrate moles into senior positions where they could actually be a part of what was going on. Even at the best of times, intelligence is very seldom an exact science; it is rarely possible to be unequivocal in deducing exactly what the enemy is doing (let alone what he is going to do) unless one has some 'eyeballs' actually on the ground – that is, humint. A number of commentators (some with direct intelligence experience) had said at the time that, given these problems, Tony Blair's dossier was far too sure of itself about almost everything. Iraq might indeed have some WMD, it might be gathering the materials needed to make nuclear weapons, it might have some 'extended-range rockets', it might even be able to load them in forty-five minutes. But how did we *know* – with all the certainty that the dossier claimed? 'Ah, we can't tell you without compromising our intelligence techniques or the security of our sources.' End of discussion. We had to take so much on trust. (Incidentally, that is another SODEM which is sometimes brought into play: pertinent information can be withheld on grounds of 'national security' or 'protection of sources' or 'commercial confidentiality'. One has no way of knowing whether the reason for the embargo is genuine or merely convenient. It is the Whitehall Loop again.)

The fact is that, as far as the dossier is concerned, we now know that the doubters, including Dr Kelly, were right. Apart from the claim that the world would ultimately be a better place without Saddam Hussein, there were few assertions in that document which events have subsequently confirmed as accurate – there were no nerve gases, no anthrax spores, no ricin, no botulinum toxin, no mobile laboratories, no nuclear materials, no extended-range rockets, no nothing. In short, with Downing Street's interfering help, some of our senior intelligence people got things badly wrong. Indeed, they could not have got them more wrong. Which must be particularly galling for the members of those same intelligence services a little lower down the ladder who were quietly voicing their doubts from the beginning – and who were either ignored or briskly told to shut up.

The absence of any of those Iraqi weapons about which we had been given such cast-iron assurances leads to that other SODEM: the decoy gambit. It is a diversionary tactic which, in this case, by bombarding the BBC with fuss and fury over Gilligan's reporting, drew attention away from the really important problem – that Downing Street, and those top intelligence people, had put together a dossier which was partial and wrong in almost every specific. The tactic was successful: for every square yard of newsprint which examined the issue that really mattered, there seemed to be at least an acre about the row between the government (Alastair Campbell leading the charge) and the BBC. Journalists loved it. With a few honourable exceptions, they willingly allowed themselves to be decoyed. Of course, at its simplest, the answer (it is worth repeating) to the question about what really went wrong is straightforward: one or two of those top intelligence people got far too close to Number 10. That may have been a good career move, but it was a lousy way to run an intelligence service.

The MOD has also come in for criticism. Some, but not all, has been justified. Obviously, officialdom had a problem: if Kelly was not identified, there was no way of showing that Gilligan had grossly misquoted his source. But the way the MOD (with Number 10) handled the 'outing' of Dr Kelly was too sly by half. For a start, it did not even tell him what it was doing. At an early stage, presumably to preserve some proprieties, it put together a statement, which, while not actually naming Kelly, gave any number of helpful clues about his background. Then someone made the suggestion that inquiring journalists (already armed with those clues) might take part in a guessing game. 'If the correct name is given,' the press office was told, 'you can confirm it.' Bingo. This presumably would allow the MOD to claim that it had not actually disclosed Kelly's name, merely confirmed it – another example of that SODEM wherein officialdom publishes a literal but misleading truth. In the event, journalists got to Dr Kelly via a rather different route. Then everyone knew. The fact is that it had already been decided to 'out'

Kelly – so that he could be placed before the Foreign Affairs Committee, where, under cross-examination, it was calculated that he would prove the case against the BBC and Gilligan.

Then there was the role of the man at the very top of the MOD. First, Geoff Hoon told the Hutton Inquiry that he had had nothing to do with the whole affair; he had left the handling of it to his department's civil servants. But when Alastair Campbell's diary was 'published' at the Hutton Inquiry, it became obvious that the Minister of Defence had been as much involved as anyone else.

Since his death, Kelly's friends have argued that he was harshly and inconsiderately treated by his MOD bosses, that they failed in their 'duty of care'. Certainly, with hindsight, they might have done better – particularly in the method of his 'outing'. But it is surely rather unworldly to think that any boss is going to be sympathetic to an employee who, in his view, has let the side down – least of all when that side is the government and/or Whitehall's civil service. Employers have never been supportive of whistleblowers. Further, while Kelly was certainly licensed to talk to journalists, he was pushing his luck if he thought he could tell a defence correspondent that, on a particular and much-debated aspect of defence, his masters had, in effect, been guilty of something near a hoax – and then expect the correspondent to ignore what he had said. You do not agree to meet a journalist unless you accept that he may be interested in what you have to say and, who knows, may publish some of the things you tell him.

Kelly also seems to have been surprisingly innocent on one other point. Given the furore that arose immediately from Gilligan's *Today* disclosure, he was surely misguided to expect that his name would not, sooner rather than later, become public – with accompanying and inevitable media interest. Too many people inside the MOD would have known – or, at the least, have had strong suspicions – for it to have become anything but a very leaky secret. And there was also the possibility that some of his colleagues – other scientists or intelligence personnel – conscious that they themselves might come under suspicion unless the real mole was unearthed, would quickly be able to work out (and then 'leak'?) who Gilligan's informant had been. One way or another, his name was always going to come out.

Had the poor man lived, Kelly would surely have been strongly disciplined for such a breach of the civil service code – 'the rules'. He may even have sailed too close to the Official Secrets Act. His employers must have been suspicious from the start, but perhaps what saved him in the early days was that they reckoned if they did not treat him too harshly they could expect him, for his part, to be a supportive witness before the Select Committees. When, because of Susan Watts's records and tape, it did not work out like that, Kelly probably realized that he could now expect little mercy. What might have followed? The sack? Loss of pension? Disgrace? Again, maybe these concerns weighed so heavily on his mind that, just two days later, this respected scientist seems to have decided that he had had enough.

AND THEN THERE WAS the BBC.

While what went on in the BBC might not, at first, be thought absolutely central to my thesis that Whitehall's tactics are too often much less than straight and true, given that the Corporation quickly became – after 06.07 on 29 May 2003 – the central *target* of those tactics, the subject has obvious relevance. Further, whereas Whitehall usually deploys its SODEMs as part of a *defensive* strategy, in this story they were used in an offensive role. Intention: if we cannot quite sink the BBC, then we must so destabilize it that it no longer remains a threat. It must be severely disciplined.

More specifically, if the BBC could be forced to apologize 'for getting it wrong' (Alastair Campbell's words), the serious credibility problems faced by Downing Street would be much diminished – an object most earnestly and obviously to be desired. So one cannot really avoid looking at the BBC's part in this story. Further, given that I worked there on and off for over thirty years, I have an obvious interest. I may also have an obvious bias. But at least the reader knows what to look for.

The BBC had been seen as the enemy of the government for some time. It often is – by whichever party is in power. Go back only as far as the Falklands campaign and you find Bernard Ingham, Mrs Thatcher's press secretary, on the phone attempting to bully senior BBC news personnel two or three times a week. His successor, Alastair Campbell, would exactly understand his frustrations. And his methods.

The basic complaint is always much the same: the BBC is arrogant, self-absorbed and does not identify often enough with the government's point of view. The complaint goes back at least as far as Suez. Indeed, it goes back much further – to 1926 and the General Strike. The BBC is seen as insufficiently supportive of 'the national interest' – which, too often, is shorthand for 'what the government is trying to do'. During the Falklands campaign, the Corporation even got into trouble because it sometimes chose to refer not to 'our troops', but to 'the British forces', in almost the same breath that it referred to 'the Argentine forces'. That was too even-handed by far. But things got more serious than that.

Now, here is an irony: the BBC's first and immediate reaction when under attack is exactly the same as that of Whitehall: it denies the charge. Of course, behind the scenes (in both Whitehall and Portland Place), there is a scramble of activity to find support for the denial already issued. At the BBC, producers and reporters are sent for by executives, executives are sent for by more senior executives, the offending programme (or sequence) is minutely re-examined, the entrails of memos and e-mails are scrutinized, and, who knows, lawyers alerted and dead files exhumed to find supporting precedents.

If the row is big enough, the most senior executive of all, the Director General, will get involved. And if the row is even bigger, the BBC governors will want to know what is going on. They certainly did in this case. Not since the *Real Lives* furore of 1985 (another instance of the BBC being 'unsupportive' of the government – in that case, in the matter of Northern Ireland) had there been such an onslaught by government. And, as often happens (and not just with the BBC), the more bullying the attack, the more stubborn grows the resistance to it. Which is one reason why, in these very public rows, positions on both sides become ever more firmly locked.

In this particular story, there was an additional complication: Alastair Campbell, the man who led the assault, had long become a serial complainant. BBC editors had grown weary of his almost daily bombardments; he had cried 'foul' so often that broadcasters had developed an immunity to his increasingly strident attacks. So when he complained about Gilligan's *Today* report, it is not too surprising that he was handled with less than the full attention that he and others in or near government thought he deserved. With hindsight, the downgrading of the man who had too often cried wolf was an obvious error – by everyone in the BBC right up to Director General Greg Dyke and the governors. But at the time, an attitude of 'Oh, it's that bloody man Campbell again' probably seemed reasonable enough. Big mistake – even if, with hindsight, one can see how it happened.

Senior news executives were summoned to brief the board of governors. From what they told the board, there seemed no reason to modify the Corporation's stance. With the corroboration inherent in Susan Watts's notes (though, strangely, Watts herself never quite saw it that way), the head of news was presumably able to assure the governors that Gilligan's report had reasonably reflected, in its essentials, what he said his mole had told him. So the governors publicly held firm. But behind the scenes there were some doubts. One governor, Dame Pauline Neville-Jones, who before retirement had reached one of the very highest ranks in the intelligence services (Chairman of the Joint Intelligence Committee) did some research among her old colleagues and returned to tell the BBC's Chairman, Gavyn Davies, that Gilligan's still-anonymous source was most unlikely to have been 'one of the senior officials in charge of drawing up the dossier'. Nor was it probable that he was really a member of the intelligence services. That alone may be enough to account for the fact that it was now noted within the governors' own circle that 'careful language had not been applied' throughout by Gilligan.

Perhaps the governors, for the best of motives (never crumple before a bully) had decided too quickly that the BBC was 101 per cent right in every detail. Should they have interrogated their executives a little harder? Yes. Should those executives have questioned their subordinates and Gilligan more closely? Yes. Should Greg Dyke have got 'stuck in' much earlier? Yes. In fact, all those people now agree that they did not react quickly or investigate thoroughly enough. But, for all that, with the evidence now available from the Hutton Inquiry, the three basic allegations in Gilligan's story have been proved 98 per cent correct: that the dossier contained unwarranted exaggerations in which Number 10 had a very considerable involvement; that some of those same exaggerations had caused real concern among intelligence personnel; and that the

'WMD in forty-five minutes' claim, if not absolutely and knowingly 'wrong', was, in the way its misinterpretation by the public was deliberately left uncorrected, highly duplicitous. In that last comment – 'if not absolutely *wrong*, highly duplicitous' – lies the only room for a Gilligan error of substance. Two per cent? Maybe.[6]

Further, there is some irony in the fact that while Gilligan has been much criticized for basing part of his 29 May report on information given him by 'a single uncorroborated source [Kelly]', the actual inclusion of that claim in the dossier was similarly based on 'a single uncorroborated source' (someone in the Iraqi officer corps). We now know that the BBC's single uncorroborated source was much more accurate than the single uncorroborated source relied on by the JIC and Downing Street.

So the governors, led by Chairman Gavyn Davies, nobody's fool, were surely right to have stood strong. True, as has been observed, the BBC would have made a more convincing case if it had shown that it had reacted to the government's charge more quickly and investigated more thoroughly. Perhaps this lapse was at least partly due to an attitude of 'Oh, it's that bloody Campbell again'. Additionally, the BBC governors' position was not helped when, rather late in the day, it suddenly became known that Kevin Marsh, the editor of *Today*, in an e-mail to his immediate boss, had expressed doubts about aspects of Gilligan's professionalism.

> The story was a good piece of investigative journalism marred by flawed reporting. The biggest millstone has been the loose use of language and lack of judgement in some of the phraseology.

One can see what Kevin Marsh means. Nevertheless, while one can differentiate between a broadcast report and the earlier investigation on which that report is based, the comment does seem to say that 'this car is a good piece of automotive engineering marred by wobbly wheels'. And, rather oddly, the e-mail was sent on 27 June – four weeks after the

6. Is this the reason why more of the intelligence personnel who had doubts about the validity of the dossier's claim of 'WMD ready in forty-five minutes' were in the MOD than in the other intelligence arms? Certainly, there has long been a degree of tension, rivalry almost, between the MOD's intelligence unit and MI6. They are meant to come together at the over-riding Joint Intelligence Committee. But it does not always work like that.

broadcast. In any case, one might have thought that with a potentially inflammable item like Gilligan's, where it would be known that the government would dissect every nuance (it monitors all news and current affairs broadcasts), the duty editor of *Today* would, the evening before, have instructed Gilligan to work out most carefully and to write down the key elements in his report (if not fully to script it) and then to run through it with him/her on the phone.[7] Interestingly, John Humphrys' studio introduction to Gilligan *was* scripted and, presumably, checked with that morning's producer beforehand. Or with the duty editor. It too could have been improved in terms of precision:

> Our defence correspondent, Andrew Gilligan, has found evidence that the government's dossier on Iraq that was produced last September was cobbled together at the last minute with some unconfirmed material that had not been approved by the security services.

One might have thought that if Gilligan were later to be criticized for 'loose language' and 'lack of judgement', those same reservations might also have been levelled at Humphrys' scripted introduction – which, presumably, had had prior approval. Or, alternatively, one might have thought that both parts of that early morning 'two-way' were a reasonable reflection of what Gilligan said he had been told. Perhaps, in his comments, the editor of *Today* was being a little too wise a little too long after the event.

Anyway, despite doubts about some details of Gilligan's reportage, the BBC governors did not back off. Maybe they took the view (to run together a few useful clichés) that at the end of the day and at that

7. Another point on which Gilligan and *Today* have been criticized is that they made no attempt to check the story with Downing Street or the MOD, let alone to give a spokesman a chance to reply. An approach might have been wise for form's sake, but no more. It would almost certainly have brought nothing but a total denial. Indeed, it is possible that Downing Street's reaction (via Alastair Campbell?) would have been so violent that the story would have been killed. Of course, some would argue that that is exactly what should have happened. Lastly, Gilligan has been criticized (not least by his boss) for being a loner who did not report in to the *Today* offices often enough. A fair point. But it is rather in the nature of investigative reporters that they don't hunt with the pack; they are often rather secretive creatures who don't share their research until they are ready to break a story. For any editor, that is a problem.

moment in time, whichever way you cut it, the long and short of the bottom line was that we went to war because we had been persuaded that Saddam Hussein possessed an arsenal of deadly gases, poxes and toxins – some of which could be on their way via long-range rockets within the hour. Further, that that 'narrative' was strongly doubted by some people in the intelligence community. Assuming that Tony Blair did not know how far from the truth his dossier was (and we are not talking just 'details' here), then one has to say that senior personnel in the Joint Intelligence Committee, helped by members of the kitchen cabinet, had given him (and the rest of us) a very bum steer indeed. With an intelligence blunder on that scale, one might expect heads to roll or, at the least, to move sideways – in the best civil-servant tradition. But because they were telling the boss, the Prime Minister, what he was so desperate to hear, it seems that heads will almost certainly stay where they are – despite any criticisms that Lord Hutton may make.

But it is little wonder that the government were out to get Gilligan, and, thereby, the BBC. If nothing else, the furore of indignation – which went on for most of the summer – was a diversionary tactic to cover up the issue that really mattered: if the JIC and Downing Street really believed everything that they put in the dossier, then subsequent history shows that they were less than wholly competent. If they did *not* believe it, but put it in anyway, they were something much worse.

A LAST WORD OR TWO: it would be hypocritical to pretend that I was 'against the war'. I thought at the time that Saddam Hussein's regime was so evil and the likelihood of his being able to develop chemical and biological weapons (though perhaps not quite to the level of long-range WMD) for future blackmail, terrorism and international mischief on the grand scale was so great that his removal – by force if necessary and despite the risks – was justified. I judged that the only reason he had allowed the UN arms inspectors back into Iraq was because of the threat posed by the coalition forces gathering along his border. Even so, he was obviously up to every trick imaginable. So, if he thought the coalition was just bluffing, it was time to call his bluff. Further, I was not much bothered or surprised by the fact that the UN did not want to get involved. Better a swift decisive war now without the UN (and the

French) than, possibly, a long messy one later – probably still without them. Maybe that was simplistic. If so, I was in some good company.

As I see it (and at some risk of repetition), back through the autumn and winter of 2002–03 Tony Blair had an almost insurmountable problem. Rightly or wrongly, he had already committed the nation to a war – but without the democratic mandate to do so. So now he had to persuade us to go with him. But too many people needed something far stronger than regime change or even the possibility that Iraq might have some chemical and biological weapons. So Number 10 encouraged the intelligence teams, and particularly the overriding Joint Intelligence Committee, to find whatever horrors were needed to do the job. In other words, the intelligence, in the form of the final dossier, had to fit a decision already taken. One is reminded of the aphorism that, too often, 'democracy is about the process of manufacturing consent'. Official disinformation was, through the autumn of 2002 and the winter and spring of 2003, very much part of that 'manufacturing' process. So, whatever the outcome and verdict of Lord Hutton, his inquiry has opened to public view and discussion the entrails of what would otherwise have been a still-hidden narrative of official dissembling and, in parts, cover-up.

Maybe Tony Blair did the right thing, but we now know that he got hold of (or was given) some very dodgy reasons for doing so.

Addendum

This chapter was finished a week before Lord Hutton published his findings. A thought: just because it is not 'done' to question an umpire's decision, that does not mean that the umpire must, inevitably, always get it right. Anyway, thank the Lord for juries.

A second thought: in early May 2004, John Scarlett was appointed head of MI6.

THE ILOIS

'The purpose is to maintain the fiction'

These steps should be ordered and timed to attract the least attention and should have some logical cover where possible worked out in advance. Even if these steps are taken with the utmost discretion and careful planning we must anticipate that they will become known and arouse suspicions as to their purpose.

A Foreign Office 'Memorandum of Guidance', 11 May 1964

We agree that there is a prospect that the ignorance and confused thinking prevailing on the matter could enable us to dodge the real issues.

A Foreign Office signal to the UK Delegation at the UN, 21 February 1969

In the matter of the Ilois, there may be an awkward problem of presentation. Meanwhile, the less said the better.[1]

A Foreign Office minute, 17 April 1971

THE ILOIS? WHO, WHAT and where are they? Coming originally from Mauritius, the Seychelles and perhaps from Madagascar, they had lived and worked for several generations on the Chagos Islands, a remote scatter of atolls in the middle of the Indian Ocean. These lonely outposts of the Empire had come into British possession as part of the victor's small change at the end of the Napoleonic Wars. Ever since that time, the Governor of Mauritius, over 1200 miles away, would send someone over to have a look once a year or so. That was how they were governed.

The Ilois (patois for 'islanders') earned a little cash by working for absentee Mauritian landlords in the coconut plantations on the three inhabited islands. They harvested the nuts, dried the 'meat' into copra,

1. The documents from which these and other, subsequent quotations are drawn all come from the FO/BIOT files 1967–72.

and processed the oil – prized for use in cosmetics and confectionery. Between times they fished in the lagoons. They grew vegetables, and kept chickens, pigs and goats. A small ship journeyed over from Mauritius now and then to collect the copra. It was a very simple life. The occasional visitor thought it idyllic. The world was somewhere else.

Then the Ilois got caught up in the Cold War.

Back in the mid-1960s it was obvious that Britain could no longer afford any serious defence commitments east of Suez. In any case, the Empire was dying. Singapore had gone. Aden and Mombasa were going. Mauritius and the Seychelles were also imminently for independence. But with British influence running down, who would fill the vacuum and vastness of the Indian Ocean? Who would safeguard the West's oil tankers coming out of the Gulf? Britain and America were nervous that the Russians, through their hugely expanding navy, would try to gain control; they were already making overtures to various Marxist-leaning regimes – Aden, Somalia, Zanzibar, Mozambique. The Chinese, too, were signing 'friendship treaties'. So to counter this potential threat the Americans approached the British (or was it the other way round?) with a plan to lease the main island of the Chagos group. They were looking for somewhere to establish what they called 'an austere communications facility'.[2]

The biggest of the Chagos Islands is Diego Garcia. Being on the way to nowhere, it is one of the most remote inhabited islands in the world. But within its horseshoe-shaped lagoon of about fourteen miles by four, one could anchor as many ships as one might wish. On the enclosing atoll a runway might be built which could take any planes then flying. Furthermore, such a base would be strategically placed right in the middle of the Indian Ocean, yet remote enough to leave the Americans undisturbed. To Harold Wilson's cabinet – or those of the cabinet who were told – it seemed a good idea. Diego Garcia would join places like Ascension Island and Lakenheath: British-owned, American-run. The 'rent' would go some way towards paying for the American Polaris missiles

2. The Americans originally had their eyes on Aldabra atoll. It genuinely seemed to have no indigenous 'belongers'. But word got out and the wildlife lobby mobilized: Aldabra was the home and breeding ground of a rare species of giant turtle.

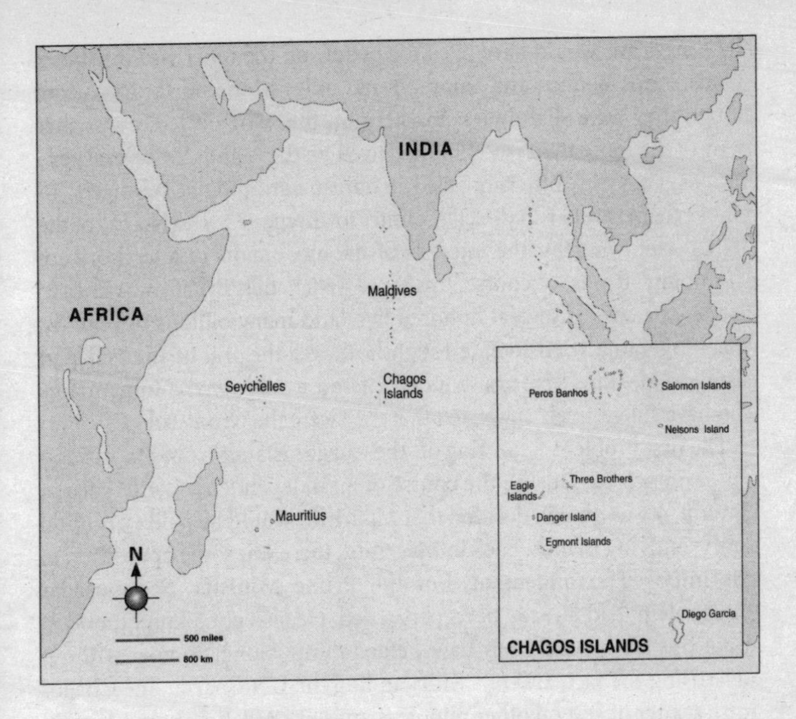

with which Britain planned to arm some of her nuclear submarines. And self-interest went beyond that: there was comfort in knowing that the policing of the Indian Ocean would be in safe and friendly hands.

But there were two problems. First, for nearly 150 years the Chagos Islands had been ruled as a far-flung outpost of Mauritius. Now, with Mauritius about to become independent, it would be contrary to the UN Charter for Britain to split off and retain the Chagos archipelago for her own use. Chosen pieces of a former colony could not be picked off and retained by the vacating imperial power. According to the Charter, signed by Britain, to do so would be a 'disruption of the territorial integrity' of the newly emergent nation. The second problem lay in the firm demand of the Americans that, for reasons of security, the island should, in the jargon of the times, be 'swept' and 'fully sanitized'. This was a way of saying that the inhabitants of Diego Garcia would have to be removed.

The Americans would have liked the people on the other two inhabited islands, Peros Banhos and Salomon, 140 miles to the north, to go too, though they were slightly less insistent on this. The difficulty was that many of the more than 1500 Ilois had lived on the islands for several generations. They were officially called, in bureaucratic pidgin, 'belongers'. To remove them would run directly counter to another Article (No. 73) of the UN Charter, whereby 'the interests of the inhabitants of a territory are paramount'. It was, of course, this same Article that Britain was later to invoke, at a cost of several hundred lives and many billions of pounds, when Argentina tried to ride roughshod over the will of the Falkland Islanders. The Ilois were not so lucky. There are even some commentators who have subversively suggested that they were the wrong colour.

The first problem – splitting off the Chagos Islands from Mauritius – was easily solved. During the course of an independence conference in London, it was quietly decided that Mauritius would be paid £3 million for the outlying islands. Back in Mauritius, there was some opposition to this imposed arrangement, but the Prime Minister, Seewoosagar Ramgoolam, had already been persuaded. He also got a knighthood at about this time, which may have helped things along. So now, without advertising the fact, and not withstanding the UN Charter, the Chagos and a scatter of several other remote islands like Aldabra (home of giant turtles) and Agalega became the British Indian Ocean Territories (BIOT). We had created a new colony. Which is, presumably, why Whitehall hoped that 'ignorance and confused thinking [might] enable us to dodge the real issues'. Nevertheless, one could argue that in the effort to contain the tyranny of communism and to maintain the safety of the 'free world', a few overly legalistic UN corners might reasonably be cut. Realpolitik was what mattered. Besides, Mauritius was not much interested in its far-flung appendages. In short, the end justified the means.[3] But there was another 'real issue' which was not so easily solved. Or justified. What was to be done about the resident Ilois?

3. There was another argument about why the transfer to Britain should have been kept quiet: the Russians would certainly have used the truth to embarrass the 'imperialist' British both at the UN and among the more volatile politicians in the emergent nations of East Africa. Who knows but India might also have made life difficult.

For the British to be seen, at the behest of the Americans, forcibly removing the inhabitants of Diego Garcia and the other two islands would cause all kinds of embarrassment – and not just at the UN, with its emphasis on the paramountcy of local wishes. Who knew but that some MPs might become overly inquisitive. Indeed, one internal Foreign Office note is quite specific: 'The less said the better – Mr Dalyell is interested and may kick up a fuss.' In fact, Tam Dalyell's Parliamentary Question was already on its way. Off and on he has been asking them ever since – for well over thirty years. Even now he is not wholly satisfied. Doubtless he will be submitting more questions.

Anyway, back in 1967 Whitehall hatched a plan. While it was not quite illegal, it was of very doubtful morality. The copra plantations would be bought from the Mauritian owners and then shut down. It was reckoned that once the Ilois realized there was no more work, they could be persuaded to remove themselves without too much fuss. They would be resettled in Mauritius. The scheme was spelt out by the top mandarin at the Colonial Office, Denis Greenhill (later Lord Greenhill of Harrow) in a note to the British Delegation at the UN:

> The object of the exercise is to get some rocks which will remain ours; there will be no indigenous population except seagulls who have not yet got a committee. Unfortunately, along with the birds go a few Tarzans and Man Fridays who are hopefully being wished on Mauritius.

Political correctness had not yet been invented. Obviously everything depended on keeping this rather transparent plan out of the strong light. However, if by some unfortunate chance word leaked out of what was really going on, it was important to have a contingency plan to put people (including Mr Dalyell?) off the scent. Cover-up is not a term recognized in Whitehall. But a conspiracy by any other name would still smell as bad.

The scheme was a simple one. But it moved forward the strategy – 'the line to be taken' – from being merely immoral to being undeniably illegal. The plan required that inhabitants of Diego Garcia and those other two islands – Peros Banhos and Salomon – would be designated as mere contract labour 'imported' from Mauritius for just a few years at a time. Thus the tiresome business of the UN Charter with its emphasis on self-determination and the rights of 'local inhabitants' could be avoided. So began a whole series of confidential notes, memoranda and signals between Whitehall, our delegation at the UN, and the British High Commissions in Mauritius and the Seychelles. One official, in a note he obviously never thought might be read more than three decades later, commented, 'We are being asked to cook the books.' Exactly. Another official went into the recipe in a little more detail:

> The Colonial Office is at present considering the line to be taken in dealing with the existing inhabitants of the British Indian Ocean Territory (BIOT). They wish to avoid using the phrase 'permanent inhabitants' in relation to any of the islands in the territory because to recognise that there are any permanent inhabitants will imply that there is a population whose democratic rights will have to be safeguarded and which will therefore be deemed by the UN to come within its purlieu. [The solution will be] to issue them with documents making it clear that they are 'belongers' of Mauritius and the Seychelles and only temporary residents of BIOT. This device, though rather transparent, would at least give us a defensible position to take up at the UN.

Obviously the authors of these various memoranda – who, incidentally, all went on in time to get their CMGs, knighthoods and even peerages – never dreamt that their thinking would see the light of day more than thirty years later. Maybe it is unfair to lay bare their deceits. But, given the ultimate fate of the Ilois, it would be even more unfair to leave them hidden.

In July 1968, not long after the Chagos Islands had been secured under the Union flag, Foreign Secretary Michael Stewart sent a four-page confidential explanation to Harold Wilson. It would, of course, have been written by one of his advisors, who now got down to the detail:

> The UN General Assembly may object that the interests of the local population are being ignored, but we have been able to resist such arguments by pointing out that the inhabitants consist mostly of migrant workers from Mauritius and Seychelles . . . Resettlement will involve some small expense but it is not expected that there will be any financial difficulty with this. When the arrangements are complete, and they may be complicated by a recently completed survey

> which found that 128 individuals (about 34% of the total population of 389) are second generation inhabitants of Diego Garcia, we would propose, as agreed at the time of the creation of BIOT, to deny, if necessary, the competence of the UN to concern itself with a territory which has no indigenous population . . . The matter will be easier to handle at the UN if the proposal to develop the island does not become publicly known . . . until after the end of the next session of the UN General Assembly.

One sees here the cover-up of the original lie being firmly cemented in place. Furthermore, the paragraph contains a gross underestimate of numbers. This must have been deliberate, because only eight years earlier – before it became important to pretend that there was no 'indigenous' population – the then Governor of Mauritius, Sir Robert Scott, had made a brief visit to Diego Garcia and the two other inhabited islands; he came up with the very different estimate of about 1700 inhabitants. In his book *Limuria*, Sir Robert made this further comment:

> At least a quarter of the population in 1901 consisted of temporary labourers. Today [1960], this part of the population amounts to less than one eighth, although admittedly there is an indeterminate proportion of islanders still doubtful whether they are permanent or not.

Likewise, in a Central Office of Information film shot during the Governor's visit, the commentary states that the people 'are native to these islands'. So, despite the official dissembling, there can never have been the slightest doubt in Whitehall that a significant proportion of the inhabitants of Diego Garcia, Peros Banhos and Salomon were 'belongers'. They had been there for several generations. Indeed, a formal BIOT report made as late as June 1968 records that on Diego Garcia 'there are 354 third generation belongers . . . they would not normally be thought of as temporary inhabitants'. The register of births and deaths for the Chagos, so far as they go, now lodged in the FO's files at Milton Keynes shows that 354 is a quite considerable underestimate. If Sir Robert Scott's figures are to be believed, there were probably three or four times that number.

Finally, the unblinking blatancy of the lie under which 'the natives' were to be removed and then barred from any return is exemplified in the advice proffered by the FO's Legal Department when it was asked for help in drafting the necessary Ordinance which would give legal authority for the 'clearance' of the islands. Here is the first paragraph of that advice:

> The purpose of the Immigration Ordinance is to maintain the fiction that the inhabitants of Chagos are not a permanent or semi-permanent population. The Ordinance would be published in the BIOT Gazette which has only very limited circulation. Publicity will therefore be minimal.

The phrase 'to maintain the fiction' says it all. Well, most of it.

FAMILY GROUPS OF ILOIS HAD long made the occasional trip to Mauritius in the steamer taking away the copra. They would go to spend some of the money earned in the plantations, to see the bright lights, to do some shopping, perhaps to visit a doctor. Then they would get the next ship home – even though the return might mean a wait of several months. But in the late 1960s several such visiting family groups found that they were not allowed to board the ship home. They had been 'removed' on the grounds that their contracts with the plantation owners had expired. But most of them had never had contracts. Angry but helpless and homeless, they were left to fend for themselves.

In 1970 the Head of the Indian Ocean Department at the Foreign and Commonwealth Office in Whitehall was Eleanor Emery. She had first learnt about the Chagos 'problem' a few years earlier when she had been the Counsellor at the British High Commission in Ottawa. In a cable to London she had warned that some time before, in a different but parallel context, Canada had 'specifically condemned the transfer of sovereignty without the consent of the inhabitants'.[4] So, unless the Canadians could be hoodwinked (Miss Emery did not use that term), Britain could not rely on Canada's support if things came unstuck at the UN. It was obviously becoming ever more important that nothing should be done which might let the secret out. By 1970, Miss Emery, now promoted and back in Whitehall as the boss (the Commissioner) of BIOT, was much more directly involved in the bamboozling business. But she was not acting merely on her own initiative; she was following the official line laid down

4. The FO/BIOT files 1967–72.

earlier by the Colonial Secretary, Anthony Greenwood. He was in no doubt that the Article of the UN Charter about 'progress towards self-government' should be disregarded: 'We should not accept the responsibilities laid on the administering government under this Article of the Charter.' So that no one should be in any doubt, he then stated that 'we propose to avoid any reference to "permanent inhabitants" . . . it is essential that there should be no doubt that the individuals are, and are accepted as being, belongers of Mauritius and the Seychelles'.

A few months later Tam Dalyell gave notice that he intended to ask a number of what were obviously going to be awkward Parliamentary Questions. And, as a consequence, one or two journalists were also sniffing around. So, given that Diego Garcia was very much Miss Emery's immediate responsibility, she put together what was officially labelled 'a memorandum of guidance'. In Whitehall-speak this was 'a memo on the line that should be taken'. No doubt she had Mr Greenwood's directive propped up in front of her. Maybe she herself had drafted it at an earlier stage. Her memorandum had a restricted circulation. But not that restricted. One can assume that it would have been read by most Foreign Office ministers and at least a couple of dozen FO officials – in Mauritius and the Seychelles, in the UN, in the Washington Embassy, in the British Information Service, in the FO's Defence Department, and across the road in the MOD. Miss Emery's task was to make sure that everyone would be humming the same tune. She began by drawing attention to 'a recent revival of public interest in the British Indian Ocean Territory'. She meant that Mr Dalyell and a few others were about to make a nuisance of themselves. Miss Emery then got to the nub of what she had to say:

> We shall continue to try to say as little as possible to avoid embarrassing the United States Administration . . . [To say nothing of the British Administration.] Apart from our overall strategic and defence interests, we are also concerned at present not to have to elaborate on the administrative implications for the present population on Diego Garcia of the establishment of any base there . . . We would not wish it to become general knowledge that some of the inhabitants have lived on Diego Garcia for at least two generations and could, therefore, be regarded as 'belongers'. We shall advise ministers in handling supplementary questions . . . to say that there is only a small number

> of contract labourers from the Seychelles and Mauritius engaged to work on the copra plantations.
>
> Should an MP ask about what would happen to these contract labourers in the event of a base being set up on the island, we hope that, for the present, this can be brushed aside as a hypothetical question at least until any decision to go ahead with the Diego Garcia facility becomes public.

Together with a retort that a question is 'irrelevant', the SODEM of dismissing difficult inquiries on the basis that they are hypothetical (because 'Her Majesty's Government has yet to consider the matter', or words close to that effect) is familiar to any student of the Whitehall handbook. Being translated, both replies mean that decisions have already been made – 'but because we are on shaky ground we don't want to talk about them'. And, in the passage quoted above, the term 'administrative implications for the present population' is a neatly non-emotive phrase for the forcible removal of that population.

So, in the cause of containment (and getting a set of Polaris missiles on the cheap), Parliament was deceived. And an estimated 1700 Ilois on three of some of the most remote inhabited islands on earth were about to be forced from their homes. But perhaps (again), given the strategic exigencies of the time, one should not be too censorious. Maybe it is the matter-of-fact blatancy of the deception that really lifts the eyebrows. If only as much thought had gone into the problem of the dispossessed Ilois as went into the construction of the cover-up. If only Whitehall had stopped short of their callous abandonment. A US Congressional Committee was told that it was 'fortuitous that Diego Garcia has no local population whatsoever'. In fact, at about that time, what remained of the allegedly non-existent population on Diego Garcia – some had already been persuaded to leave, while others had been barred from coming back – gathered under the palms to listen to a BIOT administrator who had made the 1200-mile voyage from Mauritius to give them the final news:

> I told all the inhabitants that we intended to close the island in July . . . a few of the Ilois asked whether they could receive some compensation for leaving 'their own country'. I kicked this into touch by saying that our intention was to cause as little disruption of their lives as possible.

These were simple people; they did not know what to expect. Or how to protest. Presumably, they hoped that their colonial masters would look after them. Is it too extreme to compare the efforts made on their behalf with those made in support of those other islanders, of whom there was a very similar number, in the Falklands? Our moral and legal obligations were the same to both.

Some weeks after that gathering under the palms – with their concerns now firmly punted into the long grass – the Ilois packed up a few belongings in boxes and hessian sacks, strung together some clanking bundles of pots and pans, shut the doors on their houses, held a last mass in the island's small church, and put down their donkeys and the village dogs. Two mares and a stallion escaped. Then, with only what they could carry, they were ferried out to the waiting ship. Four miles away, on the other side of the lagoon, the Americans had arrived.

A week later, on docking at Port Louis in Mauritius, the Ilois were met on the quay by the friends and relatives who had preceded them. The news was not good: no jobs, no money, nowhere to live. The British had paid £650,000 'in full and final settlement of HMG's obligations'; it worked out at less than £400 per head. But it was not a handout to the families; the money went to the Mauritian government to defray the costs of resettling the Ilois. Inevitably it got caught in the bureaucracy of administration and there were many delays. The Ilois themselves got nothing: no compensation for the loss of their jobs, homes and land. They got no direct help at all. As sometimes happens, Whitehall had successfully brainwashed itself into believing its own deceptions – that the Ilois really were only Mauritians on contract. So, having dumped them on the dockside, British responsibilities had ended.

Apart from now being abandoned, their problems were compounded by other factors. First, 20 per cent of Mauritius' working population was unemployed. Second, the Ilois had no wage-earning skills other than working in coconut plantations and processing copra. But Mauritius did not have a copra industry; it was a sugar island. Third, some of the Ilois were only semi-literate and this, combined with a transition from a mainly barter economy to one based on cash, left many of them hopelessly confused. They also spoke a patois peculiar to their home islands, so they were quickly recognized by the many unemployed

Mauritians as rivals for the same few unskilled jobs. There was hostility. Within weeks, according to a number of contemporary accounts, many of the Ilois were living rough or in lean-to shacks made of corrugated iron and sacking. They were destitute. The more desperate young men turned to drink (and the petty crime needed to pay for it), some of the young women to prostitution.

Within the first year, there were several suicides. It is said that some of the older Ilois went down with the most forlorn of all ailments: a broken heart.

A few of the more literate exiles put together a petition that they took to the British High Commission. 'Although we were poor there, we were not dying of hunger. We were living free. Here in Mauritius we don't get anybody to help us. We are at a loss not knowing what to do.' They asked that each Ilois family be given a house, a plot of land and some kind of work – as they had had back home. If these things were not possible, could they go home to their own islands? If not to Diego Garcia, what about the two islands that the Americans did not seem to need: Peros Banhos and Salomon? The High Commission passed the petition to the Mauritian government. After all, the British had already made a 'full and final settlement', so the plight of the Ilois was now someone else's problem.

It took a few years, but eventually the predicament of the Ilois found the support of some Mauritians, particularly the main opposition party, the Mouvement Militant Mauricien (MMM). No doubt the MMM had found a cause with which to make life difficult for the local government. But Whitehall became worried when it started to ask questions about the validity, under international law and the UN Charter, of the way Britain had 'purchased' the Chagos, and the way the Ilois had then been removed from their island homes. In the wider world beyond Mauritius, there was further potential for embarrassment. A roving reporter from the *Washington Post* had come across the story. David Ottaway wrote about what he called 'this act of mass kidnapping'. His article prompted a Congressional Committee to ask some questions. It was told 'the entire subject of Diego Garcia was considered classified . . . in response to British sensitivities'. In London the occasional question was being asked in the Lords and in the Commons – Mr Dalyell had now been joined by others. The London *Sunday Times* ran a long feature article in September 1975: 'The Islanders that Britain Sold'. And a Methodist preacher from Kent, George Champion, shamed by what he saw as his country's treatment of a remote and voiceless minority, began a rather remarkable one-man campaign to arouse the public conscience and spark some eventual justice for the Ilois. He preached, he wrote articles, he sent letters, he made a fuss. He even mounted a solo picket once a month on the Whitehall pavement outside the Foreign and Commonwealth Office; his placard just said 'Diego Garcia'. People sometimes stopped to ask what Mr Garcia was supposed to have done. Or not done. When Mr Champion told them, they too were ashamed. Either that or they hurried on, unconvinced there was anything they could do about the problem.

In Mauritius the Ilois were now desperate. They held forlorn demonstrations and hunger strikes. They resisted (and went to jail) when the police came to pull down the unlicensed shacks they had built. They even set up a small protest camp in the entrance to the British High Commission. The Mauritian government commissioned a survey: it found that there were at least three times as many people claiming Chagos ancestry as had been acknowledged by BIOT. The government let Whitehall know its view that the British had not adequately discharged their responsibilities.

Something must have pricked (just a little) the conscience of the Foreign Office, because in 1979 it decided to try another 'full and final settlement'. This time the amount was £1.25 million. But there was a condition: each Ilois had to sign a binding agreement to renounce any claim ever to return to the Chagos Islands. Some of the most destitute families signed without appreciating what they were doing. One imagines that it was a case of 'if you want some money, then sign here'. But when other Ilois realized what was happening, they sent the English lawyer charged with the arrangements back to London – with a flea in his ear. Strangely, it was a law firm started by this same lawyer, Bernard Sheridan, which later became the legal champion of the Ilois.

That same year, a small group of Ilois and some Mauritian friends determined to revisit their homeland. Knowing that a landing on Diego Garcia was pointless – there were more than 2500 US servicemen there by now – they headed for Salomon, about 140 miles north of the

American base. In the eight years since it had been abandoned, the island's coconut plantations had become overgrown. But the houses were still habitable, the fresh-water wells were in reasonable order, there were plenty of fish, pigs, wild chickens, coconuts and vegetables. The party stayed several weeks. The visit had shown that with a contract to supply a few hundred tons of copra and oil each year, a return to the old life would be possible. The problem was that, according to an executive decision taken 7000 miles away in Whitehall at the time of the 'clearances', they were breaking the law by even visiting their islands.

Back on Mauritius there were more protests. A long-awaited report on the condition of the Ilois, commissioned by the island government, was damning in both its direct and inferred criticism of the British.[5] Unfortunately, Whitehall was not persuaded. After all, to have acknowledged that the cover under which the Ilois were expelled had been the purest fiction would have been seen as a direct comment on the morality of those who had devised that cover ten years earlier. It would have been 'letting the side down'. It seems almost impossible within Whitehall to change earlier decisions without admitting earlier mistakes. And it is part of the lore of the place that neither ministers nor top civil servants make mistakes.

If the Americans insisted (as they did) that Diego Garcia was cleared, why could the 'belonger' inhabitants not have been more generously compensated and offered help to settle on Peros Banhos and Salomon? At least they could have been given the option. For that matter, why did the Ilois have to move at all? Most of them had lived and worked four or five miles away on the opposite side of the atoll from that part of Diego Garcia on which the Americans had now built their base and runway. And given that the Americans brought in workers from the Philippines almost from the start, security can hardly have been the priority they claimed then or since. Indeed, in 1981 sixty Mauritians were shipped in to help on construction work. So what was going on?

Over 2000 American servicemen are normally stationed in the 'austere communications facility' of Diego Garcia. During the Gulf War and again during the Afghan campaign against terrorism, the population

5. The Sylva Report of May 1981.

rose to at least 4000. The runway has long been extended to 2 miles – to take B52 bombers. The lagoon is home to every type of US naval ship, from submarine tenders to landing craft, from cruisers to tankers, from ocean-going tugs to requisitioned freighters (loaded with military supplies and ready to go). Ashore, beside all the military installations, there is a chapel, a hospital, a bowling club, a rod 'n' gun club, a nine-hole par-3 golf club, a baseball diamond, an Olympic-size swimming pool, a workout gym, a movie house, a radio station, a Post Exchange, ice-cream parlours, launderettes and numerous well-stocked warehouses. The US Navy Diego Garcia website promises incomers that 'You can look forward to a fun-filled tour . . . with unbelievable recreational facilities and exquisite natural beauty'. In the airport lounge there is a red phone box from Olde England. Other attractions include an internet café where you can 'check your investments while investing in a pizza'. The electricity needed to desalinate up to a thousand tons of seawater each day (let alone to power all the air-conditioning) would satisfy a fair-sized city. They drive on the right.[6]

On the highest water tower, overlooking the satellite tracking dishes and the communications antennae, is painted the slogan, 'Welcome to the Footprint of Freedom'. The greeting should not be taken literally; a welcome is the last thing on offer if one should arrive as an unauthorized visitor. The only way that a 'civilian' can get to Diego Garcia is illegally, by yacht. In 1984 the journalist Simon Winchester joined a small Australian schooner in southern India and persuaded the female skipper 'to give it a go'. As he relates in his book *Outposts*, some weeks and over a thousand miles later the yacht sailed into the lagoon. Unexpectedly, the American tug which guided them in was very hospitable; the crew handed across a crate of beer and a carton of frozen strawberries as soon as the anchor was down. It was the British, roaring up in a launch marked 'BIOT', who were the problem. Two khaki-clad gents stepped across onto the yacht and demanded her immediate departure. They knew all about Mr Winchester because he had applied in London some months before and been unequivocally turned down. Now here he was

6. These and other details were gleaned from someone who served in Diego Garcia, and from the official US Navy website: www.dg.navy.mil/index=us navy.

anyway – cheeky fellow. The Australian skipper formally quoted the maritime convention whereby a ship can claim refuge if in trouble; there were several things that needed 'fixing'. The BIOT men were not persuaded. But it was getting dark; they relented. The yacht would have to leave at dawn the next morning. Mr Winchester never put a foot ashore.

The make-up of the British 'presence' on Diego Garcia varies from year to year but typically consists of a dozen or so Royal Marines, a few RN ratings and, at one time, three or four London policemen. There are also one or two BIOT personnel seconded from the FO in London. In overall charge there is usually an RN Commander who is the Queen's representative in all respects – Magistrate, Registrar of Births, Deaths and Marriages, Inspector of Customs, Postmaster and Conservation Officer. Occasionally, a senior personage from Whitehall hitch-hikes in for a few days on an American C-130 bringing in supplies from Singapore. Perhaps the visitor and the other 'Brits' on station are there to remind the Americans who actually owns the place. But, other than that, there must be very little for these people to do. A few years ago the Marines kept themselves busy by restoring the plantation manager's small chateau on the far side of the atoll. It is to that part, deserted now for over thirty years, that some of the Ilois would like to return.

If one forgets about the Ilois, the world probably is a safer place because of what Diego Garcia has become. Even so, in Whitehall the place is never officially referred to as a 'base', merely as a 'facility'. But, at least, the adjective 'austere' seems to have been dropped.

ON A MONDAY AFTERNOON in April 2001, one would have found an Ilois, Olivier Bancoult, sitting on a banquette in the House of Commons tea-room. He was there as the guest of two MPs, Tam Dalyell and Jeremy Corbyn. A little earlier, together with his lawyer Richard Gifford, they had all been along the passage for an official meeting with the Foreign Office, in the person of a junior minister, Baroness Scotland. The session had been arranged to see what amends the Government planned in the wake of the successful action Mr Bancoult had recently brought against the Crown for the way it had forcibly removed him and his family from his home thirty-three years earlier. They had expected Baroness Scotland to be sympathetic; after all, she was of mixed race herself, with a West

Indian background. Instead, they got the impression that she thought the whole affair rather tedious and that the Ilois were given to whinging. However, for all that, she reluctantly recognized that the Foreign Office, having lost the case and been shown up rather badly, now had no choice but to make the right noises. But time would soon show that, even at that level, redress was going to be inadequate.

Olivier Bancoult was four years old in 1968 when he made the long voyage to Mauritius with his parents and younger sister, Noelie. They were taking Noelie to hospital; she was eighteen months old. A cart had run over her leg and crushed it. Sadly, the injury and the long journey so weakened her that she died during treatment. After the family had buried her, they went down to the dockside to check the sailing date of the next ship home. They were told that they would not be allowed to make the journey. The shipping clerk was unmoved by Mrs Bancoult's entreaties. He had his instructions: 'The islands are closing down.' So not only had the family lost their daughter, they had also lost their home and all their possessions except the clothing they had with them. There was not even a means of contacting their friends and relatives who were still on the island: there was no telephone and mail was no longer being accepted.

In a long statement submitted to the High Court in 1999, Olivier Bancoult said that his mother never really recovered from the shock. His father could find no regular work and he died a few years later. His family's story was fairly typical of the experience of the exiled Ilois. What was untypical was what, against the odds, Olivier Bancoult had made of himself. He was hardly into his teens when he realized that he had to get an education. He even started to learn English – a French patois is the 'natural' language of Mauritius. At only twenty he started the Chagos Refugee Group. There had been other Ilois groupings but they had never amounted to much; besides which, they had all been established by Mauritians.

In the mid-1980s there was a last attempt at a 'full and final settlement' by Whitehall. This time the amount had grown to a tempting £4 million. But with the number of Ilois now swollen by births to nearly 2000, the sum still only divided out at about £2000 per head. This, though about three times the average annual wage in Mauritius at the time, was not much in exchange for one's birthright, one's home and one's job. Consequently, despite being in desperate need, a number of Ilois families refused to sign the 'renunciation' form. They still hoped to return to their island homes. By now they knew that it was not the Mauritians but the British who were wholly responsible for their plight. Moreover, though it was late in the day, they realized that they were subjects of the Crown and entitled to British passports, as issued in British Dependent Territories – like the inhabitants of St Helena or the Falklands. It was this knowledge that directed the women to demonstrate once again outside the British High Commission. It also alerted some of the Ilois, on the advice of a local Mauritian lawyer, to the possibility that they might stand a chance of legal redress in the British courts.

But these things take time. First, they had to find an Ilois in whose name the legal action could be mounted – a plaintiff. Olivier Bancoult was an obvious choice. Then there was the need to get legal aid in Britain. That involved finding a London lawyer who would handle the application. Richard Gifford (of Sheridans, the legal firm that had been involved since the late 1970s) took it on. Following on, counsels' 'opinions' had to be sought in order to convince the Legal Aid Board that funding the action was worthwhile – that it would have a good chance of success. Then there was the process of 'discovery' under which the Foreign Office had to surrender all its files of thirty years earlier. After that there was the careful preparation of the case itself and meetings with counsel. Rather late in the day the Treasury Solicitor tried to argue, on behalf of the FO, that because the events in dispute had happened in a British Indian Ocean Territory, no British Court had the necessary jurisdiction. The case should be heard before the High Court of BIOT. This, due to some colonial quirk, was 'situate' in Cheltenham. Somehow, Richard Gifford got round that one. But it all meant delay.

Eventually the case (a judicial review) was heard in the autumn of 2000 before Lord Justice Laws. The deceits so clearly revealed in the original FO files (and quoted in this chapter) meant that, from the start, the case did not go well for Whitehall. Of the various arguments that Olivier Bancoult's team could have deployed, they chose to assert the fundamental illegality of the 1970 Ordinance (a mere executive decision taken in someone's Whitehall office) which had removed the Ilois and then barred them from ever returning to their islands. The team claimed that this was in clear breach of that oldest of all British legal precepts, the Magna Carta:

> No man shall be taken or disseised [*sic*] or exiled or in any way ruined except by the lawful judgement of his peers or by the law of the land.

Counsel for the FO tried to suggest that literally, legally and figuratively Runnymede was a long way from the Chagos Islands. But the plaintiff's team pointed out that as recently as 1982, in a case involving a 'Native American' tribe in Alberta, Lord Denning had reaffirmed that the 'agreement' between King John and his barons in 1215 'has always been considered the law throughout the Empire. It is a law which has long followed the flag.'

In the end the court found unequivocally for Olivier Bancoult. Lord Justice Laws, having perused all the dissembling FO memoranda from three decades earlier, dryly observed, 'I found the flavour of these documents a little odd; it was as if some of the officials felt that if they willed it hard enough they might bring about the desired result, and there would be no permanent population on the Archipelago.'

However, it should also be said that he acknowledged the way that the FO had opened their incriminating files. Perhaps that had something to do with the fact that Robin Cook, the Foreign Secretary at the time, had tabled a number of Parliamentary Questions about the plight of the Ilois when in opposition. Now in office, he could hardly order his minions to be obstructive. This may also be why the FO decided not to appeal against the judge's finding. Either that, or the FO recognized the innate weakness of its case.

So what next? The first move was really up to the Foreign Office – which is why Olivier Bancoult was seeing Baroness Scotland that afternoon. But the FO was caught in a classic bind. It had signed a fifty-year agreement with the Americans in 1966 under which it guaranteed that the Chagos Islands would be cleared of all inhabitants. Thirty-four years on it found (surprise, surprise) that the clearance had been illegal, and that the inhabitants and their descendants must be allowed to return. While it worked out what to do, it commissioned a £55,000 study into the feasibility of repopulating Peros Banhos and Salomon. The

Americans were not happy, and wrote a stiff note to the British Government:

> Resettlement would immediately raise the alarming prospect of the introduction of surveillance, monitoring and electronic jamming devices that have the potential to disrupt, compromise or place at risk vital military operations.

One senses a degree of overstatement here. What are the Americans doing on Diego Garcia that requires such a 'fully sanitized' environment extending for nearly 150 miles in every direction? Stretching out so far, the circle of prohibition encloses the islands of Peros Banhos and Salomon. Where else in the world does the US require such a wide radius of total exclusion? Surely the other two islands could be repopulated, with the Americans over-flying or visiting them at unannounced intervals to make sure that no one was setting up 'monitoring or jamming devices'? Anyway, what is to stop a hostile power from sailing a surveillance vessel into the area and making trouble? As long as it was in international waters, it would be very difficult to police.

In fact, Britain would still seem to have some leverage, albeit meagre, to persuade the Americans to modify their stance. First, the initial lease for Diego Garcia was for fifty years. This presumably ends in 2016. So could we not explain to our allies that, for an extension of another fifty years, it would not come amiss if they could be just a little more understanding? Or, alternatively, when next they ask the landlord for permission to expand the base or to lengthen the runway, could not that same landlord expect an 'accommodation' vis-à-vis the Ilois? Where there's a will . . .

THROUGH 2001 AND 2002, following the judgement of Lord Justice Laws, it became apparent that 'will' has been in short supply. Whitehall's reaction has been determinedly minimalist. Within the FO sits the BIOT Commissioner. One must wonder if he and his small staff are writing the sort of dissembling memoranda their predecessors composed over thirty years ago. Perhaps; perhaps not. But why should one think that they are likely to be any different? Is someone, even now, suggesting that 'if this feasibility study can be dragged out for a year or two, maybe Mr

Bancoult will lose credibility among his supporters, and then perhaps the steam will go out of this Ilois drive to go home. How real is it anyway?' Far-fetched? Not really. What is certain is that the Ilois have been held at arm's length from having any say in the study examining the feasibility of *their* return to *their* islands. And, so far, indications are that the government is going to comply with its legal obligation in the most parsimonious and delaying ways possible.

A confirming hint of this came at that meeting with Baroness Scotland; she firmly rejected any possibility of compensation or a grant-in-aid to subsidize a return to the islands. What had the Ilois done with all that money they had been given in 1984? Had they run through it already? Someone tried to point out that when you have no training, no job and no housing, £2000 a head does not go very far. Anyway, what about their thirty years of exile? And they needed money to restore their derelict islands. It did not go down well.

A few months later things did not go any better in negotiations with the BIOT Commissioner. There was no question of any return to Diego Garcia and, of course, the events of 11 September have merely reinforced that. As for getting back onto Peros Banhos and Salomon, things did not look good there either. The Americans were firmly against any kind of transit through their airfield – the Ilois had hoped that this might have provided a way of getting to and from the other two islands. Building an airstrip on either of those islands was also out of the question – no money. No money either for a ship. So no hope of starting any copra co-operatives. What about fishing? In fact, two fishing boats sailing from Mauritius, but manned mainly by Ilois, had been 'caught' by a BIOT patrol boat and warned off under threat of a fine and imprisonment. The fact that this was in direct breach of the London judgement made no difference – until legal pressure was brought to bear on BIOT in Whitehall. Only then was a signal sent to Diego Garcia telling the local BIOT officials to back off.

There are just over 500 'survivors' from those who were forcibly removed from the Chagos Islands, and more than three times that number of children born to one or more Chagos parents. Obviously, it would never be possible for all of them to go home; many would not want to. Yet for those who do want to return, the future does not look good. It would seem that while BIOT cannot now legally stop them going back to the two northern islands, it can still make that return so difficult that it is most unlikely to happen.

In working toward that end, the authorities are using the most potent weapon in the bureaucratic armoury: red tape. The procedural possibilities for delay are almost endless. For example, before any Ilois not actually born in the Chagos can be considered eligible for return, let alone for any compensation, full family details are required: birth certificate, marriage and birth certificates of the parents, and a will if either or both parents have died. The data must be properly compiled through a central agency in Mauritius and then forwarded to London. No funds have been allowed for the compiling or administration of all this paperwork. In any case, some of the data simply does not exist. Never did. One sees the zealous hands of the Treasury Solicitor's Department at work. 'With the best will in the world, if we are going to do a proper job, we just can't rush these things.'

In November 2001, provoked by the way Whitehall was procrastinating, the Ilois planned a demonstration in Port Louis. It was a year since Olivier Bancoult and his supporters had won their case in London. But in that twelve months nothing had happened. So 500 people camped for a week at the gates of the British High Commission. The increasing embarrassment worked – up to a point. An appointment was made for Olivier Bancoult to visit London and, with his lawyer Richard Gifford, to talk things through with Baroness Amos. She was more sympathetic than her predecessor, Baroness Scotland, who had moved on to the Lord Chancellor's Office. She promised, within limits, to do what she could to speed things up. But, judging by the number of civil servants who flanked her, she was likely to find those limits set very tightly. This supposition has since been confirmed . . .

The best hope now may lie with the UN. The UN Human Rights Committee has examined the evidence and heard the testimony. Its report seeks the accelerated compliance of the UK – under its obligations in the International Covenant on Civil and Political Rights. So far nothing has happened. We will have to wait and see.

IT IS EXTREMELY RARE THAT an outsider, a mere civilian, gets the opportunity to leaf slowly through the classified files of a government department. It is rarer still when most of those papers are marked 'Restricted' or even 'Secret – Guard'. Normally, it only happens when the papers are judged to be so old and harmless (and all the key players long dead) that they can safely be released to the Public Records Office. Even then it is not unknown for certain documents, perhaps more embarrassing or revealing than the rest, to be held back or 'disappeared'. Just occasionally, the files are opened when, as a consequence of the legal process of 'discovery', the Ministry which 'owns' them is compelled to disclose documents (or photocopies) ahead of an impending court action. Even more unusual is a situation where a Ministry voluntarily produces documents – sometimes in what it supposes will be the support of its own case. That is what seems to have happened to what are loosely called the 'BIOT Papers, 1967–72'. Photocopies of those papers rest thickly on a shelf in the office of the London solicitor who steered Olivier Bancoult's claim against Her Majesty's Government to eventual success. The process took Richard Gifford seven years.

Some of what those papers reveal has already found a place in this account. But four further points are interesting. The first is that the Foreign Office played the game according to the rules: it appears to have held nothing back, none of the papers seem to be missing. Of course, whether credit should accrue for merely behaving honestly (even though very late in the day – some would say over thirty years late) is a nice question. But the temptation to lose some of the more revealing papers must have been there. On the other hand, there would have been very little point in removing just some of the papers. There would still have been too many others. Yet if *all* the compromising papers had been detached, the files would have been so thin as to be quite unbelievable. Perhaps, short of applying for the rather discredited device of a Public Interest Immunity Certificate (on what grounds?), the FO had no choice but to comply. Additionally, it seems that the Foreign Secretary at the time probably played a role. Robin Cook, when in Opposition, had tabled a number of questions over the years about Diego Garcia and the Ilois. Now that he himself had become the relevant minister, he may have pushed his minions further towards transparency than they might normally have wanted to go.

The second point is that, among all the many memos from people in Whitehall who knew what was planned for the Ilois, hardly anyone even hints at a doubt or qualm. Maybe the civil servants were simply acting on the instructions of their masters, the ministers. But the excuse that one was 'only carrying out orders' has seldom been held to be an adequate defence of doubtful activities, let alone illegal ones. Anyway, one is surprised at the will, zeal even, with which the civil servants seem to have set about their task of deception. Yes, it would have been a brave man or woman, someone out of tune with the surrounding culture, who dared to question the plan to secretly remove the long-term inhabitants of a British territory from their homes. But in a file of over 100 FO memos, letters and signals, one finds just two notes of hesitation. In the margin of one memo an official tentatively asks, 'Aren't we batting on a rather sticky wicket here?' And elsewhere one finds this minor comment: 'We have a certain old-fashioned reluctance to tell a whopping fib, or even – depending on the number of permanent residents – a little fib.' Realpolitik, in both the global sense and in terms of personal careers and mortgage payments, was what mattered. But does that excuse the enthusiasm?

The third point is that the story of the Ilois is the only one in this book where a web of fiction was constructed as a matter of deliberate policy to hide an intention. In other words, the cover-up was put together *before* the activity it was meant to disguise. Much more usually the dissembling comes afterwards. First comes the cock-up or worse, then comes the hush-up. Then, when that starts to unravel, there comes the cover-up – partly to hide the hush-up, partly to bury the initial blunder. The story of the Ilois is an exception to the normal sequence.

Lastly, there will be senior civil servants who will be quick to claim that the deceiving memos quoted in this account are wholly exceptional to the normal way of working in Whitehall. They were, it will be said, a response to the very special circumstances of the Cold War.

Maybe.

SINCE THE CHAPTER ABOVE WAS finished in the autumn of 2002, it would no longer be accurate to claim that the story of the Ilois is the only case in this book where a narrative was constructed to disguise or conceal some *future* plan – rather than as a cover-up to disguise some blunder (or worse) that had already happened. One must now also include significant parts of the dossier that, as discussed in the previous chapter, took us to war in Iraq. That said, *this* chapter is about the Ilois and 'what happened next'.

For an understanding of what followed, we should briefly dip back to the 'verdict' of the High Court's judicial review: Lord Justice Laws determined that the original BIOT Ordinance ('. . . the purpose of this Ordinance is to maintain the fiction . . .') that had banished the Ilois from their ancestral homes was unlawful; it was '*ultra vires*'. But, strangely (to most laymen anyway), it was not within the Court's remit to decide or even to recommend whether any compensation or restitution of the right to go home should be ordered. Nevertheless, the Foreign Office moved immediately – to promulgate a replacement Ordinance 'allowing' the Ilois to return to all their islands *except* for the one that really mattered: Diego Garcia. Quite why that particular aspect of the new Ordinance should not also be unlawful has never been explained. But, lawful or not, there was no way that the Ilois could take the Foreign Office up on its limited 'generosity': they had no money, no ship, no work, no nothing.

So the movers and shakers in the Ilois community decided to go back to the English courts – this time to get some hard cash. After more than two decades in Mauritius, some of them had moved on from being the innocents they were when they first began life in exile. Perhaps, also, they were encouraged by the theory (if not the practice) of their victory at the judicial review. So now they aimed to obtain personal compensation (in addition to the rather paltry amount they had gained back in the early 1980s) for homes they had lost and for their many hardships ever since. In legal terms, they sought damages; they accused the British government of deceit, negligence, misfeasance, and wrongful exile. Some intended to use their 'winnings' to alleviate their poverty in Mauritius; others wanted to go back and rebuild their lives on two (at least) of their islands – Peros Banhos and Salomon. To that end, they would need money to buy or charter a small ship, and to pay for building materials. Some, looking north at the success of tourism in the Maldives, imagined similar possibilities for themselves.

Anything legal takes time. It takes even longer when the 'other' side tries to shut down the whole case on invented grounds. For example, the

Foreign Office initially argued that there was no case to answer because it had not been responsible for the removal of the Ilois in the first place. That decision, it said, had been made by the plantation managers on the purely commercial grounds that copra production was no longer economic. But, while the arguments caused by this and other ruses delayed the proceedings, they did not ultimately stop them.

Eventually, the case began on 9 October 2002 in the Law Courts on the Strand – in Court 73, later to be used for the Hutton Inquiry. Being a civil action, there was no jury. The judge who presided and who would eventually make a judgement was a bewigged Mr Justice Ouseley. Bewigged also were the clerks and barristers. What the thirty or so Ilois made of it all one can only guess. Their wrinkly walnut-brown faces (most were well into their late fifties or beyond) looked somewhere between bemused and jetlagged. They had only recently arrived from Mauritius. It was a cool autumn and most of the women, many with socks and flimsy sandals on their feet, sat with layers of thin cardigans pulled tightly over their cotton frocks. The men were mostly in sweaters under lightweight suits. Almost from the opening cross-examination of the first witness there were problems: very few of the visitors spoke anything but Creole. So interpreting went slowly to and fro; hesitations and misunderstandings were many. Sometimes the answers had little to do with the questions. Ten working days had been allowed for the case; it took nearly forty.

Given that, at the end, counsel for each side took a week to sum up, and that the judge's account and his eventual judgement ran to more that 240,000 words (nearly twice the length of this book), there is no hope of giving here more than the briefest outline of what happened.

Boiled down to essentials, the government's argument was that in 1982 it had made a generous settlement of £4 million (in addition to the £650,000 paid out ten years earlier). Each Ilois, on receiving his or her share (£2000-plus each), had been required to sign or thumbprint a 'receipt'. To anyone who could read English, the document's meaning was (and still is) clear: the payment was made on condition that 'in consideration of the compensation paid to me I renounce all claims that I have against the Government of the United Kingdom'. It went on for a few more lines in the same vein. There was, to be fair, no 'small print' other than in the negative sense: nowhere did the form specify the actual amount of money paid out to the individual. In court, the barrister for the Crown (strictly speaking, he was appearing for the Attorney General and the BIOT Commissioner) was able to show a large number of thumbprints and what passed for signatures.

In contrast, the Ilois argument was that many of them had not properly understood what they were agreeing to. These were, after all, still a mostly illiterate people. Many subsequently claimed that they had thought they were just signing a receipt for some cash – a handout to compensate them for some of the hard times they had suffered. They maintained that the form, which was printed in a language they could not understand (let alone read), was never properly explained to them. They said they did not understand that they were signing away all further rights, that this was a 'full and final' settlement – not only against any further payments, but also against any hope of ever returning to their islands. Anyway, if they did not sign, they would get nothing. So, in a phrase they would not have understood (even in their own language), the government had them 'over a barrel'. There had certainly been some negotiations, but not really with the Ilois. The discussions had been between the two governments involved – Mauritian and British. For the islander, it was take it or leave it. No thumbprint – no money.

It was up to counsel appearing for the Crown to demolish the Ilois witnesses. It was often a contest with something of the cat and mouse about it. Time and again, with that smiling but rather smug politeness that lawyers often employ, the Crown's barrister derided the notion that the Ilois witnesses (fifteen took the stand in slow succession) had not known perfectly well what they were signing back in 1982. Surely the offer and its ramifications would have been discussed and argued over among the Ilois community for weeks beforehand. And what about those Mauritian newspapers (in French and English) which had carried items about what was intended? Had no one read them? Or had no one asked that someone else read and translate them? Surely, as counsel rather wearily implied on numerous occasions, it was simply not believable that the Ilois did not know what was happening. Anyway, there were old photographs of the community at various meetings called by Ilois leaders. The judge was also, in his occasional interjections, inclined to show his lack of belief in several witnesses. His impartiality seemed to lapse momentarily when, at one point, in a slip of the tongue, he said of the government's 'offer' back in 1982, 'We weren't offering a return [to the islands].' In that one word 'we', he had rather obviously allied himself with the Crown's point of view. On noticing the raised eyebrows of Richard Gifford, the solicitor who had been working for the Ilois for years, the judge quickly corrected himself: 'I saw Mr Gifford frown when I said "we". Am I right? I think so, yes. I *meant* the British government.' But he had rather given the game away.

Over the succeeding weeks, any observer sympathetic to the Ilois would have been worried by the way things were going. The Ilois lacked guile. Not so the legal team for the Crown. The cross-examination of Mr Saminaden is an example of the way a witness would be ambushed. Back in Port Louis, this retired blacksmith lived in three rooms with several of his married children and their families. Like the other Ilois, he said that he had put his thumbprint on the form assuming that it was a receipt for money. He was interrogated hard. What was his job? Blacksmith. So presumably, in that job, he sometimes went to a metal store for supplies – iron bars, perhaps? Yes, of course. Did he put his thumbprint on a chit for the bars? Yes. How did he know that he was getting the right number of bars? By counting them. So he could count? Yes – up to a hundred. So where were the numbers on the so-called receipt he had signed? There weren't any. So surely, given that the form did not mention any specific sum, he must have realized that he was signing a renunciation of his rights rather than a receipt for a specific amount of money. Gotcha. Or, to be more formal, QED.

At one stage, the judge asked why, if the Ilois really thought that they had not signed away their rights in 1982, none of them had taken legal action against the British government much more promptly. Why wait nearly two decades? That seems a fair question until one recognizes that many of them may not have realized (as they had long maintained) that, in the eyes of the British government, they *had* signed away their rights. The judge's question also seems to overlook the distance in culture (and geography) between the poorer quarters of Port Louis and the Inns of Court on the Strand. After all, even when all parties to an action live and have their being entirely in England, it can take years for a case to come to fruition. The judge came close to suggesting that the islanders only had themselves to blame for not seeking legal recourse many years earlier. Either that, or they were hesitant and not too sure of their case anyway.

At the end of eight weeks, Mr Justice Ouseley had to curtail proceedings. Through no fault of his own, his court schedule – laid down by those above – had long since required him to move on to other cases. So final submissions had to be made in writing. Then, with the judge busy in other courts, there was a pause of ten months. Eventually, Mr Ouseley found the time to write his judgement. No one could complain that he was anything but painstakingly conscientious; he went into the whole history of the affair since the late 1960s. At over 300 pages, the document is not a light read. A crowded court, including some Ilois who had lately taken up residence in England, listened to the part that mattered: the judgement.

The judge found against the Ilois. It became very clear that he simply had not believed many of their key witnesses – particularly their fundamental claim that they had not realized they were signing a formal renunciation of any possible return to their islands or any further money. It is worth listing some of his more trenchant comments:

> He [the Ilois witness] was asked about the 1982 Agreement. I considered that he was very reluctant to give straight answers to obvious questions about what the Ilois thought was going on . . .

> There is no doubt that she was not answering the question, not because she did not understand it, but because she understood it only too well. The implications of answering the question truthfully were that the Ilois knew very well what the negotiations were about.

> His understanding of events was long past the point at which he could be regarded as a reliable witness.

> She was very evasive about why she had made no effort to find out what was being said in English from those who could speak English . . . It is perfectly clear to me that she was in a position to enquire readily what was going on and it is quite incredible to suppose that she did not ask . . .

> The only consistent pattern to her answers was their evasiveness and their contradiction.

It would be unfair to say that, at every point, the judge found unequivocally against the Ilois. He said that the £4 million 'settlement' of 1982 'was evidently not generous'. He further acknowledged that they had been shamelessly treated by successive British governments.

> Many [Ilois] were given nothing for years but a callous separation from their homes, belongings and way of life and a terrible journey to privation and hardship. Ill-suited to their surroundings, poverty and misery became their common lot for years. They alone were made to pay a terrible price for the defence establishment on Diego Garcia.

It was an eloquent comment, but of little comfort to the Ilois. In their view, the judge might as well not have bothered. They could not understand how he could recognize the heartless way they had been treated and yet, at the same time, deny what they saw as their legitimate plea for justice and recompense. The cynic will say that their real problem was that they confused natural justice with what is, too often, the normal working of the law. The cynic might be right.

In a sentence of two, the judge made it clear that he thought it would be a waste of public money for the case to go any further.

> Ill-treatment does not require a hopeless case to be allowed to continue . . . Justice does not require an obviously unmeritorious case to be allowed to proceed.

Perhaps the last words in this sad story should be those of Richard Gifford, the solicitor who has battled on and off for over ten years for the Ilois cause: 'The Crown appears to have held that the government of the day did nothing wrong and that it did not know that what it was doing was unlawful.' The islanders were remarkably philosophical, he added: 'When you have been kicked around for thirty years, you get used to setbacks.'

The Ilois are now talking of an appeal – if not within the English legal system, then, who knows, within the American system or the European Court of Human Rights.

THE *BELGRANO*

'Some minor discrepancies'

Will the Minister reaffirm that there is no question of proceeding with any proposal contrary to the wishes of the islanders? Surely, they must be of paramount importance.

Rt Hon Peter Shore MP in the Commons on 2 December 1980

The answer to the Right Honourable Gentleman's question is 'Yes'. There are about 1800 *islanders. I make it clear that we shall do nothing which was not 'endorsed' by the islanders. I agree that is the predominant consideration in this matter . . . Their wishes must be of paramount importance.*

Rt Hon Nicholas Ridley, Minister of State, Foreign Office,
replying to the above question

PETER SHORE AND NICHOLAS RIDLEY were, of course, talking about the Falkland Islanders. But one can make another connection between the Ilois and the Falklanders, or, more accurately, with the campaign fought in their defence. It is connected with the *Belgrano*, the Argentine cruiser whose sinking early in the Falklands War in May 1982 was to become so controversial.

The juxtaposition of the stories of the Ilois and the *Belgrano* allows one to 'compare and contrast' the very different consequences of two official fictions. In the first, a series of lies was told which denied the existence of any 'belongers'. Almost certainly, everyone involved derived some satisfaction from a job effectively done. Presumably, their careers prospered. Certainly *Who's Who* shows that, on retirement, they all wound up with CMGs, knighthoods or better. Their deceit was sustained for over thirty years – and would be in place yet had it not been for Olivier Bancoult and his lawyers. But, in the case of the Argentine cruiser, another fully authorized fiction was fed to Parliament for more than two years – until it eventually became too much for one civil servant to stomach. Clive Ponting blew the whistle. No honours for him. Instead, he wound up at the Old Bailey. True, he was acquitted. But he was out of a job. Who said that honesty carries its own rewards? Or, just as pertinently, that dishonesty carries its own punishment?

First, the background.

Argentina had long claimed the ownership of the islands she called the Malvinas. In early May 1982, after years of fruitless negotiations with the British, she decided to settle the matter by force. She invaded. Now, in shock and against all reasonable odds, Britain resolved to respond. After all, under the UN Charter the wishes of the 1800 islanders were held to be paramount: they had always been adamant in denying any proposition that they might one day live under the Argentine flag. That was the justification for what followed. Within days Mrs Thatcher was persuaded (though, by all accounts, she did not need much pushing) to order an improvised naval task force to steam 8000 miles to the South Atlantic. Perhaps the threat would be enough to persuade the ruling junta in Argentina to see sense. If not, the troops assigned to land and retake the islands would follow – as soon as enough ships could be mustered to carry them.

By late May, while waiting for those troops to arrive, British naval ships had taken up position to the east of the Falklands. Presently, it was learnt that one of our nuclear-powered submarines, HMS *Conqueror*, operating much closer to the Argentine shore, was shadowing a cruiser and two destroyers. They were reportedly heading in the general direction of our warships. The cruiser was the *Belgrano*. A decision was made to sink her.

The execution of that order was very arguably the defining moment of the Falklands War. But contrary to popular and parliamentary myth, it was most definitely not the first serious act of conflict between the two countries. Nor, it seems, was it a decision taken by a peevish Mrs Thatcher solely to scupper a last-minute peace 'initiative'. If the truth had been told from the start – though, because we were at war, the details might have been limited – much embarrassment, confusion, suspicion and anger would have been avoided.

IF ONE IGNORES THE FACT that Argentina 'started it' a month earlier when they made their armed takeover of the Malvinas, the war really began in the very early hours of 1 May.[1] At 03.40 Falklands time, a single Vulcan bomber targeted Stanley airfield with twenty-one 1000-pound bombs. If that is not a *de facto* declaration of war, it is difficult to know what is. With numerous air-to-air refuellings, the bomber had come 3750 miles from Ascension Island. Now, with more refuelling, it had to get back. At the time it was by far the longest bombing sortie ever attempted.[2] The airfield runway was certainly damaged, though not as severely as had been hoped. But as Admiral Woodward, the man in charge down there, tells it in his book *One Hundred Days*, the Vulcan had another purpose: 'The arrival of the bombs formally announced that Margaret Thatcher's government were not best pleased with the antics of Galtieri's forces.' Nearly two decades later, in conversation at his kitchen table, he makes the point more bluntly: 'Down there, as far as we were concerned, the gloves were now bloody well off.' He emphasizes with some vehemence that the order to sink the Argentine cruiser came later. 'Quite a lot had happened by then – the retaking of South Georgia; the sinking of their sub (the *Santa Fé*); that Vulcan raid; and I'd sent Harriers and warships inshore to bombard Stanley airfield and Goose Green. And, of course, their air force had had a go at us. Blood had already been spilt.'

Obviously, he is right. Shortly after the Vulcan raid, the task force's command ship, HMS *Hermes*, launched twelve Sea Harriers armed with both air-bursting ordnance (to keep the Argentine anti-aircraft gunners' heads down) and runway-busting bombs. One group went for Stanley airfield again; the other group went for the airstrip at Goose Green. It was on the aircraft's return from those two raids that Brian Hanrahan, the BBC journalist, told the world: 'I counted them all out and I counted them all back.' With security very much in mind (no point in telling the enemy that our air 'force' was perilously small) the comment had been partly suggested by Admiral Woodward.

1. The British had retaken South Georgia a week earlier, but no lives had been lost on either side during the recapture.
2. The sortie involved seventeen in-flight refuellings because, of course, some of the tanker aircraft (Victors) had themselves to be refuelled from other tankers in order to get back to Ascension. The Vulcan bomber flew non-stop for 7500 miles – the equivalent of Heathrow to Chicago and back.

Later that same day, three warships detached from the task force and went forward to bombard the airfield. The idea throughout was to deny the enemy the use of the runway as a forward base from which the Argentines' fast jets could attack our naval task force. The Argentines later admitted to fifty casualties; it may have been more. It was only a matter of hours before they replied – with some forty aircraft. Operating at the extremity of their range from the mainland, most of them had to turn back before they could reach our ships. As it was, they lost two Mirages and a Canberra.

Given all this 'activity', it is not surprising that even today Admiral Woodward gets rather abrupt if one makes the error of assuming that the 'shooting' war only began when the *Belgrano* was torpedoed – a full thirty-six hours after that Vulcan bomber turned for home. Or after those Argentine aircraft were shot down. 'That is a mistake,' he says, 'which people who should know better are fond of making.'

In emphasis, he makes the point that timing was the all-important factor. 'The whole campaign had to be run to a precise schedule if we were to stand any real chance of success. London – Mrs T. and her lot, the naval command, and then the Marines and the Paras – everyone had agreed several weeks earlier that we *had* to start the campaign no later than 1 May. And we had to finish it by mid-June. That's just six weeks – start to finish. Tight. Very tight. Any delay in starting, even by a day, would reduce our chances – which, let's face it, were not too brilliant anyway.' So, in mid-April, while the ships had paused at Ascension Island, it had been firmly agreed in signals to and from the War Cabinet that if American shuttle diplomacy for a peaceful solution had not paid off by, at the very latest, 30 April, the war would have to begin the next day, on 1 May.

The timetable was determined by the approaching southern winter. It was already mid-autumn by the time the task force got down to the Falklands. The sheer wear and tear of being continuously at sea in the Roaring Forties, and the lack of any maintenance beyond quick, seaborne running repairs, would have had an ever-increasing impact on the fighting effectiveness of British ships and aircraft. And their crews. With gales and near-freezing temperatures expected on two days out of five by mid-June, the fleet's endurance was going to be very limited – six or seven weeks at the most.

The same factors applied, perhaps even more so, to our land forces once they were ashore. For the moment, the Marines and the Paras were still coming south from Ascension Island, and anyway, time had to be allowed (ahead of any landing) for the clandestine gathering of intelligence about the dispositions of the enemy. But once on shore, the troops would be almost totally exposed, without even tents, for much of the time.

All this would have been keenly appreciated by the Argentine high command. They knew, just as surely as did Admiral Woodward, that every day the British were forced to delay beyond 1 May, for whatever reason (but most obviously by continued diplomatic ping-pong to find a settlement), would be wholly to their advantage. It was in their interests to stall. Hence, beside bombs, that Vulcan raid carried the message that the British were not taken in by Argentine prevarications. So the war, though formally never actually declared, had already begun well before *Conqueror*'s torpedoes were fired.

That there were also other perceptions about the sinking, then and ever since, is in no doubt. The heavy loss of life on *Belgrano*, and the raising of the stakes, both political and military, divided opinion. There were also worries about several legal aspects of the action and, thereby, the possible reaction of the UN and the 'international community'. Further, the Argentine cruiser seemed such an easy target that her destruction was seen by some as being inherently unfair, unsporting, 'not quite cricket'. But the fact that she was so ill prepared was no one's fault but her captain's and, beyond him, the Argentine navy's. Lastly, an idea took hold among some critics that the sinking had no tactical relevance, that it was solely designed by Mrs Thatcher and the War Cabinet to show Galtieri and his junta (and the Americans?) that they could forget about any chance of a 'peaceful settlement'.

In fact, from the moment Argentine forces came ashore at Port Stanley four weeks earlier, a negotiated conclusion to the dispute was unrealistic. They were not going to get out; we were not going to let them stay. So, whatever else they may have been, *Conqueror*'s torpedoes were yet another demonstration of the British will to win. To that extent, Mrs Thatcher's critics were right. But, as we will see, it was both simpler and more complicated than that. Historically, largely because of mishandling in Whitehall at the time and, even more significantly, long after the shooting was over, the sinking of the *Belgrano* grew to become the most contentious incident of the war. It classically illustrates what happens when a government's politicians and their civil service advisors become needlessly trapped in the dissembling concrete of their own pouring.

ALTHOUGH SHE WAS FORTY-THREE years old, the 13,500-ton cruiser *Belgrano* was one of the two most formidable elements in the Argentine navy; the other was the British-built (1945) aircraft carrier *Veintecinco de Mayo*. *Belgrano*, which had started life as the US heavy cruiser *Phoenix*, was well armed, with fifteen 6-inch guns, eight 5-inch guns, twenty 40-millimetre Bofors quick-firing anti-aircraft guns and two systems of Seacat anti-aircraft missiles. She also carried a modern radar system that could be used to guide aircraft onto their targets. Lastly, she was protected by a belt of 4-inch armour – which would, at the least, have blunted the effect of any missiles launched from our destroyers. She may have been old, but she was not the toothless rust-bucket that she has since become in some accounts. At the time there was a rumour that she was equipped with Exocets. Her two accompanying destroyers certainly were; they had eight apiece. These missiles, which carried miniature radars to lock onto their targets, had a sea-skimming range of over 20 miles.

In any close engagement with the British task force, now patrolling to the east of the Falklands while it both softened up the Argentine garrison and landed secret 'recce' parties ahead of the invasion force, *Belgrano* and her escorts might have been heavily outnumbered. They might have been severely damaged, even sunk. But, if well handled, there was no telling what harm they might have done first. Moreover, if an Argentine attack had been properly co-ordinated from the north and south (*Belgrano* and co. from the south, the carrier and co. from the north), Admiral Woodward and his captains would have had some very real problems. To guard against just this type of danger, the Navy had much earlier asked Mrs Thatcher's War Cabinet for authority to send three nuclear-powered (not nuclear-armed) submarines to patrol off the Argentine coast and around the islands – to watch for and, with sensitive sonar equipment, to listen for any emerging elements of the opposition.

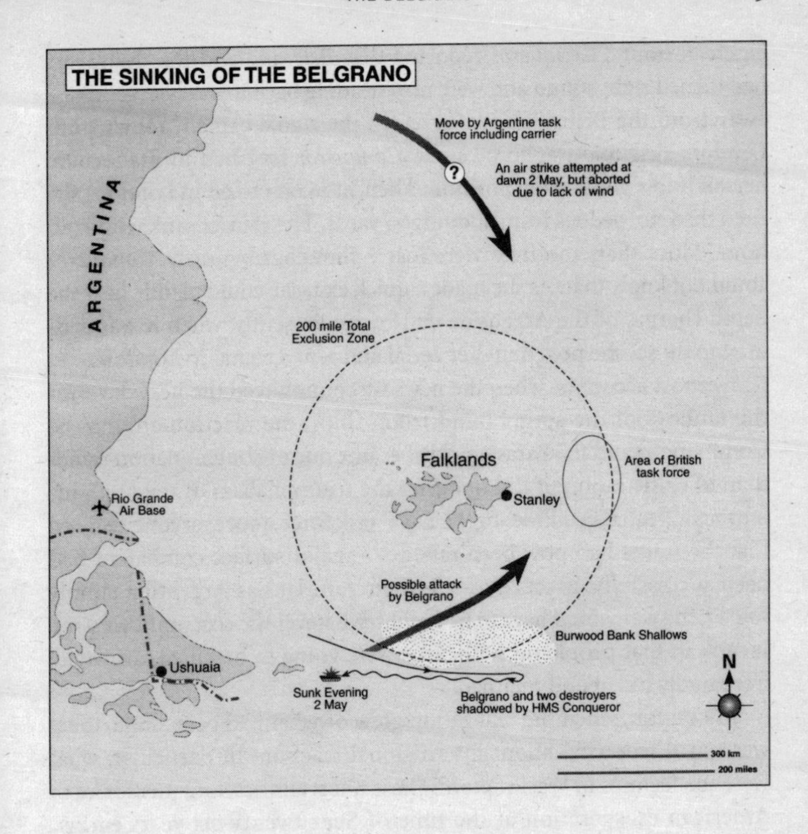

These submarines reported direct to the C-in-C in Northwood. Admiral Woodward makes no secret, then or now, that he would have preferred to have had them directly under his own command.

Off Tierra del Fuego one of those patrolling submarines, HMS *Conqueror*, sighted an almost stationary tanker. She was obviously waiting for someone. The submarine's CO, Commander Wreford-Brown, decided to see what happened next. Presently he was rewarded. *Belgrano* and two destroyers turned up and took on fuel. Then they moved off. *Conqueror* signalled to London that she was shadowing them. They were heading east in the general direction of the British task force at a rather unbelligerent 13–14 knots. After following and watching for eighteen hours, *Conqueror* reported that *Belgrano* and the destroyers had turned right round and were now heading back towards Argentina – away from the British ships. Presently, the signal came through from London: *Belgrano* was to be sunk. *Conqueror* first had to manoeuvre herself into a good firing position. Then, at 16.00 (20.00 in London) she fired three torpedoes from about 1200 yards. The cruiser sank within an hour. More than 300 lives were lost – though, obviously, *Conqueror* could not know that. As she made a quick exit, she could plainly hear the depth charges of the Argentine destroyers. Presently, when it was prudent to do so, she poked up her aerial and sent a signal to London.

By most accounts, when the news was announced the next day over the tannoys of the southbound troop ships, the reaction among the Commandos and the Paras quickly became one of contemplation rather than of exhilaration; it did not echo the triumphalism of the *Sun*'s infamous 'GOTCHA' headline. In the naval task force, too, everyone realized that the stakes had now been raised – a major surface combatant had been successfully attacked, not just aircraft. Unless Argentina simply folded, the war would have to be fought, whatever the cost, until we won. It sank in that people on both sides were going to be killed, drowned, irreparably burnt and maimed.

In London, when the realization grew of what had been done, there was much worrying about international reaction. In particular, what were the feelings in Washington? These uncertainties, and memories of American exasperation at the time of Suez twenty-six years earlier, almost certainly played a part in the official obfuscations that were to follow.

In Argentina the loss of *Belgrano* was such a psychological shock to the junta that their navy never put to sea again. On that ground alone, the sinking would seem to have very considerable *post hoc* justification. With the full benefit of hindsight, it can easily be argued that had *Belgrano* not been sunk, and had the Argentine navy played its proper role, the outcome of the whole campaign might have been quite different.

That is a bare-bones version of events. Apart from those few elements that are obviously conjectural, it is a true account – as far as it goes. But it does not go very far; there are some serious omissions. Above all, in light of subsequent theories and rumour, it does not tell who, why and how the final decision was made to 'take out' *Belgrano*. But, for all that, it is more accurate than the account given to the House of Commons by the Minister of Defence, John Nott, two days after the sinking:

> [On] 2 May at 20.00 London time, one of our submarines detected the Argentine cruiser *General Belgrano*, escorted by two destroyers. This heavily armed surface attack group was close to the Total Exclusion Zone and was closing on elements of our Task Force which was only hours away. We knew that the cruiser had substantial firepower, provided by fifteen 6-inch guns with a range of 13 miles, and Seacat anti-aircraft missiles. Together with escorting destroyers, which we believe were equipped with Exocet anti-ship missiles with a range of more than 20 miles, the threat to the Task Force was such that the Task Force commander could ignore it only at his peril.
>
> The House will know that the attack by our submarine involved the capital ship only and not its escorting destroyers, so that they should have been able to go to the assistance of the damaged cruiser. We do not know whether they did so, but, in so doing, they would not have been engaged.

The statement was short on a number of facts. Unless one assumes that Mr Nott was genuinely ignorant (a view not entirely dismissed by some servicemen), one must conclude that the paucity was deliberate. If his statement was *meant* to be misleading, the deception may well have been justified. We were at war; deceit and guile are just as much weapons as Exocet missiles or torpedoes. Also, there was world reaction to consider. Nevertheless, it is worth listing the mistakes (or were they fictions?) because, long after the war, when they were no longer necessary (if, indeed, some of them had ever been), they could not be changed. The cement had set. As a consequence, the errors or fictions had become the MOD's 'true' version of events. Once so established, they became as immutable as a Papal bull. Even two years later, to question them from outside the MOD was secular heresy. From inside the MOD it was treachery.

First, it is not true to say that 'at 20.00 London time, one of our submarines detected the . . . *Belgrano*'. The truth is that *Conqueror* had been shadowing *Belgrano* for at least thirty hours before she was sunk. Second, and more seriously, the Argentine ships were not 'closing on elements of our Task Force which was only hours away'. True, one could argue that for a time the distance between the Argentines and the British had been 'closing', but hardly to the extent, in common parlance, of only being 'hours away'. Anyway, at the time she was sunk, *Belgrano* and the destroyers had certainly not been 'closing'. On the contrary, they had been steaming away from the British for over ten hours. The two task forces, Argentine and British, were then probably over 250 miles apart. Third, it was untrue that 'the attack by our submarine involved the capital ship only'. One of *Conqueror*'s torpedoes, though probably aimed at *Belgrano*, just missed, hitting one of the destroyers instead. It failed to detonate (Mr Nott probably did not know this). Fourth, though less importantly, how were the destroyers to know that if they had gone to assist the *Belgrano*, 'they would not have been engaged'? Lastly, *Belgrano* was more than merely 'damaged'; she was abandoned and sinking. Nevertheless, did these inaccuracies matter? One could argue that in times of war (declared *de facto*, though not *de jure*, by that Vulcan) even the House of Commons cannot always expect the whole truth.

But there was another problem: the cruiser was outside the Total Exclusion Zone. This was a circle of 200 miles radius, centred on a point in the middle of the Falkland Islands. By British decree, any Argentine ship or aircraft within the TEZ was liable to attack. So what was the point of having a TEZ if one was going to torpedo a ship outside it? In fact, ten days earlier, with an imminent British attempt to retake South Georgia, the Argentine junta had been warned in the following terms:

> In announcing a Maritime Exclusion Zone [the MEZ was an earlier version of the TEZ], Her Majesty's Government make it clear that this measure is without prejudice to the right of the UK to take whatever additional measures may be needed in the exercise of its rights of self-defence under Article 51 of the UN Charter. Any approach on the part of Argentine warships or military aircraft which could amount to a threat to interfere with the mission of British Forces in the South Atlantic will encounter an appropriate response.

Whether such an 'extension' was legal in international law, and whether the 'self-defence' section of the relevant Article in the UN Charter adequately covered the torpedoing of *Belgrano*, may be debatable. (In fact, neither side ever formally 'declared' war, so, strictly speaking, *everything* they did was illegal.) But it can be argued that the British warning was clear, and that the junta had been carefully and formally told of it through the Swiss Embassy in Buenos Aires. Unless the junta thought we were just bluffing, it should not have been in much doubt that its ships *would* be attacked within the TEZ, and that they *probably* would be beyond it. So, whether strictly legal or not, it seems most unwise of the Argentine navy, under the notably bellicose Admiral Anaya, to have despatched a cruiser and two destroyers on the chance that the British, having already shown that they were in a no-messing mood, did not mean what they said. Indeed, the British had already indicated beyond doubt that they were not bluffing when, during the retaking of South Georgia (600 miles beyond the TEZ) a week earlier, they had attacked and so damaged the Argentine submarine *Santa Fé* that she had to be run ashore to avoid sinking. So, with *Belgrano* it cannot have been a case of the Argentines not getting or misreading the British message. They either ignored it or decided to take a risk.

So how was the decision to sink *Belgrano* arrived at?

After the war, it became apparent that it largely followed on a judgement made by Admiral Woodward, the man-in-charge in the South Atlantic. To this day he queries the confusion over what he sees as a straightforward naval narrative – and over his even more straightforward decision. Back then, he knew from the signals coming from *Conqueror* (directed to both Northwood and to him) that the Argentine cruiser and destroyers were steaming eastward from Tierra del Fuego – in his general direction. He also knew that one of the more modern items of 'kit' in *Belgrano* was a powerful, long-distance radar, which might be used to find outlying pickets of his task force and, thereafter, to guide in attacking aircraft. He was worried about the possibility that another Argentine naval force might move towards him from the north – our other submarines had failed to find the Argentine carrier and her escorts. In fact, the carrier carried a squadron of Skyhawk fighter-bombers, which she had *already* attempted to use against the British task force.[3] Although Woodward did not know about this at the time, he insists that the possibility of being caught between the two Argentine groups was very real. The danger would be greatly reduced if *Belgrano* could be removed from the equation. But speed was critical. He could not risk the probable delay involved in the normal naval protocol of 'requesting' his superiors in Northwood to 'consider' ordering *Conqueror* to sink *Belgrano*. They might take too long in the considering. So instead, to demonstrate the urgency (and despite the fact that *Conqueror* was not under his command), he signalled direct to the submarine – telling her commander to engage *Belgrano*. He surmised that *Conqueror* was submerged and would probably not pick up his signal (stored on a satellite) for some hours. But he knew that the signal (in cipher) would be picked up almost immediately by Northwood. There, as he reasoned at the time and later wrote in his book, 'Such a breach of naval discipline could imply only two things – either Woodward has gone off his head or he knows exactly what he is doing and is in a very great hurry. I rather hoped that they would trust my sanity.' They did.[4]

Admiral Sir Terence Lewin, Chief of the Defence Staff, was on his way to Chequers for a meeting of the War Cabinet. It was the morning of Sunday 2 May. In light of Woodward's signal and his own instincts, Sir Terence's advice to the politicians was unequivocal. He later said that he told the meeting, 'Here was a chance to knock off a major unit of the Argentine Fleet.' There was almost certainly more to the discussion than that. Among other considerations was the knowledge that, although the American Secretary of State, Alexander Haig, had just about despaired of

3. At dawn on 2 May, ten hours *before* the *Belgrano* action, the Argentine carrier had already tried to fly off her Skyhawks to find and bomb the task force. But it was an unusually calm day and the carrier had an engine problem – she could not make more than 20 knots. So she was unable to generate sufficient wind over her deck to get the laden aircraft (fully fuelled and each loaded with three 500-pound bombs) into the air. The carrier abandoned the attempt and returned to port. This was not known by Admiral Woodward until a little later.
4. Apparently, Admiral Woodward did not find out until late in 2001 that the Chief of Defence Staff (Admiral Lewin) was already asking the War Cabinet for permission to change the Rules of Engagement. This would have had the effect of enlarging the Total Exclusion Zone considerably.

trying to put together some kind of deal (and seemed quietly about to side with Britain), the Peruvians were still trying to broker a last-minute compromise. How would it look to the world if Britain deliberately 'torpedoed' this very last chance for a settlement? And had done so under circumstances where critics were bound to question the legality of the action? But someone at Chequers (Admiral Lewin?) would surely have made the point that, in accordance with the timetable agreed weeks earlier, the war had already started – the previous day. Further, one imagines that Mrs Thatcher might have observed that 'peace' negotiations, under various brokers, had been going on for weeks already; so why was the current attempt by the Peruvians likely to be more successful than any of the others? And what about 'our boys' down there with the winter coming on? Furthermore, how would it look if Woodward's 'request' (with Lewin's support) was rejected, only to have *Belgrano* run amok (then or later) among the task force while, simultaneously, the *Veintecinco de Mayo* launched an aerial attack from the north?[5]

So, with the news from the South Atlantic, and the previously agreed timetable in mind, the evidence seems to be that the War Cabinet judged that the time for diplomatic bargaining had run out. In Argentina, despite the fact that the shooting war had begun thirty-six hours earlier, it was clearly in the interests of the junta to pretend that it was still responsive to negotiation. With winter now beginning, every day of procrastination would make the occupying force that much harder to shift. And if the junta was *not* pretending, how was anyone to know? Even if President Galtieri was genuine and did want to agree to some kind of compromise (as now seems possible), there were strong indications – based on reliable intelligence – that other members of the junta would not have agreed. Certainly Admiral Anaya, head of the enemy's navy and the driving force behind the invasion in the first place, would never have allowed a settlement. And the Argentine public, by now high with Malvinas fever, would not have stood for it either. On the British side,

5. In fact, two days later a pair of 'naval' Etendards (flying from a land base) found and sank HMS *Sheffield* with Exocet missiles. In announcing this fact to the Commons, John Nott inadvertently told the Argentine air force that its improvised and quite untried 'marriage' of Exocet missile to an Etendard fighter was effective. Someone on his briefing staff had not been thinking.

having sent ships and troops 8000 miles to the south, there was a deep reluctance to call the whole thing off for what would be seen as some half-baked 'accommodation'. Having marched her men to the top of the hill, Mrs Thatcher was not, if she could help it, about to march them down again. So, with all these factors in mind, the War Cabinet came to a decision. A scrambled phone call was made to Northwood authorizing that a 'sink' signal be sent to *Conqueror*.

It is known that the submarine had been having problems with her aerial mast. This, and the fact that she had to poke the mast above the surface (not something she could do if shadowing close to *Belgrano* and co.) in order to access the satellite on which the coded signal was 'stored', would account for some of the hours that passed between the time at which the War Cabinet authorized the order and the moment it was received in *Conqueror*. Further time would also have passed while *Conqueror* manoeuvred herself into a suitable firing position. Altogether, there was an eight-hour gap between the order leaving Chequers and its execution in the South Atlantic.

During that time (or perhaps earlier), it is thought that *Conqueror* signalled to Northwood that *Belgrano* and co. had reversed their course and were now steaming back towards Tierra del Fuego. Until the signal logs and other records are released after thirty years in 2012 (if then), we will not know what reaction there was in Northwood – if, indeed, there was any. It has been argued, though by very few in the Navy, that *Belgrano* and co., now heading west, were no longer a threat to the British ships. But it has also been argued – very forcibly – that the mere existence of *Belgrano* and those destroyers was a potential danger which Admiral Woodward and his captains, with a great many other things on their minds, did not need. Furthermore, with night coming on, if *Belgrano* and co. had suddenly turned around and accelerated into the night at 20+ knots, they could have reached the British task force 250 miles away before dawn. At that time of year the nights are fifteen hours long.

Additionally, if the Argentines *had* turned round and headed towards the British task force, their course would have taken them diagonally across the shallows of the Burdwood Bank. In some places the Bank is only 300 feet deep; in a few it becomes even shallower. No submarine commander will run the risk of charging (submerged) at 20 knots through such waters. Further, at that speed, a submarine has to be more than 200 feet down in order not to leave a visible surface wake. Lastly, at that speed, it is difficult to shadow by sonar – the submarine herself is generating too much interfering 'noise'. In short, across the Bank, *Conqueror* might easily have 'lost' the Argentine ships. This possibility was clearly recognized in the Navy and, specifically, by Admiral Woodward – though it has been much disputed by others who do not understand the operation of those submarines.

Anyway, no withdrawal of the order to attack was made. *Belgrano* was torpedoed at about 16.00 (20.00 London time). The first news in the London papers was picked up from reports in Buenos Aires.

Looking back through the relevant *Hansards*, and the books and articles which covered the *Belgrano* affair during the ensuing weeks, months and years, one wonders why John Nott, the Minister of Defence, was not more straightforward in his initial statement to the Commons and in his later answers to questions. Mrs Thatcher, too. Why did Nott have to go into detail – half-truth detail? Time and again one or the other tried to justify the sinking with the unnecessary formula that *Belgrano* and the destroyers were, during the hours immediately preceding the torpedoes, positioning themselves for an attack on the task force: 'There was every reason to believe the *Belgrano* was manoeuvring to a position from which to attack our surface vessels.' Elsewhere, there was the repeated assertion that *Belgrano* had made 'frequent changes of direction' – presumably part of the 'manoeuvring' referred to above. Though she was undoubtedly zig-zagging, her mean course was indisputably away from the British. And there was always the claim that the Argentine ships and the British had only been 'hours apart' – which, while a rather elastic phrase, implies to most people that an engagement was imminent. Lastly, there was the implication that the sighting and the sinking had been almost simultaneous and that, therefore, the torpedoes must have been fired on the initiative of the commanding officer of *Conqueror*.

In her book written a decade later, *The Downing Street Years*, Mrs Thatcher suggests these 'facts' were merely 'minor discrepancies' and therefore did not matter. This seems disingenuous. At the least, they were half-truths. So why? Part of the answer may lie in the undoubted political nervousness about what had been done. And one imagines that there were straightforward 'humanitarian' qualms in terms of the several hundred conscript Argentine seamen known to have been lost. Nevertheless, why could the questioners not have been told that the War Cabinet assembled at Chequers had listened to professional naval advice? Yes, it had been a hard decision. Then Mr Nott might have added that he was sorry that he could not say more, and until the war was over that 'explanation' would have to do. Of course, some MPs and public figures would have objected that the sinking was an unnecessary escalation of hostilities, and that it breached the 'minimum force' formula of the UN. But those mutterings were being made anyway. If the government had told the truth – though, for the time being, a necessarily limited version of it – it would not, once the war had ended, have been stuck with a string of inaccuracies it then had to defend so unconvincingly. The British public will accept almost anything if told that it is 'on the advice of the Navy'. But once journalists and maverick MPs suspect a smoke screen put up by politicians, they will inevitably suppose the worst – even if, sometimes, it is not really there. They will start to do their own digging, which, in turn, will lead them to ask increasingly awkward questions. This then means that, unless the original dissembling or muddle is going to be admitted (most unlikely – though in this case it could so easily have been), what started as a hush-up (even a necessary one) grows over the months or years into a full-blown cover-up. This then has to be defended long after all need for it has disappeared.

One of the most obvious problems with cover-ups is that they are very difficult to get out of. Better not to get into them in the first place.

Another problem with cover-ups is that everyone who is involved has to tell exactly the same story; they all have to be 'on message'. For many reasons, including individual consciences, this is difficult to arrange. Anyway, there are almost always people who, outside the loop of the original hush-up (the conspiracy?), unknowingly give the game away – or enough of it to start others asking questions. In the *Belgrano* affair, the ship's captain, Captain Bonzo, was obviously not in the loop. When interviewed immediately after the war, he was quite sure where and in what direction his ship had been heading when sunk. Admiral Woodward, in a lecture to the Royal United Services Institute four months after the conflict was over, told how he had urged Northwood HQ to authorize the sinking. The commander of *Conqueror* also said that it was not his decision to sink *Belgrano*; he was acting on orders from Northwood. Furthermore, perhaps without realizing what he was doing, he told how he had shadowed the Argentines for thirty hours. These divergences from the official version of events aroused Tam Dalyell to put down the first of a barrage of Parliamentary Questions.

As a ranging shot he first asked what course *Belgrano* had been on when torpedoed. Given that the Argentine navy had let that particular cat out of the bag, there was no point in denying that she had been on a westward heading – away from the British ships. But the official answer contained the information that 'the cruiser and her escorts had made many changes of course. At the moment she was torpedoed she was on a course of 280°.'

This reply was quite true. But it was also misleading to imply that *only* at the particular moment of being torpedoed was *Belgrano* heading westward. This was obviously meant to reinforce the earlier assertion that she had been 'manoeuvring to a position from which to attack our surface vessels'. Consequently, a few days later Dalyell asked for more details. Again, he got the answer: 'It is not possible to give precise details, but her movements were consistent with indications that she and her escorts posed a threat to the Task Force.' Again, from a naval viewpoint this was true. But, from a lay or parliamentary perspective, it would have been much 'truer' to have said that the Navy and, even more specifically, Admiral Woodward considered her a threat whatever she was doing and whatever 'her movements' were. The answer might have made the point that the position, course and speed of an enemy ship are all secondary to its capability, and to what may, in ten minutes' time or tomorrow or next week, become its intentions. Yes, the loss of Argentine life was tragic. And perhaps the sinking broke some aspects of international law. But if *Belgrano* and her destroyers, replenished in Ushuaia, had returned a few days later and sunk a British ship with an equally tragic loss of life, what would the reaction have been? Where then would parliamentary sensitivities have stood about international law?

Instead, long after the war was history, the ministers continued to dig themselves into a deeper and deeper hole. The most public and famous manifestation of the scramble to keep up the smoke screens came in May 1983, when, eleven months after the sinking, in a BBC TV 'election call', Mrs Thatcher came up against Mrs Gould. This geography teacher was articulate and determined; she knew what a compass heading was and, more importantly, in the case of *Belgrano*, what the reciprocal of that heading was: 'But Mrs Thatcher, the *Belgrano* was going *away* from the British Fleet.' It was one of the few occasions in her long reign when one saw the Prime Minister rattled and quite out of her depth. It was embarrassing. And wholly unnecessary. Some have suggested that she genuinely did not understand what the *Belgrano* affair was all about. But it is difficult to believe that the Prime Minister, ignorant though she was about nautical matters, had not taken the trouble to get herself briefed on a controversy that had never gone away. Again, why not admit *Belgrano*'s course, but then simply say, 'The Navy reckoned her to be a threat *wherever* she was'? Perhaps the answer to that question is that too many politicians, when in doubt, have a default setting on their mental circuit boards marked 'Dsmbl'. Mrs T. certainly reverted to that setting that evening.

Before the General Election of June 1983, Tam Dalyell had few allies in his questioning. Undoubtedly there was the feeling, particularly on the government benches, that he did not deserve any answers – honest or otherwise. This dated back to the days when the naval task force was still steaming south. Dalyell's was one of the dissenting voices in the Commons. He forecast that the nation would get itself 'into a British Vietnam . . . there will be massive casualties . . . the fleet should turn around and come back to Portsmouth and Rosyth as soon as possible'. With hindsight, he agrees that he did not cover himself with glory. But that was never his object. His object is summed up in just two sentences drawn from a statement he made while the task force was steaming south:

> In a campaign like the Falklands, you have to distinguish between what you want to do and your capacity to do it. Invading the Falklands: do we have the means?

It was a legitimate question. There *was* cause to be concerned. The Navy was worried. The top command of the RAF was more than just worried; it was against the whole idea. With just eighteen Harriers going south, air superiority or even (to use the phrase of the time) 'an adequate air situation' against a country that could put more than seventy jets in the air was a very real anxiety. And the task force's ability to defend itself was going to be badly handicapped by a defence 'economy' made four years earlier: the Navy now had no aircraft or helicopters equipped with airborne early-warning radar.[6] Further, at the time, no one could know that Argentine misjudgement would result in at least eight of their bombs failing to detonate after they had buried themselves in our ships. And what, for example, if the Exocet that sank the fully laden *Atlantic Conveyor* had found one of the targets for which it was really intended: *Hermes* or *Invincible*? That one missile could have shifted the odds overwhelmingly in the Argentines' favour. As it was, the loss of that supply ship with her cargo of tents, food, ammunition and, above all, three Chinook helicopters was almost catastrophic. However, in the end superb training, astute thinking on the spot, guts, nerve and not a little luck prevailed.[7] We won. Tam Dalyell was wrong. But no one should doubt his motives or patriotism. Unfortunately, patriotism does not

6. The Navy lost its last early-warning Gannet aircraft when HMS *Ark Royal* was scrapped in 1978. Thereafter, our remaining (and much smaller) carriers were fitted with 'ski-ramps' (for Harrier take-offs), which made them impossible for conventional aircraft. Plans to fit early-warning radar to Sea King helicopters were forestalled by the defence cuts and economies of the late 1970s. It was very nearly a disastrous decision.
7. At times, luck or something close to it was with the British. For example, had Argentine intelligence been just a little better, they might have delayed the invasion by six months – until the defence cuts being made by Mrs Thatcher and Mr Nott had resulted in the sale of *Hermes* to India and *Invincible* to Australia. Also scheduled to go were 8000 men, nine frigates and destroyers, and the two amphibious assault ships *Fearless* and *Intrepid*. Without those men and ships, the retaking of the Falklands would have been impossible. And was it luck or good management by the British that, as part of its space-tracking and satellite programme, the US had built a 10,000-foot runway on Ascension? Without that long runway, which made the island an effective staging point (apartheid made Capetown/Simonstown unavailable), it is difficult to see how the Falklands expedition could ever have got under way. For a few days in April 1982 Wideawake Airfield handled more aircraft movements in a day than any military airport in the world. And what about the Argentine bombs that, incorrectly fused, did not go off? Maybe luck comes to those who deserve it.

give immunity against sometimes getting things wrong. Yet that is no reason why one should subsequently be denied the truth.[8]

After the election of June 1983, other MPs joined the questioning. John Morris, a lawyer and the shadow Attorney General, pointed out the inconsistencies and contradictions in the official narrative. The discrepancies encouraged his suspicion that the sinking had been designed to close the door on any chance of a negotiated peace. He called for an inquiry. In the Lords, Lord Hatch raised many of the same concerns, not least the matter of ministerial accountability to Parliament. And the obligation to tell the truth. This was fifteen months after the sinking.

The questioning never really went away. In a famous exchange, nearly two years after the events in question, Dalyell bluntly asked the Prime Minister who was lying – she or the commander of *Conqueror*. The Speaker ordered him to rephrase the question. So he stepped round the forbidden 'L' word and instead asked who was telling the truth. Mrs Thatcher's problem was that the commander of *Conqueror* had not, right at the beginning, been briefed on the official story – that he had sighted *Belgrano* only a very short time before she was sunk. Was this meant to imply that the decision to torpedo had been taken on the spot, there and then? The truth was that *Belgrano* had been shadowed for at least thirty hours and the final decision had been taken by the Prime Minister and her War Cabinet at Chequers. She did not answer the question, but replied, 'The full facts were given in several replies in the House . . . All the facts are there.' This is a standard rebuttal when the truth is seen as a possible embarrassment. Sometimes one hears a variation: 'There is no new evidence. All the relevant facts are in the public domain.'

By now the credibility gap was so wide (and, one might add once more, so unnecessary) that the parliamentary denials only further reinforced

8. A personal note: the reader should know that the author and Tam Dalyell were friends at university, and have been in spasmodic touch since. While the author disagrees with this longest-serving of all MPs (over forty continuous years) on many aspects of politics and national affairs, he is nevertheless an admirer. In an era when far too many MPs go the way the whips tell them to, the presence of so few independent spirits is to be deplored. The few we have must be treasured and respected – whatever their views. In any case, Tam Dalyell's integrity is accepted as a parliamentary 'given' by all sides of the House.

suspicions, and so widened the gap even further. The government had itself to blame. The Shadow Cabinet and, in particular, the Shadow Defence Minister, Denzil Davies, took up the issue. Whether the motivation was to get to the truth or to make life difficult for the government (probably both) does not matter. Ministers still have an obligation to tell the truth. There are few exceptions to this duty, but in this instance, now that the war was long over, even fewer applied. Those that did still pertain would have been mostly concerned with Government Communications Headquarters (GCHQ) and the covert help in intelligence and weaponry we had received during the war from the Americans. These details could have been held back without diminishing any of the essential truths.

In early 1983 Michael Heseltine replaced John Nott as Minister of Defence. For his first year in office he had not been much concerned with the *Belgrano* problem. But by early 1984, he and his advisors recognized that the official narrative was coming apart. It was apparent that several MPs knew a good deal more than they were revealing.[9] The potential for embarrassment – in that Ministers had misled the House – was growing. Better perhaps to tell the truth, or as much of it as would be compatible with ongoing security factors like the GCHQ material. So an MOD Assistant Secretary (a rank more senior than it sounds) was instructed to prepare a paper on the whole tangled story. Clive Ponting was a high-flyer: his diligence and flair had already earned him an OBE at only thirty-four. For his work on the *Belgrano* he would have needed (and was almost certainly given) access to all the relevant documents, including the classified signals between Northwood and the South Atlantic, and the intercepts made by (or passed to) GCHQ of signals between the Argentine high command and ships in its navy. There would also have been information derived from reconnaissance satellites – part of the long-standing co-operation between British intelligence and its American equivalent.

Clive Ponting took about ten days to do the research. The more he read, the more he was struck by the gap between the authorized version of events and what had actually happened. His report was highly classified; only six copies were made. As Ponting tells it in conversation and in his

9. There were 'leaks' routed to Tam Dalyell and others by some who had first-hand knowledge of the facts. It seems they were offended by the official deceptions.

book *The Right to Know*, he presented his paper – almost immediately dubbed 'The Crown Jewels' – to a top-level meeting with the Minister, Michael Heseltine. Those present included the Minister for the Armed Forces, John Stanley, and the MOD's top civil servant, Sir Clive Whitmore. Also there for some of the time was Admiral Sir John Fieldhouse, who had been Commander-in-Chief at Northwood during the campaign. Early on, as Ponting tells it, the Admiral wanted to know why an official despatch in which he had clearly stated that *Belgrano* had been trailed for thirty hours had been altered to read as if she had been spotted only shortly before being sunk. Nobody could (or would?) tell him. But, if Ponting is right, that unanswered question further confirms the allegation that there was a cover-up. It also highlights an important aspect of that stratagem: the precise timing of various events, and the signals reporting them, had been fudged. The discussion lasted all morning. It is recalled by Michael Heseltine in his recent autobiography, *Life in the Jungle*:

> My overwhelming impression . . . remains one of surprise. Here were the principal characters who had given Mrs Thatcher very clear advice to sink *Belgrano*, and yet on many of the details so soon after the event they were arguing among themselves.

Internal arguments are a frequent feature of muddled cover-ups. Clive Ponting certainly recalls the debate, but says that it was less concerned with the details of what had actually happened than it was with how to shore up the deteriorating believability of the official version of events. According to Ponting, John Stanley thought the surest way of solving this problem was simply to deny that there was one – by pulling down the shutters and refusing to answer any further questions on the grounds that 'everything is classified'. Someone pointed out that this would look rather lame so long after the events in question. It would also, in light of the information made public more than a year earlier by both Rear Admiral Woodward and Commander Wreford-Brown (of *Conqueror*), put both officers in breach of the Official Secrets Act. Would they now be prosecuted? In the end it was agreed that there really was no alternative but to end the charade. Later that day, Michael Heseltine and Sir Clive Whitmore took 'The Crown Jewels' over to the Prime Minister to get her agreement for a more open policy.

Evidently, Mrs Thatcher agreed the new approach, but only as long as a way could be found to limit the personal and political embarrassment inherent in acknowledging that the version of events put about since the end of the war had always been less than true. That might have worked within a few weeks of the war's end. But it was far too late for that now. Some disguise was still called for. Today it would be immediately recognized as 'spin'. Ponting was given the task. He found this not only difficult but rather distasteful. Nevertheless, he managed to draft replies to both Denzil Davies and Tam Dalyell that, while going rather further than before, did not draw too much attention to the previous dissembling and half-truths. He thought he had come as close to squaring a difficult circle as was possible. So he was disappointed when someone higher up the MOD chain of command decided that the replies he had so carefully drafted were not to be sent to Dalyell and Davies after all. Instead, Heseltine wrote a letter (on the advice, no doubt, of his immediate advisors) brusquely saying that he had nothing to add to the information previously made available. It was back to the cover-up, or something very close to it.

Maybe a clue to this reversion to the original narrative can be found in a comment made some months later by Heseltine to the Select Committee on Foreign Affairs:

> It was apparent to me that if we were to move down the route of following the detailed analysis which was being requested, we would end up with yet more requests for yet more information.

To political sceptics, this may not seem a strange thing for a minister to say. Certainly, in its accurate reflection of Whitehall policy (in answering Parliamentary Questions, never provide any more information than is strictly necessary), it has a certain honesty. However, that was all well in the future. Back in the spring of 1984, Ponting had a problem. It was partly a matter of conscience and partly one of common sense. He was sure that Dalyell and a few others already knew a good deal about the cover-up – in which they had identified a conspiracy rather than a mere cock-up. Dalyell was most unlikely to give up until he had dragged it into the open. So the truth was going to come out in the end. When it did, there would be embarrassment and recrimination all round. And

Ponting did not see why he should have to stand too near that fan. But meanwhile there was the worrying way that individual MPs and, thereby the Commons as a whole, were still being misled. The deceit was obviously known to a range of senior MOD civil servants. But none of them was prepared to say anything; to do so would have been to commit the considerable civil service sin of 'letting the side down'. After all, 'a line had been agreed' more than two years earlier. So, with no support, Ponting could do no more than urge, once again, that on grounds of expediency (even if morality did not come into it) it would be better to 'come clean'.

However, as before, he was strongly opposed. The Minister for the Armed Services, John Stanley, repeated the formula that all information beyond that already given out (much of which was misleading) was 'classified'. Ponting, from his research for 'The Crown Jewels', surmised that while there were indeed some details which were classified, the facts needed to give honest answers to Tam Dalyell and others had been declassified a long while back. To pretend that their non-disclosure was vital to the nation's safety was simply dishonest. Security was being used as a cloak to cover the discomfort of certain ministers, not least the Prime Minister. After a good deal of thought, Ponting sent a short, unsigned letter to Dalyell telling him that the information he wanted was not classified and that he should go on pressing for it.

Perhaps as a consequence, the correspondence between Tam Dalyell and Michael Heseltine went to and fro all through the summer. Heseltine's replies evolved into a fixed formula which, strangely, did not much use the 'security' argument. Instead, he said that because Dalyell's real aim was to show that *Belgrano* had been sunk to scupper the last-minute chance of a peace agreement (being brokered by the Peruvians), there was no point in giving Dalyell the information he was asking for:

> My refusal to answer the many detailed questions you have put to me rests on the fact that . . . your purpose is to demonstrate your belief that *Belgrano* was attacked in order to destroy the prospects for peace and not because she posed a threat to the task force. Since, as the Prime Minister made clear in her letter of 12 April to you, your contention is simply not true, I remain of the view that there is nothing to be gained from providing the detailed answers you are seeking.

In short, because I don't approve of what I think you are trying to do, I am going to deny you the answers to which you, as an MP, have a constitutional right. Heseltine did not pretend that aspects of national security lay behind his refusal; he just did not approve of the line of questioning.

One is surprised that Heseltine, who is nobody's fool, did not see that the official tactics were in the end likely to be self-defeating. The more Dalyell and others were fobbed off, the more certain they became that there was a conspiracy to hide the real reason, as they saw it, that *Belgrano* was sunk. There was no way now that they were going to believe that the torpedoes had been fired because the Navy wanted them fired – even though, at the time, it had clearly suited Mrs Thatcher to go along with, and approve, that want.

The narrative now shifts slightly. During the summer of 1984, the Commons Select Committee on Foreign Affairs had begun hearings on the future of the Falkland Islands. This inevitably touched on the Peruvian peace plan (basically, a form of lease-back) and its possible demise with the sinking of the *Belgrano*. The question here was the same as the one Tam Dalyell had long been driving at: had the sinking been ordered to silence the tiresome Peruvians, and thereby to end Argentine tactics to drag the 'negotiations' further into the winter? Or had it been a solely tactical decision to 'take out' a perceived naval threat? One wonders why no minister ever explained that it was almost certainly a combination of *both* reasons. If someone had so explained, there would undoubtedly have been a short-lived furore and a repetition of some earlier headlines – 'Thatcher Torpedoed Peace Prospects'. But an explanation about, first, Admiral Woodward's concerns and, second, the approaching winter could hardly have been denied. Such an answer might not have satisfied Tam Dalyell now. But, right or wrong, if a straight answer had been given early enough, it would have gone a long way to reducing the potential for ministerial embarrassment. And have saved endless trouble.

The Select Committee wanted answers about the exact timings throughout the *Belgrano* affair. When had different naval signals been sent and received? Had news about the latest 'moves' in Peru, New York and Washington been received in London before or after those signals?

This worried Number 10 and the top echelons of the MOD. It was difficult enough to refuse such information to one or two individual MPs, though, if desperate, one could imply that they were only in it to score political points. But to refuse answers to a cross-party Commons Committee was more difficult. The argument about 'national security' would be unconvincing; Select Committees quite often hear such information in closed session. A senior civil servant, Michael Legge, was given the task of 'drafting round the problem'. No doubt he took advice – though not from Ponting.

The Legge Minute ran to several pages. Most of it was concerned with maintaining consistency, as was made clear in the opening paragraph: 'We have borne in mind the statements made to date by Ministers on the subject of *Belgrano*.' In translation this seems to mean that 'we have already taken a line on this matter and we are therefore stuck with it'. Given this inhibition, the paper could propose few changes or additions to the authorized narrative. To have done so would, wrote Legge, 'provide more information than Ministers have been prepared to reveal so far about the *Belgrano* affair . . . I therefore recommend that we should avoid these difficulties by providing the Committee with a more general narrative.' (A variant on the 'say very little' tactic?) It was apparent to Ponting that the Committee was going to get no further in its inquiries than Tam Dalyell and Denzil Davies. It worried him that his department, the MOD, could be so obstructive when, more than two years after the events in question, very few issues of national safety or security were involved.

Sometimes a cliché says it all. Ponting was torn.

On the one hand there was an ingrained duty of loyalty to his department, colleagues and ministers. On the other was obedience to a Whitehall 'commandment': a civil servant should never be knowingly involved in a process that misleads Parliament. The two 'loyalties' were not compatible. So what to do? As Ponting tells it today and, no doubt, as he told it to himself then, there were not many options. He could just shut up – that is what his superiors would have told him to do anyway. He could urge a rethink within the MOD. But he had tried that before – and been turned down. Or he could find a way of letting a responsible journalist know what was going on. But that was not really an option because it would inevitably detonate media interest in a problem that he hoped could be more quietly resolved. In the end he decided that the only option he could 'live with' would be to send another anonymous envelope to Tam Dalyell and trust the MP to decide how to handle things from there. Inside that envelope were two papers; both were unclassified. One was a somewhat filleted copy of the Legge Minute. The second contained the answers to the questions the MP had been asking in March. Ponting hoped the 'leak' would not be traced back to him, but he took some comfort that, if it were, there was a ruling of some years earlier which just might cover his dilemma. It had arisen when a Select Committee had asked very specifically what would happen if a civil servant passed information to that Committee because he/she believed that earlier information had been misleading. The Treasury, which has the final word on these things, had been surprisingly reassuring:

> There would be no breach if the sole publication were to the Committee or to the House since the publication would in that event amount to a proceeding in Parliament and would be absolutely privileged.

Tam Dalyell got Ponting's papers in his House of Commons mail. It largely confirmed what he already knew. He had not received straight answers to his questions. But, again, what to do? He kept the thing to himself for over a week. Then, judging that the Select Committee on Foreign Affairs was probably also going to be misled, he decided to give the paper to the Chairman of the Committee, Sir Anthony Kershaw. He knew, of course, that Sir Anthony was a Conservative and therefore was likely to be broadly supportive of the official position. Nevertheless, he thought that his confidence would be respected and that his paper was safe enough. But some days later he was stunned to learn that Sir Anthony had sent the paper back to the MOD. Maybe there was an informal agreement with Michael Heseltine: the Minister got the paper; Sir Anthony got the Minister's consent to appear before the Committee later that year. The Minister passed the paper to the MOD Police with instructions to trace the leak. It was not difficult. Ponting was already known for his doubts about the way the *Belgrano* affair was being handled.

Ponting met the MOD halfway by offering to resign. It seemed that that would be the end of the matter. But two weeks later the Attorney General turned away from such a solution. Ponting was arrested, fingerprinted, phone tapped and was formally charged under the Official Secrets Act. So much for the earlier Treasury note about 'absolute privilege'.

Part 1 of the Official Secrets Act is concerned with espionage – spying. Ponting was charged under Part 2 of the Act; it deals with the unauthorized disclosure of information. Dating back to 1911, Part 2 was a 'catch-all'. Nowhere does it adequately define 'unauthorized' or, for that matter, 'official secret'. Perhaps the omissions were deliberate. In theory, Part 2 covered any and all information that a civil servant might come across in the course of his work. So, if the Attorney General so decided, it could even apply to the revelation that the latest lavatory paper in the MOD was unperforated. More seriously, this was the first time that a prosecution had been brought under the Act for passing information to an MP. Perhaps it was hoped to deter anyone else from thinking about a similar 'betrayal'.

The fact that the MP had previously been fed bogus information was obviously going to be a useful element in Ponting's defence. His legal team would argue that it was very much 'in the public interest' that MPs, individually or collectively, should not be deceived on matters no longer relevant to the security of the nation. It seemed likely that the prosecution would, in effect, argue the exact reverse: that the unauthorized disclosure of information was, under any circumstances, a breach of trust and, as such, against the national interest.

During the five months that Ponting was suspended, and before the case came to trial at the Old Bailey, there were some interesting developments. Mrs Thatcher's Press Secretary, Bernard Ingham, was reported to have said that it was the government's hope that 'an appropriately severe member of the judiciary would be on hand to hear the case'. So, if the government got its way on the choice of judge, this would be as close to a political trial as it is possible to get in the United Kingdom. At the same time the Attorney General, Sir Michael Havers, was unwise enough to get involved in a BBC radio discussion about the case, during which he was even more unwise to make the following comment:

> This is simply a matter of a very senior civil servant disclosing matters which I say he had no right to disclose.

One might have thought that this comment, with its unequivocal assertion of guilt – a matter normally left to a jury – came close to contempt of court. But in deciding not to admonish himself, Sir Michael may have taken into account the fact that, besides being one of the nation's most senior law officers, he was also a politician and a working colleague of those ministers closely associated with the case.

Elsewhere, the Campaign for Freedom of Information organized a fund to help with legal expenses. The National Council for Civil Liberties (NCCL) and, bravely, Whitehall's own First Division Association – the 'staff union' to which senior civil servants belong – came in with support. So, too, did the three Opposition leaders: Neil Kinnock, David Steel and David Owen. The press, of course, took a delighted interest from the start. One of the most pertinent reports appeared in the form of a 'spoof' letter from Denis Thatcher in *Private Eye*'s 'Dear Bill' column. It was as near the mark as any of the more erudite broadsheet editorials:

> Did you see that uppity quack Owen has been sounding off about the *Belgrano*? My advice was to come clean and say 'what the hell is war about if it isn't torpedoing a boatload of Argies before they steam in and do the same to us?' But for the Boss this is a very sore point, her finest hour, etc, and any word of criticism brings on the heebie-jeebies. In this I think she was encouraged by Tarzan, and they have now decided to string up some little Whitehall paper-pusher, rack, thumbscrews, the whole works, just because he photostated a few memos and sent them down to Halitosis Hall.

As it often does, *Private Eye* had the political dimension about right. Perhaps, to mix some metaphors, it really was a parliamentary storm in a teacup that, because it had not been straightened out early enough, was now out of control. John Nott and Mrs Thatcher had been less than straightforward about *Belgrano* right from the start. Michael Heseltine came in later. How far, at the beginning, it had been deliberate or just an incompetent muddle caused by poor briefing and too many other things to think about, no one really knows. Those involved had some justification while the war was being fought. But once the war was over, no one on Mrs T.'s side of the House seems to have had the guts to tell her that she was continuing to mislead Parliament – 'any word of criticism brings on the heebie-jeebies'. So, from then on, with suspicion growing by the month, things just got worse and worse.

They finished up at the Old Bailey.

The trial began in late January 1985 – not far short of three years since *Belgrano* had gone down. It lasted ten days. The prosecution went first. The thrust of its case against Ponting was that, although his passing of information to Dalyell had not risked national security, it was a breach of official confidence and, as such, was against 'the national interest'. 'What would happen if every civil servant who disagreed with his seniors or his Minister were to do a Ponting?' That question was implied throughout. It ignored the fact that telling, and not telling, the truth was involved. At one stage, despite earlier assurances to the contrary, the prosecution asked that the trial should go into closed session. The judge, Sir Anthony McCowan, granted the request. In some of his early comments he seemed to show that he was the 'appropriately severe member of the judiciary' the government had wanted. The 'in camera' session was mostly concerned with various intelligence appraisals at the time of the sinking. Some of the information had been (and still was) classified, but it had little to do with the charge against Ponting; he had not passed on anything that was classified. The session probably just confused the jury. Back in open court, various senior civil servants, ex-colleagues of Ponting, were called. Some were more accurate in their testimony than others.

Things livened up one day when the judge summoned Tam Dalyell into the well of the court and gave him a blast for having suggested to *The Times* that it was John Stanley, the Minister for the Armed Forces, who earlier had ordered the alteration to Admiral Sir John Fieldhouse's despatch that had said that *Conqueror* had trailed *Belgrano* for thirty hours before being torpedoed. Given the significance of the *sub judice* rule, the judge had a point. Maybe Dalyell had one as well.

Things livened up further when Ponting took the stand. Counsel for the prosecution would have preferred to deny him any chance of making the point – persuasive to any jury – that, for whatever reasons, a Prime Minister and two successive Ministers, John Nott and then Michael Heseltine, had misled Parliament. But it was impossible to keep this out of Ponting's cross-examination answers. It was central to the whole story. After all, without the Ministers' misleading answers, there would have been no point in Ponting taking the risk of making his 'corrective' leak; there would have been nothing to correct. So the prosecution suggested that he had been politically motivated: he had 'leaked marvellous ammunition' to Tam Dalyell, whom he knew to be an arch critic of the government's decision to go to war over the Falklands, let alone its decision to sink the *Belgrano*. Ponting managed to make the point that Dalyell was a duly elected MP and, as such, regardless of his views, he had a right to be told the truth – unless there was a very good 'national security' reason otherwise. In any case, if one was going to talk about motivation, what about the government's bending of the facts to save itself political embarrassment during the previous two years? Elsewhere, there came the suggestion that Ponting had acted out of pique: he had been annoyed that his recommendations to the ministers had been turned down. Ponting gave as good as he got. He did not accept that 'the national interest', which he had allegedly damaged with his disclosure to Dalyell, was synonymous with 'the government's interest'. Pious though it might sound, he implied that there *was* a higher duty – to the sovereign body of Parliament.

At times these exchanges were quite lively. They went on all day. It was difficult to tell how the jury was taking it all. But they must, at least, have pondered the defence's argument that Parliament had been misled long after there was any 'security' need to do so.

The jury would have also wondered at the appearance of Merlyn Rees for the defence. Yes, he was now a member of the Opposition, but here was someone who had been Secretary of State for Northern Ireland and then Home Secretary. In the latter office he had charge of MI5 – so he knew something about security, leaks and 'the national interest'. Interestingly, the prosecution could not muster any minister, past or present, to lend weight to its case. Perhaps it was told not to try.

On the stand, Merlyn Rees found an early chance to make a telling point: 'If I'd thought there'd been a breach of security, I would not have come along this morning.' That was strong enough, but it was a little later in his cross-examination that his words must have really worried the prosecution:

> Loyalty to a Minister and a Government must be there, but the loyalty to his nation is greater. If a civil servant found himself with a crisis of conscience, and no channels offering reasonable prospect of redress, should he simply resign and say nothing? If those were the circumstances, I would put truthfulness to Parliament above all.

Counsel for the prosecution did the best he could with Merlyn Rees; he suggested that the final decision about such matters must surely rest with the relevant minister. Merlyn Rees agreed that if 'the national interest' (i.e. security) really were the issue then, yes, the minister's decision would be the one that mattered, 'but not if it is the political embarrassment of the government'. He really did not need to say much more.

There was another big gun rolled out by the defence. Professor Sir Henry Wade was a Cambridge don and a constitutional lawyer. He had a worldwide reputation in the area of government and administration. The latest in a long line of books he had written was called *Constitutional Conventions*. The title was entirely appropriate to the case. In a nutshell, he said that without a written constitution, the good governance of Britain was dependent on the observance of long-standing conventions. As was the relationship between the government of the day and Parliament: 'The conventions could not exist unless Ministers give truthful answers to Parliament.' Indeed, truthful answers were one of the conventions. So, while trust between a minister and his civil servants was very important, that between the minister and Parliament was imperative.

The judge was not impressed by either of these witnesses. Indeed, Sir Anthony's body language had betrayed his sympathies from the start. Now, rather obviously, he did not bother himself with making any notes during the testimony of the ex-Home Secretary and the Cambridge professor. From an early stage it seemed to Ponting and his legal team that the judge's mind was made up. To give just one example of his utterances during the proceedings: 'If the Crown is right, there isn't any scope for an acquittal . . . he [Ponting] was clearly not acting in the interests of the state . . . He was not acting in the interest of the government.' The judge evidently held the view that the interests of the state and the interests of the government were the same thing. But this was exactly what the trial was really about.

The reaction of counsel for the prosecution to one of these interjections was interesting. 'M'Lord, I am very reluctant,' he said, 'that in this of all cases you should finish up directing the jury to convict.' This was extraordinary. One might have thought that this was exactly what the prosecution would want – until one realizes that the government and the Attorney General would, in the face of widespread media accusations, wish to avoid any confirmation that this was a politically motivated trial. So the message must have gone out to back-pedal. It would look better if the jury was allowed to make up its own mind with a minimum of obvious direction from the judge. But no one seems to have told the judge.

When the judge came to sum up, he may have thought that he needed to nullify the persuasive closing speech from Ponting's counsel. And his references to the points made by Merlyn Rees and Sir Henry Wade were dismissive. As before, he equated the interests of the state with the interests of the government and thereby with those of a relevant minister. There was little about the expectation of MPs that they should, except under very limited circumstances, always be told the truth. Not a word about the possibility that Ponting might, just possibly, have been concerned about that expectation. Instead, he seemed to imply motives of resentment, rancour and disappointment. At first, Ponting and his legal team were dismayed. But, as he now recalls, the longer the judge ploughed on, the more it seemed that his inherent views would become obvious to the jury.

One never quite knows with juries. Did they feel that the judge had pushed them too hard towards a conviction? That, in his summing-up, he had rubbished the testimony of Sir Henry Wade too vigorously? Did they feel that Section 2 of the Official Secrets Act was an overly convenient catch-all? Or were they swayed by the closing speech from Ponting's counsel? Were they unpersuaded by the evidence coming from some of the civil servant witnesses? Were they bothered by ministerial lack of candour – despite the claimed justification for it? Were they curious about why no minister had appeared as a witness for the prosecution? Were they concerned that the interests of the state and those of the government were held to be the same thing? Were they puzzled that no one had really explained to them just why Parliament should have been denied the information some of its members had pressed for? Maybe, once they retired, they asked themselves all these questions.

They were out for less than an hour. Their verdict was unanimous: not guilty. And Ponting got his costs. The government was pole-axed. That evening the news led the bulletins on both ITN and BBC. The next day's papers were almost unanimous: whatever they had to say about Ponting (he got mixed reviews), ministers and their officials had made a mess from beginning to end. The government had been the author of its own misfortune.

In arriving at its conclusion, the jury probably did not know of Winston Churchill's observation nearly fifty years earlier. He, too, back in the 1930s, had been leaked a stream of information about the inadequacies of the country's defences – which were then denied by the relevant ministers. His subsequent comment has current pertinence:

> The Official Secrets Act was devised to protect the national defences and ought not to be used . . . to shield Ministers who have strong personal interests in concealing the truth.

If, today, one goes to a copy of *Who's Who*, one finds that all those civil servants who either acquiesced or played a part in laying a smoke screen around the *Belgrano* affair have retired. All seem to have wound up with the honours, knighthoods even, that are the rewards given to, and expected by, good team players in Whitehall. Likewise, their colleagues across the street in the Foreign Office who must have known what was really happening to the Ilois. But not Clive Ponting. True, he has his OBE. But he had that anyway. On his evidence one might conclude that integrity is all very well, but as has already been observed, and will be again, there is no point in taking it too far. And if, by chance or design, someone *should* take it too far, they should certainly not go looking for any reward for doing so.

If that last observation is thought to be either too pious or too unsophisticated, one is reminded of the small boy who, having pointed out that the emperor was not wearing any clothes, was admonished in a whisper by an old man standing nearby, 'Of course not, lad. But get real.' It is a commentary on our public expectations that, too often, we are resigned to such weary cynicism. We just shrug and don't even hope for better next time.

CHINOOK – ZULU DELTA 576

'Absolutely no doubt whatsoever'

We will of course be having a very major inquiry into the causes of this accident and that will take place over the next few weeks.

Malcolm Rifkind, Secretary of State for Defence, 3 June 1994

I have this afternoon placed in the library of both Houses a summary of the findings of the Inquiry into this tragic crash, which claimed the lives of 29 people. On all the evidence, it was concluded that the cause of the accident was that the two pilots had wrongly continued to fly towards the Mull of Kintyre below a safe altitude in unsuitable weather conditions. This constituted a failure in their duty and, regrettably, therefore, it was concluded that both pilots had been negligent.

Malcolm Rifkind, Secretary of State for Defence, 15 June 1995

I am puzzled that although we did have several meetings after the Inquiry had reached its conclusion of gross negligence, neither then nor at any other time was I given any indication that there had been serious problems with that type of aircraft. On the face of it, if an aircraft crashes and the MOD are at the time in legal dispute with the manufacturers because of matters relating to the aircraft and its operational capability, that is information that should at least be shared with an inquiry so that they themselves can judge whether it might or might not have contributed to the accident.

Malcolm Rifkind on ITN, 13 October 1999

THE PASSENGERS ARRIVED FROM various parts of Northern Ireland during the late afternoon. It was Thursday 2 June 1994. As they gathered in the small RAF waiting room, there would have been the usual welcoming banter and laughter. Most of them knew each other. They would have chatted about the agenda for this conference at Fort George. There were several sets of golf clubs – in the hope, no doubt, of a quick nine holes during a long summer evening. At about 5.15 p.m. they were called to put on their orange survival suits. One can guess that there were the normal good-natured jokes about how the RUC (or was it Special Branch?) always managed to grab the newest and brightest ensembles. Then, after a short safety briefing which some of them knew almost by heart, they went outside and were bussed across the tarmac to Zulu Delta 576.

The two pilots, Flight Lieutenants Tapper and Cook, were already in the cockpit working through their checks. Tapper was in the left-hand seat. He was the NHP – the 'non-handling pilot'. He was also in overall command. Cook was in the other seat; he was the handling pilot. The forecast showed much of the Highlands to be in cloud. Because of that, and an icing restriction on their type of Chinook, they would be flying at between 100 and 1000 feet – low for a fixed-wing aircraft but quite routine for a helicopter. The first leg of the flight would be straightforward. So would all the others. It would take ZD576 across to Scotland, arriving at a point just short of the lighthouse on the tip of the Mull of Kintyre. From there they would parallel the coast north to Fort William. Then up the Great Glen to their destination at the army base of Fort George. It would be a flight under Visual Flight Rules (VFR), or what pilots sometimes call Mark One Eyeball. At the same time, the aircraft's position would be available on its Global Positioning System (GPS). This, receiving signals from three or more fixed satellites, plots an instant position to within less than 100 metres anywhere in the world.

With the twenty-five passengers all aboard and settled they were ready to go. The engines were started and, as the hum wound up to an almost deafening whine, the twin rotors began to turn. After more checks the Chinook taxied forward. The pilots paused briefly while Aldergrove control tower was asked for clearance. A few seconds later the sound of the rotors changed again. Slowly, ZD576 lifted and then, tilting forward, climbed and accelerated away. As she banked round to the north, the ground crew walked back to the hangar; they would not be needed again until she was home from Fort George with the last of the daylight four hours later. The tower logged the time of departure as 5.42 p.m.

Seventeen minutes later a yachtsman and his friend watched ZD576 pass low and close ahead. The yacht was about 2½ miles south-west of the

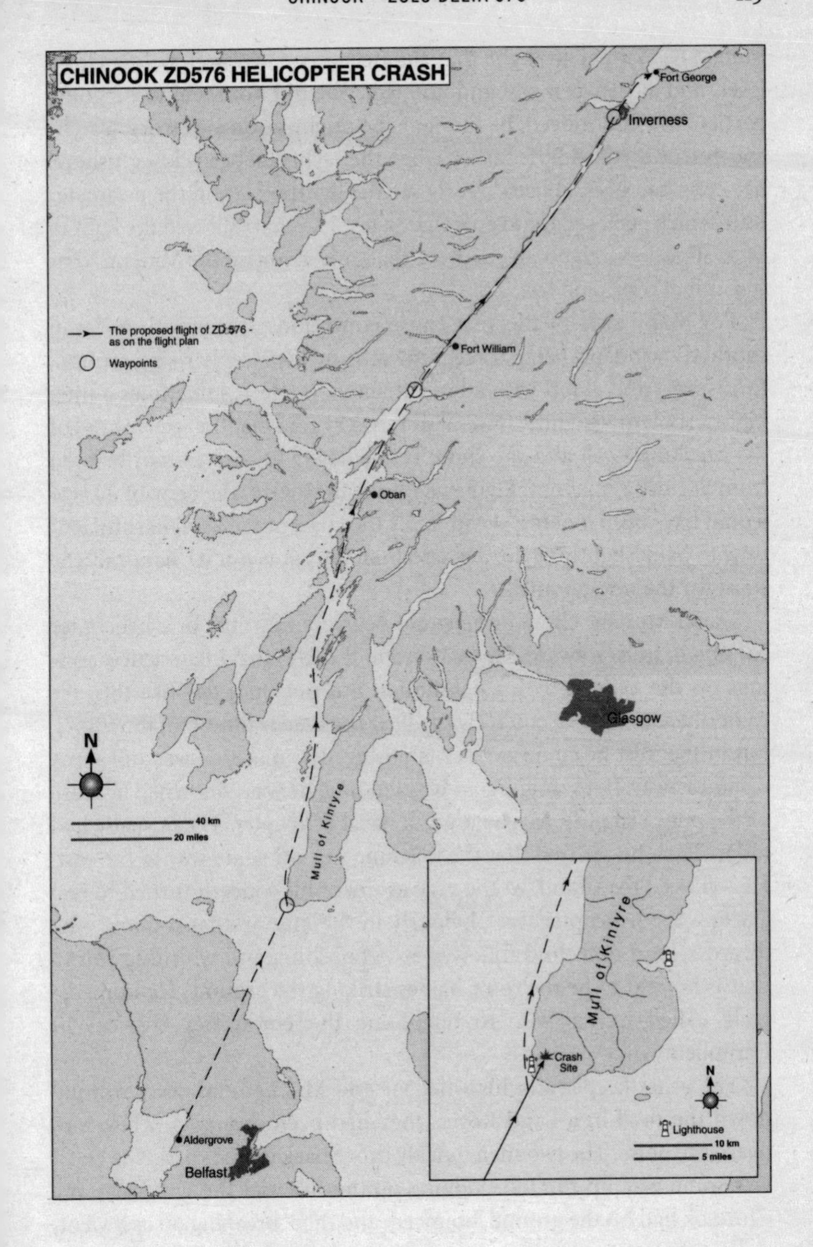
CHINOOK ZD576 HELICOPTER CRASH
Fort George
Inverness
The proposed flight of ZD 576 - as on the flight plan
Waypoints
Fort William
Oban
Glasgow
N
40 km
20 miles
Mull of Kintyre
Aldergrove
Belfast
Mull of Kintyre
Crash Site
N
Lighthouse
10 km
5 miles

Mull. The skipper thought that the helicopter was 'well below cloud level', and at between 200 and 400 feet. She did not seem to be going particularly fast; indeed, he thought she might be on a practice search-and-rescue sortie. A little earlier, when the yacht had been closer inshore, her crew had been able to 'clearly see the lighthouse and the perimeter wall' which enclosed the keepers' cottages. The chart showed the light to be at almost exactly 300 feet. Above that, mist mantled the Mull up to its summit at over 1400 feet.

For many days of the year those conditions are typical. A damp southerly wind, on being forced upwards by the steeply rising ground, forms mist and cloud with a base at about 300 feet, sometimes a little higher, sometimes a little lower. But it is very rare that the white water of the breaking swell and the shore immediately behind cannot be seen from at least a mile out. Flying as low as they were, the crew of ZD576 would have been looking ahead to see the coast of the Mull in sufficient time to bank slightly to the left, and then (as pilots put it) 'handrail' the coast for the next 70 miles.

David Murchie thought he could hear the murmur of a helicopter coming in from seaward. He was used to the RAF making practice landings on the helipad by his lighthouse. But not on a day like this. He went outside. Now he could clearly hear the louder thump of the rotors, but in the mist he could not see anything. The machine was still some distance away. If it was going to be a landing, he was concerned because of the poor visibility. Maybe it was a naval helicopter. They usually had radar. Then he realized that the machine was off some way to the east. He followed the sound. At the very moment his concern turned to real alarm – the helicopter was obviously in the mist and far too low – he 'heard a loud dull thud followed by whooshing and whistling sound that I thought to be the rotor blades striking the ground'. He immediately called to his wife to telephone the emergency services in Campbeltown.

The other keeper and his wife, Mr and Mrs Lamont, were coming down the road in a Land Rover; they had been shopping. They, too, heard the noise. The two men quickly drove back up the road. The crash was some way up the hill. Judging by the fire and the wreckage, the Chinook had hit the ground, bounced, and then, breaking up as it went, finally stopped about 300 yards further on. Much of the debris was alight; the rest was spread over a wide area. Scattered among the debris and the burning heather were huddles of orange bundles. The dark smoke mixed with the fog. It was obvious that in a crash of that severity there would be no survivors. But both men, and two holiday cyclists who emerged out of the mist, felt that they had to try to make sure.

An hour-and-a-half later, at 7.26 p.m., BBC1 broke into its schedule. There had been a crash of an RAF helicopter 'in western Scotland'. It was thought to be carrying a number of passengers. It was not known if there were any survivors. 'We will bring you further news as it becomes available.'

IT IS PROBABLY BEST TO go back to the beginning. Or even a little before the beginning.

The Chinook is a remarkable machine. With fuel and crew it weighs nearly 13 tons; it can lift a further 10 tons. Built by Boeing, it has been flying with the United States Army, and later with at least twenty other forces, for nearly forty years. CH-47s first saw active service in Vietnam, where they were used for heavy lifts and rapid troop deployment – forty-five fully armed infantrymen at 130 knots. More than 1000 have been built and they are still in production. They cost at least £20 million apiece.

The RAF got its first Chinooks in the late 1970s. Given that the new aircraft's main role was as a troop transport, there was an attempt by the Army (there always is) to wrest control away from the RAF. Such was the rivalry that, as far as helicopters were concerned, the two services hardly talked to each other for nearly a year. The RAF won. But it had to promise that it would always give the Army's needs the highest priority. Since then, Chinooks have been used in the Falklands, the Gulf, Lebanon, Bosnia, Kosovo, Sierra Leone, Afghanistan, Iraq and, of course, Northern Ireland. They have been versatile and reliable machines – though, like all helicopters, the downtime for routine maintenance is high.

Back in the mid-1980s it was realized that a time was coming when the whole RAF fleet of thirty-two Chinooks would need modernizing. So by 1988 contracts were being drawn up to start shipping the aircraft back to the Boeing factory in Philadelphia. At a rate of seven or eight a year, they would be stripped out and virtually rebuilt. It was hoped to have most of the fleet upgraded and back in operation by 1993. The update of the whole fleet would cost over £150 million.[1]

Knowing what was being planned, various companies in the component business approached the MOD with proposals for 'improvements'. One such was a consortium led by Textron-Lycoming, who made the engines. The improvement would be a computer system which, by electronically sensing the power needed by the rotors in any given manoeuvre, would feed exactly the right amount of fuel into the engines to give the required power. The estimate was that the RAF would not only have a much more reliable fleet, but that there would also be big savings in fuel and maintenance.

The MOD knew that other computerized fuel systems had been developed by various manufacturers around the world. Airbus had specified one for all its new aircraft. Boeing's 767 and 777 had it too. And Concorde. But developing the software for a helicopter would be much more difficult because, unlike a fixed-wing aircraft, a helicopter accelerates or decelerates by tilting the angle of the 'disc' formed by its rotating rotors, not by speeding up or slowing down the speed of those rotors. In a Chinook, the rotors turn at a constant 225 rpm – whether the helicopter is just sitting on the ground or whether it is in a vertical climb. The difference is solely in the pitch of the rotor blades – varying between zero pitch (in a sense, flat or feathered) when sitting on the ground, or full pitch (for maximum 'bite' on the air) when lifting straight up. But, obviously, more engine power, much more, is needed when the rotor blades are working at full pitch than when they are feathered. The proposed computers (one for each engine) would not only measure out the exact amount of fuel needed for any manoeuvre, they would also ensure that the power of both engines was exactly matched and in harmony. And that the rotor speed was held at a constant 225 rpm. The system was very

1. Partly to save money, it was decided not to fit cockpit voice recorders (CVRs – about £12,000 apiece) or the much more sophisticated 'black box' data recorders (about £250,000 apiece). A CVR records more than just what the pilots are saying to each other. For example, from the CVR recovered from the civilian Chinook G-BWFC lost in the North Sea on 6 November 1986, investigators were able to identify gearbox failure within forty-eight hours of the crash.

sophisticated, but if the design consortium could get things right, it would be a great improvement.

The generic term for this piece of 'kit' was FADEC. It stood for Full Authority Digital Electronic Control. It meant what it said: the Fadec would be in full control of fuel flow and, therefore, of engine speed. It seemed a good idea. The contract was awarded. The Textron-Lycoming consortium now had its eye on an even bigger prize. At the time there were over 600 other Chinooks in service around the world.

The first RAF Chinook was shipped back to Boeing's helicopter plant in Philadelphia in mid-1988. It was a major overhaul: new and more powerful engines, new electronics, new hydraulics, new flight controls, new almost everything. Textron-Lycoming fitted the two Fadecs. By mid-January 1989 everything was ready for ground trials at nearby Wilmington. The tests went on for several days. Short of actually flying the thing – that would come next – just about everything that could be tested was. There were a few minor glitches but 'nothing that couldn't be fixed'. With the Fadecs there was a recurring hiccup called, in the esoteric language of these things, an 'E5 fault'. But, again, it was more of a passing nuisance than something to worry about.

On the last day the team decided to run a test on the Fadecs' fail-safe mode. To simulate a hit from, say, small arms fire, they disconnected one of the input plugs. It was a mistake. One of the engines suddenly started to accelerate. Within seconds it was running at more than 30 per cent above its safe limit. One of the Fadecs was not reacting as it was meant to and its secondary back-up system had failed. As the speed of the rotors increased even further, there was a real danger of the rotor blades flying off and one or other of the engines disintegrating. This was not fail-safe. If airborne, this 'runaway' or overspeed could have been fail-dead. The pilot saved the day by going into an emergency 'shutdown' on both engines. The whole episode had taken only eighteen seconds. The Chinook was severely damaged.

The MOD was angry. This was not a matter of changing to the spare wheel and then quickly back on the road. While the fault was almost immediately identified as being in the software (it was that 'E5' again), putting it right would be much more complicated. A correction to one part of a software program can have almost endless knock-on effects on other parts of the package. And then there would have to be a whole set of new tests. The MOD would be looking for compensation. The RAF would be stuck with too many Mark 1 Chinooks overdue for their mid-life rebuild. The Army would be getting irritable.

The MOD set up its own inquiry into what came to be known as the 'Wilmington incident'. It ordered that 'a full reappraisal of the Fadec system be carried out by the contractor'. Someone must have pointed out that it never makes much sense to rely too heavily on a contractor to check the quality of its own work. So, rather late in the day, the MOD commissioned a top software consultancy in Britain, EDS-Scicon, to assess the quality of the rewritten software program.

With the update programme badly delayed (some said by nearly three years), the first four Mark 2 Chinooks were not shipped back to Britain until late in 1993. Their first port-of-call was the MOD's test centre at Boscombe Down. Here, as with all new or heavily modified aircraft, test pilots and engineering boffins would put the helicopters through their paces. This is no quick 'round the houses' process. It is meticulous and painstaking; it can take months.

One of the aspects of the 'new' Chinooks which, almost from the start, worried the electronics section at Boscombe Down was the Fadec. It had certainly been much revised, but they still did not like it. The 'language' in which the software was written did not allow them, even with their sophisticated equipment, to make a complete top-to-bottom appraisal. Nevertheless, they could 'read' quite enough to have concerns. They agreed with a report by EDS-Scicon that 'latent errors' in the system might 'still have serious implications'.

The top echelons of the RAF and the people at the MOD's Procurement Executive were in a jam. The programme of upgrading the fleet of Chinooks had already been badly delayed. Now, if Boscombe Down was to have its way, there were going to be even further hold-ups. But with commitments to the Army in Ulster, Bosnia and the Falklands, plus training, normal maintenance and aircraft over at Boeing, the RAF needed the 'new' Chinooks in service as quickly as possible. At the time fewer than half of the RAF's thirty-two Chinooks were 'operationally available'.

Thus for the RAF and the MOD it was a case of 'needs must'. Someone must have suggested that the quickest way out of the mess would be to release the Mk2s for squadron service but with several operating restrictions. The major limit would be to reduce the normal 'cargo-load' from 10 tons to 5 tons. This meant that if one of a Chinook's two Fadecs failed and thereby caused the relevant engine to be shut down, the aircraft could still manage safe flight on the remaining engine. But this solution ignored the possibility of an engine and rotor runaway – a repeat of the 'Wilmington incident'. Indeed, in that kind of situation, if airborne, the lighter the load, the *more* dangerous the 'bolting horse'. One of the other significant restrictions would be to bar the Chinook from flying in conditions where icing might occur. The aircraft was fitted with de-icing equipment, but there were aspects of the gear that did not satisfy Boscombe Down.

So, given the urgent need, a decision was taken at a senior level within the RAF and the MOD to adopt this solution of imposed restrictions. It was not the first time in its long history that the reservations of Boscombe Down have been over-ridden. But it is rare when a 'safety-critical' component is involved.

The test teams at Boscombe Down were not happy to see an aircraft being passed for squadron service before, in their view, it was ready. And, as someone sourly observed, it seemed a pity that, having spent many millions, the resultant helicopter was, for the time being, 50 per cent less capable in terms of load carrying than the one it was replacing. In any case, there were still problems. In March 1994 Boscombe Down suspended flight trials on a new Chinook while some of these faults were rectified. After some days, flying was resumed – only to be stopped once more on 1 June. The Fadec equipment was still misbehaving. In the words of the relevant report, the software was 'unverifiable'. In fact, according to a memorandum from the Director of Helicopter Projects, during the three preceding months there had been five airborne incidents 'due to Fadec malfunctions [and] there had also been other incidents on the ground'. On one occasion an engine flamed out and testing was further delayed. On other occasions warning lights flashed; the fact that they often turned out to be false alarms ('spurious captions' is the official term) was not always immediately apparent.

The processes of Boscombe Down can sometimes be almost too perfectionist. RAF realists (or cynics?) have occasionally observed that if they waited until Boscombe Down was happy with every last fault, no new aircraft would ever reach the squadrons. Pending an eventual answer, temporary restrictions sometimes have to be written into the appropriate flight manuals – as now with the Chinook Mk2.

One of the first of the new machines to enter operational service was ZD576. For two months it flew various tasks in England and was used as a vehicle for pilot conversion courses. Then, on 31 May 1994, it was flown from RAF Odiham, the home base of all Chinooks, across the Irish Sea to the RAF detachment at Aldergrove outside Belfast.

FLIGHT LIEUTENANTS TAPPER AND COOK were the pilots waiting at Aldergrove and assigned to fly ZD576. They would have wanted to check through her fault-and-maintenance log as soon as the aircraft landed. What they read confirmed what they had already heard on the grapevine: during the two months that ZD576 had been operational, there had been a number of problems. Some were mere glitches, others were more serious. On one occasion there had been a brief mismatch in power from the two engines. Yet such a variation in torque was one of the very things the newly fitted Fadecs were meant to prevent. There had been a break of a fixing point within the housing ('the broom cupboard') of the flying controls. The fracture had allowed one end of a 7-inch spring to come free. True, the spring was only there to provide the pilots with a feeling of 'balance' on the lever (the 'collective') that controls the pitch of the rotor blades. It was not 'safety-critical'. But that was not the issue. If the spring had become detached at *both* ends, there was a real chance that it could have fallen and interfered with the control rods and bell cranks which, in the lower half of 'the broom cupboard', were particularly close together.[2] The log also showed that there had been several instances of warning lights coming on. Some had been traced back to one or other of the two Fadecs. Only a week earlier several such lights had flashed – indicating a failure on No. 2 engine. The

2. On 11 May the OC Engineering and Supply Wing of RAF Odiham had originated a signal about a loose spring found the day before in ZD576. 'Detachment of the bracket could present a serious flight safety hazard with the danger of a detached bracket fouling adjacent flying controls. Date/Time: 11 May 94 0930.'

aircraft had diverted to Luton, the nearest airport. The fact that, in the event, these had been false alarms would have been of little comfort. All pilots are trained to be wary of making assumptions about 'false' alarms; one day they might be the real thing.

The day after ZD576 arrived at Aldergrove, both pilots and another officer took it on several short flights in the immediate area of the airfield. Although they were completely familiar with the Chinook Mk1, some weeks had passed since they had completed their short Mk2 conversion course. Like drivers in a different car, they wanted to make sure that they were 'up to speed' on all aspects of their new aircraft. They were concerned to find that the temperature gauge for the 'power turbine inlet' was obviously misreading. As a forewarning of possible overheating, the gauge is an important indicator on any turbine-powered helicopter (which means all service aircraft). Furthermore, in the Chinook Mk2, that particular temperature point is one of the key 'inputs' to the Fadec. In the event, the fault cleared itself. But, alongside the other concerns, even the temporary failure did not boost confidence.

Earlier, Tapper had phoned his parents in Norfolk. They talked of this and that. He let slip to his father that he was not too happy with the prospect of flying the new Chinook. Cook, too, had talked in the same way to his father – a retired Concorde pilot. It is officially recorded that Tapper asked the commanding officer of the RAF detachment at Aldergrove if the 'old' Chinook (i.e. the Mk1) that the new machine was replacing could be kept on for a while. But such was the shortage of serviceable Chinooks throughout the RAF that this was not possible.

Neither Tapper nor Cook was normally given to nervousness. They each had completed about 3000 hours of service flying. Both were experienced Special Forces pilots. That is as high on the ladder of helicopter skills as any operational pilot can go. Temperamentally, too, according to both official and informal accounts, they were very stable. 'Extremely professional', 'very safe', 'deeply conscientious' are some of the comments apparently listed in appraisals by more senior officers.

The other two members of ZD576's aircrew were equally highly regarded. Graham Forbes, the Special Forces 'crewman leader', was known to be meticulous in working out navigational detail so that he could confirm the pilots' every move. Far from regarding this as interference, Special

Forces pilots see it as part of the teamwork they value so highly. Indeed, in an SF aircrew, each member is not just encouraged to crosscheck his colleagues, he is positively expected to do so. Sergeant Kevin Hardie was also someone who 'was trusted implicitly'. This was a top team. None of them was likely to be voicing a concern for any but the most genuine and serious reason. The fact is that they simply did not have full confidence in their equipment. But that, in the RAF or any other service, is not cause enough to refuse an assigned task.

The next day, 2 June, the crew of ZD576 flew a series of local Northern Ireland sorties for the Army. The task for late that afternoon and evening was the 400-mile round trip to Fort George.

THE BBC'S *Nine O'Clock News* was five minutes late because of a party political broadcast.

> Good evening. An RAF Chinook helicopter with twenty-nine people on board has crashed in the west of Scotland. It hit a hill in thick fog. An eyewitness reported hearing a loud explosion and seeing a fireball when it hit the hillside. Police say people have been killed, but the fog is hampering rescue operations and the search for survivors. The helicopter is said to have had civilians as well as military personnel on board. It was flying from Aldergrove Airport near Belfast and came down on a hill near a lighthouse at the end of the Mull of Kintyre.

During the next nine minutes, Michael Buerk was able to add some details about the emergency operations triggered by that phone call from Mrs Murchie just over three hours earlier. But of the crew and passengers, all he could say was that there 'was no confirmed news of anyone being found alive'. Five service helicopters were on the scene, one with an RAF search-and-rescue team; they reported very poor visibility. Fire engines and ambulances had arrived from nearby Campbeltown. The town had launched its lifeboat to search the cliffs. A Nimrod surveillance aircraft had been alerted to take station high above the Mull – to co-ordinate radio communications. Glasgow Royal Infirmary was on standby. The RAF had already appointed a Board of Inquiry.

At the crash site the local police from Campbeltown had been first on the scene. One of their duties was to guard the still-smouldering debris until the specialists arrived the next morning. The exact disposition of everything would undoubtedly provide some clues about the sequence of events.

The next morning, inspectors from the civil Air Accidents Investigation Branch (AAIB) and a three-man RAF Board of Inquiry flew in. Some came direct by helicopter, some to the nearby RAF airfield at Machrihanish.

About a third of the debris was badly burnt. The rest varied in size from a man's fist up to parts which, though shattered and twisted, were still quite recognizable – the engines, the rotors, parts of the cockpit and fuselage. The experts from the AAIB laid out a grid of coloured tapes to provide known reference points for a series of precise measurements; they took hundreds of photographs. They took notes. They conferred with the three officers of the RAF's Board of Inquiry. The bodies were removed.

Now in broad daylight, there seemed to be no apparent reason, not even a hint, as to why the aircraft should have flown into a hillside at what, according to the still readable ground-speed indicator in the cockpit, was a speed of about 147 knots. There were no witnesses. And the aircraft had no cockpit voice recorder or 'black box' flight data recorder.

It was not as if the aircraft, with a few more feet of altitude, might *just* have cleared the steep hill ahead. It would have taken hundreds of feet. Anyway, the flight plan filed back at Aldergrove showed that there was never any intention to over-fly the Mull; to have done so would have put ZD576 into icing conditions. The pilots planned to skirt the Mull by paralleling its western coast at low level. The whole thing was inexplicable.

Within a few days the remains of ZD576 were back in Farnborough, where, in the hangars of the AAIB, they were laid out for investigation – a process that was to take many months. At the same time the RAF's three-man Board of Inquiry – a Wing Commander and two Squadron Leaders (one a helicopter engineer) – started to take evidence from more than twenty people. They ranged from the lighthouse keepers and the yachtsmen to engineer officers, squadron commanders and other Chinook pilots. Written evidence was submitted by weather forecasters, by air-traffic controllers, by computer engineers, even by the Officers'

Mess waitress who had served Flight Lieutenant Cook his breakfast. There were reports from experts in aviation medicine, aircrew psychology, magnetic anomalies and electronic interference.

In Farnborough the staff of the AAIB was making no quick assumptions. Some of ZD576's components had to be sent back to the original manufacturers for analysis and reports. Some were taken to specialist metallurgy laboratories. Others were minutely inspected where they now lay. Every instrument that had survived from the navigation, flight, radio and engine systems was tested and retested. Somewhere among the thousands of pieces there might be a clue as to what had happened. Or, more significantly, *why* it had happened.

After some months a report was received from Philadelphia. At the request of the MOD and the AAIB, Boeing had been asked to carry out a series of Chinook simulations to try to gain an insight into what was happening immediately before the crash. But when Boeing's report came in there were a number of difficulties in matching it with other indications found in the wreckage and with impact marks and debris distribution on the ground. There was disagreement about the speed at impact. There were other inconsistencies. For example, the Boeing simulation analysed the rotor speed as having been abnormally low. But the wreckage showed (according to the AAIB) that the rotor speed at impact was very slightly *above* normal. The simulation indicated that the engines had been at one power setting, the wreckage suggested another. There were other discrepancies. Nevertheless, the Boeing Simulation Report formed a significant part of the evidence presented to the RAF Board of Inquiry. Despite its inherent problems (which, later, Boeing partly acknowledged), the Report was not officially challenged. But unofficially, when it was released to a wider readership, it was regarded as potentially misleading by some of the very same civilian and RAF experts on whom the MOD was relying for advice in other areas of its helicopter operations

The RAF Board of Inquiry visited the AAIB at Farnborough several times and made itself very familiar with the detective work going on there. Eventually, in January 1995, over the signature of the Chief Investigator, Tony Cable, the AAIB's Report was completed. With all the witness evidence collected, and the AAIB analysis and the Boeing Report in front of them, the three officers on the Board had to look for an answer to the only question that really mattered: did the cause of the crash lie in pilot error or technical failure or a combination of both?

The AAIB Report runs to nearly seventy pages, plus accompanying photographs and diagrams. It goes into meticulous detail on almost every aspect of the wreckage. At the end it makes a number of recommendations, not least that voice and data recorders should be fitted to all Chinooks. Another suggestion is that certain 'flight control components' should be more firmly 'bonded'; this is engineering talk for securing that spring, and others like it, more firmly. But as to what caused the crash, the AAIB Report came nowhere near providing enough firm data on which the RAF Board of Inquiry might base a definitive conclusion.

Not surprisingly, given the state of the wreckage, the AAIB had been unable to find evidence of any 'pre-impact' fault among the hundreds of moving parts and dozens of systems which go to make up a Chinook. All the same, the AAIB was very careful to say that lack of such evidence could not be taken as proof that no 'pre-impact' malfunction had occurred. Some debris was just too damaged (or simply missing – vaporized in the extreme heat) to judge one way or the other. The comments on that balance spring are typical:

> Most attachment inserts on both flight control system pallets had detached, including the collective balance spring bracket that had previously detached from ZD576's thrust/yaw pallet, with little evidence available to eliminate the possibility of pre-impact detachment.

The key phrase is, of course, the last one: there was 'little evidence' to show that the spring which was found 'detached' had not come away from its attachment *before* the crash – 'pre-impact'. If it had, the consequences might have been catastrophic. Elsewhere, the same cautious theme reappears:

> No evidence of a control jam was found, although such a possibility could not be excluded given the level of system damage.

Thus, while the AAIB found no evidence of a control jam, 'such a possibility could not be excluded'. Some might interpret its reservation more strongly. Many RAF Chinook pilots did. And still do.

If one talks to some of those pilots, they will suggest that the following sequence of events is possible. With a helicopter flying straight and level, the pilot (or the autopilot system) only needs to make very minute control movements to keep the aircraft in that attitude. It is as if one is driving at a steady 70 mph on a dead-straight motorway on which there is no other traffic; only the smallest corrective adjustments to the steering are needed. But, unknown to the pilot, that spring has fallen down. Now, when he nears the Mull and comes to bank away to the left (or the driver attempts to ease off onto a slip road) he finds he cannot move the steering (in a helicopter it would be the cyclic), or he can only move it in the wrong direction. He has a major problem.

If this was what happened aboard ZD576, the situation would have been yet further complicated by the fact that the aircraft might soon be into cloud – because it cannot turn away. Chinook pilots point to that spring which had come within a thick whisker of falling down before. They point to the uncertain AAIB testimony: 'No evidence of control damage was found, though such a possibility could not be excluded given the level of system damage.' Lastly, there are those anomalies between the Boeing simulation and the data derived from the damaged rotors, the engines and other indicators. The suggestion is that these inconsistencies can only be explained if the normal relationship between the control 'settings' and the aircraft attitude had broken down. In short, if they point to anything, it is to the possibility of a control jam.

Another possible scenario concerns one of the two Fadecs. One of ZD576's Fadec computer units was far too badly damaged by fire to allow any investigation. So it was just not possible to know whether it might have provoked an engine 'runaway' – similar to the one in that Wilmington 'testing' incident. Alternatively, the engine may have been rapidly surging up and down, or 'hunting'. With the new, improved Fadec these things were not meant to happen. But the fact is that they had done so several times in other Mk2 Chinooks. Indeed, one of the most experienced Chinook pilots in the RAF, Squadron Leader Burke, the unit test pilot at RAF Odiham, experienced two runaways within twenty-four hours some months earlier.

He was working on attachment to the Boeing plant in Philadelphia. Along with an American pilot, he was taking a newly completed Mk2 aircraft through its RAF acceptance trials when, suddenly and without warning, one engine went into an overspeeding runaway. 'Luckily, we were on the ground. But for some seconds we were fairly busy. Had we been airborne near low cloud and steep hills it might have been a different story.' The very next day the same thing happened again. But this time the two pilots had made sure that there were Boeing and Textron engineers watching closely. A thorough investigation was carried out but no reason for the runaway could be found. On the third occasion (and thereafter) the engines behaved perfectly. But the Squadron Leader wrote a lengthy report after each of the two emergencies; he lodged them with the RAF officer in charge of the liaison team at Boeing.

A runaway can occur with no warning. If one had happened in ZD576, coincident with the intended change of course – a bank of between 12° and 14° to the left – the handling pilot would have immediately raised the collective lever as far up as it would go. This action, by putting maximum pitch on the rotor blades, would have increased the load on the rotors, which, in turn, would have slowed them and the runaway engine back to a safer speed. But the engine might still have been accelerating back and forth in uncertain surges, which would have made the pilot's task doubly difficult. Yet containing the rotor speed is the absolute priority, because above 330 rpm, centrifugal force will cause the rotor blades to fly off.[3] At this point it is immaterial whether or not there is a hill somewhere in front. A crash will be inevitable. However, there is now another problem: with the rotor blades at something like full pitch, the aircraft will be climbing, and, at the same time, accelerating forward. So ZD576 would have been gaining speed and moving upwards towards cloud. Moreover, the few pilots who have had major rotor runaways have reported that the aircraft shakes so violently that the flight and engine instruments are almost impossible to read. One pilot says that it is like trying to watch a film which is jumping in the gate of the projector. The conditions cannot be simulated. So, until it happens 'for real', a pilot will never have experienced it.

3. The engines are fitted with governors ('limiters') but they had never been fully trusted. In any case, under certain circumstances there might be emergencies when all possible power was required – beyond the limiters.

Why, it may be asked, as soon as the engine runaway (if such it was) became evident, did the pilot not bank away from the Mull? Why, instead, did he try to rectify this critical problem while still flying straight on? There are two possible reasons – or a combination of both. Every helicopter pilot knows that, in an emergency and if he still has power, he must immediately return to (or hold) the aircraft in level flight and, if possible, in a slight climb. At the same time, for the five to twenty seconds of the emergency, the pilot handling ZD576 would have been totally occupied with the only problem that mattered: the 'safety-critical' priority of 'braking' the rotors. If he does not do that, the rotors may fly off, in which case he and everyone else will be dead anyway. By the time he had got the rotor speed back under control – if, indeed, he succeeded – he may have been in cloud. Now, still climbing (to hold down the rotor speed) and in the appalling vibration, he would probably not have been able to read his instruments. Further, he may well have been disorientated. He sees the heather of a hillside immediately in front; two seconds or even one second later he has hit the hillside and the aircraft is breaking up.

Had the engine overspeed (if such it was) begun twenty seconds earlier, who knows but ZD576 might be flying today.

Another possibility centres on the autopilot computer or the sensors that feed into it. Numerous Chinooks had experienced 'uncommanded flight control movements' (UFCMs). The nomenclature is exact: terrifyingly, the aircraft suddenly has a mind of its own. It does not respond to the pilot. Instead, it does its 'own thing'. Then, just as suddenly, it can return to normal. But, as with 'uncommanded movements' on a home computer, there is sometimes no trace of what caused the problem. Several pilots of supersonic fighters (which are also heavily computerized) have made the point that had they been killed in a crash for which no cause could be found in the debris, it would probably have been put down to pilot error.[4]

There is at least one other possibility: the AAIB inspector found 'four fine metal slivers up to 0.2 inch long' on one of the 'servo valve screens'

4. In a parliamentary answer to Martin Bell MP on 3 December 1999 the MOD revealed that RAF Chinooks had suffered thirty-five UFCMs in the previous six years.

in the hydraulics of the 'flight control system'. There was also 'a considerable quantity of very small metallic particles' in the system. The AAIB inspector did not think that any of this had 'contributed to the accident'. But, at that time, he was not to know that those slivers might have had more significance than he or anyone else imagined.

In other directions, evidence derived from 'debriefing' the aircraft's GPS (it survived the crash) seemed to show that, between eighteen and twenty-two seconds before impact, one of the pilots (almost certainly Tapper) had 'asked' the GPS to give him a new reading – the course and distance to the second waypoint (87 miles up the coast). In other words, the pilots could see that ZD576 was nearing the end of its first leg and that a slight change of course (between 12° and 14°) was now required. The significance of the waypoint change is twofold. First, it implies that the pilots intended to change course rather than to fly straight on into the cloud ahead. Second, it indicates that, up to the time they made that routine change, the pilots must have been unaware of any technical problem. This fact is absolutely central to the controversy that has enveloped the whole affair ever since – as will become apparent.

One of the mysteries is why ZD576 did not initiate a 'Mayday' distress signal. Perhaps things just happened too quickly. In fact, the radio transponder, which when tuned to the right code would automatically have sent such a signal, was found by the AAIB to be within just two 'clicks' of the emergency frequency. Perhaps the vibration was so violent that the relevant crew member (possibly Forbes) had difficulty selecting the distress code.

Having read, heard and, no doubt, pondered all the evidence many times, the RAF Board of Inquiry had the Solomonic task of coming up with reasonably definitive 'findings'. Yet there were no survivors, no witnesses and no voice recorder, no 'black box'. Further, in a number of important areas there was no conclusive evidence from the AAIB; the inspector had been unwilling to say that, in his own words, 'pre-impact malfunction' could be 'positively dismissed'.

It is obvious from any reading of the Report by the RAF Board of Inquiry that its three investigating officers were in the deepest of dilemmas. In terms of lives lost, this was the most serious peacetime accident the RAF had ever suffered. They would have felt themselves under pressure, perhaps unspoken, to come up with a definite conclusion – to get to the bottom of what had happened. Of course, there *was* the possibility that Tapper and Cook, with Forbes's acquiescence, and careless of all their years of training and experience, and forgetting that they had only just called on the GPS to give them the course for the next leg, suddenly and collectively decided to abandon their agreed flight plan and, instead, to climb at high speed into cloud. But it seems unlikely. Many find it inconceivable.

Against *that* scenario there was the possibility that one of several malfunctions might have caused or contributed to the crash. Random incidents in the known history of the few Mk2s in squadron service at the time confirmed the possibility. Nor could the AAIB's report be used to deny it. But there would be major problems if the three officers on the Board of Inquiry even hinted that ZD576 (and by implication the other 'new' Chinooks just coming into squadron service) had some serious and unresolved technical problems. It would be seen by the high command of both the RAF and the MOD as confirmation of what a number of Chinook aircrew had been quietly saying for some months: that the Mk2 was being introduced into squadron service too soon. And from that, there would follow two key questions – though, limited by its brief, the Board could not ask them. First, who exactly had authorized such a situation and, second (and more specifically), who had then sanctioned the flight of twenty-five key personnel in a Mk2 on 2 June? Even an allusion to those questions in the Board's report (or anywhere else) could be taken by the senior officers collectively or individually involved in those decisions as an unwarranted comment on their judgement. Because no such direct allusion was made, an important question has never been adequately discussed. Was the flight of ZD576, with those high-profile passengers, seen – in part anyway – as useful confirmation of the confidence in the decision to put the Mk2 Chinook into operational service? Senior officers will regard that question as offensive. Perhaps the question is best put the other way round: if that Mk2 Chinook had *not* been used for that flight and, say, a fixed-wing C-130 Hercules transport used instead, might not *that* decision have been seen by some as confirmation that there were, indeed, still some official doubts about the Mk2? Certainly, such important passengers and the choice of aircraft would have been formally reviewed and approved at the 'tasking conference' held every morning at the HQ of No. 1 Group at RAF Upavon. There would have been similar approval at the parallel conference in Northern Ireland at Lisburn. No one would have been in any doubt about what was proposed. And that leads on to the next problem.

There has long been unease at a state of affairs whereby senior RAF officers, who in some circumstances would seem to have a direct or indirect 'interest' in the verdict of a Board of Inquiry, are involved in the appointment of that Board and in agreeing its terms of reference. It would be thought ludicrous if the management of an airline, after a serious accident, had the sole right to appoint the only investigating body. But the RAF's position is rather worse than that. Senior RAF officers (management) are empowered to overrule the findings of their own Boards if they think they can come to a 'better' verdict. And against that 'senior' verdict there is no appeal.

Back in 1986 this very problem prompted Lord Trefgarne, then a Minister at the MOD, to ask for a report on the whole uncomfortable situation. The AAIB's senior Accident Inspector, W.H. Tench, was appointed to investigate. After nine months he reported that the disquiet seemed to be largely justified. In a report running to nearly 10,000 words, perhaps the following passage best catches the essence of Mr Tench's conclusions:

> The pervasive nature of the involvement of some Station Commanders, AOCs, senior Staff Officers and even Commanders-in-Chief is an unwelcome intrusion upon what should be the complete independence of the Board of Inquiry . . . the opportunities for staff officers to influence the Board's interpretation of evidence, or even their findings, must throw some doubt on the complete freedom of the Board to draw its own conclusions.

The high command of the RAF took no notice of the Tench Report. So it is still quite normal for senior 'reviewing' officers to be kept informed on an almost daily basis about the progress and thinking of a Board of Inquiry. It would be extraordinary if information did not also flow downward – with the reactions and advice of the senior officers to what they are hearing about a Board's deliberations. In time those senior officers will see a preliminary draft of a Board's report. If they think that the Board's conclusions are wrong or not clearly enough drawn, they can order a rewrite.

The reviewing officers in this case were Air Vice Marshal Day and Air Chief Marshal Wratten. Even if the three investigating officers on the Board of Inquiry did not experience any pressure from above, they evidently still felt that they could not ignore the uncertainties of the AAIB Report or the promptings of their own judgement. Nor, presumably, could they set aside the problems experienced with the 'new' Chinooks. No amount of pretending that they were not there would make them go away. The Board's report reflected this conclusion:

> The Chinook HC2 had experienced a number of unforeseen malfunctions, mainly associated with the engine control system, including undemanded engine shutdown, engine run-up, spurious engine failure captions, and misleading and confusing cockpit indications. The Board found no evidence that any of these malfunctions had occurred on Chinook ZD576's final flight. Nevertheless, an unforeseen technical malfunction of the type experienced on the Chinook HC2, which would not necessarily have left any physical evidence, remained a possibility and could not be discounted.

In effect, like the AAIB, the three-man RAF Board was saying that the lack of evidence for engine or other malfunctions could not be taken as 'proof positive' that no malfunction had occurred. Nevertheless, the Board were inclined to the view that the aircraft appeared to have been handling normally and was under full pilot control just prior to impact. This thinking seems to have been based partly on the Boeing simulation and its claim that the aircraft had been put into a flare (an emergency braking, pull up) just seconds before the crash. In fact, there was evidence in the wreckage that some of the controls might not have been 'handling normally': the collective lever had been found to be fully raised and the yaw control was hard over.[5] Lastly, deliberately to fly

5. Yaw control is equivalent to rudder on a fixed-wing aircraft. In both types, except at very low speeds, a turn is achieved by banking the whole aircraft. Yaw control in a Chinook is certainly not used above 20 knots. Yet ZD576 was travelling much faster at impact. So why was the control in a 'hard over' position?

upward into cloud (any cloud) was certainly not normal. For all that, Boeing's evidence of an emergency flare, if accurate, implied that there had been no major difficulty with the controls.

The Board's verdict was indefinite. It leant uncertainly towards pilot error. But it could not bring itself to say so with certainty. It proposed a scenario in which the pilots did not realize that they were so close to the Mull, but at the same time attempted to climb over it. But in advancing this as a hypothesis (rather than a definitive explanation) of how an experienced crew might have made such a basic mistake, the Board seemed to be confirming its own lack of conviction in the theory. It also pointed out that there were other possibilities that could not be ignored:

> There were many potential causes of the accident, and despite detailed and in depth analysis, the Board was unable to determine a definite cause.

This conclusion is repeated four pages later, though in terms which are now rather more critical of the 'command' pilot. Reading the Board's conclusion, it is clearly being pulled, or driven, in two opposing directions:

> The Board were unable to positively determine the sequence of events leading up to the accident, and therefore concluded that although Flt Lt Tapper made an Error of Judgement in the conduct of the attempted climb over the Mull of Kintyre, it would be incorrect to criticize him for human failings based on the available evidence.

That, evidently, was as far as the Board felt it could go. It cleared Flt Lt Cook absolutely. And, against Flt Lt Tapper, the 'Error of Judgement' was, as the RAF officially defines these things, only 'an honest mistake accompanied by no lack of zeal'.[6] Given that the Board also found that 'it would be incorrect to criticize him for human failings', one can sense its dilemma. While giving weight to its own doubts, it may also have wished to reflect the more severe thinking of its senior reviewing officers – which would later be set out in their written examination of the Board's verdict.

6. The RAF defines an Error of Judgement as 'an honest mistake, accompanied by no lack of zeal'. This is a long way short of Negligence, which is subdivided into minor, gross, reckless and disobedient.

The Board's rather fractured logic shows how severely it must have been torn. But the Board was not alone in being pulled in two directions.

Appended to the Board's conclusions is a three-and-a-half page report by the Group Captain who was the officer commanding the RAF's Chinook base at RAF Odiham, the home of ZD576 and her crew. He had been instructed by Air Vice Marshal Day to review the Board's findings and give his own analysis. His is a very strange document indeed. For 95 per cent of its length he argues strongly against the Board's hypothesis (hesitant though it is) that the Chinook was flown into the rising ground of the Mull due to Flt Lt Tapper's 'Error of Judgement':

> The Board opine . . . that the crew, faced with the expected deteriorating weather, consciously elected to make a climb on a track over high ground and in so doing used a speed and power combination that is unrecognisable as a Chinook technique. I find this difficult to believe; such actions would go against all the crew's instincts and training. Moreover, it is the very antithesis of the professionalism and careful planning that had gone on beforehand. Even taking into account the factors which the Board feel could have deceived the crew into believing a high-speed cruise-climb would have given them sufficient clearance over the Mull, I, and the few senior Chinook operators that I felt able to consult, find this suggestion incredible.

There is more in the same tone. He cites the possibility of what he calls 'engine control system malfunctions' (i.e. Fadec faults) as causing the pilots 'to inadvertently enter cloud and then fail to take the correct procedure for an emergency climb in a timely manner'. Bravely, he comes down against the suggestion that Flt Lt Tapper was guilty of an 'Error of Judgement' with, as we have just seen, the comment, 'I, and the few senior Chinook operators I felt able to consult, find this suggestion incredible'. And yet, amazingly, right at the end of his report, he suddenly reverses those strongly held reservations and points directly at Flt Lt Tapper:

> In carrying out that mission, Flt Lt Tapper, as captain of the aircraft in peacetime, had an overriding duty to ensure the safety of the aircraft, its crew and the passengers. While there may, arguably, be some mitigating circumstances, I am regrettably drawn to the conclusion that he failed in that duty.

So he no longer finds such a conclusion 'incredible'. But if anything is incredible, it is surely this 180-degree change of mind. No reason is offered as to how he gets from one conclusion to its opposite. There is a clear, yet unexplained, contradiction. Yet on reflection, perhaps the contradiction *does* have an explanation. The OC Odiham's conclusions, like those of the three-man Board of Inquiry, may have reflected his knowledge of the views of the two reviewing officers.

As has already been mentioned, the conclusions of an RAF Board of Inquiry are always reviewed by at least two senior officers. Sometimes they will modify the Board's 'verdict'; only rarely will they deny it. But now, if the three-man Board had held back from an unequivocal criticism of Flt Lt Tapper, and cleared Flt Lt Cook, there was no such hesitation on the part of the two reviewing officers. Air Vice Marshal John Day and Air Chief Marshal Sir William Wratten obviously felt that the Board's verdict was inconclusive and fudged. Towards the end of a four-page examination of the Board's Report, Air Vice Marshal Day concluded thus:

> While aware of the difficulty of attributing negligence to deceased aircrew, I am nevertheless forced to conclude that Flt Lt Tapper was negligent to a gross degree. I cannot avoid the conclusion that Flt Lt Cook was [also] negligent to a gross degree.

Air Marshall Sir William Wratten's conclusion is no less condemnatory:

> The actions of the two pilots were the direct cause of this crash. I also conclude that this amounted to gross negligence.

The verdict was the equivalent of manslaughter – of twenty-five people. The basis of the Air Marshals' verdict is straightforward. They say that the pilots were going much too fast (at an air speed of 135+ knots, which, with a 15+ knot tail wind, gave a ground speed of 150+ knots) to avoid the steeply rising ground of the Mull they knew lay immediately behind the low cloud ahead. They had left everything too late. If, as the Air Marshals claimed, the pilots had intended to climb over the Mull, they could not now gain height anything like fast enough. If, as in their flight plan, they had intended to turn along the coast (a thesis the Air Marshals did not favour), they had simply run out of room to make the turn. Either way, they were almost bound to hit the steeply rising ground. So, whatever the precise sequence of events, the only fact that mattered was that the pilots had, with almost criminal carelessness, misjudged their distances. It was far too late to begin a climb over the Mull – if that is what they intended. And it was too late to make a coastal turn – if *that* is what they intended.

Hence, a verdict of gross negligence was inevitable.

But how do the Air Marshals know that the pilots delayed their turn or their climb until it was too late? Where was the 'too late' point? That information was 'milked' from the aircraft's undamaged GPS equipment by the manufacturers. This showed that the crew had asked the GPS to give them the new course when, assuming a 150+ knot ground speed, they were only 600 metres out from the shore. They obviously would not have bothered to adjust the GPS if they had been aware of any technical problems. But the subsequent 'milking' of that GPS for 'historic' data by the manufacturers was a complicated and multi-stage process. Computer experts are dubious that it can be done without minor errors occurring at each stage – until the final and accumulated inaccuracy can become quite considerable. The manufacturers themselves acknowledge the problem. But, despite this potential for inaccuracy, the Air Marshals insist on a distance of 600 metres as the basis for their calculations. That distance was, they said with emphasis, not an estimate. It was 'a known fact'.

Their reasoning means that the possibility of a control jam, a Fadec runaway or any other technical failure is totally irrelevant because, if any fault had happened (a very big 'if' in the view of the Air Marshals and the MOD), it could not have done so until *after* the point of no return – until after the point at which the pilots calmly asked the GPS for the new course. But by then it was too late. So the 'gross negligence' had already occurred. In short, if any technical fault had *then* happened, it could not have *caused* the catastrophe. In any case, the Boeing simulation showed that the pilots had made an 'emergency flare' four seconds before impact. This demonstrated that the controls were fully responsive and that, therefore, the pilots were in effective control.

It is a convincing argument – until one listens to some Chinook pilots. First, they point out that ZD576 was not making a square-on approach to the shoreline; it was coming in at an oblique angle. So it was *not* too late to make the slight turn of between 12° and 14° to parallel the shoreline. In fact, one does not need to be a pilot to work it out. A-level physics will do. A calculation involving speed, angle of bank and G-force shows that such a turn (at a reasonable 30° angle of bank) was comfortably within the Chinook's capability. Second, the pilots may well have intended to slow down as they went into the turn; this would have even further reduced the turning arc. Third, the official assumption that ZD576 was travelling at about 150+ knots (ground speed) at the time of the waypoint change was just that: an assumption. It seems to be based on various interpretations, not least the speed (about 150 knots) that the aircraft was doing at impact. But this is not a reliable indicator of the speed nearly a mile earlier, at the time of the GPS change. A Fadec runaway could account for both an acceleration and a climb. Fourth, while the lighthouse (rising from 260 to 300 feet) was certainly in cloud, there was no evidence at all that the base of that cloud came lower than 250 feet. Indeed, the yachtsman's evidence was that it did not. Furthermore, in the area immediately ahead of ZD576 as she approached the Mull, the profile of the coast is less steep than around the lighthouse – which is 1000 metres to the north. This could mean that there may have been no cloud at all until at least 200 metres inland (i.e. along the 250-foot contour). In which case, not only would the coast and the immediate hinterland have been clearly visible, but a clear turn would have been even easier. Fifth, as already mentioned, there must be doubts about the accuracy of the 600-metre calculation; ZD576 may have been further out. Lastly, the unexplained anomalies in the Boeing simulation raised questions about its overall validity – particularly about the emergency flare which, according to the Air Marshals, showed that the pilots were in full control. One Chinook pilot sums up his reactions to the gross negligence verdict as follows:

> We're not talking high-speed jets here – or even propeller-driven aircraft. For a Chinook there was plenty of time to turn onto the new course. Anyway, they were turning through less than 15° – they'd have made that in two seconds. No problem. There is just no way they'd have flown straight on – up that hill and into cloud. Remember, there were three of them involved. They worked together. And they weren't idiots. Obviously they had a problem when they came to change course – the aircraft didn't respond.

Interestingly, seven years later members of a Lords Committee, flying in an RAF Chinook, asked that the aircraft should be flown – at the same speed, course and height as ZD576 – up to that same waypoint change and then turned to fly along the coast. Admittedly, there was no cloud on the Mull. But the helicopter was able to perform this simple manoeuvre without any difficulty – 'quite adequately' was the term actually used by a member of that Committee.[7] Similarly, it is known that several pilots, disbelieving the official theory, have unofficially tested the turning circle of a Chinook through that 12° to 15° turn at 150 knots – without exceeding a 30° angle of bank, which is the normal limit when carrying civilian passengers. No problem. One is surprised that the Air Marshals did not order an official test for themselves.

But much of this is jumping ahead of the chronology. We should go back.

ONE MUST ASSUME THAT BOTH the Air Marshals thought hard before arriving at their verdicts. They say they did. Yet it seems to have been remembered by neither of them that, according to one of the RAF's own regulations (set out in its Air Publication 3207), a verdict of pilot negligence (let alone *gross* negligence) can only be introduced against deceased aircrew where 'there is absolutely no doubt whatsoever'. It is not possible to devise a higher level of proof. Yet many people with first-hand experience of Chinooks felt that the official case was shot through with doubts. Some had been identified by the three-man Board, by the AAIB and, apart from the last two sentences in three-and-a-half pages, by the Group Captain OC RAF Odiham. But the Air Marshals obviously persuaded themselves that no one else's doubts mattered – no matter how well qualified those doubters might be. They were adamant that any technical problems – which they regarded as dubious in the extreme – were wholly irrelevant. The fatal mistake of not turning away sooner (or climbing) had occurred well before the pilots made that routine GPS change.

The Air Marshals subsequently, and in some irritation, claimed that their duty required them to be wholly unbiased. One would hope so. But

7. House of Lords Select Committee on Chinook ZD576. Oral evidence, September 2001, page 145 (HMSO, November 2001).

there seemed to be an implication that more junior ranks (including the three-man Board of Inquiry?) had been unduly swayed towards their two dead colleagues. Maybe and maybe not. But the Air Marshals did not recognize that their own positions also carried a risk of bias. The Tench Report had made this very point nearly ten years earlier. A Commons Select Committee was later to make it again in the following terms:

> We strongly recommend that the Board of Inquiry process should be revised to ensure that those officers who have management and command responsibility for aircraft and the personnel involved do not influence or control the findings of Boards of Inquiry.

No one seems to know exactly how the 'absolutely no doubt whatsoever' regulation came about. So one must guess. At some point in the history of inquiries into fatal RAF accidents it may have been pointed out that everyone, except the dead pilot(s), has the opportunity to defend themselves – designers, builders, component manufacturers, maintenance engineers, air-traffic controllers, weather forecasters, training instructors, airfield managers, the MOD's Procurement Executive and, not least, senior RAF officers. Only the pilots are missing. So, to redress the balance, someone with a sense of justice must have suggested that negligence should only be attributed where 'there is absolutely no doubt whatsoever'. There cannot be a higher burden of proof; it is far higher than that ('beyond all reasonable doubt') required in a criminal trial.

For the families of the two dead pilots, the days following the official verdict were filled with part anger, part near despair. Unlike almost all other legal processes, there was no appeal against the Air Marshals' verdict. Manslaughter. It was absolute and final. And there was evidently no way that any of the MOD's mandarins or ministers was prepared (or would have dared?) to modify, let alone to set aside, the verdict. Even the suggestion of such a move would have brought about an unholy row with the high command of the RAF. There are occasions when the 'integrity of command' is held to be paramount.

Then, by a quirk of the British constitution, there appeared a means whereby the dead pilots and their families might have their say. ZD576 had gone down in Scotland. This made the whole affair subject to the

Fatal Accidents and Sudden Deaths Inquiry (Scotland) Act. This allows, indeed it requires, a more rigorous investigation than is usually the case in a coroner's court south of the border – where the verdict of a service Board of Inquiry is often accepted without too many questions.

It is said that discreet inquiries from the MOD went north to the Lord Advocate's department in Edinburgh. Did there really have to be a full inquiry? With counsel for each of the interested parties? Why was Scotland so different from the rest of the country? These questions had to be discreet because it would never do (given all that derives from the 1689 Bill of Rights) for the Crown to be thought to be trying to nobble the judiciary.

Presumably Edinburgh explained that there really was no choice. After all, twenty-nine people had lost their lives. And lost them in Scotland.

Thus early in 1996, in a courtroom in Paisley, a court was convened. The Sheriff (i.e. judge) was Sir Stephen Young. He quickly established that he knew what he was doing. He was patient and painstaking. He was also a yachtsman, which was not as irrelevant as it might seem: he did not need help with the technicalities of GPS waypoints or drift or transponders or compass headings or the variables inherent in meteorological forecasts and visibility. And if there was something he did not understand, he went on asking questions until he did.

At considerable cost, the Tapper family had engaged a barrister. The Cook family also made sure that their son was legally represented. Earlier, the MOD's Earl Howe had advised that such expense would not be necessary because the interests of both pilots would, in effect, be represented by the MOD's QC. Unbelievably, it did not seem to occur to Earl Howe or his advisors that the MOD's QC would immediately have found himself in the deepest conflict of interest. Did Whitehall really believe that its QC, perhaps by changing wigs, would be able to move from a position of defending the RAF verdict of pilot negligence to one of contesting that same conclusion? Surely nobody could be that stupid. Anyway, both families ignored the 'advice' and paid their own way.[8]

In fact, all the 'interested' parties – the Crown, the MOD, Boeing, the

8. Information supplied by Captain John Cook, the pilot's father.

families of the dead passengers, the dead pilots – had their own Advocates or QCs. Over a period of sixteen days, evidence was taken from thirty-eight witnesses. Some of them had not been called by the RAF Board of Inquiry, so they had not been heard anywhere before. Perhaps the most impressive testimony of all – and it seems likely that the judge found it so – came from two Chinook pilots. Because they were members of the Special Forces flight, they were not referred to by their real names. Through one long day and into the next, the answers from Flt Lts J and K, in response to sharp questioning from the MOD's QC (who was, of course, in court to ensure that the official verdict of gross negligence was not undermined), show that these two men were more than just highly intelligent: they had very incisive minds indeed. Flt Lt J was the Deputy Commander of the Special Forces flight as well as its Safety Officer; he had also trained Tapper in parts of the Special Forces helicopter 'syllabus'. Both J and K had been flying Chinooks for ten years, and both were obviously deeply sceptical about the way the Mk2 Chinook had been introduced into 'frontline' service:

> We were certainly uncomfortable with being told that the test pilots [at Boscombe Down] were not flying the aircraft any more because they were uncertain of its operability, and [yet] the line pilots were continuing to fly it. It did seem slightly the wrong way round. It was an uncomfortable position.

Later, Flt Lt K expanded on the same theme:

> [There was] an apparent lack of knowledge at higher level as to what was likely to happen to aircraft systems in any given set of circumstances, and I mean specifically the Fadec-related problems

When it came to a specific analysis of the crash on the Mull, both pilots made it clear that they found the official verdict unsupportable. As one of them put it, 'The pilots were found guilty because not proven innocent.' Given the very senior source of the verdict, this was brave stuff. But it must also be acknowledged that it would have been possible, though most unwise, for the RAF to have refused permission for J and K to appear. When asked what he thought of the conclusion that the crash had occurred because Tapper had negligently selected an 'inappropriate rate of climb to over-fly the Mull', K just looked across at the QC and replied, 'Unlikely in the extreme.' He also rejected the alternative thesis that there had been no room to turn. He advanced a theory of a control jam. He explained that he himself had suffered a minor version of what he thought was a far more likely explanation for the crash of ZD576:

> I have experienced one control malfunction which forced us to land the aircraft immediately because of the severity of the control restriction. The lights in the cockpit started to flash on and off. The hydraulic pressure cycled between zero and maximum; there was vibration felt through the airframe. The aircraft was becoming difficult to control. Control inputs were occurring which were undemanded. We landed as soon as possible . . . in the first flat area available to us. No fault was ever found.
>
> A control jam is not the sort of thing you can train for, because if that sort of thing occurs there is nothing you can do about it. You just have to wait until the jam clears itself – if it does.

When Counsel for the MOD suggested that K's evidence might be coloured by the fact that he had been a colleague of Tapper's, he replied, 'I am here as a Chinook pilot who does not for one moment accept the findings of the Board of Inquiry' (he was referring to the verdict of the Air Marshals rather than to that of the three-man Board). Elsewhere, he told the court, 'I have a desire to get to the root of this crash. It does nobody in the RAF, particularly flying Chinooks, any good to have this crash unsolved.' These replies were cool but deeply felt, and if they sometimes seemed to border on being belligerent, it was presumably because there was, as he said, 'a feeling of injustice across the whole Air Force'. This was brave; it was also impressive.

Curiously, neither of the two Air Marshals appeared at the Paisley inquiry. Much later, one of them was publicly to claim that he would have welcomed the opportunity but that it had been denied. This is an extraordinary assertion. It implies that if the MOD (through its counsel) had suggested to the Sheriff that one or both Air Marshals should be called, the proposal would have been refused. If any such 'bar' on their appearance was made, it must have been imposed at a very high level in the MOD, not in Paisley. Why?

The evidence heard over those three weeks covered all the possibilities. Then the Sheriff 'retired' to ponder and to write his Determination. It ran to a detailed 123 pages. The Sheriff seems to have focused on three questions. First, how could anyone be sure 'beyond all reasonable doubt' (which was a very much lower threshold than the 'absolutely no doubt whatsoever' required from the Air Marshals) that the pilots had suddenly and inexplicably changed their minds from the low-level flight plan they had filed before departure to one where, on reaching that waypoint change just short of the coastline, they deliberately decided to climb over the Mull through cloud. And, second, if that had not been their intention, how could anyone be sure that they had not been the victims of a technical problem which had only become apparent at the moment of, and as a consequence of, an attempt to change course? Lastly, he looked at a suggestion which had been there since the beginning: that due to poor visibility and a small navigational error, the pilots did not know exactly where they were and had flown into cloud because of incompetence. He suggested that this came nowhere near being demonstrated 'absolutely beyond doubt'.

If the answer to the first two of those questions was negative – and Sheriff Young evidently thought that it was – the official verdict became difficult to sustain. He was obviously unconvinced that pilots with their level of training and experience could have got things so completely wrong. He clearly thought that there were several legitimate answers to the mystery – answers which did not depend on pilot negligence. But with no cockpit voice recorder (CVR) and no conclusive evidence of malfunction before or after impact, he (like the Board of Inquiry before him) found it impossible to come to any finite conclusion. Indeed, he wrote that with no CVR fitted, 'the competence and skill of the crew are unavoidably but invidiously called into question in a speculative manner'. The key sentence in his report is brief and unequivocal:

> It has not been established to my satisfaction that the cause of the accident was that found by the [RAF] Board of Inquiry.

One might have thought that this one sentence, let alone the rest of the report, coming from a judge with no agenda or position to defend would have caused second thoughts back in Whitehall. But within the bureaucratic mindset (which usually does have a position to defend), 'second thoughts' are too often held to indicate a weakening of resolve rather than a reappraisal of the evidence – or lack of it. The MOD, along with the Air Marshals, evidently persuaded themselves that the proceedings in Scotland were an irrelevant irritation. So the hopes of the parents of Flt Lts Tapper and Cook, who had fought so hard for their sons and who read the unambiguous Scottish 'acquittal', were not fulfilled.

The media was now intrigued by a situation in which two legal processes under the Crown, one civil and one RAF, had come up with opposing verdicts. Investigation was made easier by the fact that, under John Major's 'open government' policy, the fifty-five-page report of the RAF Board of Inquiry had, quite early on, been made available to the families of those killed. This was most unusual. Normally, only the final verdict of a Board of Inquiry is published; the evidence and the background reasoning are closely restricted. So one can imagine the families' anger when they discovered how the Air Marshals had overruled the verdict of the three-man Board of Inquiry – which had exonerated Flt Lt Cook altogether – and replaced it with one of their own: gross negligence by both pilots. One can also imagine the consternation of the Air Marshals and the MOD, who, having thought that the proceedings would remain secret with only the final verdict released, now realized that the whole process would be subject to the most thorough and public questioning. Upper echelons in both the RAF and the MOD would have most roundly cursed John Major and his policy of 'transparency'. Without his meddling, and the parallel release of the AAIB Report, the whole affair of ZD576 might have been as surely buried as those who had lost their lives on the Mull. The irony is that the Prime Minister may have supposed that by being so open, the verdict would seem the more convincing in the eyes of the public. It did not work out that way. No wonder Channel 4 commissioned a full-length documentary on the whole affair.

Investigative documentaries can take a long time to come to fruition. Eventually, in January 1997, the film was transmitted. As is sometimes the case with a journalistic investigation, it brought a number of interesting people out of the woodwork. One such was Malcolm Perks.

He was a computer consultant for several makers of aircraft engines, including Pratt & Whitney and Rolls-Royce. Over the years he had been directly involved in the design and development of Fadecs for a variety of engines, both civil and military. He was widely recognized as one of the world's leading experts on the design and application of these systems. On a January evening in 1997 his wife pointed out that there was a TV film coming on about the Chinook that had crashed some years before. She knew he would be interested because two years earlier he had been contracted by the MOD to be their consultant and expert witness in a case they were bringing against Boeing and Textron-Lycoming. Indeed, he had made three transatlantic trips to testify at the hearings in the US. He had advised the Washington lawyers who had been retained by the MOD on the best way to present the technicalities of the case. The case concerned the Fadec 'runaway' on that first Chinook at Wilmington.

He was surprised that the documentary people had not been in touch with him during their research because, while he thought the programme had done a good job, there was one very significant gap. He wrote to Channel 4. In time the letter was passed to the film's director, David Harrison, who by then was something of a lay expert on the story of ZD576. Harrison immediately saw the significance of what Malcolm Perks was saying.

Evidently, the MOD had sued Boeing for faulty procedures in setting up that 1989 test in Wilmington and, even more relevantly, it had sued Textron for inadequate design and preparation of the relevant Fadec software. The damages sought by the MOD ran to millions of dollars. But the MOD had evidently not told either the RAF Board of Inquiry or the Scottish Inquiry; it had not even told the AAIB investigators. And, of course, there were still problems with the Fadecs – as evidenced by doubts at Boscombe Down.

When the MOD was questioned about this apparently serious omission – it might even be seen as the deliberate withholding of important evidence – the reply came back that any early problems with the Fadecs were quite irrelevant to the crash of ZD576: 'We have nothing to hide.' For confirmation, the MOD pointed to the findings of the Board of Inquiry and of the two Air Marshals. There was nothing, said the MOD, about Fadec in that verdict. Given that the Board of Inquiry had not been told about the early computer problems, this is not too surprising. This argument, in which the MOD deliberately disappears up its own fundament, has the Alice in Wonderland quality that is a recurring characteristic of the MOD. It is a heavy-duty example of the Whitehall Loop.[9]

When Malcolm Perks's information about the problems of Fadec was shown on *Channel 4 News*, the MOD came up with a categorical denial: the legal action against Textron had had nothing to do with the software; it had been because the *test* procedures at Wilmington had been at fault. In short, there had been no problems with the software – which is why the MOD had not told anyone about its legal action. So now it was 'not relevant' on two counts. First, there had never been any significant problems with the Fadec itself; it had been the test procedures which had been the trouble. Second, Fadec had played no part in the crash of ZD576.

It is worth following the MOD's account of its legal action in some detail because it contains very serious and all-too-typical examples of official fiction. A good place to begin is with the testimony of Dr John Reid, the Minister for the Armed Forces, when, rather late in the day, in March 1998, the Commons Defence Committee set up a hearing on the procurement aspects of the Chinook programme.[10] On being questioned about the MOD's action against Boeing and Textron, this was the Minister's answer:

> It was not, repeat not, on account of a failure of software . . . We sued them for negligence in their test procedures. We did not sue them because of the failure of the Fadec software. This is one of the misconceptions that has been allowed to flourish. So there was a case, the

9. Despite the official assertion/verdict that technical problems, even if they had occurred, were totally irrelevant because pilot negligence had preceded them, information about those problems should still have been passed to the Board – because, *at the time* the Board was hearing evidence, it could not know how the Air Marshals would later conclude. Therefore, whatever the Air Marshals decided subsequently, the history of Fadec should have been disclosed.
10. House of Commons Select Committee on Defence hearing of 4 March 1998. Report published 13 May 1998.

RAF Board of Inquiry was aware of the case, but the case was essentially against Boeing and Textron-Lycoming for negligence in their testing procedures, not against the software.

In two respects this was not just economical with the truth. It was bankrupt with it. If Dr Reid did not know he was lying twice over, then someone among those who briefed him would surely have known, and should have stopped him – 'No, Minister'. The first lie was in the firm assertion that the Board of Inquiry knew about the legal action against Boeing and Textron-Lycoming. But just one year later, Dr Reid's successor as Armed Forces Minister, John Spellar, in a written answer to an informed inquiry from Robert Key MP, had to make a belated admission:

> It is not possible now to establish if the investigators [the RAF Board of Inquiry] were informed at the time of this case.

In a letter to Martin O'Neill MP, the same Minister had to admit that the AAIB had not been told either:

> The AAIB advise that they were not aware of this litigation at the time of the accident investigation.

Dr Reid's other and even more serious fiction lies in his assertion that the MOD was only suing for inadequate test procedures and 'not, repeat not' for faulty software. Dr Reid was to repeat this assertion on *Channel 4 News* and elsewhere on several occasions. The MOD's initial thinking may indeed have been focused on the test procedures, but things quickly broadened from there. A legal submission prepared by the MOD's Washington lawyers in July 1991 gives the game away; the submission was written on information supplied by the MOD:

> In the design, development, manufacture and testing of the Fadec system, Textron was negligent and failed to use the skill and care contractually required of it, and otherwise breached its contractual obligations in numerous ways.[11]

As if that were not proof enough, the MOD had contracted Malcolm Perks to be its technical witness in its case against Textron. His report, as

11. This passage is drawn from the MOD's 'Brief before the American Arbitration Tribunal', dated 1 June 1995.

submitted to the MOD in December 1994 (six months *after* the crash of ZD576 but well before the final deliberations of the Board of Inquiry), details the software failings which led to the near destruction of that first Fadec-fitted Chinook at Wilmington:

> The malfunction was the result of faulty computer software design that caused an uncontrolled rush of fuel to one of the helicopter's engines during ground testing and an uncontrolled run-up of engine speed that severely damaged the helicopter . . . The Fadec designed by Textron and its subcontractors failed to meet established industry standards of airworthiness.

And if yet more proof were needed that Dr Reid was seriously misleading the Defence Committee in claiming that testing was the sole issue, it comes in a letter written by a senior MOD official to David Harrison, the producer of a (by now) second Channel 4 documentary. On 2 August 1999 Martin Fuller, Head of Secretariat (Air), wrote as follows:

> The claim against Boeing was formulated solely on the grounds of negligence in conducting the test, but the claim against Textron went wider alleging that Textron failed to use due care in the design, development, manufacture and testing of the FADEC software system. MOD made the wider claim against Textron because, self-evidently, there must have been a failure of the system to perform to specification to begin with, for the damage to have resulted during testing.

As one might expect, elsewhere in Mr Fuller's letter he emphasizes that the Chinook that crashed at the Mull was 'fitted with a very different standard of software' to the one in the Wilmington accident. He does not address the fact that Boscombe Down and EDS-Scicon were no happier with that later version than Malcolm Perks had been with the type fitted at Wilmington. Neither was reckoned to be airworthy.

Thus from three different directions Dr Reid is shown to be wholly wrong in his confident claim. Yet neither the MOD nor Dr Reid has ever apologized for misleading the Defence Committee and, thereby, the public. Nor, even more importantly, has there ever been any proper explanation as to why details of the software problems in the Fadec were never communicated to the RAF Board of Inquiry or to the Fatal Accident Inquiry in Scotland or to the AAIB inspectors. One must guess.

There were other 'mistakes' in the testimony offered by the MOD to the Defence Committee that day. At one point, by way of emphasizing the unlikelihood of any malfunction aboard ZD576, one of Dr Reid's advisors, Air Vice Marshal Jenner, referred back to a much earlier incident:

> There has only been one previous RAF Chinook accident. It was in 1988. It was at Hanover Airport and it involved, very unfortunately, the aircraft hitting one of the ground buildings in error, no question of any other malfunction.

When, after the Committee hearing, it was pointed out to the Air Vice Marshal that his statement was 'quite simply wrong', he wrote to the Committee with accurate information. Not counting ZD576, he acknowledged that there had been eight Chinook accidents; five of them had been caused by technical faults. It is strange that an Air Vice Marshal, knowing that he was almost bound to be questioned by the Committee about the reliability of the RAF's Chinooks, could have been so ill informed. It makes one wonder about the quality of advice given to ministers.

At another point in the hearing, Dr Reid told the Committee that he had spent two days in preparation. He should have spent much longer. On frequent occasions he misled both himself and the Committee by quite misunderstanding the nature of the technology he was talking about. For example, he sought to reassure members of the Committee about Fadec by telling them, 'Fadec is a widespread system . . . used by the Dutch, the Americans, the Royal Flight . . . some people suggest [it] is peculiar to the Chinook'. The 'some people' were about right. Dr Reid did not seem to realize that the term 'Fadec' is generic – like gearboxes or pneumatic tyres. There is a whole variety of Fadecs made by different companies (at least five) around the world; each type of Fadec is very specific – like gearboxes or tyres – to the application for which it is designed. Those applications will vary greatly. Further, the relatively few then fitted in American and Dutch Chinooks were different from the ones in RAF Chinooks. And the ones fitted by Airbus, the Royal Flight and in at least a dozen other fixed-wing aircraft were quite different from anything fitted in any helicopter. So because other Fadecs were relatively reliable in other applications, it did not follow that the ones made for the RAF's Chinooks would be equally trouble-free – which was the Minister's simplistic contention.

In another direction, Dr Reid maintained that Chinooks' Fadecs were not 'flight safety critical' – which shows that he (and what about his advisors?) never understood the problem. The people at Boeing who install the things acknowledge that they are critical. They should know. So should the MOD, because in the documents prepared for its action against Textron there appears the claim that 'the Fadec software was truly critical in maintaining safe flight'. Was the MOD telling the court in America one thing while it told the Select Committee the opposite?

Dr Reid had told the Committee in his opening address that he 'welcomed the opportunity to explain and inform. There has been a lot of ill-informed speculation. There have been a lot of misinformed statements.' Far from reducing the body of misinformation that morning, the Minister and his MOD advisors (it is unfair to blame the Minister for everything) had significantly added to it.

But they were far from finished. At one point Dr Reid explained that even though the first of ZD576's two Fadec units had been destroyed by fire, it was known from the other, undamaged Fadec that the first one would have been working properly because 'if one was working normally, the other was working normally'. But that is absolutely not how the two Fadecs in a Chinook work. Dr Reid cannot have read the AAIB Report during his two days of homework. Of the semi-destroyed unit, the Report had said, 'Fire damage prevented assessment of [its] functionality and had destroyed its memories of the operating programme and exceedance [*sic*] and fault history.' In short, the AAIB did not know whether that particular Fadec had been working properly or not. Yet Dr Reid and his civil servants knew.

When one of the Committee asked the Minister about those two runaways experienced by Sqn Ldr Burke, he implied that they must have been very minor incidents – if indeed they had happened at all. Anyway, why had the Sqn Ldr not followed regulations and filed reports on them? He had heard of the Sqn Ldr's allegation some days earlier and, accordingly, had authorized a search for such reports in the MOD. They did not exist.

Unknown to the Minister, Sqn Ldr Burke was sitting in the 'audience'; he was quite cross. After the hearing he made a small fuss. The truth was that someone had not looked for his reports in the right place. One report was found some days later; it gave a full account of the first incident. Fortunately, because both pilots had been vigilant, the offending engine had been shut down very quickly. So, in a sense, Dr Reid was correct in calling it 'a minor incident'. Catastrophe had been averted. The report on the second runaway was never found.

Sqn Ldr Burke was now retired and blowing his whistle. He had been a helicopter pilot for thirty-one of the thirty-seven years he had been in the RAF. For fourteen years he had been the unit test pilot at RAF Odiham, the home of all Chinooks. He probably knew more about the virtues and vices of the Chinook (both Marks) than anyone on this side of the Atlantic. Indeed, his Station Commander had once written that his 'air-testing skills on the Chinook are unique'. In his time he had coped with almost every known Chinook emergency. And a few unknown ones too. He had also flown the aircraft operationally in the Falklands and Northern Ireland. He knew far too much about the Mk2 (and conditions at the Mull – which he had flown over many times) to agree that the only possible explanation for the crash of ZD576 lay in pilot error. So he was both very well informed and a maverick. That is always a dangerous combination where officialdom is concerned.

Earlier, in light of his 'unique' experience, he had been asked by Tony Cable, the man running the AAIB investigation, for help in setting up some static tests at RAF Odiham. To this end, with the help of two experienced fitters assigned by the AAIB, he used ground power to activate the flight controls of a hangar-bound Chinook. The idea was to try to replicate some of the reactions of the controls to various alternative 'explanations' (including the anomalous Boeing simulation) of the crash. There was nothing clandestine about what he was doing. But just when the results were getting interesting, he was told to stop. Furthermore, the Deputy Station Commander of Odiham ordered him, with some embarrassment, not to talk to anyone, colleagues or enquirers, about anything to do with the accident. And that would include any mention of those earlier runaways in America. He should also understand that there was no question of his being allowed to volunteer any information to the Board of Inquiry (or, later, to the Scottish Inquiry). This order was doubly strange because, on earlier occasions, he had been specifically nominated by the RAF as the best person to advise several coroners' inquests and boards of inquiry on some of the more obscure aspects of helicopter flight characteristics. Now he was barred from any such role.

But four years later, upon retirement, the gag was off. When MPs had asked the Minister questions derived from the Squadron Leader, Dr Reid went out of his way to refer to him as merely a '*supposed* expert'.

Largely as a consequence of the whistle-blowing of the two 'supposed' experts, Sqn Ldr Burke and Malcolm Perks, the whole subject of Fadec was bound to come up at the Defence Committee's hearing. The Minister and the MOD were in a difficult position when it came to explaining the refusal of Boscombe Down to 'verify' the thing. The chosen 'line' was to claim that the problem lay not in the inadequacy of the software, but in the inadequacy of the equipment at Boscombe Down to interpret that software. This ignored the fact that Boscombe could 'read' quite enough to conclude that there were serious software faults. It further ignored the fact that EDS-Scicon, under contract to the MOD, was just as critical of the Chinooks' Fadecs as Boscombe Down had been. So now, presumably for good measure, the Minister threw in the thought that the views of Boscombe Down did not much matter anyway:

> All that Fadec has not satisfied is an internally imposed test procedure which Boscombe Down believe they should apply because they consider that their role is to give unequivocal advice to the operators of the aircraft.

In fact, of course, the application of 'internally imposed' tests (very carefully devised) and the giving of 'unequivocal advice' is what the experts at Boscombe Down have always done. It is what they are paid to do.

Whether these various examples of Dr Reid's ignorance that day were due to his own initiative or to his briefing one cannot tell. It made little difference. The result was the same; it gave added impetus to suspicions already aroused: why was the MOD so busy smoke-screening if, as it always claimed, it had nothing to hide?

There is one other curiosity in Dr Reid's discourse: when one of the more sceptical Committee members, Menzies Campbell, asked him how the RAF's 'gross negligence' verdict squared with the 'absolutely no doubt whatsoever' requirement, the answer was extremely odd. The Minister seemed to suggest that sophisticated grown-ups, like all those present, would well know that 'absolutely' did not really mean 'absolutely'. 'It seems to me,' he said, 'there are two ways to look on the word "absolutely". The first one is a philosophical discussion. Can there ever be an absolute?' Dr Reid satisfied himself that there could not. When he got to his second way of looking at the word, he was able to persuade himself that it did not apply in the case of ZD576. Menzies Campbell, who is both a Scot and a lawyer, tried to cut through this fudge by intimating that the Scottish Sheriff had not had the same philosophic problems as the Minister. Neither, before the two Air Marshals 'reviewed' its verdict, had the three-man Board of Inquiry. But it was all water off the Minister's back. He seemed, in a roundabout way, to say that the normal usage of language did not really count in the official estimation of things. Like Lewis Carroll's Humpty Dumpty, it was a case of: 'A word means just what I choose it to mean – neither more nor less.' In Whitehall it is often that way.

It was a lengthy hearing. But it was no secret that some time earlier the 'rules of engagement' for this session of the Defence Committee had been 'co-ordinated' with the MOD – via the Labour Whips. It was almost certainly agreed that the Minister would only appear if he was given a fairly gentle ride. Even more important, Bruce George, the Committee chairman, would have the major hand in writing the Committee's Report. He rather gave the game away at the very beginning of the hearing when, in his short opening address, he was less concerned with welcoming the Minister (as is customary on these occasions) than with 'reminding' the other Committee members that they were not to be too pressing in their questions about ZD576:

> The Committee has decided, and has repeatedly reaffirmed, that we do not intend to seek to challenge or endorse the findings of previous inquiries into the accident. I hope all members of the Committee present here will respect that collective decision.

Some Committee members, like Menzies Campbell and Crispin Blunt, did not recall having been party to such a firm agreement. They seem to have found the arrangement rather too cosy.[12] It was to get even cosier when the Committee's Report, published some weeks later, appeared to do exactly what the Chairman had earlier asserted it would not do, i.e. 'we do not intend to . . . challenge or endorse the findings of previous inquiries . . .'. A sentence near the end reads as follows:

> We have considered the evidence suggesting that the crash of ZD576 pointed to fundamental flaws in the design of the Chinook Mk2 or its components. We have found no compelling evidence of this.

So, if there was no compelling evidence of fundamental flaws in the Chinook's 'design . . . or its components', the only remaining explanation would seem to lie in the human factor, the pilots. Which would seem to be an endorsement of the official verdict.

Elsewhere, too (just one more example), the Chairman was curiously persuaded by the MOD evidence. The Committee's Report carries this strange comment about the role of Boscombe Down:

> We are concerned by the failure of Boscombe Down to give final approval to the Fadec software. We conclude, however, that this is a management failure, and are persuaded by the evidence that this absence of approval raises no safety-critical questions.

Quite how the Select Committee was 'persuaded' that Boscombe Down's report raised 'no safety-critical questions' is not explained. But Boscombe Down got criticized for doing, once again, what it was being paid to do. The folk at the MOD and at the top of the RAF must have been well pleased with the Committee's Report. It is almost as if they had had a hand in writing it.

THERE HAD ALWAYS BEEN MEDIA interest in the 'Chinook affair', but through 1998 it gathered authority and momentum. The 'ill-informed speculation' of journalists became ever more irksome to the authorities. It was also becoming increasingly clear to anyone who went digging that the MOD had withheld an even greater range of information –

12. This interpretation was confirmed in correspondence with the author in March 2001.

'irrelevant' material – than had originally been thought. The list was impressive.

The AAIB investigators, the Board of Inquiry and the Scottish Inquiry had not been told that six weeks before the crash, one of ZD576's engines had been replaced under circumstances that had nothing to do with routine maintenance. They had not been told that within the undamaged Fadec, as returned to its manufacturer (Textron) for post-crash analysis, one of its code faults – dismissed by the manufacturer as just 'a typical nuisance fault' – was the self-same 'E5' problem that had triggered the engine runaway in Wilmington. They had not been told that, at the very time the AAIB had been relying on Textron-Lycoming's technical competence for an analysis of that Fadec, the MOD was suing that same company for what amounted to technical incompetence. (The MOD won damages running into several million dollars.) They had not been told that the MOD's consultants, EDS-Scicon, had identified fifty-six serious 'category 1 anomalies' in the first 20 per cent of the Fadec software it had examined. They had not been told that in 1994 Chinooks had suffered six 'uncommanded flight control movements' and five in 1995. They had not been told that the day before ZD576 crashed, Boscombe Down had suspended flight testing on their Mk2 Chinook and had earlier written a confidential memo to warn the MOD that the Fadec software was 'unsuitable for its intended purpose'. Presumably, the MOD held that all this information was irrelevant.

If any one of these 'irrelevancies', let alone all, had been withheld from the defence in a criminal trial and then subsequently brought to light, the prosecution would have been in deep professional trouble. And the verdict would have been set aside.

Anyway, if the AAIB investigators and the RAF Board of Inquiry did not know about those things, one can hardly blame the MPs on the Defence Committee for not knowing either, and for not putting all the right questions to the Minister. It is quite possible that the Minister himself did not know about some of these things. He would not be the first MOD Minister to be denied the opportunity to decide for himself what was, and what was not, pertinent. An earlier Minister for Defence was now beginning to make this very point.

Back in 1995 when he was Minister for Defence, Malcolm Rifkind had, he reasonably assumed, been thoroughly briefed by the RAF and his senior civil servants. Based on that briefing, it had been his unpleasant duty, as the Minister, to tell the Commons that 'it was concluded that both pilots had been negligent'. Three years later, and out of office, he was concerned to realize that he had not been told the whole story. Obviously those who had briefed him in 1995 had decided that there was no need to worry the Minister with some of the details. In the best tradition of the Loop, they, not the Minister, had made the decision about what was relevant. Mr Rifkind was not appreciative:

> I am puzzled that although we did have several meetings after the Inquiry had reached its conclusion of gross negligence, neither then, nor at any other time, was I given any indication that there had been serious problems with that type of aircraft. On the face of it, if an aircraft crashes and the MOD are at the time in legal dispute with the manufacturers because of matters relating to the aircraft and its operational capability, that is information that should at least be shared with an Inquiry so that they themselves can judge whether it might or might not have contributed to the accident.

So why had the MOD been so careful not to pass on any of that information? For an answer one must look back to the reasoning of the Air Marshals. It had always been fundamental to their verdict of gross negligence that, in the extremely unlikely event that a technical fault had occurred, it could have played absolutely no part in the crash. Therefore, any such problem, with the Fadecs or control jams or electromagnetic interference or anything else, was a total irrelevancy and should be kept right out of any and every discussion – even with the Minister.

Up until now, although the Air Marshals had spoken forcefully within the senior levels of the MOD, they had kept quiet as far as the wider world was concerned – presumably on the grounds that only exceptionally do serving officers 'go public'. But with so many people asking questions, they were now forced to explain. They had, of course, long convinced themselves that all the allegations about possible malfunctions were not just 101 per cent irrelevant, but mischief-making to boot.

The only factor that was germane was that the pilots had placed themselves too close to the Mull. Nothing else mattered. To make their point (in an article in the Royal Aeronautical Society's magazine, *Aerospace International*[13]) Air Chief Marshal Sir William Wratten used an analogy of a motorist on a motorway driving too fast into fog. He hits a stationary car and is killed, or, at the least, is badly injured. The Air Marshal reasonably argues that the fault lies entirely with the motorist. There was, judging by the skid marks, nothing wrong with his brakes. Nor, given that he had swerved to avoid another car, was there any problem with the steering. But (and this is the Air Marshal's key point) it would not have mattered one jot if, quite unbeknown to the driver (maybe it was a rented car whose service history was unknown to him), there *had* been something wrong with the brakes or steering (or a fault in a Fadec or a loose spring or whatever). The fault was still entirely the driver's because he had not slowed down in plenty of time when he saw fog ahead. This was the nature of the pilots' 'gross negligence'. It seems a persuasive analogy. But one does not need to be a pilot to see where it comes unstuck.

Using Sir William's narrative, consider the problem if the driver, seeing fog ahead, finds that his accelerator is jammed. However, he has a clutch. So he can disengage the now violently over-speeding engine. He then brakes, steers his way across onto the hard shoulder and kills the ignition. All is well. But, of course, the only way a Chinook pilot can 'brake' a runaway engine is by applying maximum pitch (with his 'collective' lever) on the rotor blades. This will immediately start him climbing but it will not slow down his forward movement. Indeed, with the rotors now acting more powerfully, he will be going faster. So he finds himself climbing and accelerating forward – towards the fog/cloud.

No doubt Sir William would not be moved. He will say (indeed, he does say) that the pilot(s) should have turned away before ever getting near the fog. So how near is 'near'? The two Air Marshals say, based on data which is at least arguable, that 'near' was 600 metres. They argue that, given the turning circle (at the maximum permitted 30° angle of

13. The letters and articles are found in *Aerospace International* for April, July 1998, Dec 1999, Aug, Sept, Oct 2000.

bank) of a Chinook, that is not enough. But they have been able to find few, if any, Chinook pilots to agree with them. Why therefore did the Air Marshals not order some actual flying tests to settle the matter? Anyway, who is to say that ZD576 would not have slowed down going into the turn? But supposing, unbeknown to the pilots that day, a spring had worked loose some minutes before and fallen down between the myriad control rods. In straight and level flight the fault would not have been apparent. It would only have become so when the pilots tried to turn. At that moment (and not before) they would have found that the 'steering' had jammed. Or maybe they could only turn in the wrong direction. Moreover, other flight controls were behaving wrongly. Or perhaps the problem lay in a sudden Fadec runaway . . .

The Air Chief Marshal's analogy of the car driver can be extended. Suppose the police checked Hire-a-Car's workshop records of that particular car and other similar models in the fleet, and found that there had been earlier instances of jammed accelerator linkages or jammed steering. Indeed, one such problem had almost caused a major accident at a place called Wilmington. Suppose it was further found that the owner of Hire-a-Car was suing the car manufacturer about earlier faults in that model. And lastly, supposing it was found that, despite his knowledge of those faults and the legal action, the owner of Hire-a-Car was still hiring out that particular model of car to the public. The narrative raises interesting questions about who ordered or condoned the entry into service of the Chinook Mk2 while, in effect, the owner was suing the manufacturer and, more important, there was a list of known problems with the aircraft. Indeed, one of those problems was reckoned by the owner's own test organization to be so worrying that it had grounded its test aircraft.

One can go further. Supposing the Motorway Police, not knowing about the discoveries made by their colleagues in the Hire-a-Car workshops, decide to bring charges against the motorist (he was merely badly injured in the crash) for dangerous driving. Some might think there was a conflict of interest if it was then found that one of the magistrates on the bench that day was also one of Hire-a-Car's senior managers. He might, if he were to observe the proprieties, wish to disqualify himself – as the Tench Report had recommended. No such move was made. Two

Air Marshals sat in magisterial judgement. Moreover, theirs was a judgement against which there was no appeal.

In the media debate that grew through 1997 and 1998, neither of the Air Marshals nor the MOD was prepared to give an inch. Indeed, they became quite bad-tempered about the whole affair. Their investment in the gross negligence verdict was total. When the Royal Aeronautical Society's monthly magazine *Aerospace International* ran a short article in January 1998 summarizing news reports that the Fadec had been put into service with 'unverifiable' software, Air Chief Marshal Sir William Wratten should have let it go. Instead, he wrote to the editor:

> There is no way whatever by which an unserviceable Fadec could compel pilots to fly at high speed and low level towards high ground which is covered in cloud. To those uneducated in aviation matters, this . . . may be difficult to grasp. To your readership, however, I would expect it to be self-evident.

Publication of those comments brought a number of dissenting letters from readers who were evidently 'uneducated in aviation matters'. They included an ex-Boscombe Down test pilot, a former CAA flight standard inspector (on Chinooks), and the top computer expert (Malcolm Perks) who had earlier been the MOD's principle witness against the makers of the Fadec. They, and others equally 'uneducated', all testified (as one of them put it in the magazine) that 'an unserviceable Fadec might indeed compel pilots to fly . . . towards high ground . . .'. Sir William and the MOD let it be known that it was none of the Society's business to question the judgement of two senior RAF officers. In the end Sir William resigned from the Society. And took all serving RAF officers with him. One gets the feeling that he exited muttering something about 'damn cheek' and 'bloody civilians'. What we know for certain is that he wrote a parting article categorizing all criticism as 'wilful ignorance'.

That was not clever. Someone now pointed out that Sir William's thinking was that of someone who had no experience of flying helicopters. He had come up through the RAF as a 'fast jet' man. To a person educated in that culture, the idea of a pilot flying at 150 knots until he is only 600 or 700 metres from a hill before angling away is incomprehensible. But helicopter pilots will tell one that they do it all the time. Anyway, unlike a fixed-wing pilot, they can (and do) slow down in seconds.

Simultaneous with these developments, three senior members of the Royal Aeronautical Society's 'Flight Operations Group' were making their own independent review of all the evidence and circumstances. They were vastly experienced professional airmen; again, one was a helicopter expert. At the end of a long and very thorough report, they concluded that this was 'certainly not a case in which there was absolutely no doubt whatsoever'.[14]

By now, other specialist journals had become involved. The trade magazine *Computer Weekly*, digging hard and using the Freedom of Information Act in the US, published a series of articles culminating in a devastating 140-page critique of the MOD and the RAF.[15] It was mostly concerned with the technical aspects of Fadec and the way the MOD had failed to 'own up'. One of *Computer Weekly*'s revelations from the US concerned what was almost certainly the most extraordinary manoeuvre ever 'performed' by a Chinook. In April 1997 a US Army Chinook, on manoeuvres at 1100 feet above the Texas Panhandle, suddenly went completely out of control. It did a snap roll. For what must have seemed a lifetime, but was really only a few seconds, the pilots could get no logical response at all from the flight controls. Nothing would 'bite'. They were convinced that they were doomed. But they went on fighting to regain some kind of command. 'Never, never give up trying to fly the thing' is a very basic pilot motto. Then, quite suddenly, when they were less than 300 feet above the ground, everything came right-way-up and returned to semi-normal. They managed to put the aircraft down in a wheat field.

A day or two later, with the Chinook trucked back to base, the experts pulled it apart. They could find nothing wrong. There was 'no evidence of any malfunction'. If the aircraft had crashed and the crew been killed,

14. The report was co-authored by three pilots: Captain MacDonald, a retired airline pilot and Air Accident Investigator; Captain Hadlow, a retired airline pilot and ex-armed forces helicopter pilot; and Captain Kohn, a retired airline pilot, an aviation consultant and Regulatory Authority Inspector. Their report is usually referred to as 'The MacDonald Report'.
15. 'RAF Justice' by Tony Collins (*Computer Weekly*, May 1999).

it might have been put down to pilot error. Only later was it found that there were some small metal slivers in the hydraulics of the flight controls. The conclusion was that the 'metallic contamination' might have been responsible. But no definitive cause could be found. A US Army newsletter of 1998 told how after another 'no-known-malfunction' crash had been blamed on pilot error, it was later officially conceded that a momentary power failure might have affected the Automatic Flight Control System. No one could be sure. But the dead pilots were cleared. The Army's Analytical Investigation Branch at Corpus Christi, Texas, found that there had been a number of incidents involving 'uncommanded manoeuvres or flight control lock-ups' in airborne Chinooks. When specialists tried to reproduce these faults, they were often unable to do so. Even on the mundane level of a home computer, it is a recognizable problem. The thing 'crashes' or makes some 'uncommanded manoeuvre'. Frustration ensues. One way or another, though it may take several minutes, one gets the thing working again – but with no real idea of what went wrong in the first place. A helicopter pilot does not have 'several minutes'.

The relevance of all this to ZD576 is obvious. So, too, is the conclusion that 'metallic contamination' may have played a part in the bizarre behaviour of that Chinook in Texas. One rereads the comment made over three years earlier in the AAIB Report on ZD576:

> Examination [of the Lower Control Actuators] revealed no anomalies apart from a considerable quantity of very small metallic particles in residual fluid in parts of the boost actuator . . . and the presence of four fine metal slivers, up to 0.2 inch long on one of the servo valve screens.

Any engineer will confirm that metal slivers 'up to 0.2 inch long' could be large enough to constitute a hazard even if, as here, they had been caught on a screening gauze. It is why such filters are cleaned at regular intervals. The MOD and the Air Marshals deny that the American experience has any bearing on ZD576 because, of course, the crash at the Mull happened because the pilots did not climb or turn away soon enough. This ignores the questionable calculations on which that hypothesis is based. Likewise it denies the ability of the pilots to slow down. But then any factor which does not fit the official verdict has always been dismissed as 'irrelevant'.

In retirement, Air Chief Marshal Sir William Wratten has been able to respond to media criticism rather more vigorously than before. Some of his comments have provided glimpses behind the scenes of the official reasoning. From the several examples available, there was a revealing interview on the BBC's *Newsnight* (1 December 2000). He was being questioned about his 'overruling' of the conclusions of the three-man Board of Inquiry. He made this comment:

> These are young officers whose experience of these matters does not match those of their senior commanders . . .

Apart from the fact that in terms of both the flying and engineering of Chinooks (one of the Board was a Chinook engineer officer), the Board's collective and practical experience considerably outweighed that of Sir William, one asks why he made the comment at all. The answer is simple. While Sir William and Air Vice Marshal Day were certainly empowered to overrule the Board of Inquiry's doubts, not even the Lord above could airbrush those doubts out of existence. They were there – indelibly. The only way to cope with this very awkward fact was to imply that the Board's doubts were of little account – because the three officers concerned were young and inexperienced.

If Sir William truly regarded the Board members as lacking enough experience to conduct an investigation into the most serious of all the RAF's peacetime accidents, one must wonder at the competence of 'the senior commanders' who appointed them in the first place. Secondly, when it suits the official thesis, the Board members are deemed to be inexperienced. But when it suits another argument, they are deemed to be thoroughly competent. In this instance the MOD's press office had been briefed by the Air Secretariat three years earlier, so that, when the news media posed questions about the Scottish Inquiry's lack of support for the RAF verdict, the official counter should include the following comment:

> The RAF Board of Inquiry comprised members with first-hand knowledge of Chinooks who conducted an exhaustive investigation.[16]

16. Questions and Answer Brief for/by MOD Press Office, *circa* 21 March 1996.

So, perhaps they were not quite so inexperienced after all. You pays your money and the MOD or the Air Marshals makes the choice.

DURING THE LATE 1990S and through into 2001 there were several developments that pushed matters towards the ultimate goal. Once again, a television report played a part. Quite by chance, the life peer Lord Chalfont happened to see an item that worried him. He made contact with people who were close to the affair. The more he heard, the more concerned he became. An ex-army officer with a notable war record, and a respected thinker over several decades on matters concerned with defence, he started asking questions. Eventually, in May 1997, he initiated a short debate in the House of Lords about what he saw as a major miscarriage of service justice. The MOD, through its Minister in the Lords, was unyielding.

Lord Chalfont was not deterred. Now a cross-bencher but having once been a Labour minister in the Foreign Office and, more recently, Chairman of the All-Party Defence Group, he was very familiar with the machinery and, more importantly, the machinations of Whitehall. He understood the pressures, restraints and advice ('No, Minister – the less said the better') under which ministers must often reply in debate. In 1999, together with a number of other people in both Houses of Parliament and beyond, he formed the 'Mull of Kintyre Group'. This was less an overt lobby group (though some very pertinent questions were asked in both Houses) and more a discreet attempt to reason with ministers in the MOD. They were courteously received. But that was as far as it went.

Then in July 2000, during yet another Lords debate triggered by Lord Chalfont, concern was expressed by a former Lord Advocate, Lord Murray. He had carefully examined the findings of the Board of Inquiry and, in particular, the verdict of the two Air Marshals. He now suggested that those two officers, in setting aside the 'absolutely no doubt whatsoever' requirement when, very clearly, a properly constituted Board had had quite considerable doubts, had probably 'misdirected themselves'. This was the first time that anyone with real legal authority had looked at the saga from that angle. The MOD did not respond.

However, the mandarins and ministers were wrong if they thought that, by pretending they had not noticed Lord Murray's comments, they could thereby avoid the difficult questions. Four months later, and nearly two years after the Commons Defence Committee had fired its blunt arrows, another Select Committee thought to mount a sharper investigation. This was the Public Accounts Committee (PAC).

There were a number of MPs of all parties who had been dissatisfied with that earlier 1998 report of the Commons Defence Committee. How far they spurred the PAC to take over where the Defence Committee had inadequately left off one can only guess. But a cross-party letter to the Chairman of the PAC must surely have played its part. It came from Menzies Campbell (a Liberal Democrat who had been a member of that earlier Defence Committee), James Arbuthnot (Conservative) and Martin O'Neill (Labour). The letter was quite short. One could choose from a number of points made by the three MPs. Perhaps their final one will illustrate the tone and message:

> There is no proof that Fadec caused the crash; nor is there any proof that it did not. But there is persuasive evidence that the computer software problems had not been resolved before ZD576 flew into the Mull of Kintyre. This raises doubts that all responsibility for the crash belongs to the pilots. We would be grateful if the Committee would investigate these matters further.

Malcolm Perks, who had been contracted by the MOD to be its expert Fadec witness six years earlier, now sent the PAC Chairman his own detailed history of the whole Fadec debacle. After making the point that the affair had been a managerial and technical mess since almost the beginning, he gave examples. Again, one will suffice:

> The writing had been on the wall for years that this Fadec's software was of doubtful quality, but the necessary actions had not been taken. In the end . . . MOD overruled their experts [i.e. Boscombe Down and EDS-Scicon] and went ahead anyway with its release into [operational] service. Reasons for rejecting advice should not include, 'It's not the answer I wanted.'

Computer Weekly also submitted a long memorandum. While acknowledging that other possibilities might have been behind the crash, its focus was obviously on the Fadec problems. It made any number of telling points. Again, one such point – less oblique than it seems – will do:

> It is currently more than a week after a computer failure brought down the London Stock Exchange for nearly an entire day, and the bug that brought down the system has not been identified because it has not been possible to replicate the exact problem. The inability to identify the bug is despite the forensic skills of some of the most expert software specialists in the USA and the UK.

Well briefed and armed with a more thorough understanding of the problems – and the nature of earlier MOD smoke screens – the Public Accounts Committee questioned four very senior members of MOD staff at some length. It seems that, this time, no soft-pedalling pact had been pre-agreed with the MOD. Perhaps this was why no minister came forward to answer questions. Neither did anyone from the RAF volunteer. The four officials got a rough ride. To a large extent they were paying the price for Dr Reid's obfuscations of nearly two years earlier. But, as some of the officials now before the PAC had played a part in briefing the Minister on that earlier occasion, one need not feel too sorry for them. On several occasions the exchanges were angry and bad-tempered. Or, in the preferred idiom, 'There was a robust exchange of views.'

When published, the conclusions of the Committee were damning. It was critical of the MOD and, by direct implication, of senior command in the RAF at almost every point. Below are a few of the paragraph headings from its analysis:

- The Chinook Mark 2 acceptance process and outcome were flawed.
- At the time of the crash of ZD576 the Chinook Mk2 fleet was experiencing widespread and repeated faults caused by the Fadec software.
- There was, at the time of acceptance into service, and still is, insufficient independent assurance on the performance of the Fadec software which is critical to safe flight.
- The process for convening and conducting RAF Boards of Inquiry is unsatisfactory.
- The finding of the RAF Board of Inquiry into the crash of ZD576 does not satisfy the burden of proof required.

- Negligence should only be found when it is definitely the cause of the crash, not simply as a last resort in the absence of any other more convincing explanation.

THERE ARE TWO PARTICULAR AREAS of the findings worth looking at in a little more detail. When the Committee came to comment on the MOD's attitude towards the Scottish Fatal Accident Inquiry, it did not tiptoe round the issue:

> The Fatal Accident Inquiry worked to a lesser burden of proof in determining cause, its findings being based on a balance of probabilities rather than no doubt whatsoever. However, against even this burden of proof the Sheriff could not agree with the Board of Inquiry's findings of gross negligence. We are surprised that the MOD has not taken on board this learned legal judgement. Indeed, we believe that the Department should recognize the Court's superior standing over its own domestic procedures. We regard the Department's preference for the results of their own procedures as constituting unwarrantable arrogance.

Lastly, it spelt out in some detail why it was critical of RAF procedures as well as those of the MOD:

> The officers reviewing the findings of the investigating board had command responsibility for the management and provision of the support helicopter fleet. They would therefore have an interest in ensuring minimal disruption to the fleet, particularly in the light of the problematic acceptance process. We believe that the reviewing officers reached their conclusions in good faith; however, their position as commanding officers for the helicopter forces leaves them open to allegations of conflict of interest and reduces the perceived objectivity of the findings of the Board.

The Committee repeated what the Tench Report, long ignored, had pointed out fourteen years earlier. The Minister for Defence, Geoff Hoon, found the Committee's Report 'superficial'. Was that a way of making the point that the Committee's Chairman, David Davis, was a Conservative? But then many of the flaws and mistakes which characterize this whole narrative had occurred when the Conservatives were in office. Consequently, it was hardly a party matter. What had not changed from one administration to the next was the grip exercised, the arguments advanced, the fudge peddled and the deceits practised by those in both permanent and transitory office at the MOD.

In March 2000 Lord Chalfont tried another tack. He initiated a Lords debate in which he proposed that the House should set up an *ad hoc* Select Committee to re-examine the whole affair. This was an unusual proposal. It was the last thing the MOD wanted; it would be an unwarranted intrusion in a matter which was nothing to do with the Lords, who would not understand the details anyway. Members of the Government's front bench, led by the responsible Minister in the Lords, Baroness Symons, spoke powerfully against it. So did Lord Craig. As the commanding officer of the RAF (Chief of Air Staff) in 1985, he would have played a central part in rejecting that report by W.H. Tench recommending that senior RAF officers should divorce themselves from accident investigations in which it might be thought that they had a direct interest. Little wonder that sixteen years later he should make the point that a re-examination of the official verdict on ZD576 would, as he told the Lords, 'only serve to undermine [a] sense of respect and trust' in senior officers. By now one had the feeling that what mattered to senior RAF officers above everything else was preserving 'the integrity of command'. But Lord Craig (and he was not the only one) did not seem to recognize that, within the RAF, in the matter of ZD576, 'respect and trust' for some senior officers had already become diminishing assets.

The MOD was worried. While it had managed to disregard the Sheriff in Scotland, ignoring the findings of a Lords Committee which would be comprised, no doubt, of four or five senior lawyers (ex-judges, probably), would be more difficult. But some of the arguments advanced by those who doubted the official case were very strong indeed. If, for example, in that earlier Lords debate Lord Murray had brought his legal mind to bear on the 'absolutely no doubt whatsoever' problem with the comment that the Air Marshals had probably 'misdirected themselves', another legal mind was now no less critical in a slightly different direction. The short speech of Lord Ackner, an ex-law lord no less, is a good example of the way an incisive legal mind works. A single paragraph is enough to give the flavour:

Towards the end of his observations, the Air Marshal stated: 'It is incomprehensible why two trusted, experienced and skilled pilots should, as indicated by all the available evidence, have flown a serviceable aircraft into cloud covered high ground.' My Lords, if it is 'incomprehensible' then he does not understand how the accident happened. And if he does not understand how it happened, he is not in a position to exercise the very limited jurisdiction which has been given to him.

Having heard nearly two hours of debate, the House of Lords voted that a Select Committee should be set up. There followed a hiccup when the Lords Liaison Committee – a standing body charged with the organization of Select Committees – came back a few weeks later to recommend *against* setting up such a Committee. The main argument was that this Committee would be acting as a quasi court of appeal. As such, it would be a dangerous precedent. However, the House as a whole evidently felt that this argument would have been much more convincing if there had already existed some mechanism for an appeal – as there is in almost all others areas of our judicial system. But, against the manslaughter verdict of the two Air Marshals (who had no legal qualifications), there was no suitable mechanism. The House of Lords, in full session, was unhappy. On a vote it decided that it *would* have its Select Committee.

A few weeks later, in a crowded room overlooking the river, the five-member Select Committee held its first hearing. This was a formidable crew, chaired by Lord Jauncey, a former judge at the Scottish Court of Appeal. Three of the others were QCs, and the fifth was an engineer who held honorary scientific degrees from nine different universities.[17]

If the measured questioning of the witnesses was any indication, the Committee had done its homework on the dozens of papers and reports, official and unofficial, which had accumulated over the previous seven years. Through five long sessions first one Lord then another slowly questioned a string of witnesses: the Wing Commander who had been the chairman of the RAF Board of Inquiry, the Squadron Leader in charge of converting pilots to the Mk2, the two Air Marshals, Tony Cable

17. The five Committee members, under the chairmanship of Lord Jauncey, were Lords Bowness, Brennan, Hooson and Tombs. Lord Tombs was the engineer.

of the AAIB, Mr Holbrook (the yachtsman), the three authors of the MacDonald Report and Sqn Ldr Burke. Rarely did anyone get questioned for less than an hour; sometimes it took much longer. The fathers of the two pilots, Michael Tapper and John Cook, were also given the opportunity to address the Committee. And there was a hearing for an RAF Special Forces pilot – one of the two 'anonymous' witnesses in Scotland nearly six years earlier.

From the many hours of testimony it is difficult to pick out the most significant moments. There were a number. If, when it came to the turn of the two Air Marshals, their Lordships' patience was rather tried, they did not show it. Well, hardly. The two officers asked for the opportunity to begin with a lengthy and uninterrupted presentation, aided by a set of thirty-four slides. The Lords listened patiently. Once again we learnt why the pilots 'grossly breached the rules of airmanship'. As always, any possibility that a technical problem might have had a role was rejected.

At numerous points in the question and answer session that followed their slide presentation, the Air Marshals stressed that their reasoning was entirely based on known facts, not hypotheses. Speculation was for other people – their critics. Thus: 'We know that about twenty seconds before impact with the ground, the crew made a waypoint change.' Or: 'We know that they had chosen to fly straight over the Mull because they had set up this 1000-feet-a-minute rate of climb.' Throughout their testimony Sir John and Sir William repeatedly fell back on this same formula. 'We know for a fact that . . .' Or: 'What is for sure is . . .' Or: 'The Boeing simulation tells us that . . .' Air Marshal Sir John Day summed up this belief: 'The judgement I have made about gross negligence . . . is based on what I *know* happened from the facts I have described to you.'

Despite the Committee's efforts to give nothing away, it was not difficult to detect a note of scepticism, disbelief even, from this or that Lord as they listened to and then questioned the Air Marshals' certainties.

The fact (if, in this context, one dares to use the word) is that many of the Air Marshals' 'facts' were very shaky indeed. For example, at one point Sir William came up with the key assertion (indeed, nothing could be more 'key') that when the pilots made the waypoint change, 'they could not see the Mull'. Similarly, Sir John maintained that 'somewhere in that 600 metres, before they coasted in they were in cloud'. Of course, if that had been the case, the pilots would have been foolhardy in the extreme and their guilt never in any doubt. However, as Lord Jauncey rather quietly commented, 'I do not think there is any evidence of that.' One of the other Lords then pointed out that the yachtsman had been able to see the Mull from well offshore. This assertion by the Air Marshals (and both of them paraphrased it elsewhere in their testimony) was compounded by seven of their diagrammatic slides. In a most vivid way, these revealed their mindset. The slides showed the Chinook about to nose into a large cloud that was depicted as extending hundreds of metres out to sea. One must assume that this error represented the Air Marshals' honestly held but entirely mistaken mental picture of the accident's circumstances. No wonder they were adamant about negligence.[18] Those slides explain a great deal about the official verdict. One looked to see what the Committee members thought. They gave little away.

At one point in the testimony of Air Marshal Sir John Day there was an almost audible intake of breath from some of the retired pilots in the 'audience'. He had suggested that, because the AAIB's analysis found no evidence that ZD576's engines had been under emergency power at the moment of impact, this was a sure sign that there had been no control jam. Afterwards, in the corridor outside, there was much muttering about this assertion. The fact is that emergency power is only relevant in certain types of difficulty. If, for example, the pilot of any aircraft even begins to suspect a control jam (or a car driver thinks that his steering has locked), the last thing he does is to apply emergency power; it will almost certainly make his problem worse – perhaps to the point of disaster. Did the Air Marshal not know this? 'Worrying, very worrying' was all that one of the several retired RAF pilots could find to say afterwards. It was an adequate summary. In fact, when Captain Cook, the father of Flt Lt Cook (the 'handling pilot' in ZD576), came to appear briefly before the Committee the next day, he put the Committee right.

18. When the author wrote to Air Marshal Sir William Wratten asking if there was an explanation for the slides' inaccuracies, he was told that he was concentrating on an irrelevancy. The MOD's Air Secretariat were not much more help.

As a pilot of nearly forty years' experience, from RAF Meteors to BA Concordes (on which he had been the pilot training manager), his comments probably carried some weight.

Committee members made two allusions to the gap between the obvious doubts of the RAF's three-man Board of Inquiry and the Air Marshals' own unequivocal certainties – all derived from the same evidence. The officers were not able to help except to repeat the implication that the Board was inexperienced – 'young' was the euphemism now used.

They might have wanted to use the same adjective to describe Witness A. This was the same Special Forces pilot who had spoken so convincingly in Paisley; he was now a senior Squadron Leader and had recently been decorated for his skill and courage in a widely reported

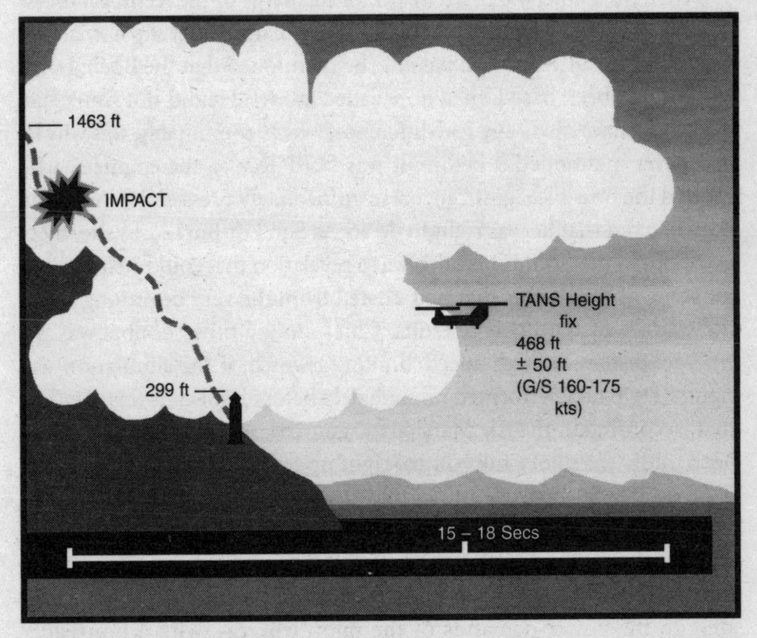

One of the MOD slides showing, in diagrammatic profile, the coastline, the Mull lighthouse, the cloud and the sea. But there is no evidence whatsoever that the Chinook entered cloud well out to sea . . .

incident 'in an operational theatre'. In answer to a string of questions he made it clear that he could not support the official verdict at any point. He was the more convincing because he was never in the least confrontational or attacking. The following question and answer gives some slight feel of his testimony – which, in all, lasted for forty-five minutes:

> Lord Jauncey: Can you think of any reason why, having changed the waypoint, the aircraft should have continued on its existing course at apparently a slow rate of climb to the Mull?
>
> Witness A: That is the crux of the matter. I cannot think of any reason why the crew would have elected to do that unless they were not doing it of their own volition.

When Mr Cable, the AAIB inspector in charge of the technical investigation at Farnborough, came to give his evidence, he let slip a small but significant detail. Almost in passing, he mentioned that the Boeing simulation had been based on 'a non-Fadec model'. He did not think that this would have made any real difference, which, presumably, was why he had never mentioned it before. It was Lord Tombs, the engineer, who spotted the possible significance. He immediately pressed the inspector. It turned out that he was right to do so. As Sqn Ldr Burke was shortly to point out to the Committee, this was a revelation that could well account for some of the doubts that had existed from the very beginning about the validity of the Boeing results. Chief among those doubts was the emergency flare (a high-speed 'braking') which, if the simulation was right, ZD576 had performed immediately before impact. It was this flare that, according to the Air Marshals' argument, showed that ZD576 had been under the pilots' full control right up to the moment of the crash.

'I was really shocked,' Burke told the Committee, 'to learn that the simulation had been carried out using non-Fadec Chinook data.' He wondered why the MOD had 'chosen to keep very quiet' about it. He explained that the engines of a Mk2 Chinook will react almost immediately to the power demands of the pilot, whereas, with a non-Fadec Chinook (i.e. the Mk1), there is a small time lag. This difference only becomes apparent when the helicopter is subject to a very rapid power change or manoeuvre, which, of course, does not happen in routine flying. But it can certainly happen in an emergency. In the context of the crisis in which one might suppose that the pilots of ZD576 found themselves, it meant that the official interpretation of the final part of that flight could be seriously flawed. It raised yet another area of doubt (as if there were not enough already) about the official verdict.

This small but important difference between the two Marks of Chinook was something that Mr Cable, not a Chinook or even a helicopter specialist, would not have known. It was something that Air Marshal Sir William Wratten, who had no piloting experience of helicopters, might not have known. It was something which Air Marshal Sir John Day, an officer who did have Chinook experience, certainly should have known. It was something that someone in the helicopter 'office' within the MOD *must* have known. And which they should have told the Board of Inquiry and the Air Marshals. Yet one wonders if it would have made any difference to the view of the Air Marshals.

The testimony heard by the Lords Committee ran to over 200,000 words.[19] Two HMSO 'blue-backs' not only contain the verbatim transcripts of five long afternoons, but also a quantity of written submissions, including several from the MOD and the Air Marshals. Malcolm Perks, now working in Canada, responded in writing to a request from the Committee for his thoughts on the Fadec problem. Having been the MOD's chosen expert, he now found no difficulty in envisaging a 'transitory runaway'. He further made the point that 'the evidence of the wreckage does not support the reconstruction of circumstances leading to the crash, much of which is based on the Boeing simulation'. The disparity was something that had worried him from the beginning. But now, with the knowledge that the simulation had not been done on a Fadec 'model', he had a specific explanation for it.

Through December 2001 and then January, the Committee considered the accumulated evidence. While no one who had been to the hearings was going to tempt fate by being too loud in their forecasts, there was a clear feeling that the Committee would not have too much difficulty in coming to a conclusion. After all, ultimately all they had to do was decide whether there was any room for any doubt. If there was,

19. Lords Select Committee on ZD576 – oral evidence (HMSO, November 2000).

even at the most marginal level, then the official verdict which depended for its validity on being 101 per cent watertight – 'absolutely no doubt whatsoever' – could not stand.

In the event, when the Report was released at 11.00 a.m. on 5 February (there was a small queue waiting for the sound of Big Ben), it emerged that the Committee had gone much further than anyone might have anticipated. Written in the rather flat and unemotional tones one would expect, the Report was damning of the official case at almost every point. Of all its criticisms, those directed at the Air Marshals were the most trenchant. It found that their reasoning and, therefore, their verdict were almost wholly derived from a string of assertions which were far from being 'the certain and undoubted facts' that they were so unequivocally claimed to be. The Committee cited five of these 'facts'; each was central to the official case. It then demolished them. For example, both the Air Marshals had placed much emphasis on the certainty that the pilots must have been in full control right up to the point of the crash, because 'we know for a fact . . . that some four seconds before impact the crew started to flare the aircraft'. The Committee was wholly unpersuaded: 'Not so. The Boeing simulation, using assumptions now shown to be incompatible, produced this result. On no view could it be described as fact.' Elsewhere, Sir John Day had claimed that the two pilots must have 'chosen to fly straight over the Mull – we know that because they had set up a 1000-feet-a-minute rate of climb'. Again, the Committee flatly contradicts this 'certainty': 'There is no evidence that they had chosen to over-fly the Mull; indeed the making of the waypoint change suggests the contrary.' Time and again the Report finds the four or five 'known facts' on which the official case was wholly based to be quite unsubstantiated:

> Sir John Day's conclusions must be weakened by his reliance on matters which he treated as facts but which have been demonstrated to our satisfaction to be not facts but merely hypotheses or assumptions.

At one point the Committee appears (sardonically?) to thank the MOD for sending, very late in the day ('when the first draft of our Report was almost complete'), the formula for calculating the radius of the turn necessary for ZD576 to clear/not clear the coast. (In fact, the Committee had already obtained the formula for itself.) The formula shows (at the officially assumed speed) that a crash was a likely consequence. But besides commenting that the speed is an 'assumption', the Committee points out that the MOD's calculations 'do not take account of the possibility that if the crew, on initiating the turn, had reduced speed, the radius of the turn could have been greatly reduced'. In one of the very few places where the Committee allows a touch of irony to peep through, it comments, 'The formula was helpful in demonstrating the dramatic effect of a reduction in speed in reducing the [turning] radius.'

On almost every one of its thirty-eight pages the Report is critical of the Air Marshals' judgement and, by clear implication, of the MOD's parallel and unremitting advocacy. By the time one reaches the final page the Committee's 'determination' is a foregone conclusion. The Committee makes a point of stating that it was unanimous:

> It is not our role to determine the likely cause of this accident, and indeed on the evidence which we have heard and read it would be impossible to do so. We are nevertheless satisfied on the evidence before us and against the standard of 'absolutely no doubt whatsoever', that the Air Marshals were not justified in finding that negligence on the part of the pilots of ZD576 caused the crash.

That afternoon Lord Chalfont chaired a press conference. When asked what they wanted 'to happen now', the fathers of the two pilots said the same thing. They wanted the official record of their sons' gross negligence 'expunged from the record'. No more. But certainly no less. After all, their sons had been roundly 'acquitted' by the Scottish Inquiry, by the Commons Public Accounts Committee, by the Flight Operations Group of the Royal Aeronautical Society, and now, most thoroughly of all, by the Lords Committee. And that said nothing of the doubts expressed by a number of distinguished legal brains or, for that matter, by the original three-man RAF Board of Inquiry before it had, in effect, been overruled by the RAF's high command. The MOD would now be constitutionally obliged to reply to the House of Lords – though within months rather than days. Of course, before that, the media demanded an immediate, same-day reaction.

It fell to the unfortunate Adam Ingram, Minister for the Armed Forces, to try to answer the harrying questions of the *World at One*, *PM*, the *Ten O'Clock News* and *Newsnight* – and that was just the BBC. It was a thankless task. One's heart went out to the man; he was trying to defend a situation which was both indefensible and absolutely not of his making. With only the most basic knowledge of the story, he had obviously been briefed to play for time with the usual response: first, 'we will need space to study this report', and second, 'the Committee appears to have found no new evidence or new facts on which to base its conclusions'. This, being one of Whitehall's standard SODEMs, was to be expected. Nevertheless, one might have thought that the 'discovery' that the simulation (on which so much of the official verdict was based) had, in effect, been done on the wrong aircraft might have been considered as a 'new fact' – among several others. The only real surprise was that the Minister did not bother to claim that the Committee did not understand the many complicated technical factors involved. That, no doubt, would come later.

And what about the Air Marshals? Sir William Wratten had already retired. Sir John Day was now a full Air Marshal and in line to become the next Chief of Air Staff, the senior post in the RAF. He had earlier let it be known within the MOD that he would probably resign if the Lords Committee and subsequent events went against him. In order to work round this and other deeply embarrassing possibilities, several worried conferences were convened within the MOD. One conclusion was that, in an attempt to restore some credibility to both the Air Marshals and to itself, the MOD should commission Boeing to do another of its computer-based simulations. Despite the fact that this would at least now be based on the right aircraft, critics reasonably asked if Boeing was likely to come up with results which acknowledged any significant error in its original calculations. Furthermore, Malcolm Perks (the MOD's chosen 'computer' witness in its earlier legal action against Boeing and Textron-Lycoming) wrote a detailed letter to the Lords Committee and the MOD in which he pointed out that a simulation can, at best, only produce an approximation which, even then, is subject to interpretation. It can never be definitive, nor, despite the certainties expressed by the Air Marshals and the MOD's Air Staff, can it be used to produce results about which there is 'absolutely no doubt whatsoever'.

Consequently, those outside the MOD (with, presumably, the tacit support of the Lords Committee) were now insistent that, as well as the results of Boeing's new simulation being made public, both the data and the calculations from which those results are derived should also be fully disclosed. They let it be known that they would have a team of experts standing by to rigorously examine and fine-comb all the figures and computations. Nevertheless, it may be difficult for anyone outside Whitehall to tell if the MOD – to whom Boeing will exclusively pass its findings – has filleted out any inconvenient details before making them public. In similar cases in the past it has done so both covertly and overtly – sometimes on its own in-house claim that some of the data is 'commercially confidential' or 'not in the interests of national security'. It could do so again. The fact is that those who have followed the long saga of ZD576 have long since exhausted any trust they once might have had in the good faith of the MOD.

In another development, the Commons – no doubt prompted by the Lords Report – held a full-blown debate.[20] This was unusual in that it took place at the instigation of the Opposition on one of those relatively few and, therefore, precious days when it is entitled to choose the subject of debate. As David Davis, a Conservative, pointed out when he opened the proceedings, 'This is a virtually apolitical subject, there is no ideology involved, no party difference . . . the original decisions that we are seeking to put right were taken under a Conservative administration . . . we are seeking simply to correct a miscarriage of justice that has gone on for too long'. Because of the 'broad cross-party agreement on this issue . . . we will not seek to divide the House this evening'. Impressively, over the next two-and-a-half hours party allegiances were quite ignored as speaker after speaker pointed to the weaknesses in the official case. The cast list was imposing: Menzies Campbell, Tam Dalyell, Martin O'Neill, John Redwood, James Arbuthnot, Lady Hermon, David Trimble, Frank Field, Robert Key, Henry Bellingham and James Gray. Several returned to the very basic point that there was simply insufficient evidence to sustain a verdict of guilty on even the criminal law's requirement of 'beyond all reasonable doubt', let alone the RAF's 'absolute'

20. *Hansard*, 19 March 2002.

requirement. Only one back-bencher, John Wilkinson, spoke (rather bravely) in support of the official verdict. In reply, Geoff Hoon, the Minister, did his best. But time and again he was pushed into defensive replies that, as a practised lawyer, he must have recognized were at best inadequate and at worst evasive and entirely unconvincing. In that, he performed no differently to anyone else who had been saddled with trying to defend the official findings in the case of ZD576.

According to journalists who have been discreetly briefed by the MOD, it is apparent that officialdom is not going to give an inch. So a debate in the House of Lords seems inevitable. And, no doubt, there will be another debate in the Commons too. Consequently, Lord Chalfont has, for a second time, written directly to the Prime Minister pointing out that these debates are likely to encompass matters well beyond ZD576 itself, such as 'the constitutional position of government departments vis-à-vis Parliament, natural justice, human rights, etc'. In short, which is the sovereign body? Parliament or the MOD? Interesting. No one in Whitehall will be able to say that they were not warned . . .

And there, as this book has to meet a publishing deadline, we must leave the story. Only one point remains – it will already be obvious to everyone except, it seems, to the Ministers, their MOD advisors and, of course, the two Air Marshals. For that reason alone it is worth repeating. At the press conference following the release of the Report by the Lords Committee, Michael Tapper put it very simply:

> The reputation of my son and of Flt Lt Cook is no longer in question; it is now the reputation of the MOD which is the issue.

One might stretch charity to the limit and suggest that the MOD does not realize the nature of its problem. But that would be too simple. The MOD is well aware of its difficulties. What it cannot bring itself to do is to admit any possibility that it and the Air Marshals might be even slightly mistaken, let alone that they are almost wholly in error. As so often in Whitehall, the investment in an official version of events is now so great that any reappraisal is impossible. Once again, the place is stuck in the concrete of its own pouring. Honour and honesty have become secondary to sticking to a long-agreed 'line'. No one in authority has the guts to break ranks. So the MOD will go on making statements claiming that it is wholly right and everyone else is wholly wrong. In this, it will not even convince itself.

SINCE THE CHAPTER ABOVE was finished in the autumn of 2002 there have been three interesting developments relevant to the story of ZD576. The first is best intimated by a written Parliamentary Question put by David Davis a year later, on 5 November 2003.

> David Davis: To ask the Secretary for Defence if he will make a statement on the release to service of the Mark 3 Chinook helicopters.

While the bare facts that prompted that question are straightforward, their potential for the embarrassment of the MOD, not least in the matter of ZD576, is enormous.

First, the bare facts: between July 2001 and May 2002, the RAF took delivery of a batch of eight new Chinooks. At the time of writing (May 2004), it has had no operational use from any of them so far.

Now, the detail: in late 1995, the MOD (Procurement) contracted with Boeing for a variation of the Chinook. It would be known as the Mark 3. Each one would cost over £24 million. The first (of eight) was scheduled for delivery in late 1998; the others would follow over the next eighteen months. They were primarily (but not solely) designed as 'special operations' aircraft – equipped for deep penetration into hostile or, at least, uncertain territory. As such they would have extra fuel tanks, a forward-looking infra-red searchlight and a whole array of specialized electronics too secret to be talked about. Much less secret is the fact that each aircraft would have 'new and improved' Fadecs.

Delivery of the first of the new aircraft was over two years late. *Jane's Defence Weekly*, a journal with its ear firmly to the ground on these things, reported that 'according to the MOD, the delay has been caused by software problems'. Within the RAF's helicopter squadrons, where the tragedy of ZD576 is still far from forgotten, there were those who quietly observed that 'software problems' sounded all too familiar. Others, higher up the RAF's managerial ladder, were more concerned that the delay almost certainly presaged a further slippage in the delivery schedule of the other seven aircraft. That premonition was well founded: the last of those eight aircraft was not shipped out from Boeing until May 2002 – two years late. Whether this was Boeing's fault or that of the MOD (with late specification changes?) or both is not clear.

Anyway, Air Vice Marshall David Niven, CO of Helicopter Command, had cause to be worried. The Mark 3s, he said, 'can't come too soon' as 'there is a perceived shortfall in airframes [i.e. helicopters] due to new key tasks created by the formations of 16 Air Assault Brigade, the commissioning of two new amphibious ships and the late running Merlin Mk 3 programme'.[21] In short, just as with the Mark 2 nearly ten years earlier, there was real pressure to get the new Chinooks into squadron service as quickly as possible – as soon as Boscombe Down had cleared them for operational flying. But therein lay a problem: Boscombe Down was being sticky. Which would seem to be one of the reasons why today, more than eight years after the contract was placed, and well over two-and-a-half years after the last of the batch was delivered to the UK, the RAF has still not flown any of its Mark 3s operationally.

In a letter replying to that question from David Davis – a letter written by the MOD's Air Secretariat but signed by Adam Ingram, the Minister for the Armed Forces – the MOD blandly avoids any hint of a problem.

> Of the eight helicopters procured, one temporarily remains at Boeing to support any future upgrade programmes. The remaining seven aircraft have, since their delivery in 2001, been undergoing full Military Aircraft Release (MAR) trials at Boscombe Down – part of the standard acceptance procedure for all aircraft. Of the seven helicopters at Boscombe Down, three are actively supporting [i.e. being used for] the MAR trials; the remaining four aircraft are in storage pending their Release To Service clearance.

In translation, this means that over two-and-a-half years after the last of the batch was delivered, the new Chinook was still undergoing acceptance trials. Clearly, this is not as it should be. Certainly, such delay is not 'standard procedure'. Elsewhere, in its 2001–02 Performance Report (Annex F), the MOD is equally cool in attributing the hold-up (though it does not

21. The Merlin is a troop-carrying helicopter built by Westland; it is single-rotored and smaller than the Chinook.

seem to recognize it as such) to the necessity of fitting a combined cockpit voice recorder and flight data recorder to each aircraft – as strongly recommended by the inquiries following the crash of ZD576. Because of this requirement, the MOD reports (on one of the very few occasions when it actually uses the word 'delay') that the Mark 3's 'full operating capability will be delayed until 2005'. That is four years after delivery. This is all the more amazing given that a CVR/FDR unit is essentially no more than a 'bolt-on' component; it is not an integral part of any other system – with the knock-on and delaying effects that that would inevitably involve. Fitting such a unit is relatively straightforward – certainly it is not a job that need take more than a week or two. To many observers it is extraordinary that seven £24 million aircraft should (if one is to believe that Performance Report) remain grounded and useless for yet a *further* two years (until 2005) for lack of CVR/FDR units. After all, it is nine years since it was decided that all Chinooks should be fitted with such units. If it really is the case that not enough units were ordered from the manufacturer (to equip all the aircraft), it is a revealing indictment of the procurement abilities of the MOD. It is akin to building a fleet of tank transporters but forgetting to order the proper heavy-duty tyres.

To many people who take an interest in these things, the official reasoning about those CVR/FDR units is just not believable. They look for some other reason to explain why, after nearly four years, none of the seven aircraft in the UK will have entered service. There does not seem much doubt that the real problem lies within Boscombe Down. Given that the test personnel at that establishment are rightly (but inconveniently) unlikely to spill any beans, and that the MOD appears not to recognize (not publicly anyway) any significant problem, one must rely on detective work and an informed hunch or two.

One obvious possibility points toward that 'new and improved' software. By far and away the most significant item of software in a Chinook is the Fadec – one to each engine. Despite the improvements made to that software since 1994, and despite the Air Marshals' verdict on ZD576 (that Fadec played no part in the crash), it is no secret that the equipment still occasionally goes into a 'run-up, run-down or torque split'. In lay language, that means that, with little or no warning, one or other of the two Fadecs can cause an engine to accelerate, decelerate or to lose synchronization between itself and the other engine. These things are uncomfortable enough in benign flying conditions, but, if the terrain or the weather or the even the enemy are unfavourable, things can become hazardous very quickly.

A popular narrative among those who take an unofficial interest in these things goes like this: when Boscombe Down expressed its doubts (and that may be putting it mildly) about the Mark 3, for whatever reason, there could be no question of the MOD and the RAF high command reacting in the way they had in the case of the Mark 2. This time they could not, in order to get the new aircraft into service, simply overrule Boscombe Down by introducing a weight restriction (or whatever) and then hoping for the best. If any aircraft thus 'released' were later to crash due to an equipment failure, it would inevitably and very publicly bring the still-simmering controversy surrounding the injustices of ZD576 back up to boiling point. The corporate embarrassment to the MOD and the personal humiliation of the two Air Marshals (now retired) would be enormous. So, better not to take the risk. Instead, four of the new aircraft would be tucked away in a hangar and the other three would be involved in a continuing but increasingly desultory programme of trials. Anyway, whatever the theories, there is no doubt that helicopters worth nearly £200 million are now doing nothing useful. If any MP or journalist starts to ask difficult questions, they will be told – in the well-worn tradition – as little as possible. But whether the MOD will be able to withstand the probing of the Public Accounts Select Committee (PAC), which, in the spring of this year (2004), is set to examine the whole Mark 3 story, is another matter.[22]

In fact, it is very doubtful if any of the Mark 3s could fly operationally even if a 'release' were suddenly to come through tomorrow. Given that they were (and still are) of no use to the RAF, they have been cannibalized to provide spares for the earlier marks of Chinook flying in Iraq and Afghanistan. Some of their classified equipment has also been transferred

22. The Public Accounts Committee may also be asking questions of the MOD about the 'cold storage' of some dozens of Apache helicopters. These are primarily designed as anti-tank aircraft. But it is said that there are not enough pilots trained to fly them and, also, that there is a problem with their anti-tank rockets – 'debris' from the actual firing can sometimes 'interfere' with the tail rotors.

to squadrons in the Middle East. There has even been a failed attempt to see if the Americans would like to buy them back from the MOD/RAF.

We have not heard the last of the official absurdities that surround the Chinook – both the Mark 3 and ZD576.

THE SECOND DEVELOPMENT in the story of ZD576 derives from Boeing's second computer simulation of ZD576's flight path and pattern immediately before the crash. Unlike the first simulation, this new one was properly based on a Fadec-equipped Chinook. To the surprise of some, the results and the data from which those results were derived eventually became available (from Boeing) for detailed inspection by critics of the original simulation. All the experts who have examined the new information (except, it seems, those in the direct employ of the MOD) are agreed that this second simulation is more accurate, thorough and revealing than the first. Even Boeing agrees, with some embarrassment, that its earlier statistics – quite apart from the fact that they were based on the wrong helicopter – were 'unfortunate'.

The plain fact is that the second simulation differs from the first in all those areas – speed, height, power and aircraft attitude – on which the two Air Marshals relied in order to 'confirm' their case against the pilots. The flight path during the last thirty or forty seconds of ZD576 was almost certainly quite different to the one on which the official verdict is based. For example, the second simulation shows that the air speed at the moment of impact may have been nearly 20 knots slower than that first postulated (130 knots rather than almost 150 knots). Again, the first simulation proposed a 'mid-range' power output from the engines; the second indicated that they were at full, even emergency power. The first had ZD576 at 468 feet (plus or minus 50 feet) as it approached the coast; the second showed that this figure might have been wrong by as much as 50 per cent. In another area, Boeing acknowledges that the angle of bank (at the moment of impact) as postulated in the first simulation is not consistent with the evidence of the wreckage – a point made by a number of Chinook pilots since the very beginning. There are other discrepancies.

In short, the new data throws even greater doubt (if that were possible) on the claim by the two Air Marshals that their verdict of gross negligence was based 'certain and undoubted facts'. If the second simulation is to be believed, every aspect of those official 'facts' is shown to be wrong. But the MOD's Air Secretariat and the Air Marshals remains quite impervious – as in so many other examples in this book – to any data that does not fit with its own authorized version of events. This collective blindness surely qualifies for associate membership of the Flat Earth Society.

EARLIER IN THIS CHAPTER, ONE can find the thought that 'the investment in the official version of events is now so great that any reappraisal is impossible'. That assessment is classically demonstrated once again in a third recent development. It stems from a 'deliverance' (a resolution) passed at the 2003 annual gathering of the General Assembly of the Church of Scotland. This is an important body composed of 'commissioners' from every presbytery (a group of parishes) in the land. In the view of many Scots it clearly outranks the recently devolved government of Scotland. Certainly, it is at least as well respected. (That new government, since its formation, has borrowed the Church's meeting chamber in Edinburgh for its sessions.)

By all accounts it was an impressive moment. Following a thoughtful discussion as to how best to present the case, over six hundred 'commissioners' now rose and stood silently – to signify their unanimous approval of the proposal that a letter be written to the MOD asking it 'to revisit the issue of the crash of ZD576'. The Assembly 'continued to be troubled and disturbed' by the 'verdict' of eight years earlier. Only on very particular occasions does the Assembly stand to 'register' its feelings; normally, the commissioners remain seated and merely signify their approval with a low murmur.

A letter was duly sent, which of course drew much strength from quoting the dissenting conclusions of the three judicial and quasi-judicial bodies that had already examined the affair: Sheriff Young's Fatal Accident Inquiry, the House of Lords Select Committee and the Commons Public Accounts Committee.

The MOD's reply, when it came some weeks later, was as full of inventions and self-serving sophistries as ever. It is worth listing a few of the more blatant examples because they neatly encapsulate what one is up against when trying to talk to the flat-earth official mind about almost anything. Black becomes white, in becomes out, and up becomes down.

First comes the patronizing Putdown-cum-Invention: 'The MOD has every sympathy for the families of both the crew and the passengers. It has to be said, however, that the repeated review of the accident, with accompanying media interest, can only add to the grief of the families.' Where is the evidence for this convenient assertion? (It is one often advanced by official bodies anxious to see embarrassing bygones discreetly buried and forgotten.) In fact, in the aftermath of ZD576 it seems that no one involved in lobbying for justice has been asked by any relative to desist. If anything, the contrary would seem to be the case: many relatives evidently draw some comfort from the fact that the scandal has not been buried. Obviously, when it suits, the MOD will make these things up as it goes along. It invents.

Elsewhere, under the heading of Blatant Sophistry, is an attempt to downplay Sheriff Young's damning criticism (in his FAI finding) with the risible assertion that 'the purpose of the FAI was somewhat different from that of the RAF Board of Inquiry; the former being to determine the cause of death, whilst the latter was to ascertain the cause of the accident . . .'. Absolutely not so – another invention. The cause of death (as shown on the death certificates) would have been 'multiple injuries', or a close synonym for that phrase. Sheriff Young did not need to hear sixteen days of evidence to work that out. The fact is that he was every bit as interested in the *cause of the accident* as was the RAF. While he was unable to come to a firm conclusion, he was very specific when he came to comment on the verdict of the two Air Marshals: 'the competence and skill of the crew are . . . invidiously called into question in a speculative manner'.

Another MOD invention: it says that the Sheriff's findings 'do not justify setting aside the conclusions of a very thorough RAF investigation, carried out by experts with first-hand experience of Chinooks'. This is worse than a mere half-truth. The 'verdict' of the three-man Board of Inquiry (experts every one) was indefinite; in its own words, 'There were many potential causes of the accident and despite detailed and indepth analysis, the Board was *unable* to determine a definite cause'. So the three-man Board most certainly did *not* conclude that the pilots had been guilty of 'gross negligence'. Neither did the CO of RAF Odiham, the home base of all Chinooks. Nor for that matter did the Air Accident Investigation Branch. The *only* people who found the pilots guilty of gross negligence (i.e. manslaughter) were the two Air Marshals, one of whom (ACM Wratten) had never flown a Chinook in his life. That leaves just one man, AVM Day, who could reasonably claim to be an expert on the Chinook. Even so, his experience was on the Mark 1, which, of course, was not equipped with Fadec.

In the same inventive vein is the MOD's concluding assertion: 'There is not a single known fact that does not fit the conclusion that this tragic accident was a controlled flight into terrain.' This nonsense is, of course, merely parroting the two Air Marshals. And they, as we already know, were utterly and unanimously demolished on this exact point by the House of Lords 'Chinook' Committee; it underlined 'a reliance on matters treated as facts which have been demonstrated to our satisfaction to be not facts but merely hypotheses or assumptions'. The Air Marshals' 'hypotheses' and 'assumptions' had, of course, been largely based on that first, and suspect, Boeing simulation. (When the results of the second simulation were released in 2002, the Lords Committee saw no reason to go back and revise its earlier strictures.)

If the MOD supposed that its reply would bamboozle the elders of the Church of Scotland into silence, it underestimated the Scots. Indeed, they felt angry and insulted that anyone could think them so stupid. MPs were alerted and a further letter was drafted.

> The MOD seems to demand that the normal juridical rules be turned on their head by insisting on evidence to prove innocence. No such evidence is necessary.
>
> To presume, in the face of the Fatal Accident Inquiry, the House of Lords Committee and the Commons Public Accounts Committee, that the MOD came to a correct judgement on this matter is certainly to display a lack of humility . . .

We will see. The Church of Scotland is not likely to give up – which, given the myopia of the MOD, is just as well.

On 2 June 2004 a commemorative service was held at the cairn that now stands on the crash site of ZD576. Ten years have passed. Let's hope that justice, though slow in coming, will finally be delivered.

GULF WAR SYNDROME

'We have nothing to hide'

We do not believe it is a syndrome. It is just some symptoms we don't have an explanation for.

Lieutenant Colonel Douglas Hart, a Pentagon spokesman, 1993

A common feature of the media coverage has been its alarmist nature. Investigations of the allegations have revealed them to be a mixture of unsubstantiated rumour, incorrect information or repetition of earlier allegations which have been fully investigated and found to be unsupported by the facts.

MOD statement, 9 December 1994

The MOD's Medical Assessment Programme appeared to be trying to find a diagnosis not related to the Gulf War. When none was found, they were not interested in looking beyond that with an open mind. Having an open mind in medicine and science is essential.

An army doctor (reservist) who served in the Gulf

THE MEETING HAD BEEN a waste of time. Indeed, some thought it a disaster. They emerged down the steps of the MOD, just off Whitehall, and clustered on the pavement for a few minutes before dispersing across London to various main-line stations and then home. They had hoped for better; they were disconsolate and rather angry. 'You'd think that we were making it all up,' someone said. 'They didn't want to know,' commented another.

The meeting had ended a few minutes earlier. On one side of the long table had sat the minister, Nicholas Soames, flanked by eleven civil servants and advisors. On the other side were seven ex-servicemen and women who, three years before, had served in the Gulf. They had hoped to bring a doctor or a scientist or perhaps a lawyer with them, but they had been advised by the MOD that this would 'not be necessary'. So now, on behalf of nearly 1000 ex-servicemen who had earlier formed a Gulf Veterans' Association, they were explaining their concern about what they saw as a very real problem: too many of their colleagues had unexplained illnesses which seemed to derive from their service in the Gulf.[1]

The Veterans' Association laid out its argument: that in correspondence going back more than two years the MOD seemed remote and dismissive, even obstructive. Evidence was presented to demonstrate that although, as time went by, more veterans rather than fewer were 'reporting' sick – with a widening variety of physical and neurological problems – there seemed to be a reluctance by the MOD to release medical records to help GPs and hospital consultants make diagnoses which might lead to treatment. Was it true that few such records existed anyway? Had they been destroyed? Certainly no one seemed to know just which or how many vaccines had been given to whom. And if they *did* know, the MOD was not telling: 'Regrettably, some of that information is classified.' Then there was the denial that insect sprays containing organophosphate (OP) had been used in the Gulf, let alone that they had sometimes been used in dangerous, harmful quantities. According to the MOD, no supplies of OP insecticides had been ever issued; only harmless pyrethrum-based sprays had been used in the Gulf. This assertion, given the first-hand experience of some of the veterans – they had got translations made of the Arabic labels on the containers – brought sighs of frustration. Following that, they tried raising the matter of the tablets they had all had to take against the possibility of gas attack. What about the key ingredient, pyridostigmine bromide? Among some of the troops at the time it had seemed to cause vomiting, diarrhoea, heavy sweating and even, as someone now said, 'fuzziness in the head'. So what about its less obvious, long-term effects? The confident reply was that there were no long-term effects. The same assured answer came to worries about depleted uranium ammunition: 'We've done a lot of testing of the stuff over the years. If you handle it according to the regulations, there are no hazards – short or long term.' This was probably true – as far as it went. But what about the dust and detritus of the ammunition after it had hit its target?

1. This account is based on the recollections of two Gulf War veterans who were at the meeting.

Then there were questions about the Medical Assessment Programme recently set up by the MOD at an RAF hospital in Wiltshire. What was it looking for? Was its purpose to get to the bottom of the problem, or to confirm the official stance that there was no problem?

On all these and other matters there was a good deal of distrust, and tempers became edgy at times – on the veterans' side. On the MOD side there was the studied forbearance of those who felt that they were being thoroughly reasonable, but whose patience was being stretched rather thin. They were, in any case, quite confident that they were right – and had not much to fear even if it should later be shown that they might have got one or two administrative details wrong.

Several times, as the coffee and biscuits came round again, Mr Soames, in what those facing him felt was an overly avuncular manner, set out the official argument, as he would do a little later on television: 'Of course, we are sympathetic. But we cannot accept that there is any connection between these illnesses and service in the Gulf. Yes, it is true that people who served in the Gulf are now ill, but there is no common link to any of those illnesses that can be associated with a syndrome that could be called a Gulf War Syndrome.' Mr Soames acknowledged that he was 'not a medical man' but was acting on the advice of those who were – like the staff of the MOD's Medical Services Directorate. 'Compassion must go hand-in-hand with scientific rigour' was a phrase he used. At least one of the veterans reflected that it would be more convincing if any research of 'scientific rigour' had actually been commissioned by the MOD. At one point there seemed to be a suggestion from the 'official' side of the table that some veterans might even be motivated by the smell of eventual compensation for their alleged ills. That may well have been true of a few, but did that suggestion mean everyone was thought of as a possible malingerer?

The Minister's confident formula of denials brought nods of agreement from his supporters. There was, one of them was keen to emphasize (starting with, as a veteran recalls, the standard 'May I come in here, Minister?'), no evidence that there was anything special about any of the illnesses some of the veterans were allegedly suffering; indeed, the very same complaints were found in the general population and in about the same proportions. There was disagreement from the veterans' side of the table; they had statistics which showed that this was not the case at all. Furthermore, if the implication was that the MOD really had commissioned a statistical or epidemiological study, why had the veterans not heard about it? After all, without their participation, where could the MOD be getting the raw data for such research? But the MOD people were unmoved; the unspoken implication was: 'Our experts – even if you don't know about them – are better than your experts.' Anyway, in this whole affair the Minister and his civil servants were the masters, whereas the veterans were merely supplicants, amateurs. So when all was said and done, That Was That, as it often is when 'ordinary' people attempt to tackle Whitehall.

No wonder the ex-servicemen thought the meeting had been a waste of time. Mr Soames and his entourage probably thought much the same thing.

TWO DIVISIONS OF Saddam Hussein's Republican Guard entered Kuwait City early on 2 August 1990; two armoured divisions went through the city – getting temporarily lost in the streets and highways – before they rumbled on further south. Within twenty hours it was over; there was no formal surrender or capitulation. Even though the political and military signs had been there for months, the international 'community' still managed to be both surprised and appalled by what had happened. Perhaps it was this unanimity of shock which helped President Bush, because once he had set his mind to it (with a nudge from Margaret Thatcher: 'Don't be wobbly, George'), he was able, remarkably, to stitch together a coalition force of more than twenty countries. For once, most of the western world – and parts of the eastern one, too – were in accord. But accord was one thing; getting a fighting force into position was another.

There was an anxious time early on when the Coalition was openly committed to confront Saddam militarily, yet did not have enough troops on the ground to do anything but argue the toss at the UN. Perhaps it was the US Navy and its Cruise missiles that deterred the Iraqi dictator from venturing into Saudi Arabia and overrunning the advance units of the Coalition. Given the length of the supply lines and the enormous logistical difficulties, the build-up of forces was remarkable and rapid – surely a tribute to that most American of characteristics: Can Do. By Christmas there were nearly 800,000 men deployed in the Gulf and along the Iraqi border. Nearly 700,000 were American. The British sent 53,000.

The air war began in mid-January – led, of course, by America. Each evening the world watched the view from cameras in the noses of 'smart' bombs. The ground war started five weeks later. It was over in just under 100 hours. From a military viewpoint it was one of the swiftest and most decisive of victories. The first troops were home by late March.

None of this could have been predicted beforehand, during the anxious build-up through the autumn and early winter of 1990.

During those preparations, sometime in October, the MOD quietly asked hospitals up and down the country to earmark more than 1000 beds. It was a wise precaution. If the worst came to the worst and Saddam Hussein did not back down – and it seemed increasingly unlikely that he would – the beds were to be ready to take incoming casualties from the Gulf. At the same time a high proportion of doctors and medical personnel were recalled to the Reserve Forces and readied for service. It was the same in the United States. The Pentagon flew 120,000 zippered body bags to the Gulf. Britain made do with several hundred black plastic bin liners.

Once the build-up of men and arms had been completed, and the air assault had begun, there was not much doubt that, in a conventional war, the Coalition forces would win – quickly and with a limited number of casualties. So why all those beds? Why all those body bags and bin liners? Why all those doctors and nurses? Because, in the minds of those who had to think about these things, there was one overriding concern: Saddam Hussein might do the unthinkable. He might resort to chemical and biological weapons. There was no doubt he had both. And he had the means of delivering them. Through the 1980s he had been sold the raw materials for 'manufacturing' anthrax, smallpox and plague by, among others, Britain, the US, Germany and Russia. And even earlier, he had similarly acquired the means to manufacture nerve gases. But at that time Iran, not Saddam's Iraq, was the enemy. The Americans had not forgotten the humiliation in 1979 of seeing their embassy in Tehran besieged and then occupied by the Ayatollah's 'students'. Nearly 100 staff members were held hostage for over a year. So while Saddam was at war with Iran, he 'might have been a son-of-a-bitch, but at least he was our son-of-a-bitch'.

From Russia he imported the Scud missiles to carry his gases and toxins to any destination within 250 miles of their launch. Nor had he hesitated to use poison gas: first, during his war against Iran and, later, to terrorize his own troublesome Kurds. Now, against the possibility that he might be tempted again, America let him know that she 'had a range of options' should Iraq be foolish enough to use chemical weapons against the Coalition. Would this deliberately ambiguous threat, with its hint of possible nuclear retaliation, be enough to deter? At the time there was no sure way of knowing if the Iraqi dictator would see sense. There was always the possibility that, in a suicidal fit of madness and to even the balance of forces, he might use his chemical and biological weapons again.

Against that possibility the Allies took a range of counter-measures – vaccines, tablets and sprays. These were the prophylactics which, since the war, have come under ever-growing suspicion as the cause of problems not properly researched at the time. But, as well as the prophylactics, there were other potential hazards whose full potency seems not to have been recognized until too late – toxic smoke from oil fires, nerve gases from demolished Iraqi arms dumps, and ammunition made from depleted uranium. In fact, worries about the latter were beginning to be talked about and published among scientists during the 1970s but were wishfully ignored.

It makes sense to begin with the prophylactics.

First, the vaccines. While many of the 'shots' were given in Britain before departure, such was the hurry to get men out to the Gulf that some of the vaccines were not administered until the troops were in the desert. By this stage there was neither the time nor the medical personnel for a formal programme of treatment. The priority was simply to get protective vaccines into the men as quickly as possible. Usually, it was a case of: 'Right you lot, sleeves up and get fell in for y'shots.' Not surprisingly, the normal nicety of 'informed consent' did not really come into it. One wonders why the MOD should later have insisted that it did; there simply was not the time. One took what one was given. And if you refused, your name was likely to be listed on your unit's orders. The standard procedure was for five or six injections to be given at once – both arms. Then the medical team would hurry on to the next unit. Including 'boosters', as many as fourteen injections could be given within a few days. Indeed, some soldiers were later to claim that they had had a total of eighteen jabs, with as many as ten in a single day.

It must have seemed to the troops that they were getting a cocktail of almost every vaccine known to man. Besides 'standard' shots for tetanus, cholera, typhoid, diphtheria, polio, measles and smallpox, there were others for hepatitis A and B, yellow fever and whooping cough. Then there were shots for botulinum (anti-toxin), bubonic plague and anthrax. It was known that Saddam Hussein had experimented with the last three. Lastly, there were several vaccines that were, apparently, on the secret list. One of these may have been tularaemia (rabbit fever), another may have been squalene; the latter is not a vaccine in its own right, but an adjuvant – a booster to make other vaccines more effective. In the US, as a result of independent and privately funded research, it has come under considerable suspicion. Another area of doubt centres on the fact that anthrax vaccine was combined with pertussis vaccine (whooping cough); animal experiments have shown this 'mixture' to be very debilitating – perhaps permanently so. Some of the laboratory creatures died.

The MOD has refused to publish a list of all the vaccines given to the troops. 'The information is classified' – which makes a nonsense of its reassurances three years after the war to the Commons Defence Committee that no vaccines were given without prior 'informed consent'. Ask almost any Gulf veteran, and they will tell you: 'Half the time we hadn't a clue what we were getting.' Perhaps the MOD has had second thoughts, because it has lately conceded that, in this matter of consent, troops in the Gulf were sometimes subject to what it now calls 'robust persuasion'. Anyone who has ever faced a sergeant major in full spate will know about 'robust persuasion'. They would be able to assure the Whitehall warriors that it has very little to do with 'consent', informed or otherwise.

Anyway, other than feeling 'thoroughly bloody' for a few days (the officers) or 'right fucked' ('the lads'), most people 'survived'. But some took much longer to recover. And a few reacted so violently that they had to be flown home.

Then there were the tablets. Along with the issue to every man of a respirator (gas mask) and a multi-layered, top-to-toe 'Noddy' suit to protect against nuclear, biological and chemical (NBC) attack, everyone was required to take three 'Nerve Agent Pre-treatment' tablets a day. These NAP tablets were designed, as the name implies, to pre-arm the body against nerve agents – poison gases like soman. They were primarily to give protection during the few minutes it took to get into one of those suits.

Saddam had used gas against the Kurds and the Iranians. In scientific parlance, nerve agents 'irreversibly inhibit the enzyme acetyl cholinesterase. Inactivation of the enzyme leads to the accumulation of acetylcholine at the cholinergic synapses.' In lay language, sarin, soman and other nerve agents 'block' significant parts of the nervous system – those parts which control basic body functions such as breathing, heartbeat, digestion, sweating, defecation, sight. They do this by inhibiting the enzyme which normally 'neutralizes' a nerve signal once it has delivered its message to a muscle. This 'neutralizing' is vital because without it, muscles and nerves become overloaded and overstimulated. In a sense, they become totally confused; the body goes into uncontrollable spasms that become increasingly violent. According to the dose, death follows within minutes or hours. And there is nothing gentle about this way of dying.

Research had long shown that the drug which is the key ingredient in the NAP tablets, pyridostigmine bromide (PB), is a partial answer to those nerve agent gases. It stops their 'blocking' effect – though, for a time, it can induce side effects akin to the very problems (like muscle weakness) it is meant to prevent. Furthermore, it is only effective if it is already in place *before* a chemical attack – as a pre-treatment. And, because its protective effect is short-lived, one has to keep taking it – a 30mg tablet three times a day. Given that for over forty years PB has been used at dosages as high as 600mg per day in the treatment of myasthenia gravis (a disease attacking the nerve receptors in muscles), it was concluded that the taking of a mere 30mg every eight hours by fit young soldiers was most unlikely to cause any problems. It may not have been that simple: no one had thought through what might happen when PB was taken alongside all the other prophylactics.

Next there were the sprays – the insecticides. These were used to protect against bites from insects carrying diseases such as sand-fly fever; the fever is hardly ever less than incapacitating; it has been known to kill. It was remembered from the last time that large numbers of British troops had fought in a desert, in North Africa in 1941 and 1942, that a proportion had gone down with insect-born illnesses. The desert is far from the sterile environment sometimes supposed. The most effective modern sprays contain organophosphates (OPs). These are also used in sheep dip to deter ticks and, since the use of such dips became compulsory in Britain, a number of sheep farmers have suffered mental and physical problems, some severe. OPs are chemically related to nerve gas. Therein lies the problem.

The Whitehall authorities had long claimed that if indeed there was a problem attributable to the sheep dip, it was because the farmers had failed to observe recommended precautions, and because they had obviously used the dip at strengths far greater than those laid down by the manufacturers. Anyway, the MOD asserted that while some very small amounts of OP insecticides had been shipped out to the Gulf, only the standard (and milder) NATO-issue spray was actually used. This is a synthetically produced version of an earlier insecticide derived from an East African plant, pyrethrum. Further, the MOD reassuringly pointed out that quantities of this spray are sold every day in garden centres.

There were other precautions. Even the fighting vehicles which would advance into Iraq were given a special paint – CARC, or chemical agent resistant coating. This would neutralize or at least reduce the danger from the residue of any chemical fumes or gases through which the vehicle might pass. The fact that there were some unanswered questions about the possible toxicity of CARC itself was not a priority. The troops themselves were constantly drilled in the rapid donning of their multi-layered NBC suits. And the alarm call 'Gas! Gas! Gas!' required the fitting of respirators in eight seconds. The NBC suit took longer; you needed the help of your 'oppo': it was a two-man job. Quite how one would fight in such garb was something the troops hoped that they would never need to find out.

If Saddam Hussein did decide to use elements of his toxic armoury, the forces of the Coalition would be as well prepared as science could make them. That was the idea. Obviously while all these prophylactic measures were being taken during the 'build-up', plans were being made for far more aggressive action. Once the air war started, attacks would be mounted against Saddam's communication centres, airfields and aircraft, radar stations, bridges, command bunkers and ammunition dumps. If, in those dumps, Saddam did indeed have stocks of chemical or biological weapons – and there were intelligence and satellite clues that he did – they would be 'taken out' as early as possible.

While Saddam Hussein was promising 'The Mother of all Battles', the press releases from General Schwarzkopf's American HQ were less colourful: 'We are confident that Iraq's military infrastructure will be so degraded from the air that its army will be unable to mount an effective defence on the ground.' And that, despite a few early hiccups in the air, was the way it turned out. True, the world held its breath when Saddam launched Scuds at Israel, also sending some off towards Saudi Arabia and the Coalition bases on the Gulf, but while the Scuds made the headlines, they did nothing to deflect the Coalition's purpose. Anyway, some of them seemed to have been travelling without explosive warheads. Maybe Saddam was just showing the Coalition what he could do if so minded.

So effective was the five weeks of air bombardment that when the ground forces eventually went in, some infantrymen never fired a shot in anger; some armoured units fired fewer shells in action than they had weeks before on the practice ranges; some soldiers never saw any Iraqi troops until they had surrendered. None of this is to downplay the skills of the advancing troops; at the time there were indications that Iraq's elite units, like the Republican Guard, might offer very stiff resistance. In the event, those air attacks had been decisive. Casualties were much lighter than had been anticipated – forty-nine British were killed and about 300 wounded, far fewer than in the Falklands; 198 Americans were killed and about 700 injured or wounded. Sadly, too high a proportion of both killed and wounded were due to the mistake of 'friendly fire' from the air.

Many of the men were home by early April. The reservists from the supporting arms returned to 'civvy street', the regulars to their quarters in the UK and Germany. True, there were some questions about the reliability of the SA80 rifle in desert conditions; the engines in the Challenger tanks had given trouble in the dust; our 'smart' bombs were not always smart enough; and our Tornado bombers had been too vulnerable when flown in low-level attacks. But those were problems for the top brass at the MOD to sort out. For most people, coming home brought a feeling of relief and a satisfied sense of 'been there, done that'.

THE ROYAL REGIMENT OF FUSILIERS, being an amalgamation of the Northumberland Fusiliers and other Fusilier Battalions, is predominantly a regiment of Geordies. Eighteen months after they had come home from the Gulf, a reunion was held at Castle Alnwick – the seat of the regiment's honorary Colonel in Chief, the Duke of Northumberland. Nearly 500 still serving and ex-Fusiliers turned up. The Duke made a short welcoming speech, the regimental band played through the afternoon and, over sausage rolls and strong tea, those who had now left the Army met their mates again and, as old soldiers always do, reminisced about the bad times and the good. But among the more thoughtful, gathered in small groups, there was another topic: some of 'the lads' were missing. It seemed that they had gone down with 'this Gulf thing' and did not feel well enough to come to the reunion. In fact, some of those who *had* come did not feel too good either. They compared notes. That was partly why they were there. For some it was a rather indefinable malaise and fatigue – sometimes combined with an erratic memory and patchy concentration. One breathless veteran remarked that too often he was just exhausted – like running on a very flat battery. Others agreed with him. Someone else said something about it being like AIDS without the HIV. Some had a more definable pattern of aches and pains in their joints; several complained that too frequently they just felt depressed or irritable and short-fused. Then there were stories about those who had not made it to the reunion. There was word of problems in several marriages. Two of the lads were said to be down with leukaemia. A baby had been born with thalidomide-like disabilities. And there were post-traumatic stress, the shakes, diarrhoea, rectal bleeding, eczema. Someone had run amok and gone to prison. There was even a rumour of a couple of suicides. Given that it was mostly anecdotal, there was bound to be some exaggeration. Nevertheless, it was worrying.

Nearly all of them had already concluded that their Gulf service must have had some relevance. Some had contacted the Royal British Legion. There had been several stories in the papers. Journalists had come up with terms like Desert Fever, Gulf Flu and Gulf War Syndrome. The last seemed to stick. What they wanted to do now was to meet others like themselves. What did *your* doctor say? Have you had any tests? Which ones? Why was the MOD being so unhelpful? Why do some people have problems while others are as right as rain? And why are there so many different problems? Do people get better with time? Or worse? Above all, why? And what's to be done?

Someone from the *Newcastle Chronicle and Journal* was there. The paper ran a story. A few days later, it carried an announcement of a public meeting for anyone who was interested. The organizers had to hire a bigger hall when they realized the numbers that were likely to come. Nearly 600 people turned up. It was standing room only. The Gulf Veterans' Association was formed – with an office right there in Newcastle. The British Legion got more involved. Not long afterwards, questions were asked in the House of Commons – by MPs with constituencies in the North East.

In the North West, too, there had been moves to set up some kind of centre for mutual support. Initially, it centred round Major Hill, a reservist in the Royal Army Medical Corps. He had been a senior operating theatre nurse. Before the war had even begun, he had sickened so severely that he had been evacuated by air back to the UK. Once home, he got rather better and, at that stage, was told he must have picked up some particularly virulent but passing desert bug. He disagreed. As the months went by and he failed to make a full recovery, he concluded that his problem was more directly attributable to his service than to some chance infection. It was not until after the war that he learnt there were others like him. And they learnt of him. The word spread. Major Hill, with his medical knowledge, almost inevitably found that he now became a one-man clearing house of advice for veterans centred in Lancashire and Cheshire. The National Gulf Veterans and Families Association (NGVFA) was formed. So now there were two organizations. While there was some overlap, rivalry even, over the years there has also been a good deal of co-operation.[2]

By the late autumn of 1992, there were over 1000 Gulf servicemen who in one way or another had 'registered' as being unwell. Some, thinking back, were suspicious of the mixture and number of vaccines 'thrown' at them. That was when they had first felt ill, so they were inclined to conclude that the vaccines were the problem – or at the very least, the vaccines had made them more susceptible to other problems. Others, remembering how they had felt while taking all those pills, pointed at the NAP tablets. Then there was that insecticide – wasn't that the same stuff they put in sheep dip? And what about the depleted uranium in those shells? A few said it was Saddam's Scuds. No one knew but everyone had a theory. And they all knew that they had been fit – fighting fit – before the Gulf.

In the face of the MOD's apparent apathy, there were several attempts by both the Veterans' Associations, backed by various MPs, to get the government to fund an independent inquiry. Official apathy now became official opposition. Mr Soames expressed the MOD's view to the Commons on 20 December 1994:

> In the absence of any confirmed scientific evidence that there is a health problem resulting from Gulf service, I do not believe that there are any grounds at present for such an inquiry.

Mr Soames was employing one of the MOD's favourite stratagems: the looping argument. 'We haven't got any evidence, so we would not be justified in looking for any.' Or, to put it more cynically, 'We won't look because we might find something.' Or, again, 'Because we can't find anything (not that we've looked too hard), we don't believe that anyone else

2. Major Hill's condition grew worse over the years. He had to give up the nursing home that he and his wife had built up through the 1980s. He also had to give up his role at the centre of the NGVFA. At fifty-four he died of an embolism and heart failure. Over 200 people, many of them veterans, were at his memorial service.

can.' Alice's Humpty Dumpty would have been proud of Mr Soames and his advisors.

In another document the MOD deliberately misses the point – another standard stratagem:

> In its investigations, the MOD has uncovered no evidence to support the allegations of a new or separate medical condition peculiar to service in the Gulf.

Apart from the fact that the MOD's investigations were minimal, very few people were suggesting that the illnesses were 'new or peculiar' to the Gulf – a fact the MOD knew full well. Nearly all of the 'illnesses', from lassitude though backache to leukaemia, had been around and identified for decades, some for centuries. What was being alleged was that they had, in this instance, been caused by service in the Gulf.

For three years the official answer in Parliament and beyond was always the same: there was no such thing as a 'Gulf War Syndrome'. The MOD seemed to argue that if some veterans had a problem then it must be in their minds. Autosuggestion perhaps. Almost everyone gets depressed at times, some even get tired – a few to the point of apparent exhaustion. And there is nothing unusual about feeling out of sorts, with occasional aches and pains. Ordinary civilians know all about these things – as they do about bleeding gums and premature hair loss. So why should servicemen be any different? Another thing: many of the health problems alleged by the veterans (especially the commonest complaint, chronic fatigue) showed no physical signs susceptible to diagnosis or effective treatment. This was a further indication that 'it was probably all in the mind' – like ME, yuppie flu and all those other 'fashionable' complaints about which, at the time, many doctors were quite unconvinced. Clearly this whole Gulf War 'thing' had been cooked up by some over-imaginative journalists who sensed a good story – nothing sells like a mystery, especially if one stirs in the possibility of a cover-up by Whitehall. If you tell people that they should feel sick, then some of them will. Yes, of course, there are a few returned soldiers who are genuinely ill – there always are. Anyway, how could such a wide variety of alleged illnesses be a 'syndrome', which (according to the definition chosen by the MOD) must be a condition common to all the sufferers?

That last point relied, rather typically, on semantics. The MOD had selected the narrowest definition of the word 'syndrome'. This then allowed it to argue that as a spread of problems ranging from irritability through aching joints to leukaemia and renal cancer could not possibly be a single condition stemming from a single cause, there could be no such thing as a Gulf War Syndrome. So what was all the fuss? This is the reason – despite the fact that there are other, broader definitions of a 'syndrome' – that some veterans prefer to talk about Gulf War Illnesses, in the plural.

Lest anyone supposes that the last few paragraphs have overdrawn the casualness of the MOD in the years following the Gulf conflict, it is worth quoting two paragraphs from its written submission of 9 December 1994 to the Commons Select Committee on Defence:

> In its note forwarded to the House of Commons Defence Committee on 12 October 1993, the Ministry of Defence outlined the position at that time concerning its investigations into allegations of a mystery illness affecting UK troops who had served in the Gulf conflict. This illness has been variously dubbed in the media as 'Desert Storm Syndrome', 'Desert Fever' and 'Gulf War Fever'. The note concluded that its investigation had uncovered no evidence to support the allegations of a new or separate medical condition peculiar to service in the Gulf.
>
> A common feature of the media coverage has been its alarmist nature and there is concern that this could cause unnecessary anxiety to those who served in the successful Gulf operation. Investigations of the allegations have revealed them to be a mixture of unsubstantiated rumour, incorrect information, or a repetition of earlier allegations which have been fully investigated and found to be unsupported by the facts. A number of individual Gulf UK veterans have featured in the media coverage and their stories of ill health are undoubtedly both convincing and touching. However, there has been a lack of objective scientific evidence in these articles and [TV] programmes to justify the quantum leap which is made linking their ill health to their service in the Gulf.

From that submission one is meant to suppose that the MOD had commissioned some thoroughgoing scientific research and, as it says, had 'fully investigated' the problem. It had hardly begun. Elsewhere in the same document the MOD made a number of statements of apparent fact, revealing some sloppy thinking. Under the heading 'Administration of anti-BW [Biological Warfare] vaccines', there appears the following passage:

> The Defence Committee has received a classified briefing from the MOD on this [vaccine] programme and specific details of the programme remain classified for operational reasons. This has been interpreted in the media and elsewhere as unnecessary secrecy and 'cover up', but in fact the material could still be useful to terrorists and potentially hostile intelligence services, and its continued classification is in order to protect those troops who may face a biological warfare threat in the future. There is no medical reason why the vaccines offered, which are in routine civilian use, should produce any long-term effects, even in combination.

This is purest spin. The Defence Committee was not impressed. Since when have vaccines against bubonic plague and botulinum been 'in routine civilian use'? And anthrax vaccine, though given to some sheep farmers and tannery workers, is hardly in routine use, and certainly not in risky combination with the pertussis vaccine. Furthermore, if some of the other vaccines are in such normal use, why do they 'remain classified for operational reasons'? And what does that phrase about the vaccines being 'offered' mean? It sounds as if the vaccinations were 'offered' to the troops on a voluntary basis. They were not – as any Gulf veteran, from general to private, will testify. Lastly, how does the MOD know that 'even in combination' the vaccines would produce 'no long-term effects'? There had been no 'long-term' tests of the combination, either in its own right or in association with the NAP tablets. Or, for that matter, in association with the third prophylactic, the organophosphate in the insecticide spray. There are medical scientists who see the possible interaction between those three 'insults' as what several have called 'the Triple Whammy'. They point to the well-known synergistic (i.e. amplifying) effect that several drugs in injudicious combination can have. Who knows? Certainly not the MOD.

The official assertion about 'no long-term effects' seems to be based on nothing more solid than wishful thinking. Indeed, it subsequently became known that late in 1990, just as the first troops were heading for the Gulf, the office of the Chief Medical Officer at the Ministry of Health had faxed the MOD with a very specific warning about the potential dangers of combining certain vaccines; one such was anthrax and whooping cough/pertussis. The fax was discovered in a file six years after the war. The 'directions for use' accompanying phials of plague vaccine advise that it should not be given at the same time as typhoid or cholera vaccines. Most GPs and clinics are reluctant to give simultaneous vaccinations against polio and yellow fever. And precaution against anthrax normally requires three injections spread over a minimum of five months; some Gulf soldiers received all their 'doses' on the same day.

In replying to critics it became clear that the MOD had not done its homework; it was making up its denials as it went along – and hoping no one would notice. Or that, in time, they would just forget. The tactic (if one can call it that) has been used for decades. It goes back at least as far as the British nuclear tests of the 1950s in the Australian desert, on the Portobello Islands and Christmas Island. Some of the servicemen who were involved in those experiments – those that did not develop cancers and are still alive nearly fifty years on – have long complained of skin, bone and immune-system problems for which nuclear radiation is seen to be a plausible explanation. At the same time there were experiments at Porton Down in which the servicemen/guinea pigs were told they were helping research into the common cold or malaria. Or that they were shortly to be posted to the tropics. Four decades on, in 1997, the Wiltshire Police reopened the files on several deaths and started a major investigation – Operation Antler. They have recently sent the papers through to the Crown Prosecution Service. There does not seem much doubt that we will be hearing more. For years, relatives have been consistently rebuffed by successive governments or, more specifically, by the medical establishment within the MOD. Prolonged denial by the more powerful party often results, eventually, in weary resignation by the weaker.

To return to the Triple Whammy: the scientific advisor to the Gulf Veterans' Association, Professor Malcolm Hooper, a medicinal chemist, summed up the situation when, in a long and detailed submission to that same Commons Defence Committee, he wrote:

> Never before have drugs and vaccines been administered in such quantities, in such a mixture, in such confused dosages, over such a condensed period of time, under such inadequate medical supervision . . . It is ironic that the vaccines used to protect against some of Iraq's biological weapons may themselves have caused the greater injury.

It was an accusation Whitehall has never effectively refuted. The best they can come up with seems to run along the lines of: 'Better some understandable confusion than to have run the risk of our troops being unprotected against chemical and/or biological attack.' Given the urgencies of the time, it is not a bad excuse. But it would be better, much better, if the MOD acknowledged that much more than mere 'confusion' was involved. It would be best of all if the MOD admitted that such a hurried and untested prophylactic programme carried inevitable risks – some of which have almost certainly come home to roost. It has been in its stubborn refusal to even consider this possibility, rather than in its genuine but deeply flawed efforts to prepare our servicemen for a new kind of war, that the MOD made one of its greatest public relations blunders. This is what has been called 'the cover-up'.

Things were not much better on the other side of the Atlantic. From the start, the Pentagon and Whitehall had marched in step. In the US more than ten times as many veterans thought there was something wrong with them – but then there had been more than ten times as many US servicemen in the Gulf. The Department of Defence (DOD) claimed their illnesses were wrongly attributed – that they had nothing to do with service in the Gulf. And, as in the UK, it was said that most of the fuss was generated by the media. True, in the US there were more programmes of research. Some were privately initiated and funded, others were funded by the DOD. But the US veterans were as suspicious of the latter as their British colleagues were of similar so-called research in the UK. And for the same reasons. There was another similarity too: the comments of the relevant Congressional Committee, after it had taken evidence from the Pentagon, matched those which were later to come from the Commons Defence Committee after it had heard from the MOD:

> We find these efforts irreparably flawed . . . plagued by arrogant incuriosity and pervasive myopia that sees lack of evidence as proof . . . The Federal Government all too often has a tin ear, a cold heart and a closed mind.

Nevertheless, the American public has always been rather more sensitive than the British to the needs of their ex-servicemen, especially the ones that come home 'less than whole'. They also had the saga of Agent Orange, the jungle defoliant used in Vietnam, behind them. That, too, had started with firm denials from the Pentagon that there could be any harmful effects. But when an abnormal proportion of birth defects was observed in the babies of servicemen who had handled or been close to the stuff, the DOD had to back off – a little. Perhaps it was these factors, plus a much-publicized push from Hillary Clinton, that forced the military authorities to start acting more positively. Apparently the First Lady had been appalled to learn from some army wives that, rightly or wrongly (and no one knew at the time), they attributed the defects in their own newborn babies to their husbands' service in the Gulf. The media played it for all it was worth – of course. There is the story, possibly apocryphal, of a Louisiana veteran whose thalidomide-like baby was being examined at an army hospital. The consultant physician commented that the child's defects could only be drug-induced: 'So what you been hitting, soldier?' Came the reply, 'On'y drugs I ever taken was what y'all in the military give me . . .'

Whatever the exact reasons, by 1996 the DOD had greatly increased its funding of research – to over £75 million, with more to come. The British are inclined to be superior about the way 'the Americans throw money at a problem in the hope that that will solve it', but for all the scorn, the MOD – which persuaded the Treasury to come up with just £4 million spread over three years – was happy enough to ride on the coat-tails of American research. 'A substantial number of ongoing US projects are being closely monitored' is a phrase (or its near equivalent) frequently found in statements coming out of the MOD since 1996. The translation seems to be, 'Why spend our money if the Yanks will spend theirs?' In fact, the DOD in Washington even began to fund research projects in the UK.

If, from late 1996, there was some slight easing in the Whitehall line on Gulf War Illnesses, it could have been due to a combination of reasons. Apart from reaction to the criticism coming from Parliament, there were at least two other causes. First was the realization that with the amount of privately funded research going on in the US – research that was not beholden to any government paymaster – someone over there might come up with something definitive which could blow apart a previously held 'denial' position and thereby torpedo the general credibility of the MOD. So, 'just in case', without actually giving any ground that mattered, it would be better to back off a little and appear to be slightly less rigid. And there was another factor which, without any doubt at all, dented the armour-plating of MOD infallibility: the unravelling of its long-standing denial about the use in the Gulf of organophosphates. This was the chemical that had caused the problem in sheep dip. In June 1995 in its written submission to the Commons Defence Committee the MOD was quite unequivocal:

> Organophosphate insecticides were available to British Forces in the Gulf but were not used on British personnel as the insect population was relatively low and pyrethroid [a much less toxic ingredient] was considered adequate.

The MOD continued its denial that OP insecticides had been used on or by British troops for a further seventeen months. No doubt it was mindful of a warning in the Health and Safety Executive's 1987 Guidance Note No. 17 which points to the fact that OP is a nerve agent in its own right:

> Acute and subacute exposure to OP pesticides can produce harmful effects in man, and repeated exposures at lower doses may cause insidious cumulative toxicity.

Earl Howe, Jeremy Hanley and Nicholas Soames, all Ministers at the MOD, voiced their successive assurances about the non-use of OPs in answer to Parliamentary Questions on four separate occasions. Then in October 1996 Mr Soames had to come back to the Commons to announce that he had been 'misled' by his advisors – civil servants and senior officers in the MOD's Medical Services Directorate. He had only just found out the truth: organophosphate sprays had indeed been used and in considerable quantities. What he did not mention (maybe he had not been told) was that the spraying had frequently been done at unknown strengths and, in some instances, by untrained and unsupervised local labour. He apologized for having misled the House, but, of course, it had not been his fault. The House would be pleased to know that he had ordered a thorough inquiry into how and why he had been 'misinformed'. Those responsible would be disciplined. No, he was not going to resign:

> The Government wishes to be entirely open about what happened during the Gulf conflict. I wish to stress, Madame Speaker, that we have nothing to hide and absolutely no reason to do so.

'So, that's all right then' was the inevitable comment among Gulf veterans. In fact, the relevant people in the MOD must have known the truth about OPs for some considerable time. And they could have known right from the beginning, years before, if, less blinkered, they had bothered to ask the right questions. Indeed, the insecticide despatched from the UK had quickly run out. So instructions were given for supplies of insecticide to be locally purchased in Saudi Arabia. Much of it was OP-based, but neither the quality nor the strength of these local materials was known. All this could have been learnt if Nicholas Soames and his supporters had taken seriously the assurances of the veterans at that 'waste of time' meeting more than two years earlier.

The deceit had begun to unravel when a letter to a Gulf veteran included (by mistake?) a copy of a 'restricted' internal MOD memo – Briefing Note No. 3, dated 19 July 1996. The note confirmed that organophosphate sprays had been used in the Gulf. Perhaps the person who sent the letter did not realize the significance of the enclosure. Perhaps he did. Regardless, the veteran told his MP. A little earlier, an independent team at the Southern General Hospital in Glasgow, led by Dr Goran Jamal (an Iranian neurologist with direct experience of OP casualties in the Iraq–Iran war) had recognized the symptoms of some veterans. He had also noted that those symptoms paralleled those of some Scottish sheep farmers who had been referred to his team. The team's suspicions became even firmer when it was passed papers by a sergeant who had been directly involved in insecticide 'procedures' back in the Gulf. Lastly, the Countess of Mar, a sheep farmer and victim of mild OP poisoning herself, had begun to ask a whole series of direct questions in the House of Lords. Her questions were a creeping barrage getting ever nearer to the target.[3]

With Parliamentary Questions getting closer, eyewitnesses making ever-louder noises, that internal memo disclosed and independent medical research pointing its finger, someone in the MOD must have decided the game was up. There were also, quite obviously, a number of middle-ranking officers who had been in the Gulf at the time and would have known the facts. But they had kept quiet. Maybe they reckoned it would be a bad career move to cast doubt on the official narrative. It took a sergeant to do the job. Or was it an MOD mole who put the wrong paper in the right envelope?

Mr Soames was probably just complacent – a sin of which he had been accused more than once in earlier incarnations. Given that not long before he had been a junior minister at the Ministry of Agriculture at a time when sheep dip was making the news, he ought to have been (should have been?) thoroughly familiar with the problems of organophosphates. And he would then have recognized the symptoms that some veterans were reporting. That he did not ask the right questions or bang the right tables does not excuse him from responsibility. One of the men in charge of the MOD department which had most directly sat on the truth, the Surgeon General to the Forces, Vice Admiral Revell, retired just a few days before the storm. If he did not know the truth, he should have. Anyway, he missed the formal investigation. Some of the civil servants and officers were not so lucky. One officer was given a formal interview about 'the performance of his duties', which, in the order of these things, rates rather lower than a reprimand. Rumour was that one of the civil servants was moved 'to a less sensitive post'.

3. Between 1992 and 1997, the Countess of Mar asked more than sixty Parliamentary Questions (verbal and written) of the MOD about aspects of Gulf War Illnesses.

Mr Soames sought to make some amends in the Commons by concluding one of his statements about the 'mistake' by saying, 'We have every sympathy for those veterans who are ill, and we retain an open mind on the question of whether there is or is not a Gulf War Syndrome.' One notices the phrase 'we retain an open mind'. Retain? Since when? It was not that long since the MOD had been making those noises about 'unsubstantiated rumour, incorrect information, repetitions of earlier allegations which have been fully investigated and found to be unsupported by the facts'. Now the MOD was claiming that it had 'retained an open mind'. The inconsistency, let alone the insincerity, did not worry the people at the MOD. They probably never even noticed it. But these careless contradictions are a small indication of the casual way in which the MOD has approached the whole Gulf War Syndrome problem.

After the organophosphate episode, things could never be quite the same for the MOD. Even if its heart was not really in it, it now had at least to look as if it was trying. Within a few weeks it set up a small unit called the Gulf Veterans Illnesses Unit (GVIU) to answer questions and run a multi-page website of useful information.

In May 1997 there was a change of government. Some Labour MPs, who had not hung back in asking critical questions of the MOD when in Opposition, now found themselves on the government benches. Perhaps prompted by the ethos of New Labour, the GVIU published a document on its website called 'Gulf Illnesses – A New Beginning'. But if indeed there was a New Beginning, was it the epidemiological and clinical facts that had changed, or was it attitudes and policies? Did it really matter? The real problem was that, despite the good intentions of the political 'new broom', the senior civil servants who actually ran the MOD were the same as before; for them not to have a vested interest in defending their earlier position on Gulf Illnesses would be to admit that they might have been wrong. No chance. So a mere change of government and ministers was not enough. Trust was still in short supply.

In fact, trust had been in short supply for a long time. The story of the MOD's Medical Assessment Programme (MAP) is an interesting example of the growth of scepticism, even cynicism, on both sides. The MAP was set up at an RAF hospital in the summer of 1993 following an interview on the BBC's *Newsnight* programme, in which the then Minister for the Armed Forces, Jeremy Hanley, had invited anyone who believed they were suffering from an unexplained 'Gulf Illness' to write personally to him at the MOD. Perhaps not many veterans were watching *Newsnight* that evening, which may partly explain why, by the late autumn, only 185 veterans had applied for 'assessment'. The MOD was inclined to cite this poor response to the Minister's open-handed invitation as further proof that the whole Syndrome affair owed more to the media than to anything else. There even seemed to be a hint that the reason why relatively few veterans were willing to have a thorough examination was that some of them feared they would be 'found out' – to be making more of a few common and minor ills than was merited. But if that was the implication, it ignored a number of factors – apart from the very limited publicity given to the TV invitation in the first place.

First, most veterans had more faith in their own GPs or local consultants than in MOD doctors. This was partly due to the fact that, too often, when a GP applied to the MOD for a patient's medical history he was denied the information he needed. At least one GP was told that there was 'nothing disclosable or relevant'. One might have thought the GP could be the judge of that. Another GP only obtained his patient's records through a court order, and even then the section covering the man's Gulf service was missing. Doctors find it difficult to prescribe a programme of treatment unless they know the patient's medical history. So this apparent lack of MOD co-operation generated distrust in the alternative programme that the MOD itself was now offering. In any case, the MOD was providing neither treatment nor recommendations for treatment; it was merely making an assessment. Merited or not, there was a feeling that the MOD had something to hide.

Second, veterans who visited the MAP in its early days reported back to their friends that it seemed to have made up its mind in advance – that the people it was seeing, if they were suffering from anything at all, were afflicted with 'nothing more than some stress'. In short, it was all in their minds; if any aches and pains were involved, they were psychosomatic. Undoubtedly, there were veterans who were victims of stress, some much more seriously than others. To tell these people that they were suffering from depression, anxiety and extreme fatigue was hardly telling them anything they did not already know. To others who knew very well that they were also physiologically sick, and that in their view their illnesses were almost certainly due to Gulf service, such a diagnosis was insulting. They did not bother to go back. Their reaction may not always have been justified, but in such matters justification comes a poor second to perception. The word spread.

Third, as some veterans pointed out, it was difficult to believe that the MOD was taking them seriously when, within weeks of that TV invitation, the waiting time for an appointment at the MAP was ten weeks. The MOD had allocated just one consultant to the job. Even then, Wing Commander Coker, a specialist in internal medicine with a further degree in chemistry, was made available for just two days a week. During that time he could see (on his own estimation) only ten 'patients'. By late January, the waiting list for an appointment had stretched to more than four months – to June. Many veterans felt this was evidence enough that the whole thing was an MOD charade rather than a genuine attempt to solve the mystery of their illnesses. So was it worth going? Given that the MOD had made its general scepticism known since the beginning, the veterans had cause to be doubtful. Some of them, having made an appointment, then allowed their doubts to get the better of them; they cancelled or simply failed to appear. This did not shorten the waiting list. And it wasted Wing Commander Coker's time. But if the Ministry was misunderstood, that was mostly its own fault.

Lastly, there was the location of the Assessment Programme – at an RAF hospital in Wiltshire. For anyone travelling from Scotland or even from northern England, the rail or car journey was not a matter of 'there and back in a day'. Or even two days. For someone suffering from muscle weakness or chronic fatigue the journey to and from Wiltshire was more than just another challenge to be overcome. There were even some veterans (perhaps suffering from severe stress?) who were allegedly put off by what, to them, was the nightmare of having to cross London by tube. Given that they and others may have felt fairly 'bloody' anyway, this might not be as far-fetched as it seems. A few were in wheelchairs. Until some MPs made a fuss, the veterans were expected to pay their own fares and then apply for – and wait over three months for – an eventual refund.

The long and the short of it was that the Medical Assessment Programme was set up and organized in a muddle. A number of veterans put their doubts about the MAP to MPs, the Royal British Legion, the Veterans' Associations and the MOD itself. The following written account is more articulate than some, but it typifies the feelings of many of the veterans who attended the MAP in its early days:

- I was discharged from the MAP with no diagnosis. Long-term follow-up should have been organized so that continuity of care was maintained.
- Despite no diagnosis, it was implied that I should see a psychiatrist with regard to my symptoms. This was distressing and unhelpful in the circumstances.
- The MAP appeared to be trying to find a diagnosis not related to the Gulf War. When none was found, they were not interested in looking beyond this with an open mind. Having an open mind in medicine and science is essential.
- I have been more or less too scared or embarrassed to seek medical advice again because I have been worried that complaining too much may effect my ability to get work and/or insurance.
- Why can't the MOD believe that their personnel are suffering? Maybe they do believe, but realize the consequences.

Those comments (and more) must carry some weight; they were made by a thirty-six-year-old doctor who had served in the Gulf as a reserve officer in the RAMC.[4]

Among the 'patients' who made the journey to Wiltshire, there was an apparent anomaly: only about 20 per cent of them were still in the services. It is true that a proportion of those who had served in the Gulf were reservists now returned to 'civvy street'. Further, in the years following the Gulf War a number of servicemen, having completed their engagements, had also returned to civilian life. Nevertheless, the ratio of civilians to servicemen was disproportionate. This discrepancy has never been properly explained. But there is hearsay evidence that some people

4. The original of this letter is, presumably, somewhere in the files of the MOD. A copy is held by the Gulf War Veterans' Association.

in the forces felt they had too much to lose in terms of their careers (and eventual pensions) by 'reporting sick', let alone in challenging the veracity of their ultimate employer, the MOD. All this has been partly confirmed by those personnel who later left the services and could then speak more freely. There are also tales of people being positively discouraged by their unit commanders from 'enlisting' in the MAP scheme. Maybe some such stories do not lose in the telling. It is difficult to know. But accusations of malingering are easy to make, difficult to disprove.

In the early days of the MAP scheme many of the veterans felt that Wing Commander Coker was too easily dismissive of their 'alleged' problems. But, as time went on, he seemed to be more understanding. Indeed, the perception of some veterans was that he had come round to the idea that their complaints were not all imagined, psychosomatic or what might be expected anyway. Maybe he had become converted. Perhaps that was also the MOD's perception. But just when the veterans were beginning at last to have some faith in the MAP, he moved. Or was moved.

Perhaps the message eventually got through to the MOD that regardless of what might or might not be the strength of its case, in the eyes of the public and of MPs on both sides of the House, it was losing the debate – chiefly because, to use two sporting analogies, a series of Own Goals and Unforced Errors had made it look untrustworthy. Late in the day it made some amends by putting more consultants onto the Assessment Programme and, later, moving it to London, where it eventually found a home in St Thomas's Hospital, just across the river from the Houses of Parliament. The numbers picked up a little. But there was still the feeling among many observers that the official response had all along, in all respects, been too little, too grudging and too late.

APART FROM THE SOMETIMES USEFUL knockabout of the Prime Minister's weekly question-and-answer session, Question Time with other ministers has a more hallowed reputation than it deserves. MPs must give a minister notice of their questions; this allows time for the answers to be put together and, if deemed necessary, for ministerial officials to operate the Whitehall Loop. So, while the Speaker normally allows one fairly short (though unseen) supplementary question, and some MPs are more skilled than others at launching this second torpedo, the system is not well designed to get at the truth. Much more effective is the relevant Select Committee. Composed of ten or so members from both sides of the House who have an interest in the subject, a Select Committee usually has the time and the expertise to go on asking questions until it gets somewhere near the facts, rather than the authorized Whitehall 'spin'. Apart from ministers, it can call almost anyone to appear before it. Civil servants do not much like Select Committees; the opportunity to employ the Loop is restricted.

Through 1995, while the Conservative Government still had nearly two years to run, the Commons Defence Committee examined the role of the MOD in the matter of Gulf War Syndrome several times. The Committee published its report in October 1995. In more than 100 pages it contains transcripts of lengthy question-and-answer sessions with senior MOD staff and representatives of the main veterans' associations; there are also written submissions from both. There are papers from the Royal College of Physicians, from the US Department of Defence and from qualified and interested scientists. At the end, the Committee, having heard all the evidence and considered all the submissions, came up with its conclusions. As far as the MOD is concerned, they are damning:

> In responding to the allegation of a Gulf War Syndrome, MOD has been quick to deny but slow to investigate. The lack of evidence supporting a link between service in the Gulf and the reported illnesses so frequently cited by Ministers merely reflects the absence of thorough research or statistical analysis. In establishing the Medical Assessment Programme with commendable speed, the Department failed to support it with the necessary resources or publicity to ensure a comprehensive and speedy exercise . . . It was only after this Committee's intervention that MOD provided the extra manpower required to advance the MAP at more than a crawl. It was only after considerably more public and Parliamentary pressure that the Department began to contemplate conducting the type of epidemiological study needed to establish whether the incidence of Gulf War Syndrome related symptoms is in any way unusual. This study is not part of a co-ordinated, long-term inquiry but seems more to

> stem from an acceptance that further inaction will not be defensible . . . MOD's response has been reactive rather than proactive and characterised throughout by scepticism, defensiveness and general torpor.

The relevant minister, Nicholas Soames, harrumphed. He found the Committee's report 'disappointing and unhelpful'. He attempted to reprimand an opposition MP, Angela Eagle, for 'making mischief' when she drew attention in the Commons to some of the Committee's more trenchant observations. He was obviously furious. How his civil servants and service advisors reacted is not reported. To be fair – though beyond necessity – there are two points they might have made in some mitigation. First, the hostilities in the Gulf had been a conflict, not a war; this apparently meant that the MOD might, under some circumstances, have been liable for 'damages'. In fact, most of the veterans involved were much more interested in getting the MOD to research and provide effective treatment than in trying for monetary compensation. Nevertheless, the MOD would have thought from an early stage that some of the veterans might mount a legal action against it.[5] So the Treasury solicitor's department would have been desperate that no admissions of any kind should be made or implied. Perhaps MOD civil servants and ministers found themselves in a position similar to that of a motorist who, despite knowing that his actions have caused an accident, is required under the terms of his insurance policy not to acknowledge any fault at all. But this analogy is rather too charitable, because the MOD not only consistently denied any fault, but it also rejected the proposition that there had been any 'accident' in the first place. It was all in the veterans' imaginations. The veterans, helped by a thoroughly wayward media, had dreamt up a false connection between service in the Gulf and their subsequent medical problems.

5. There have been several occasions when veterans have attempted to start civil actions. But in each case, cost has been a significant problem. Legal aid boards have been reluctant to authorize the very large sums that would be necessary in terms of both legal and scientific research to mount a winning challenge against the procrastinations and almost bottomless purse of a government department. Secondly, some lawyers have not been as altruistic as one might expect, and money already allocated has been wasted.

Another 'excuse' may lie in the fear all civil servants have of the Treasury. And of their bosses. No one with career ambitions or dreams of a CMG, a CB or whatever would want to be seen to advocate any policy that might involve spending real money. The Treasury rules. This, as much as 'general torpor', may account for the niggardly resourcing of the Assessment Programme and the lack of any proper programmes of research. Anyway, career prospects can come before openness. Whistle-blowing is seen as letting the side down. Never explain. Never apologize. Never admit or acknowledge. Too harsh?

The Defence Committee had drawn attention to 'the absence of thorough research'. Clearly it was beyond the means of the veterans themselves to commission a programme of proper investigation. Surely that was the government's job? Yet there were no significant inquiries being funded by the MOD. Money could be saved by leaving that to the Americans. True, there was the Medical Assessment Programme, but that was geared to cataloguing symptoms, not to providing treatment or trying to find causes. Besides which, the MAP was being shunned by a significant number of ailing veterans. This did not stop the MOD from claiming that both the types of illnesses and the number of veterans seen by the MAP were, as a proportion of the total British contingent in the Gulf, no different from those found in the same age group of the general population. This assertion must have been invented in Whitehall because, to be fair, the consultant at the Assessment Programme in Wiltshire had been careful to avoid any such claim. But in one submission to the Defence Committee in December 1994 the MOD went even further. It listed the seven most common complaints found among veterans (breathlessness, headache, insomnia, fatigue, aching joints, indigestion and backache), and then claimed that the veterans had fewer of these problems than a comparable group of the general population:

> The application of general prevalence rates [for the seven complaints] to the personnel who went to the Gulf indicate that there are in fact fewer veterans complaining of these symptoms than would be expected statistically from a similar age group in the UK.

This statement is totally misleading – as the Defence Committee was quick to point out. The MOD's only data came from those 'self-selecting' veterans who had come forward for the Assessment Programme. So, first, the MOD's assertion took no account of the high proportion of veterans who chose not to attend. This significant proportion could, therefore, be omitted from the official definition of those who were 'complaining'. Second, it ignored the fact that service personnel are likely to be physically fitter and mentally more resilient than their equivalents in the civilian population. In disregarding these factors and, thereby, 'forgetting' two of the most basic rules of statistical comparison – only compare like with like and check that your samples are properly representative – the MOD was guilty, not for the first time, of distorting the evidence to fit its thesis. Third, though less significant, the MOD was using twenty-year-old data for its civilian 'comparison'. Evidently, those responsible thought nobody would notice these stratagems. They must operate at a very low level of intellectual horsepower. Or think that everyone else does. The Defence Committee was having none of it – as the following passage from its report shows:

> The analysis of symptoms affecting the general population has an important place in any full examination of the existence of Gulf War Syndrome. However, MOD was initially unduly reliant on unsuitable statistics in its efforts to downplay the significance of the numbers reporting symptoms associated with the Syndrome and to avoid launching a comprehensive epidemiological study.

At another point, an MOD witness appearing before the Defence Committee claimed that the percentage of those veterans with post-traumatic stress was about the same as those who had taken part in 'other conflicts' (El Alamein? Arnhem? Kohima? Korea? Malaya? Aden? Suez? Ulster? The Falklands?). When the Committee asked to be sent the figures on the Falklands, the most recent of all the 'other conflicts', the MOD had to reply that it did not have them after all. To obtain them would be 'a time-consuming and expensive process which we believe would be inappropriate . . .'. So why claim an unverifiable comparison with 'other conflicts' in the first place?

The fact is that, as in so many other controversies centred on the MOD, both its verbal testimony and its written submissions are riddled with factual errors, filtered evidence, bogus alibis, selected quotes, half-truths, unsupported assertions and statements which, while literally true, are totally misleading. It is just not possible to believe that these 'mistakes' were (and are) all accidental. That is a serious charge. Some of the evidence has already been presented. The rest is not hard to find.

THE POINT HAS JUST BEEN made that the MOD has claimed on several occasions that Gulf veterans have no more illnesses, nor a greater range of them, than are found in a matched group of the population at large. The claim lies at the heart of its argument that it has no case to answer. But it has never been able to advance any even half-convincing evidence in support of its claim.

So what about the counter-claim by the veterans that their problems do indeed stem from service in the Gulf? Of course, it is an easy enough assertion to make. Yet anyone trying to prove it initially faces the same statistical difficulty as the MOD: the epidemiological data is overly dependent on those veterans who 'volunteer' for investigation. What about all those who, for one reason or another (some of which have been explained), prefer not to respond? This problem has never bothered the MOD. If the veterans had relied on the same simplistic thinking, their conclusions would be just as flawed. Knowing this, the veterans look towards research that comes at the problem from a more sophisticated direction. It *is* possible to base an epidemiological study on a sample of 'volunteers', but to be even remotely valid all kinds of esoteric statistical adjustments have to be made. Several such studies, allied with causative research, have been done in the UK and in the US. The findings of one such programme, based at Guy's, King's and St Thomas's Medical School, were summarized as follows in the *Lancet* of January 1999:

> The dominant finding was that Gulf War veterans were roughly twice as likely as members of other military cohorts to report chronic fatigue, irritability, headache and other symptoms, which were remarkably similar to those reported after the Gulf War.[6]

6. This passage is in the editorial of the *Lancet*. The full article, 'Health of UK servicemen who served in the Gulf War', by C. Unwin and others, appears in the same edition of January 1999.

Other studies have put the rate of some illnesses among Gulf veterans at up to three times that found in a matched 'control' group of, for example, soldiers serving in Bosnia. In addition to research that tried to detect if there was an increased susceptibility among Gulf veterans, there were other studies which sought to find 'causative' connections between a given Gulf 'insult' (the vaccines, NAP tablets, OPs, depleted uranium, oil smoke, etc.) and a subsequent illness. These studies were likely to be the most useful of all in proving the veterans' 'case'. In the United States alone there are at least fifty papers published in appropriate scientific journals that, in one way or another, support the veterans. Many tend to point to three particular areas of increased risk among veterans: renal cancer, lymphocytic leukaemia and motor neurone disease. While minor flaws in some papers have been found, or at least alleged, there seem to have been few serious attacks on their basic conclusions. In the UK, the same is true. One of the most notable papers sets out the Glasgow research showing the effect of organophosphates.[7]

So, if one takes the MOD and the Pentagon out of the equation – both continue to be deeply sceptical – there is a clear majority verdict among qualified research teams that something, or a multiplicity of 'somethings', happened in the Gulf to cause the veterans' problem. But what? The organophosphate sprays? The cocktail of vaccines? Those NAP pills? And if not one of those prime suspects alone, what about in combination? Or the depleted uranium used in much of the Coalition's armour-piercing ammunition? Or the clouds of toxic smoke coming off the hundreds of burning oil wells? Or the dust of the Saudi desert itself – some of it finer than talcum powder? Or the Iraqi ammunition dumps – were they attacked or blown up with the care that their suspected contents merited? And if the authorities are so sure that the Iraqis totally eschewed the use of all their chemical and biological weapons, then what were some of those 'empty' Scuds loaded with? And why did those alarms go off? Were they *all* false? If they were, they were literally worse than useless because, like crying 'wolf', they would generate a disregard for the real thing – if it ever happened. The MOD has said almost nothing about the efficacy of those gas alarms. Yet the

7. 'Adverse Drug Reaction' by G.A. Jamal, *Toxicol. Review* (1998).

manufacturers have repeatedly asserted that their alarms were at least 90 per cent reliable.

So many questions. So many possibilities.

Despite all those possibilities, there does seem to be informal agreement among many scientists and medical people on one important aspect. It has to be 'informal' (a concept obviously disliked by professionals) because there is no way that all the many 'toxic' circumstances of the Gulf can be experimentally reproduced. The consensus centres on a suspicion that it was the mixture of vaccines (a risk in itself) combined with the NAP tablets which triggered a lowered immunity in some servicemen. This lowered immunity may have been yet further diminished by stress – something which (see below) is now recognized as not only a psychological factor, but a potent physical one as well. Stress, by way of adrenalin and other substances, can alter the body's chemistry well beyond normal limits. So, with a much-reduced resistance, some servicemen may have become susceptible to any or all of the other possibilities.

In medicine, the synergistic effect of drugs is well known. Taking a single drug may produce one set of expected results. But taking two drugs together will almost certainly have a multiplying effect. Some of those results may be a long way from those intended or expected from either drug on its own. Take three or four drugs at the same time and the synergistic possibilities, while not quite infinite, will certainly include the unexpected and, possibly, the dangerous. In short, 'safe' drugs may, in combination, produce a range of quite unsafe side effects. Neither the MOD nor anyone else has yet explained why such a synergy should not be found in some Gulf veterans. It would be very surprising if it were not.

At this point there is an obvious question: why is the incidence of Gulf War Illnesses so patchy? Why some people and not others? Why, across more than 50,000 British servicemen, or more than twelve times that number of Americans, are at least four out of five apparently free of problems? One part of the answer seems to depend on where the soldier served in the Gulf and for how long. According to the veterans themselves, those who were furthest forward and led the way into Iraq show a higher incidence of problems than those who worked further back. Maybe they inhaled the microscopic particles of depleted uranium that came from the armour-piercing shells used against Iraqi tanks. Maybe they were closer to some of the Iraqi chemical weapons dumps which, only partly destroyed by bombing, were now leaking into the environment. There also appears to be a connection with the length of time spent in the Gulf. And the incidence of problems among medical personnel seems to be relatively high.

Another part of the answer to 'Why some and not others?' probably has to do with genes. None of us is quite the same. Some people are mildly allergic to red wine or cats, others quite violently so to shellfish or penicillin, a few fatally to peanuts. And, for example, in setting a three-times-a-day dosage for those NAP tablets, no account was taken of wildly varying body weights: an 8-stone nurse was meant to take the same dose as a 16-stone sergeant. In vaccinations, too. Further, while one of Whitehall's answers to the suspicions about the NAP/pyridostigmine bromide 'problem' has been to say that far bigger doses are prescribed in treating myasthenia gravis, this does not allow for the fact that giving the drug to someone who does not suffer from MG may, on that individual, have a harmful effect. One would not, for example, give insulin to someone who did not have diabetes; it might even kill them. Nor does it allow for the fact that the MG patient is not already full of vaccines. Further, MG patients are not working hard in daytime temperatures rising above 38°C and night-time ones dropping below freezing. Nor are MG sufferers subject to the stresses of going to war tomorrow – a war where the enemy may use Scuds loaded with anthrax spores or nerve gas. These things almost certainly make a difference. Indeed, stress alters the body's chemistry to such an extent that the Israelis found that their soldiers when severely 'tensioned' were three times more susceptible to the effects of the pyridostigmine in NAP tablets than were unstressed soldiers. Stress can weaken the important 'blood–brain barrier' which allows traces of PB to leak across into the brain. Neurological damage follows. The same effect has been induced in laboratory mice stressed by being forced to swim without much hope of reaching 'the other side'.

But there is another, even stronger, argument in the debate surrounding the NAP tablets: pyridostigmine had never been thoroughly tested on a large group of individuals. Consequently, there is no firm data on how different healthy individuals may react – on variations in susceptibility. This is almost certainly one of the reasons why, in preparation for the Gulf War, the US Food and Drug Administration refused to clear the drug for use by the US Department of Defence unless it was under an 'experimental-cum-research' waiver.

Returning to that cocktail of vaccines, the official 'defence' is that there was (and is) no reason to suppose that there would be problems – after all, small babies are immunized against diphtheria, whooping cough and polio. And twelve months later they get a single shot for measles, mumps and rubella. A fair point – as far as it goes. But the example ignores the doubts some doctors (and many parents) have about the 'combination' MMR vaccine. More importantly, no sustained tests had been done on mixing those Gulf vaccines (which included anthrax, botulinum and plague) either in their own right or in combination with the PBs or those long-denied OPs. So how can the MOD be so confident? One medical commentator used a computer analogy: 'With such an overload of competing information being pumped into those troops, it's not too surprising that some of their immune systems just crashed.'

There were other risks. Indeed, the US Institute of Medicine now catalogues more than twenty 'toxic possibilities'. The MOD lists none. The very sand itself has been cited by some researchers. In that part of the Arabian peninsula over which the war was fought, there are areas where the sand is so microscopically fine that the normal 'filters' of the body's respiratory system are ineffective. The dust is easily and inevitably inhaled into the innermost parts of the lungs – into the 'alveolar sacs'. The desert is not as sterile as is supposed: the dust may be carrying bacteria to which westerners have no natural immunity. The lungs cannot efficiently rid themselves of this 'insult'. The dust also has a high calcium content and, in certain susceptible individuals, this may trigger an allergy which, in turn, 'compromises' the immune system – a sort of 'AIDS without the HIV'. That is the theory, anyway. The fact that none of the Saudi troops in the Coalition have come down with any of the now-classic Gulf War 'symptoms' seems to give some support to this hypothesis. The argument is that over many generations the desert-dwelling Saudis have developed immunity. But how do we know that their apparent freedom from the problems suffered within the western contingents does not really stem from the fact that the Saudis were not injected with all those vaccines? And were not taking NAP pills? Or simply that the Saudi authorities have been reticent with statistics? We don't.

The catalogue of potential hazards seems almost endless.

IN PREVIOUS CONFLICTS IT WAS enough to get shot or blown up. But the Gulf War was different: one side was facing an enemy who might have resorted to the use of chemical and biological weapons. Had those weapons been used, resulting in the death of thousands, plus the permanent injury of many more, and had it then been found that the victims had not been given all the advance protection available, the ensuing indignation of the public would have been limitless. And rightly so. But the MOD and the Pentagon had a problem: while they had an absolute duty to provide the protection, there were suspicions (some would put it much more strongly) *before* the war that some of the means of protection might carry their own risks and that others had never been properly checked. One can appreciate the dilemma facing the MOD decision-makers back in the autumn of 1990. Something had to be done, and done quickly. But (yes, the point has been made before) it has been the subsequent refusal by those same decision-makers to admit even the remote possibility that things might have gone wrong that has done the credibility of the MOD so much damage. This denial stretched – still stretches – to the effects of depleted uranium (DU). Of course, the mere mention of the word 'uranium', in any context, is likely to generate an emotive shudder. Governments and their scientists do not care for such a reaction; it gets in the way of rational discussion. Anyway, they quickly point out that this uranium was *depleted*. So what does that mean? Basically, DU is the waste left over after the radioactive uranium-235 is taken out of uranium ore. It is the 235 which is used to fuel power stations or to make bombs. The remaining waste (DU) is still radioactive, but at a relatively low level.

DU, we are reassured by the MOD, is 'not dangerous'. Or, as the Minister for Armed Forces, John Spellar, told the Commons on 9 January 2001, 'There is no evidence linking DU to cancers or to other ill health being experienced by some Gulf veterans.' This is misleading. DU is only 'not dangerous' in the sense that you might keep a slab of the stuff in the broom cupboard – though you would be well advised not to handle it too often. But that misses the point. The fact is that when 'converted' to a dust-cloud of microscopic particles – which is what happens when a DU shell hits an enemy tank – DU can be both toxically and radiologically hazardous. In solid form DU is very hard and very heavy (nearly twice the weight of lead), so DU shells have phenomenal penetrating power against modern armour; the stuff is also pyrophoric – it burns with explosive force (at 1000°C) on impact. This, of course, is why the military likes its ammunition to be made of the stuff.

In the Gulf War several hundred Iraqi tanks and other armoured vehicles were knocked out by DU ammunition – from which billions of microscopic particles 'erupted'. These then settled on, in, around and downwind from the wreckage. Immediately after the war there was a wish to have a closer look at the enemy's armour. At the amateur level this might be mere curiosity or the wish to pick up a souvenir. At the official level there was great interest in checking just how DU ammunition had worked in battle. Iraqi tanks were 'assessed' in the desert; some were even towed away on flatbed trucks for a closer inspection. Others were blown up to deny undamaged parts for any rearmament programme Saddam might plan. Helicopters landed and took off nearby. All this activity, formal and informal, sent up clouds of microscopic dust. The dust was inhaled by those in the immediate area and, if there was even a light breeze, by others for many miles downwind.

In that same Commons speech Mr Spellar made another claim: 'Handled in accordance with regulations, DU shells present no hazards to our forces.' This confidence hardly squared with a paper put out prior to the assault on Iraq by the Radiological Protection Service (RPS), based at Haslar Naval Hospital in Gosport. It included the following advice:

> Do not allow DU residue to come in direct contact with exposed skin. Sleeves should be rolled down and two pairs of gloves (inner nylon or cotton, outer heavy PVC) should be worn. Service respirators should be worn at all times, as movement of fragments may cause the release of DU oxide which, if ingested, will cause serious health hazards. When collecting DU fragments, always wear gloves and use a scoop or an empty tin. Boxes are to be marked 'Caution Radioactive Materials – DU Fragments'.

There was a problem: very few units in the Gulf were told about these warnings. Consequently, the troops had taken no particular precautions. An August 1993 letter signed by a Mr Stainton, an MOD official, acknowledges the omission: 'The issuing of safety instructions was in some cases overlooked. This was regrettable.' That 'overlooked' seems to be a recurring theme. In February 2001, a few weeks after Mr Spellar had assured the Commons that DU was quite safe if 'handled in accordance with regulations', he had to return to acknowledge that he had been wrong when he had said earlier that all troops assigned to the Balkans had been warned and trained appropriately. They had not. Neither, ten years earlier, had most of the troops in the Gulf. In this connection it is interesting to compare the final paragraph of the Radiological Protection Service's warning (above) with a statement promulgated in parallel with Mr Spellar's Commons reply (below) a decade later by the MOD: 'DU in its massive [i.e. solid] form, as expended rounds or solid fragments, is a negligible hazard.' One wonders why, if the hazard is negligible, the RPS should have recommended that when collecting 'DU fragments' one should always wear two pairs of gloves and that boxes should be marked 'Caution Radioactive Materials – DU Fragments'. Why the caution? Mr Spellar, like Mr Soames before him, is not a 'medical man'. He, like Mr Soames, should have thumped the table and told his civil servants and scientific advisors that he needed to be told the truth – and at the first time of asking. He might have learnt that DU dust (uranium dioxide) 'works' in two ways. Like all heavy metals it is toxic, which is why lead is no longer a constituent of petrol. Second, the alpha radiation emitted by microscopic DU dust, while very weak in terms of penetration, can be carcinogenic if it is ingested in any quantity and is then in direct contact with soft internal human tissue – which it inevitably will be if one is breathing the stuff. It tends to find its way into the lymph nodes. Some research points to the possibility that cancers can appear within just a few months; others may take many years. Moreover, traces of DU can remain in the body for at least two decades. It was known from animal experiments that, as well as cancer, ingestion can cause neurological dysfunctions, damaged kidneys, bleeding bowels and birth defects. All these problems, and others, found in 'test' animals are also found scattered among the veteran population – but not found as a result of research done by the MOD's Medical Assessment Programme. The Programme has never investigated veterans for DU contamination. Evidently, the MOD does not believe there is any need to investigate. It should read its own literature. An Army medical report dated 4 March 1997 is in no doubt. It is a précis of a longer MOD document called 'The Use and Hazards of DU Munitions':

> Inhalation of insoluble uranium oxide dust will lead to accumulation in the lungs with very slow clearance – if any. Although chemical toxicity is low, there may be localised radiation damage of the lung leading to cancer. Uranium compound dust is therefore hazardous.

When this report was leaked to the press in January 2001, the MOD was in an embarrassing position. So it issued a statement that the report had been compiled by 'a trainee' and was inaccurate and of no account. The major who had actually written it was, presumably, warned to keep quiet. The MOD's problem was that the Atomic Energy Authority had also put out a very similar warning. As had the Radiological Protection Service based at the Naval Hospital in Gosport. As had the medical wing of the German Army. Maybe they were all taking their lead from the same ill-informed 'trainee'.

To add to the doubts about DU ammunition, research in America after the Gulf War showed that, depending on how it was manufactured, it might contain traces of plutonium. Indeed, it is almost certain that some of the American DU ammunition did, perhaps accidentally (or carelessly?), contain such particles. As such, it is called 'dirty' DU. Plutonium is 100,000 times more radioactive than uranium. It is known that American DU was imported for munition making. Yet Geoff Hoon, the Minister for Defence, could claim, along with the line about that trainee, that there is 'no evidence' of a link between DU and any of the illnesses suffered by Gulf or Bosnia veterans. Speculation to the contrary, he said, was 'anti-science paranoia'. That there was 'no evidence' of a link was only true in the sense that the MOD had not found one – which, given that it had not commissioned any serious research to look for one, was not surprising. This was the same Alice in Wonderland argument – 'There is no evidence, therefore there is no need to look for any' – used six years earlier by Mr Soames and his advisors. Same advisors? Maybe. (There are uncomfortable parallels with those assertions from MAFF scientists back in the early days of BSE that 'mad cow disease' could not cross the species barrier to humans.)

The MOD's credibility in the business of depleted uranium has been further undermined by its assertions that DU ammunition was not used in any quantities by British forces in the Gulf. At one stage it emphasized that only 100 rounds of DU tank ammunition had been shipped from the UK to the Gulf – and most had been fired on the practice ranges before moving up to the front. This is probably the literal truth. Yet it is misleading. Documents coming out of the Pentagon under the Freedom of Information Act show that, of the 400 tons of DU 'ordnance' (from the air and on the ground) used in the conflict, 60 tons were attributed to Britain. This, if the MOD is to be believed, must mean that each shell fired by our Challenger tanks would, impossibly, have weighed nearly half a ton. The fact is that while the official claim that only 100 DU shells were despatched from the UK to the Gulf is probably correct, our DU ordnance was considerably augmented by the Americans.

In southern Iraq, in and around Basra, UN medical observers and doctors from the Austrian Red Cross have, for the last eight years, reported a very high incidence of leukaemia, together with lung and other cancers. This is particularly pronounced among young children, who, with their rapid growth in bone and tissue, comprise exactly the age group that develops these cancers most quickly. Both the MOD and the DOD deny any connection. But there is a perception that the problem is due to the large quantity of DU dust (perhaps contaminated with plutonium?) that has become part of the environment in southern Iraq. Similarly, a part of Vieques island, off Puerto Rico, has long been used as a gunnery range by the US Navy. DU rounds (containing traces of plutonium?) have been fired there for the last twelve years. It is reported that there are a disproportionate number of people with cancer of the thyroid, uterus, liver and lungs; some say the rate is four times that which would normally be expected. The US Navy has lately abandoned the use of DU shells in its Phalanx rapid-fire cannon. Why? The Royal Navy, which uses the same weapon under licence, will also have to rethink.

Finally, on the matter of DU, a statement was squeezed out of the MOD in January 2002: the Army was shortly to be supplied with tungsten-tipped rounds for its tanks. This was not, it stressed, a tacit admission that there were any problems with DU. One has to wonder. Tungsten is many times more expensive than DU. Why should the MOD's procurement people switch from a cheap waste material to one costing up to a hundred times as much?

By now the reader may be wondering at a situation in which far more potential damage seems to have been done to our servicemen by our own side than by any aggressive action taken by Saddam Hussein. He, no doubt, relished the irony. And perhaps he took further pleasure in the fact that his efforts at making and then stockpiling his poisonous arsenal seemed ultimately, by his own lights, to have paid dividends. The Coalition had to destroy those desert stockpiles – by bombing during the war, by demolition after it.

No one seemed quite sure of what happens when one uses explosives to demolish canisters filled with deadly chemicals. The official line is that they all get destroyed – incinerated. In a letter from the Director General of Porton Down, answering a Parliamentary Question from the Countess of Mar, there is the reassurance that 'chemical agents are organic materials which are destroyed by combustion'. This is only true in theory; as such it is bad science. In practice, smart bombs dropped into arms dumps, or demolitions carried out after victory, do not guarantee that combustion is complete. What happens if some of the chemicals do not get incinerated? Where do they go? And, in any case, the very act of combustion can produce other gases that may be no less harmful than the originals. What happens to them? These questions have come back to haunt officialdom.

Of all Iraqi munitions dumps – and there were more than 100 in all – one of the biggest was at a place called Khamisiyah. In over 100 bunkers spread over an area of five by two miles the Iraqi army had stored thousands of tons of ordnance. American demolition teams from the 37 and 307 Engineering Battalions started their work in early March. Off on the south side, a mile or so distant from the main bunkers, was a quarry-like pit containing a dozen or so stacks of wooden crates. They were easily identified as holding NATO rockets which, according to the stencilled markings on the crates, had been destined for Jordan. How and why they had wound up in Iraq was anyone's guess. There were more than 1000 of them. There were also crates stencilled in Cyrillic script; these were Russian Katyusha rockets.[8]

Because of demolition priorities in the main dump, it was not until the end of the assignment that an eight-man detachment was sent over to deal with the rockets in the pit. By now the team was short of explosive charges to lay against the crates. But that did not much matter because it was reckoned that the rockets would set each other off in sympathetic detonation. The men placed the charges as economically as possible. Then they withdrew upwind.

Presently they touched off the detonators. The pit rumbled for a few seconds. Most of the rockets exploded where they were or blasted into the side of the pit. A few corkscrewed up for a few hundred feet and then, because they were unstabilized, slammed back to earth again – 'fly-outs', they were called. A plume of smoke and dust rose into the evening sky. Within a few minutes, as it got higher, it began to form into a pale yellow cloud. Someone shot a video. Then, as 'the pit' had been the final demolition task at Khamisiyah, the team climbed into its trucks and headed off across the desert back to its base in Saudi Arabia.

The prevailing winds blew to the south-west. That way lay a scatter of desert camps – the tented bases of American and British armoured and infantry units, which, now that the war was over, were packing up. Many were working in shorts and flip-flops. Their Noddy suits were packed away. They were quite unaware of events more than 70 miles to the north.

It is not difficult to guess what comes next in this particular narrative. It seems that those rockets had been loaded by the Iraqis not with their normal high-explosive load, but, unknown to the demolition team, with a nerve gas. This was confirmed seven months later when, in October 1991, a UN inspection team visited Khamisiyah. They came armed with

8. Most of the information about the Khamisiyah 'incident' is from veterans' letters held by the GVA, from an interview with Dr Doug Rokke, the US Army Health physicist responsible for DU clean-up in the Gulf, and from a paper authored by the CIA and the DOD in September 1997.

a number of Iraqi documents and with equipment sensitive enough to pick up the faint traces of sarin still in the debris of the pit.

Amazingly, it was six years later, in September 1997, before the American Department of Defence, working with the CIA, published a hypothesis of what had probably happened. Perhaps they had been prompted when, earlier, a soldier had sent his Congressman the video-tape of that yellow cloud. The Pentagon went back to computer modelling based on meteorological records taken at the time. They confirmed that the cloud had spread out and drifted away to the south for over 100 miles before it finally dissipated to nothing and could no longer be identified. Anything up to 80,000 American and British troops may have been under its path. The sarin was almost certainly at a very weak level. So weak, said the authorities, that no harm would have been done. However, while everyone knows that the gas at 'weapon' strength is an inevitable and speedy killer, the research on the possible long-term effects if it is 'ingested' at a very low, non-lethal level is much less certain. Whether the damage is passing or permanent no one knows. But, as one veteran has observed, 'By the time they make up their minds we'll all be dead anyway – which is probably the idea.'

The MOD has always been dismissive about the drift of gas from Khamisiyah. Indeed, the responsible Minister, Dr Reid, assured the Commons Defence Committee eight years later (7 September 1999) that no gas alarms had been triggered. This was the literal truth, yet wholly misleading. The reason that no alarms had gone off was simple: there were no alarms still on site. With the war finished nearly two weeks earlier, they had all been dismantled preparatory to being shipped home. Who had briefed the Minister?

The fact is that the demolition of those rockets in the Khamisiyah pit seems to have added just one more ingredient to the already unbelievably complex catalogue of possibilities behind Gulf War Syndrome. But there are at least two more items still in the catalogue.

In his scorched-earth policy of making things as difficult as possible for the advancing Coalition forces, Saddam Hussein ordered the detonation of over 700 Kuwaiti oil wells. As most of them were under strong subterranean pressure, burning and unburnt oil was shot hundreds of feet into the air. The resultant black cloud, continuously refuelled by the pressurized oil below, became thicker and thicker. Because there was very little wind – consequent on a series of atmospheric inversions – the cloud became stagnant. For days it hugged the ground over an area of more than 1500 square miles. The 'fallout' was a dense mixture of smoke, soot and unburnt oil droplets. Some of the chemicals thus suspended are known carcinogens.

At noon on 25 February troops in the US 1st Marine Division were advancing along the edge of the Burgan oilfield; they reported that they could only see a few yards ahead and had to read their maps by torchlight. The soot and oil covered their clothing and burned their throats. They were coughing up black mucus. A reporter wrote about 'the fine mist of oil particles' hanging in the air. There were other similar accounts:

> We choked on oil while breathing through our doubled up scarves. On the highway the air was so thick that our vehicle headlights could not penetrate further than 10–15 feet, and Marine escorts were needed to walk ahead of the vehicles to keep us on the highway.

An official commentary by the American Department of Defence confirms such reports:

> Troops were subjected to short-term exposures where they were literally drenched in unburnt oil and/or covered with fall-out – i.e. soot, smoke and other by-products of combustion.

It would be very surprising if, after those conditions, the health of some of the American Marines had not been affected – though whether the effects would be short or long term is another question. But the official position has always been that there is no connection between any illnesses and the oil fires. The Pentagon's and thereby the MOD's conclusion, while not denying the carcinogenic and other risks of oil 'rain' and soot-and-smoke-drenched air, seems to be partly based on an empirical study into the health of 110 professional fire-fighters employed by Red Adair and other Texan companies contracted to put out the Kuwait fires. The study showed they suffered no harmful effects – despite working at the wellheads every day for several four-week stretches. But, given that by May, June and July, when the civilian fire-fighters were at work, another official report could claim that the Kuwait atmosphere was 'no more polluted than that of Philadelphia or Houston', one might guess that conditions had changed since the days in February when the Marines had needed torches to see their maps.

In fact, even a brief study of Kuwait's climatic regime shows the difference between winter and summer. In the former there are frequent periods of temperature inversion when the wind is almost non-existent, the air is stagnant and pollution hugs the ground. In the summer months the winds are stronger, Kuwait's air is clearer and any pollution is quickly carried away. The smoke plumes of the fires on which those fire-fighters were working rose into the air for several thousand feet. Photographs show the difference between February and, say, June. There are other criticisms that can be made of the Pentagon's case, but the one just cited is probably sufficient.

There is at least one other well-documented incident about which both British and American veterans have long questioned official reassurances. In the dawn hours of 19 January 1991 there was a series of unexplained events at the port complex of Al Jubayl, a huge, 40-square-mile base for a large number of British and American 'support' and helicopter units. Al Jubayl is just over 150 miles down the coast from Kuwait. On 20 January 2000, in response to rumours which would not go away, the MOD published – nine years and a day after the events in question – a forty-page booklet, whose first paragraph sets the scene:

> Sometime after 0300 hrs on the morning of 19 January 1991, in Al Jubayl, Saudi Arabia, a number of events occurred that caused great concern to many of the troops that were stationed there in the British Force Maintenance Area (FMA). There were reports of loud bangs, a bright flash, and vapour and liquid in the air. In addition, a number of detection and monitoring systems indicated the presence of chemical warfare agents. These incidents were subsequently investigated by the Nuclear, Biological and Chemical Cell at the HQ FMA and by staff at the Chemical Defence Establishment (CDE) at Porton Down. However, the event was never formally resolved, and troops in Al Jubayl appear to have received a number of conflicting explanations for the alarms.

This, given the MOD's earlier record of denial, is a surprisingly fair summary of events that morning and of the confusion surrounding them. The booklet, compiled by the MOD's Gulf Veterans' Illnesses Unit, acknowledges that a significant number of nerve agent detectors 'alarmed' that morning. Besides reporting the anecdotal evidence of individuals – from corporals through RSMs to majors – who remember seeing flashes and hearing bangs, it quotes contemporary logs and official war diaries which also contain entries about alarms, skyward 'explosions' and flashes. It reports detector paper that turned blue, and soldiers who felt vapour droplets. It also reports a number of inconsistencies – alarms that did not go off, detector papers that did not change colour, logs that did not note anything unusual. The following entry is typical of the difficulty of forming definitive conclusions:

> Eyewitnesses from Camp 13 [in the middle of the Al Jubayl complex] described a large fireball illuminating the sky, a concussion wave, and a mist in the air. Several speak of having experienced symptoms such as runny noses, numbness, and burning sensations after the explosion, although there is no record that anyone sought medical attention for such symptoms. Some eyewitnesses say that they smelt an ammonia-like odour, but this is not mentioned in the logs. Other individuals recall that they were not wearing protective clothing and that they showed no symptoms that they had been subjected to a chemical warfare agent.

The official explanation, derived from the Americans who were operating aircraft in the area – the air war had started – is that the vapour which activated the alarms came from fuel being dumped by a damaged aircraft before it landed at a nearby airfield. The explosions were sonic booms from two other aircraft returning from a mission. Tapes and records (analysed some months later) obtained from an Airborne Warning (AWACS) aircraft flying high above the scene seemed to show that shortly after 03.30 two US aircraft flew low over Al Jubayl at 650 and 900 knots respectively. On the other hand, there is firm evidence that, among many others based at Al Jubayl, 'several individuals from a US Naval Construction Battalion were involved in these alerts and have reported health problems since their service. In fact their health problems were among the first Gulf War Illnesses-related incidents that had been reported.' Apparently there is no record of any aircraft jettisoning fuel anywhere near Al Jubayl and, in any case, the manufacturer of the alarms denies that jettisoned fuel will set them off; this was also the experience of soldiers at Al Jubayl, who later deliberately tried to trigger alarms with the vapour of aviation fuel. As for the alleged sonic booms, if that is what they were, what is the explanation for the almost simultaneous flashes in the night sky? Aircraft breaking the sound barrier do not make flashes. Lastly, a number of British veterans who were at Al Jubayl at the time were later to report health problems of the type associated with the Gulf War.

So, for every item of evidence that points one way, there is another which points in the other. After setting out the data and 'arguments' of both sides, the MOD report comes down against the possibility of a Scud attack or a sneak sortie by an Iraqi light aircraft fitted with spraying equipment. But the report does not mention the carcasses of two Scud missiles found a few hours later. One was in tidal water offshore from Al Jubayl, the other was in scrub just to the north of the complex. The warheads were semi-intact but empty, so they were clearly not loaded with high explosives. So what were they carrying? Maybe the Iraqis launched them empty – as 'frighteners'. Someone must know.

With this one most notable (crucial?) omission about the Scuds, the tone of the MOD's Al Jubayl document is, for once, not characterized by the confident denials of so many of its predecessors. It is an improvement. After nine years, it was not before time.[9]

KNOWING WHAT WE DO ABOUT the myriad chemical and biological hazards of what was by far the most toxic war in history, there can be little surprise that some troops returned with impaired health. It would have been amazing if they had not. In fact, before the war had even begun, the Americans and the British had lost – 'evacuated out of theatre' – three times as many men (700-plus) to illness as they were later to lose in the battle itself. Subsequently, after the servicemen came home, mystery

9. Eyewitness accounts tell of other Scud attacks on, for example, King Khalid Military City, Dhahran and Wadi-al-Batin. So many Coalition personnel tell of seeing Scuds and of detector alarms sounding that it is difficult to believe that they are all inventing their stories. Also, as at Al Jubayl, the official war diaries of a number of military units allegedly record these events.

and controversy began to build around two questions. First, why were so many affected? And, second, what had caused the problem?

The official answer, which covers both those questions, still says that no research has convincingly identified the cause of a so-called Gulf War Syndrome. Which is rather like saying that because no one has come up with a convincing explanation for the common cold (despite decades of research), no such thing exists. So why are all those people sneezing?

Anyway, to be looking for a single cause of 'illnesses' – which range from irritability and post-traumatic stress through chronic fatigue and aching joints to cancers and birth defects – is completely missing the point. Deliberately? Almost certainly there are different causes for different illnesses – goodness knows, the people who served in the Gulf came up against enough possibilities. Further, it is probable that a combination of drugs and vaccines induced a range of different problems in different people. Indeed, as has already been observed, it is recognized in pharmacology that as the number of combinations rises, the number of effects (and side effects) increases exponentially. So why should the MOD suppose that those NAP tablets have caused only a narrow set of reactions – and harmless ones at that? In fact, most doctors will say that PB (the key ingredient of those tablets) is one of the more difficult drugs to administer safely. This is probably why the American Food and Drug Administration was so reluctant to relax its stand on PB; it did not want to authorize a 'release' for the DOD to use it as a prophylactic in the Gulf. Nothing like enough was known about its interaction with other drugs. The Pentagon forced the FDA to issue a waiver 'in the national interest'. In Whitehall the MOD faced no such bureaucratic problems.

And then there was stress. Stress has never been fashionable. The sceptic points to those Londoners in the Blitz, or submariners, or Lancaster crews who knew they were on borrowed time after a dozen sorties. They kept going, didn't they? Yes, they did indeed. And, yes, they must have been highly stressed. But they were not full of drugs and vaccines at the same time. Does that make a difference? In truth, a number of wartime aircrew *did* succumb and had to be withdrawn from front-line service. And submariners and infantrymen and Londoners too. Some, with their nerves permanently 'shot', were 'never the same again'.

In those days the condition was sometimes ascribed, ungenerously, to 'LMF' or Lack of Moral Fibre. Before that it was battle fatigue or shell shock. The latter term is particularly appropriate. Sustained shellfire is said to be an experience terrifying beyond almost all others. Staying alive from one minute to the next becomes a matter of pure chance. But gunfire is far from the only 'assault' that can echo in the mind for years afterwards. In the Falklands the sheer intensity of close-quarter fighting had its effect. And seeing friends killed or wounded in terrible ways can, for some, leave irreparable mental scars. Months, even years later, a few of the doctors and medics who had had to deal with young men blown apart found themselves in NHS psychiatric wards. In the Gulf, too, the medics were among those keenly affected. Out in the desert a few soldiers found the weeks of waiting under the fear of knowing that Saddam Hussein had used chemical weapons on his earlier enemies was an experience that stayed with them.

Today it is usually called post-traumatic stress disorder (PTSD). Probably, of all the medical problems suffered by veterans, it is the one that is the least special to the Gulf. Men coming out of almost all conflicts have suffered from it. It seems to be random in effects and who it 'hits'. In the services, even though the condition is now acknowledged, it is still a difficult subject. There remains a reluctance to understand, let alone to sympathize, with those whose war wounds are mental rather than physical. Until very recently, military medicine concentrated on battle casualties – understandably. Now, perhaps, more attention should be given to those other victims of war whose wounds are not always open and visible. But, so far, not much impetus to that end has come from the MOD.

'ANYWAY, IF THERE IS NOTHING really wrong with me, why won't the blood transfusion people take my blood?' It sounds like a reasonable 'litmus' question from a puzzled Gulf veteran. And if the MOD says their illnesses are nothing to do with their Gulf service, why are over 2000 veterans being sent disability payments each month by the Department of Health and Social Security? Maybe the DHSS does not have a position to defend. Maybe it is not concerned with the possibility of paying out compensation. Maybe it recognizes that there is a problem. And why has the Danish Government agreed that 200 of the small contingent it sent to the Gulf should receive sickness pensions? Why should the French, who for so long denied that their forces had any problems stemming from Gulf service, lately have acknowledged that they have had some problems all along?

Lastly, there are some sceptical 'old soldiers' who, with a chest of well-earned honours and decorations, point out in letters to the broadsheets that a serviceman's life, once he goes to war, is full of risks. If you don't want to run those risks, they say, don't join up. Yes, but the dangers you face are meant to come from the enemy, not from your own side. Besides, from whichever side the hazards or the actual wounds of war derive, they are much harder to bear when your own side subsequently appears to disclaim responsibility, let alone lasting care. That, in the view of many veterans, is what the MOD has done for more than ten years. It is true that the veterans worst affected, perhaps those now in wheelchairs, seek financial help – compensation. But what most Gulf veterans are looking for is not much more than recognition of their problems and, thereafter, appropriate treatment. And there *are* treatments. They will not work for everyone because, once again, the evidence is that different people have different problems with different causes – there is no single syndrome. Yet a Corporal Lake appeared before the Commons Defence Committee in a wheelchair. Eight months later, having been to the US and been put on a regime of very intensive detoxification, he was walking again. Likewise a Sergeant Hale. Similarly some others. But it won't work for everyone. And it can cost at least £20,000 per person.

The lives of some veterans have been shortened. For others, their lives or those of their newborn children have at the least been made less whole. The fact is that, in any terms that matter, the relevant staff of the MOD – permanent civil servants, transitory ministers – have been mean in their acknowledgements and generous in their denials. That, if one talks to any veteran, is what hurts. But we are probably all to blame. We get the 'governors' we deserve. Nor have we ever been particularly generous or understanding to those returning from our wars – once they have been won. It is said that many of the wounded of Trafalgar wound up as beggars waving their stumps at passers-by. Maybe that is an exaggeration. Nevertheless, in these denials, the MOD and the rest of us are acting out a long-standing British tradition. It was well recognized by Rudyard Kipling:

> Oh, it's Tommy this, an' Tommy that, an' Tommy go away;
> But it's 'Thank you Mr Atkins' when the band begins to play.
> It's Tommy this, an' Tommy that, an' 'Chuck him out, the brute!'
> But it's 'Saviour of his country' when the guns begin to shoot.

SINCE THE CHAPTER ABOVE WAS finished in the autumn of 2002, one of the more intriguing developments in the continuing story of Gulf War Illnesses is revealed in a wisp of a comment made by Geoff Hoon, the Minister for Defence, in the Commons on 7 January 2003.

> The lesson has been learnt; there is now a process whereby individuals do not receive a number of vaccinations in a short time frame.

One might reasonably ask with some surprise, 'What lessons?' After all, for more than a decade, the official line has been adamant: the alleged illnesses among veterans were almost entirely psychosomatically induced – perhaps accelerated by a degree of stress. But that was common to all wars. Certainly, there were no lessons to be learnt. Indeed, the accusation that too many troops had received too many vaccinations (and in the wrong combinations) in too short a time was, along with all the other 'alleged' causes of veterans' problems, 'alarmist . . . and unsupported by the facts'. But now, if Mr Hoon meant what he said – that the previously uncompromising dictat had been reconsidered – one might ask what else in the list of Gulf War 'hazards', until now equally strongly denied, might be under review? What about those organophosphate insecticides, the NAP tablets, the CARC paint, the DU ammunition?

Clearly, in its preparations for a *second* Gulf War, the MOD had a problem. Or two. If it acknowledged making any significant changes from its earlier 'programmes' (in vaccines, drugs or insecticides), it would come very close to tacitly admitting that it might have got things wrong back in 1991. In short, given Mr Hoon's parliamentary reply, one might suppose that the MOD would have to concede that the claims about vaccines made by the 'damaged' veterans of the first Gulf War now had some real validity. But the sad fact is that one might go on 'supposing' for a very long time – or until one realized that Whitehall is just not susceptible to such straightforward logic.

With one particular vaccine, anthrax, it is now a matter of public and specific record that the MOD got it wrong. As was mentioned some pages back, in the month or two immediately prior to the first Gulf War, the MOD deliberately ignored an urgent warning from the Department of Health: anthrax vaccine should not be used in combination with that for pertussis (whooping cough). Trials on several hundred laboratory mice had shown that it caused 'severe deconditioning' of the animals – inducing many of the very symptoms about which, months later, after the war, some of the veterans began to complain. Anthrax is normally given (well separated from other injections) via three shots spread over a period of six months. But in 1991 there was a need to get immunized troops out to the Gulf as quickly as possible. So the vaccine was usually injected in two 'close-together' doses, plus – ignoring that warning – a booster (an adjuvant) of pertussis. Obviously, given the possibility that Saddam Hussein might use anthrax as a weapon, the MOD felt it had little choice but to take that considerable risk. One can understand the dilemma. But it is more difficult to understand the MOD's ten-year denial that the dilemma ever existed. Eventually, Lord Hunt, an ex-Health Minister who had resigned over the second Gulf War, brought the affair out into the open in October 2002 (in support of a Parliamentary Question from Lord Morris – a longtime champion of the disabled). So now the MOD was forced to admit that it had deliberately ignored the warning. But if anyone thought that admission might indicate a willingness to reconsider its earlier denials, they would (again) be misjudging the MOD.

A revealing illustration of the MOD's stubbornness is found in the story of Shaun Rusling. He had been a sergeant reservist in the Royal Army Medical Corps – called up for service in the 32 Field Hospital close to the Iraq border. Before he had even returned home at the end of the conflict, he began to feel ill. He subsequently developed severe joint pains, sweating and fevers. To these were added irritability and lassitude. After nearly a year back in 'civvy street', with his problems getting no better, he sought the opinion of four different medical specialists. It all took time but, eventually, armed with reports from those consultants, he submitted a claim to the MOD's War Pension Agency (WPA) for a full disability pension. More time went by. Then his claim was turned down. He decided to appeal the whole affair via the Services Pensions Appeal Tribunal. More time passed.

At last, in May 2002, the Appeal Tribunal, having made a thorough study of a lengthy counter-submission from the WPA, not only found for Mr Rusling, but was strongly critical of the way the WPA had earlier tried, without informing the claimant, to alter the official file on his claim. It had removed the conclusions of those four consultants who, individually and collectively, had diagnosed Mr Rusling as suffering from illnesses they considered to be directly attributable to his service in the Gulf. But after that diagnosis was forwarded to the MOD's War Pension unit, it was unilaterally changed. Indeed, when the file was produced at the Tribunal, an internal note (for MOD eyes only?) was found which read: 'The rejected label "Gulf Syndrome" has been replaced by an acceptance of the label "Symptoms and signs of ill-defined conditions".' As the Tribunal seemed to ask in its conclusions: Rejected? Accepted? By whom? Certainly not by the specialists who had examined the claimant. Nor, for that matter, by the claimant himself.[10]

In short, by amending the judgement of the four clinicians to the point where their judgement might as well have not been made, the authorities had attempted to confirm their own contention that there was no such thing as Gulf War Syndrome. And, of course, if there was no such thing, then no one could be suffering from it. And if no one was suffering from it, no floodgates could be opened to other claimants. QED.

In the particular case of Mr Rusling, the Tribunal's criticism of the way the WPA had behaved was dry and to the point.

> We note that this action has significantly increased the delay in this appeal. We conclude that the Secretary of State for Defence has failed to show beyond reasonable doubt that the Gulf war syndrome is not attributable to Mr Rusling's service.

10. It is interesting that 'signs and symptoms of ill-defined conditions' is a non-disease in that it is not to be found in the bible of these things – the WHO's *Classification of Disease*, 10th edition, ICD-10. It is a Whitehall invention.

Further, as that quote implies, the Tribunal was not impressed by the length of time it had taken to resolve the case – seven years. In assembling all the papers necessary to pursue his appeal, Shaun Rusling and his wife found that, time and again, the MOD had misplaced or even lost important documents. The delays and procrastinations were endless. For the first year or two, the Ruslings attributed these problems to mere inefficiency. But as time went on, they wondered if there might be more to it than that. After six years they were no longer wondering.

The MOD and its Pension Agency decided to appeal the Tribunal's verdict. Ten months passed before the case came to court. The hearing at the High Court lasted two days and cost the taxpayer at least £250,000. Mr Justice Newman dismissed the appeal on every count. Now (early 2004) officialdom is trying to say that only *some* of Shaun Rusling's complaints are attributable to his Gulf service; the rest are 'signs and symptoms of ill-defined conditions'. So, once again, the MOD is in the business of rewriting a formal document, namely a High Court judgement. It has presumably done this in order to prevent many hundreds of other claimants coming in on the back of the Rusling case.

Most recently, it seems that the MOD has decided to settle with Mr Rusling (up to a point and on its own terms). It makes clear that this should not be taken as a precedent for all the other claimants. It seems to argue that, because the exact nature of their health problems varies from one veteran to the next, each person will have to be considered on a case-by-case basis. That way, the process could drag on for years – 'Until,' as one veteran put it, 'we're all dead anyway'. Is it too cynical to suggest that that may be the idea?

Nevertheless, at least one other claimant has recently scored a direct hit on the MOD. Corporal Alex Izett is rather special. In 1991, as a twenty-one-year-old, he was given the full cocktail of vaccines. But then he never went to the Gulf. So he missed the possible hazards of NAP pills, organophosphates, depleted uranium or any of the other 'risks' of the war zone. But this did not save him from soon developing osteoporosis and acute depression. Osteoporosis is very rare in a man so young – though a number of other veterans also suffer from it. So what induced it? Three years ago, in response to a tiresomely persistent Mr Izett, the MOD asked one of its own 'employees', Colonel Graham Howe (a clinical director with the British Forces Health Service), to examine and report on Mr Izett. The Colonel concluded that it was the pattern of injections which had 'most probably led to the development of auto-immune-induced osteoporosis'. He could see no other reasonable explanation. That report, dated 22 September 2001, was given no publicity – until January 2004, when Mr Izett agreed to give a copy to *The Times*. As in the case of Shaun Rusling, the Appeals Tribunal had found for Mr Izett. For its part, the MOD continued (and continues) to deny that the vaccines could be a cause of any Gulf War Illness. Nevertheless, it seems that a few 'lessons' had been learnt.

At about the same time as the Tribunal published its finding for Shaun Rusling, officialdom was facing discomfort of a different kind. The setting was a crowded room in Portcullis House, hard by the Houses of Parliament. A small group of MPs, plus that constant champion of the disabled, Lord (Alf) Morris, was hosting a group of US Congressmen. Months earlier, Lord Morris and Bruce George MP had been over to Washington – uniquely invited to sit with a Congressional Committee taking evidence from American veterans and scientists. Now the Committee had come to Westminster – to question more veterans and scientists. Travelling with the American party was the billionaire and recurrent presidential candidate, Ross Perot. Over the years he has pumped millions of dollars into various programmes of 'Gulf' research. Consequently, he has been deeply unpopular with the Pentagon – because it has not been able to call the tune over the research he funds. Or its results.

For some years, the elf-like Texan has paid for a team led by Professor Robert Hayley at the Houston Medical Center. It seems widely agreed that Professor Hayley has done more research into, and knows more about, the probable causes of Gulf Illnesses than anyone else on either side of the Atlantic. Now he was invited to speak in London. The six-man MOD contingent sitting in the audience looked rather uncomfortable. The Professor politely demolished the basis of at least one British study (partly funded and often quoted by the MOD) which claimed that veterans were, with only a few exceptions, the victims of their own imaginations. Then he turned to the thinking of his own team.

He reminded the audience of the 1998 gas attack on the Tokyo subway. He pointed out that many of those who had survived now suffered from a spectrum of health problems which were almost identical to those of many Gulf veterans. He pointed especially to brain damage. The gas used in Tokyo was sarin. Saddam Hussein was known to have had stockpiles of that gas. The Professor's suggestion was that the bombing of Iraqi munitions depots in the weeks before the ground war began (and their demolition after it) had caused quantities of sarin to be released. The prevailing winds could have carried an unseen and weak 'solution' of the gas over thousands of American and British troops who were getting ready for the advance. This scenario might account for the dozens of unexplained gas alarms which sounded during those early weeks. At first, everyone had rushed to get into their Noddy suits and gas masks. But with no apparent source of the gas (no Scuds, nothing showing up on air reconnaissance) it was soon decided that the alarms must be false. And that has been the official story ever since. But if so, one might expect that the MOD and DOD would have ordered a redesign of those 'cry wolf' alarms. Yet, in over ten years, the manufacturers (mostly Czech – they are the experts) report that no such order has been made. Anyway, the Czechs are sure that their alarms are at least 90 per cent reliable.

Professor Hayley was listened to in silence. He was certainly not suggesting that he thought the 'spilling' of sarin from Iraqi arms dumps was the only cause of Gulf War Syndrome. Far from it. Nevertheless, given the clear Tokyo parallels, sarin was now a likely source of some of the veterans' problems.

The Congressmen then listened to a small group of British scientists brought together by Professor Malcolm Hooper. They spoke about their research over the years into the organic 'insults' caused by other hazards – from DU dust through multiple vaccines to organophosphates. The damage was, in their view, absolutely certain. The fact is that across the global community of medical scientists this is an ever-broader and ever-deeper conclusion. The MOD and the DOD have become the increasingly isolated 'hold-outs'.

There was other persuasive testimony. John Nichol, the Tornado observer who had been captured by the Iraqis, gave evidence. Although he is not a victim of the Syndrome, he has long been a champion of the cause. In some detail he now accused the MOD (under both the Conservatives and Labour) of indifference, of pretending that there really was no problem, of looking the other way.

One of the last and most unexpected witnesses was Mrs Samantha Thompson. Her husband, a Petty Officer in the Fleet Air Arm, had died of motor neurone disease less than six months earlier. He was forty-two. He had attributed his illness to the NAP tablets and the injections. Being at sea, it seems unlikely that he was affected by that sarin cloud or the DU. Mrs Thompson had come with her six-year-old daughter. She explained that as a widow she had had no real help from Whitehall or its agencies. And she asked how, when Hannah grew a little older, she was meant to explain her father's death. Silence. The Americans were not the only ones to be moved. Their chairman looked across to Hannah. 'Young lady, your dad is a hero to this country and to the world of freedom.' There was another brief silence. It was a very American way of putting it.

THE MOD HAS OTHER PROBLEMS too. It would be worried by what it sees happening across the Atlantic. The first cracks have appeared in the long-sustained denials of the Americans. True, the Department of Defence (DOD) has not voiced any second thoughts – not publicly anyway. That has been done by the Department of Veterans' Affairs. But the DVA, although it is a separate and full-blown Department of the Federal Government, works closely with the DOD. In that liaison, it would be most unlikely that the two Departments would not be marching loosely in step. So, perhaps to save itself some discomfort, the DOD has been content to let the DVA lead the way in announcing that there have been the beginnings of an official rethink. The increasing weight of independent research by some of the most respected scientists in the land has forced this reappraisal – at last.

It is worth looking at the text of one the DVA's statements. It came from the Department's Deputy Head when he appeared before a Congressional Committee. Years earlier, after days of listening to the evidence, that same committee had been stingingly critical of the DVA and the DOD. 'We find that when it comes to diagnosis, treatment and research for Gulf War veterans, the Federal government has too often had a tin ear, a cold heart and a closed mind.' Now (28 October 2002) a senior official in that government was to admit that that criticism had been not far off the mark.

> Clearly, the past decade has not covered the DVA in glory. However, since taking office last year, this Administration [i.e. that of George Bush] has begun to change that perhaps-deserved Congressional perception [of having a tin ear etc.] . . . . I say this in light of DVA's move to cover undiagnosed illnesses stemming from service in the Gulf War . . . . There is increasing objective evidence that a major category of Gulf War Illnesses is neurological in character . . . . We want to underscore the fact that research into Gulf War Illnesses is an area ripe for important discoveries . . . . There is money to support new hypotheses . . . . We want to send a message to veterans: science is finally beginning to unravel the mysteries of Gulf War Illnesses.

A question: can one imagine anyone from the MOD making that kind of statement? The MOD line is that there are no 'mysteries' where GWS is concerned. Never has been; it is all in the mind.

Of course, one should not be *too* confident that official American attitudes have markedly changed. And even if they really have, it will take time – years, probably – for the results to feed through. But, with the US government now funding a number of independent scientists whose earlier research has not been notably 'sympathetic' to the official line, plus an apparent disposition at least to listen to their findings, there really does seem to be some willingness to re-examine some earlier shibboleths. If the MOD is not worried, it should be.

OBVIOUSLY, IN THE WHOLE complicated argument that surrounds GWS, much interest now centres on any GWS-type symptoms which may be developing among servicemen currently returning (or already returned) from the Gulf. So far, when compared with the numbers after the first Gulf War, the proportion of 'new' veterans with health problems seems to be down. But then one remembers that after that first Gulf conflict some of the problems did not manifest themselves for two or even three years – it can take that long for some cancers and some autoimmune problems to develop. So it may be too soon to tell.

Nevertheless, we now know that the MOD did order a change to some of its more controversial procedures. It is a moot question whether this was done in the light of 'lessons learnt', or because some unit commanders reported that they were likely to have a near-mutiny on their hands if the inflexibility of the 1991 procedures was repeated. Anyway, for whichever reason (maybe both?), servicemen were now given the option of not having the full programme of injections – though, if they took up the option, they were warned that the responsibility for any consequences was entirely theirs. In some units the take-up of the vaccines was as low as 50 per cent. With the anthrax jab(s) it was sometimes even lower. In another direction, it seems that the use of those insecticides based on organophosphate was much more disciplined than in 1991. And although the taking of NAP pills was still compulsory, it is known that some servicemen (senior and junior) quietly ignored that particular discipline. These factors may have had an effect in reducing the ill health of the 'new' veterans. And there is at least one other probability which could have played its part: this time, the Iraqis seemed not to have had any cylinders of sarin gas stored in their arms dumps. In the first Gulf War there was almost certainly some sarin 'spillage' caused by Allied bombing and, immediately after hostilities, by careless demolition. Some of that 'spillage' almost certainly drifted downwind, albeit at weak levels, over and into Allied troop formations.

So, up to now, what health problems *have* been identified in servicemen coming home from the second Gulf War? And in what numbers? As has already been mentioned, so far the numbers seem to be well down. But, with two possible additions, the range of 'complaints' seems to be about the same. Beyond that it would unfair (to the MOD as much as to the 2003 veterans) to be too specific. It may also be too soon to tell. Nevertheless, the two Gulf Veterans' Associations report that between them, they receive an average of six or seven communications each week (via telephone and e-mail) from servicemen (regular and reservist) or their families. Some of the calls come from wives worried about the changes they see in their husbands.

A few of those calls have been about the two 'exceptions' just mentioned. A number of soldiers (one report speaks of over eighty) have been hospitalized with a pneumonia-like illness, the symptoms of which include congested lungs and impaired breathing. Another group of more than 150 men serving in the Royal Irish Rangers have reported long-lasting and severe gastric/stomach pain. This latter may be due to one of those (water-borne?) bugs which are fairly common 'east of Suez', but which, once in the gut, are extraordinarily difficult to get rid of. Research is, apparently, 'ongoing'. In the matter of the pneumonia-like illness, there is a strong suspicion that this is much more directly the consequence of the war's environment. Suspicion points to the heavy use of depleted uranium (in tank ammunition and artillery shells) in some areas of the advance towards Baghdad and Basra. Any troops then moving through the stuff would inevitably have been breathing it. Again, research is 'ongoing'. But it will be very surprising if the MOD admits to any responsibilities.

The Veterans' Associations suspect (but it is impossible to prove) that, just as after the first Gulf War, some regular soldiers are reluctant to report their health concerns because they are worried that the 'evidence' might be used to 'brown envelope' them – to prematurely discharge them. There have been rumours (and Parliamentary Questions) about what the MOD formally calls 'manning control'. This is a process whereby, sometimes (but by no means always) after failing a fitness test, a serviceman subsequently receives an OHMS envelope containing, in effect, his discharge papers. A soldier normally signs on for twenty-two years, but he can decide to leave at three-year intervals. The Army, in its turn, can normally 'terminate' a man's service at six, nine or twelve years. It is no secret that, pressed by the Treasury, the MOD has been examining all its options to economize. One way in which a considerable saving can be made is by stepping in at a man's twelve-year point. Otherwise, of course, he may choose to go for the full twenty-two years and then retire on a maximum pension. Expensive.

Sometimes, it really does seem to be a case of '*Tommy this, an' Tommy that, an' Tommy go away*'.

HMS *GLORIOUS*, *ARDENT* AND *ACASTA*

'An accident of war'

The Admiralty has tried to suppress the truth for forty years.

Capt. Stephen Roskill DSC, author of the 1954 *Official History of the Royal Navy in World War II*, writing twenty-six years later in 1980[1]

The loss of the Glorious *and her destroyers is one of the three great RN tragedies of the War (Convoy PQ17,* Prince of Wales *and* Repulse *are the other two) which were due to incompetence and misjudgement. And it is the one which has been the least explained.*

Vice Admiral Sir Louis Le Bailly KBE, CB, Royal Navy 1932–72[2]

The Glorious *had been detached to proceed home independently owing to a shortage of fuel and was now 200 miles ahead of the main convoy. This explanation is not convincing. The* Glorious *presumably had enough fuel to steam at the speed of the main convoy. All should have kept together.*

Sir Winston Churchill in volume one of his war memoirs, *The Gathering Storm*

AT JUST AFTER 6.30 on a February evening in 1999, a small group of overcoated pensioners leant forward to listen to the proceedings starting below. This was the Visitors' Gallery in the House of Commons. They had come from around the country to hear a debate about the circumstances surrounding the loss of fathers, brothers and cousins in a long-distant but, for them, not entirely forgotten wartime incident. The debate was merely 'on the adjournment', so the House was very thinly attended. Nevertheless, given that the events being discussed had happened nearly sixty years earlier, this was an extraordinary occasion.

1. Feature article in the *Sunday Times*, 15 June 1980.
2. Letter to the author, 6 February 1999.

KADETT SIEGFRIED GOSS was on duty high in the lookout-top. As he scanned the horizon away to the north-east, he steadied his binoculars on what he later said he thought was a wisp of smoke. Whatever it was, it was certainly not cloud. He looked again. Then he called the bearing to the bridge below. Down there, other binoculars were trained and, after the shortest of pauses, orders were given. *Scharnhorst* and her sister ship *Gneisenau* gathered speed and cautiously turned to investigate. The time was logged as 16.46; German clocks ran an hour ahead of British time. It was 8 June 1940.

Barely two-and-a-half hours later, in one of the most one-sided of the war's many naval engagements, the aircraft carrier HMS *Glorious* and her two escorting destroyers, HMS *Ardent* and HMS *Acasta*, had been sunk. In terms of the 1519 lives lost, this was probably the Royal Navy's greatest single disaster of World War II.[3] It was certainly one of its most needless. Which is probably why the official smoke screen laid down shortly afterwards has never really disappeared. Even today, more than six decades later, it seems that some of the facts are still too uncomfortable to find a place in the official narrative. Either that or it would simply be too embarrassing to change any aspect of an official account held so firmly and for so long.

Those were the closing days of the Norwegian campaign – a brave but ill-judged Anglo-French attempt to stem the Nazi conquest of Norway and, towards the end, to deny the Germans the high-grade iron ore coming out through the Arctic port of Narvik. Not for the first time with a British expeditionary force, it was an operation characterized by crippling inadequacies – in troops, equipment, training, aircraft, intelligence and, above all, in strategic thinking at the outset.

The only arm of the British services able to give a consistent account of itself was the Royal Navy. Even so, in the eight weeks that the campaign lasted, it took heavy losses – many of them from air attack. Our ships paid the price of having had a naval hierarchy which, for twenty years, had failed to understand properly the potential dangers of attack

3. The greatest loss (1415) from a single ship occurred with the sinking of HMS *Hood*. In the catastrophic loss of HMS *Prince of Wales* and *Repulse* off Malaya, 840 lost their lives.

from above. Nevertheless, the Navy did not fail in offensive spirit. It engaged the Germans wherever it could find them and, against all reasonable odds, it often got the better of them. It was in Norwegian waters that the Navy gained its first three Victoria Crosses of the War. Two were awarded posthumously.

This was also the first time in any war that aircraft carriers, HMS *Glorious*, *Furious* and *Ark Royal*, played a significant role. Their aircraft, obsolescent biplanes (with the exception of the new but under-powered Skuas), were outclassed by almost everything the Germans could put in the air. All the same, the aircrews were in almost constant action – providing defensive cover for the Navy and occasionally, when the weather allowed, flying sorties in support of the troops ashore.

Nonetheless, by the end of May it had become obvious to the War Cabinet that there was nothing to be gained by maintaining what was now little more than a toehold on a distant Arctic shore. Further, with the Germans surging across the Low Countries towards the Channel, there were other, more urgent priorities.

So the decision was made to evacuate. There were more than 20,000 troops to bring home and as much of their equipment as could be salvaged. They would have to be brought out in merchant ships and convoyed back across more than 1000 miles of unsecured sea. Thus the plan to withdraw was kept a very close secret; it was told only to those who really needed to know, and, as it turned out, it was not even told to all of them. The fear was that if the Germans learnt what was going on, they would send some of their heavier warships northward to intercept the lightly escorted convoys. Thousands of troops might have been lost. Extraordinarily, not even the officers in charge of RAF Coastal Command were told – despite the fact that Sunderland flying boats based in the Shetlands might have provided vital warning if the Germans had decided to mount a naval attack on those convoys. Actually, unknown to the British, the Germans already had a fair idea of what was afoot – they had breached enough of our naval cyphers to make an informed guess. And their reconnaissance aircraft had spotted enough of the gathering troop transports to confirm their suspicions.

Glorious had a particular role in the evacuation. She was to recover a squadron of RAF Gladiator fighters from Norway. Because the wings of

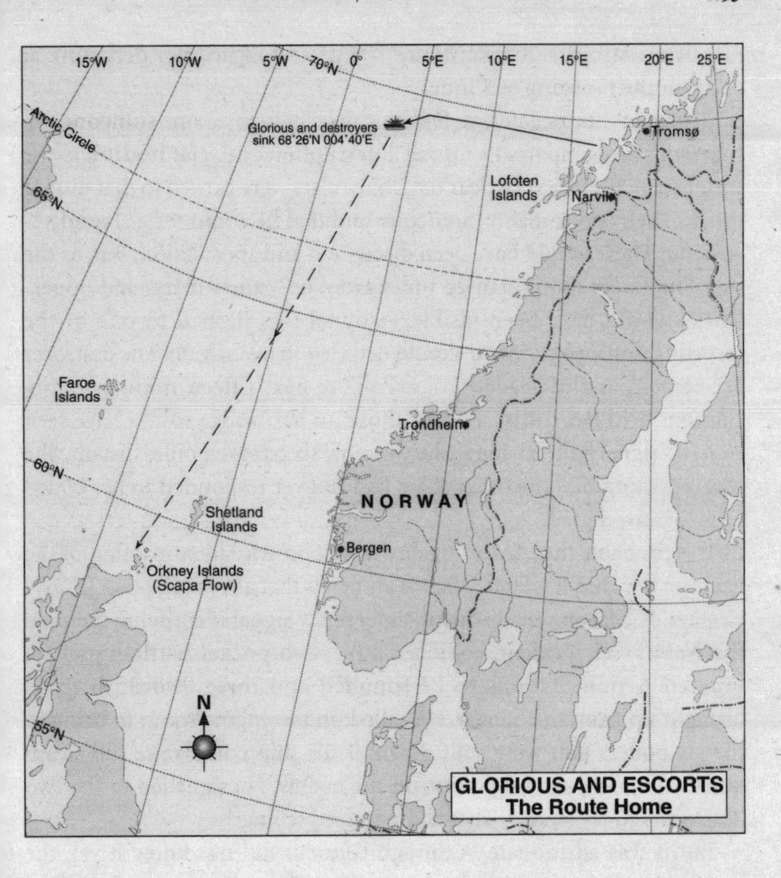

the RAF aircraft did not fold (unlike those of naval aircraft), they needed more hangar space. Consequently, to make room, *Glorious* had landed most of her own Swordfish torpedo-bombers in Orkney some days earlier. Now she carried just five Swordfish and nine Sea Gladiator fighters.

In the normal course of events *Glorious* might have been expected to form part of the escort for the last of those homeward-bound troop convoys, along with *Ark Royal*, the cruisers *Coventry* and *Southampton*, and a small fleet of destroyers. As it turned out, having taken aboard those RAF aircraft (plus another unexpected squadron), she hurriedly left for home twenty-four hours ahead of the main group – with an escort of just two destroyers. *Ark Royal* saw her go and logged her departure at 02.53 on the morning of 8 June.

Thirteen hours later, a few minutes before 16.00, someone on *Glorious*'s bridge spotted a minute interruption of the far horizon to the south-west. It was a very clear day. Binoculars were turned to that distant speck. Then (presumably) someone said that he could see a second silhouette. There would have been discussion and speculation. But, as the two ships were more than 20 miles away, only their masts and upperworks would have been visible. A signal was flashed to one of the escorting destroyers: *Ardent* should detach – to investigate. The destroyer accelerated as she headed away. For the next fifteen minutes or so, *Glorious* held her course. At last, those on her bridge would have seen *Ardent*'s signal light flashing. She was now six or seven miles distant. She was reporting that the other ships had not yet responded to her coded interrogative signal.

It is probable that *Ardent* made the first positive identification of the enemy a few minutes later. What is known is that at 16.15 Captain D'Oyly Hughes of *Glorious* made out an emergency signal identifying them, in the Navy's 'self-evident' code, as 2PB – two pocket battleships.[4] He ordered Action Stations to be sounded and three Swordfish to be brought up from the hangar. He called on the engine room to bring in the six boilers that were shut down; if his ship could raise full steam quickly enough, she might outrun the enemy. He signalled to the two destroyers to lay smoke. They did not need telling.[5]

But it was all too late. Although *Glorious* did not know it yet, the enemy vessels were not pocket battleships. They were faster, bigger and much more heavily armed. They were 32-knot battle cruisers. Moreover, *Glorious* could not fly off her Swordfish torpedo bombers without steaming upwind – towards the enemy. Anyway, it had taken ten minutes

4. This 'code' was merely an official list of easily understood abbreviations – i.e. it was self-evident. So, for example, 'PB' stood for pocket battleship. It was not in any sense a secure or secret code except in terms of the ship's position.
5. Survivors' accounts are in ADM178/201. In particular, in ADM1/19406, there is an account written by *Glorious*'s senior Warrant Telegraphist, Ernest Blackwell, when he returned home from being a POW in 1945. He tells how the captain handed him the signal identifying the enemy.

to get them onto the flight deck; it would have taken at least another ten to arm them with torpedoes.

The first salvo fell short. It was a complete surprise – the enemy was more than 14 miles distant. A few minutes later there was a second salvo: it was a straddle. The Germans now had the range. At 16.38 and at a range of over 13 miles, the third salvo found its target. The flight deck was holed and two of the Swordfish were blown to pieces.[6] *Glorious*'s only chance was to outrun the enemy. But with a third of her boilers still working up to full pressure, she was well short of top speed. Meanwhile, she was hit again and again. At about 17.00, for a few minutes, the smoke screens laid by the destroyers caused the Germans to lose the range. It was not long before they found it again.

There could never have been any doubt about the outcome. The German battle log shows that *Ardent* turned over at about 17.25, *Glorious* at 18.12, *Acasta* at 18.17. The log also shows that towards the end of the action, at 17.39, *Scharnhorst* was hit aft by a torpedo (from *Acasta*) and had to reduce speed. But once they were sure that the British were finished, both the Germans quickly made off – back to southern Norway. *Scharnhorst* needed to make urgent repairs.

In the water, those men that had not been dragged down with their ships were struggling to the few emergency rafts that had been launched. There was not much of a sea running but it was cold. Very few survived that night.

No one knew anything about the losses until the Germans made a triumphant announcement twenty-four hours later. To the Navy, the news was devastating. In the Fleet Air Arm (FAA), a navy within the Navy, where almost everyone knew everyone else, some men wept for their friends. Then, as an FAA Commander on duty in the Admiralty later recalled, they became angry:

> I had often heard mutinous remarks in the Operations Division, but that night the conversation could only be called Red Mutiny. We mourned our friends and damned the crass inefficiency that had

6. Based on the contemporary German records and an interview in Australia in 1997 with Cdr V. McBride, who, as a nineteen-year-old Telegraphist/Airgunner, was preparing one of those Swordfish.

> caused the loss of this fine old ship. Such errors showed what little influence the few professional aviators had upon current operations.[7]

The questions began almost immediately – formally within the Admiralty and much less formally in wardrooms and mess decks throughout the fleet. How had it happened? What had gone wrong? Who had been in charge? Where had the rest of our ships been? Why were there so few survivors? At the time there were few official explanations and most of them were distrusted. Indeed, the questions about the loss of *Glorious* and her escorts have never really gone away. Down the years, they have been asked by naval officers, reputable naval historians, MPs and relatives. The answers have always seemed too easy in the manner in which they explain away the things that went wrong. Officially, it was all just very bad luck; there had been no significant blunders. Which is why, in January 1999, those pensioners in the Visitors' Gallery were listening so intently to the proceedings going on immediately below.

The debate had been initiated by the Rt Hon. Alan Beith MP. Two of his constituents, in lengthy correspondence with the MOD's Naval Historical Branch (NHB), had long disputed the official version of events. From around the country they had enlisted others with similar concerns. These were not troublemakers, but people who believed that, since the beginning, they had always been told much less than the truth. Nor were they the only disbelievers. Since the very beginning, in and beyond the Navy, there had been distrust.

This was certainly not the first time the matter of *Glorious* had been raised in Parliament. In the summer of 1940, within weeks of the disaster, and then later, just after the war, questions had been asked. The tenor of the response had always seemed much the same: 'While, of course, everyone has the deepest sympathy for those who lost relatives, the incident itself was one of those tragic accidents of war which could not have been foreseen or avoided.' Now, after nearly six decades, the Minister's reply to Alan Beith was little different. Just occasionally, if one listened hard, one caught what might have been an almost imperceptible easing in the confident certainties that had always been used in the past. But in his reply – prepared and

7. A letter in the *Glorious* file in the Churchill Archive Centre.

written for him by the NHB, the keepers of the official tablets in these matters – the Minister for the Armed Forces, John Spellar, was not giving much away. He saw no reason to 'debate' the issue. Or to depart from the long-established script – which had a reason for everything that had gone wrong. Indeed, it hardly acknowledged that anything had gone wrong. Yet it was in clear error on some key facts and claimed an unmerited certainty on others. However, at least and at last, an alternative account, as presented in some detail by Mr Beith, would now be preserved in *Hansard*.

Of all the questions asked since the very beginning, by far the most important has always centred on *Glorious*'s independent return from Norway. Why, against all normal naval doctrine (then and now) centring on the principle of mutual support and protection, and contrary to all carrier practice (then and now), was this valuable but lightly armed and thinly armoured ship allowed to depart for home with an escort of just two destroyers? These were, after all, unsecured waters. Indeed, two months earlier German 'heavy units', including the formidable battle cruiser *Scharnhorst*, had been sighted (and then lost in diminishing visibility) in those very waters. Furthermore, only forty-eight hours earlier *Ark Royal* had despatched air patrols out to the south and west to a depth of 125 miles, 'as it was considered possible from intercepted messages that an enemy surface force might be in the vicinity'. The patrols had seen nothing. But that was two whole days before. Since then, 'an enemy surface force' could very easily have crept in and positioned itself across the likely course of home-bound ships.

Given these warnings, why had *Glorious* not waited just twenty-four hours to come home in company with *Ark Royal*, two cruisers and eight destroyers – which were themselves escorting that final convoy of more than 12,000 troops? Why, when the Germans found her, was *Glorious* flying no air patrols? Why did she not even have aircraft armed and in readiness on her flight deck? Why did she not have adequate lookouts posted (there was no one in her crow's nest)? Why was her crew at Cruising Stations (almost the lowest degree of readiness)? Why was she not warned that enemy warships might be somewhere along her track? Why were her urgent signals (no one doubted that she would have sent them) never heard, or if they were, not acted on? Why was the Admiral who had let *Glorious* go never questioned, or if he was, why is there no record of his answers? Why, to end it all, did the Navy break its own iron rule and not hold a proper inquiry into the disaster?

So many questions. So few answers.

IN FACT, IT IS NOT wholly accurate to say that the Navy never conducted an inquiry. Just fourteen days after the sinkings, when the few survivors reached home, an Inquiry was convened in Rosyth to find out what they knew. But as none of the survivors had been senior enough to be involved in any of the key decisions taken aboard the carrier, their evidence was of very limited use. Much of their testimony concerned their privations once they were in the water, which, while harrowing – there were not enough boats or floats to go round – did not explain why they were in the water in the first place. The three-man Board recorded that the loss of *Glorious* and the destroyers 'arose from circumstances beyond the scope of this Inquiry'; they assumed that a proper investigation into what they called 'the external circumstances' – the real causes and the background of the disaster – would, in time, be held 'elsewhere'. It never was. Nevertheless, the minutes of this inadequate debriefing were given the status of a full-blown Inquiry and stamped with the forbidding notation 'Closed until 2041'. This, of course, did nothing to allay the distrust of those who, over the ensuing decades, believed the rumour that the Admiralty was sitting on a 'secret file'. It merely added to their suspicion that there was, and continued to be, a cover-up.

In the event, when the file was 'prematurely' released to the Public Records Office (PRO) in 1993 under the Conservatives' Open Government policy, it contained little that was not already known. Perhaps the most revealing entry is a handwritten note by the First Sea Lord, Admiral Sir Dudley Pound. Having read the Inquiry minutes, he wrote, 'They seem to have forgotten they were a Man o' War.' That alone would seem to torpedo many of the easy explanations that have flowed ever since, first from the Admiralty and then, more recently, the MOD.

Returning to June 1940, the Admiralty ordered survivors to keep their experiences to themselves. There were good grounds for this. But, quite apart from considerations of security and naval and national morale, there were other reasons why the Admiralty did not immediately make a serious investigation into what had gone wrong. June 1940 was a desperate time:

the Norwegian campaign (in which *Glorious* had just played her part) had ended in a scrambled withdrawal; Dunkirk had just seen its 'miracle'; Paris had fallen and France was crumbling; Italy was entering the war; a German invasion was a real possibility. So, understandably, the Admiralty had many more urgent and immediate concerns than the whys and wherefores of the loss of *Glorious* and her destroyers – something that, in those perilous days, was already history.

Nevertheless, in reply to the questions inevitably being asked, some sort of answer had to be advanced. Some time after the disaster it was officially stated that the reason for *Glorious*'s early and independent departure from Norway was that she was so low on fuel that she could not afford to wait for *Ark Royal*, the cruisers and the destroyers. Given the urgencies of the time, that explanation – though disbelieved by many – would have to suffice. But the priorities of 1940 do not explain why, in later, post-war years, the authorities remained so reluctant to enquire too deeply – despite the questions still being raised in Parliament, in the Navy and among relatives. Could it have been that the circumstances surrounding the loss of *Glorious* and her destroyers were, and still are, too uncomfortable to contemplate? On the evidence now available, it would seem so.

According to a file in the PRO, six months after the war ended, and more than five years after the sinkings, the Admiralty received notice of some impending enquiries from a few MPs. Most of the questions were from Richard Stokes, a Labour MP for an Ipswich constituency. He had asked some of the first questions back in 1940 and, as a consequence of his interest, had long been the recipient of letters from survivors and others. Now, when the Admiralty learnt that Parliamentary Questions were on the way, it was suggested that perhaps the time had come for a full-scale Inquiry into the whole affair. But a senior civil servant advised firmly against such a move. In a memo which has echoes even today, he wrote, 'A full report at this stage would make very dismal reading and would invite Mr Stokes and other MPs to ask why this or that was not done.'[8] This seems to indicate that the loss of those three ships was recognized as something that did not need the media interest which would inevitably follow a full inquiry.

8. ADM199/480, page 145; a memo signed by R.R. Powell.

Nevertheless, MPs' questions just would not go away, and in May 1946 the Parliamentary Secretary to the Admiralty, John Dugdale, was forced to answer them. He did so with a confidence that brooked little argument. He claimed that if *Glorious* had not left ahead of the main group, 'She would have had insufficient fuel to reach British territory.' His advisors, who must have put him up to that reply, would have known from the log kept by *Ark Royal*, with whom *Glorious* was operating 'in company' almost mile by mile throughout that final sortie off Norway, that their 'advice' was untrue. The figures, together with the details of *Glorious*'s own fuel consumption (tons per mile at different speeds) as recorded in her last log to survive (March 1940), are available today in the Public Records Office. With some very simple arithmetic, which will be examined in due course, they show that she had ample fuel to reach 'British territory' – i.e. Scapa Flow. Indeed, at cruising speed she could even have reached her home port of Plymouth. The arithmetic would have been easily available to the Minister's advisors.

Not for the last time in this story, a parliamentary answer was knowingly untrue. And what about the MOD's present-day explanation: that what the Minister really meant was that *Glorious* could not have reached Scapa Flow without breaching an Admiralty 'requirement that ships should maintain a 33 per cent reserve'? If that is what the Minister meant, why did he not say so? The fact is (then and now) that whenever a warship's fuel drops to less than 50 per cent there will be concerns. But despite the MOD's implication, the 33 per cent 'requirement' was never an absolute; it was always interpreted in the light of operational priorities – as, when shown the evidence, the NHB now reluctantly admits.[9] Anyway, in the case of *Glorious* it has long been argued that the priority would have been (should have been) the safety of the ship and that, in waiting for the main group, her Captain would have been completely justified in using a small part of that 33 per cent reserve.

The Admiralty's obvious unwillingness to ask itself or anyone else the pertinent questions continued through the following decades. It is as if, by not asking any awkward questions, it could avoid awkward answers.

9. The NHB has been somewhat pushed into this acknowledgement by the testimony of naval officers who served through the war.

After all, a number of the key participants lived on for at least another twenty years. Most notably, the Admiral in overall command of *Ark Royal* and *Glorious*, Vice Admiral Wells, the man more responsible than any other for permitting that early and independent departure, lived until 1965. Extraordinarily, no one from the Admiralty ever seems to have asked him why he let *Glorious* go.

In fact, almost from the beginning, Vice Admiral Wells became a non-person in official thinking. Even in the 1999 Commons debate, the Minister told the House (reading from the NHB script) that 'tragically no officer or senior rating survived the loss of *Glorious* who was in a position to comment on navigation, operations or command decisions'. This most misleading form of words (a half-truth if ever there was one) quite ignores the fact that Wells, the man in a better position than anyone else to comment on why *Glorious* departed ahead of the main group – the most disastrous 'command decision' of all – 'survived' for another twenty-five years.

But, even in its most literal sense, the statement to the House that there was no survivor 'who was in a position to comment on navigation, operations or command decisions' is untrue. One of the key *Glorious* survivors was the man who had been in charge of transmitting her urgent signals – her 'Enemy Sighting Report' (ESR) and the several repeats of that signal. These are the signals that, tragically, were officially never heard, or at the least, 'never understood', and about which there has been confusion and dispute right from the day they were made. Yet when Warrant Officer Blackwell returned from being a POW in 1945 (he was one of four survivors picked up by the Germans thirty-six hours after the sinking), he was never called to the Admiralty to be debriefed. Instead, he seems merely to have been asked to write down what he remembered – in longhand from his home address. And that was evidently the end of it. Perhaps, again, no one really wanted to know. His report, three pages of it now in the PRO, raises any number of questions – questions he was never asked.[10] He, too, lived on for some years. Even today his testimony is ignored, except where the MOD's in-house historians take his most crucial evidence about the wavelength and the content of *Glorious*'s first

10. ADM1/19406.

urgent signal, and then, by misquoting him, get things crucially wrong – a point which will be examined in some detail later.

Time and again one is forced to the conclusion that there has been a reluctance, sometimes amounting to an outright refusal, to research too deeply or too widely, or to reach beyond the official but frequently incomplete naval records. Why? Arrogance and laziness have probably played their part, but, above all, there seems to have been a bureaucratic unwillingness to have the tidiness of the official explanation disturbed by the introduction of tiresome, inconvenient and thoroughly 'unauthorized' evidence. As this particular story is developed over the following pages, it will become even more apparent that this attitude has continued, as strongly as ever, right up to the present day – more than sixty years after the events in question.

IN TRYING TO PENETRATE the smoke screen that surrounds almost every aspect of the *Glorious* story, where should one begin? Perhaps with a retired naval captain-turned-naval historian, whose reluctant doubts eventually gave way to his even more reluctant conclusions.

Back in the late 1940s, a few years after the war, when the Cabinet Office and the Admiralty were seeking to appoint someone with the right naval and academic credentials to write the official history of the Royal Navy in World War II, the choice eventually fell on Captain Stephen Roskill DSC. When, during his researches, he came to the *Glorious* story, he had little choice but to rely on the Admiralty's explanation, including its rationale about a fuel shortage. He later acknowledged (to the author) that with three volumes to compile, five years of the war to cover, a very small staff and a deadline to meet, he was just too busy to follow up on Vice Admiral Wells.[11] Consequently, the account of *Glorious*'s loss in his official history follows the authorized 'fuel shortage' line. Nevertheless, as an officer of long experience that included time in a carrier and then service throughout the war, Captain Roskill later acknowledged that he had always been uneasy with what he felt was a rather simplistic explanation.

11. By the 1970s, when Captain Roskill realized the significance of a contribution from Admiral Wells, Wells had died.

Anyway, in the mid-1960s he was given some letters written in 1939 and early 1940 by the second most senior of *Glorious*'s Fleet Air Arm officers, Lieutenant Commander Paul Slessor (yes, the author's father). Stephen Roskill had known Slessor from the time when, under the then-Captain Wells (another coincidence), they had served together in the carrier HMS *Eagle* in the Far East in the mid-1930s. From what Roskill remembered of Slessor, he was inclined to take the letters seriously. Though they were personal letters to his wife (the author's mother), they were written in guarded, almost coded terms when touching on the events and tensions in *Glorious* during the last eight or nine months of the ship's life. They spoke of 'very trying times with our friend', and there were allusions to the captain's ignorance of naval aviation. Not many such hints, but enough. There was also a copy of a three-page report written by Slessor and the Commander (Air) the day before the ship sailed from Scapa Flow for the last time. These were the two senior FAA officers in the ship. (The 'survival' of this report is a story in itself and will be recounted in due course.)[12]

Reading the letters and the report, Roskill was alerted to the strains and disagreements that had developed between Captain D'Oyly Hughes and his senior Air Staff about the effective use of the ship's aircraft. Evidently *Glorious* had been a troubled ship. It became clear to Roskill that there was almost certainly more to the story of the final days of *Glorious* than had ever been acknowledged by the Admiralty. He began to research the matter.

Interestingly, Winston Churchill – a man not ignorant of naval matters or the ways of Whitehall – had also had his doubts. Back in 1948 in the first volume of his war memoirs, *The Gathering Storm*, he wrote sceptically of the Admiralty's fuel-shortage 'answer': 'This explanation is not convincing. The *Glorious* presumably had enough fuel to steam at the speed of the convoy. All should have stuck together.' This was no more than many naval officers were saying. But officialdom would have none of it. Indeed, more than fifty years later, in a report placed in the Commons Library following that 1999 Adjournment Debate, the in-house historians of the

12. The letters and the report are in Roskill Papers in the Churchill Archive Centre. See footnote no. 24 below for an account of how the report came to be preserved.

MOD's Naval Historical Branch were still trying to dismiss Mr Churchill's logical point. They called it 'an unreasoned argument'. Brief it may be, but unreasoned? True, Mr Churchill does not spell out his thinking, but one might have thought that his rationale was obvious: if *Glorious* had enough fuel to return independently at between 17 and 18 knots (evidently thought to be an economical anti-submarine cruising speed), she surely would have had enough to come home at the 14 knots of the convoy. Churchill had enough understanding of naval operations to know about the likely speeds.

A shortage of fuel has always been the central feature in every official explanation of why *Glorious* was detached from the 'task force'. It was repeated by the Minister as recently as 1999 in that Adjournment Debate – 'she had only sufficient fuel to return to base, allowing for the obligatory requirement to maintain a reserve of 33 per cent'. Given that this is the official explanation of why she was proceeding ahead of the main group, it is worth examining the flaws in the argument.

First, if one accepts the desirability of keeping a 33 per cent reserve (it was never an 'obligatory' requirement), no one has ever denied that *Glorious* was getting low in fuel. The argument is about whether this was the overriding reason for her 'early' (and vulnerable?) return. No contemporary signal, report, war diary entry, log notation or witness has ever been cited by the MOD's Naval Historical Branch to support the authorized account. For an organization that always insists on 'corroborative and official evidence' for any thesis which challenges its own certainties, this is inconsistent. There is nothing beyond the repeated assertion that '*Glorious* was detached because she was short of fuel. There is no other sensible explanation.'[13]

Second, the 'arithmetic', based on how far *Glorious* had steamed and at what speeds (deduced from *Ark Royal*'s log – the two ships were 'in company' nearly all the time), shows that she had enough fuel to remain on station for at least a further forty-eight hours and then to reach home, and, if need be, to operate her aircraft along the way.

13. **David Brown, senior historian in the MOD's Naval Historical Branch, made the comment in a Channel 4 documentary (30 June 1997) about *Glorious*. The comment parallels numerous other MOD statements down the years.**

Third, there is a tactical factor: if a warship's fuel is getting down to below 50 per cent of her capacity, and her Captain has therefore chosen to steam with six of her eighteen boilers disconnected – as *Glorious*'s were when sighted by the Germans – she will be unable to raise full steam quickly in an emergency. Indeed, it was this inability to accelerate and then outrun the enemy that doomed *Glorious*. So, if low on fuel, it has been long accepted that a ship will be safer within the protective shield of other warships. This is particularly so with a ship as vulnerable and as valuable as *Glorious*. As Churchill wrote, she should have stayed with the convoy.

Today the MOD's in-house historians point to what they see as a significant flaw in this reasoning: it takes no account of the additional fuel that *Glorious* would have 'wasted' while hanging about waiting for that convoy to assemble. This is a proper point, but in this particular case, *Glorious*'s Captain would have known (as, more importantly, would her Admiral and his staff in *Ark Royal*) that she would only have had to wait for twenty-four hours. From her miles-per-ton figures as listed in her last log to survive, we know that at what the Navy calls her 'loitering' speed of 11 to 12 knots, she would have burnt about 130 tons while waiting – before steaming back to Scapa Flow (about 1000 miles) at the 14-knot speed of the convoy. This would have used a further 520 tons. Thus, in total, she would have used about 650 tons. But (and it is a very important 'but'), in departing independently and ahead of the convoy, and maintaining (as Vice Admiral Wells is known to have ordered) an average speed-of-advance of 16 knots, she would have had to do nearly 18 knots – to allow for a pattern of anti-submarine zig-zags. At that speed and over the same 1000 miles she would have burnt 650 tons – no less than she would have used if she had waited and then come home with the convoy.[14] Even if

14. The ton/mile figures, as recorded in *Glorious*'s March log (her April log was lost with the ship), are as follows: at 10 knots she burnt 4 tons per hour; at 12 = 5.6 tph; at 14 = 7.30 tph; at 16 = 9.40 tph; at 18 = 11.75 tph; at 20 = 15 tph. It will be seen that a moderate increase in speed requires disproportionately more fuel. This is why waiting twenty-four hours (at her loitering speed of 11–12 knots) and then returning with the convoy at 14–15 knots would have used about the same amount of fuel as returning independently at nearly 18 knots – the speed she had been ordered to do. N.B. The theoretical ton/mile figures as set out by the Admiralty (in Confidential Book 0815B) are fractionally increased on those in her log. But the percentage of difference, being the same throughout, makes no difference to the argument.

one assumes that the convoy travelled at a slightly higher speed and that it took a rather longer route home than the one taken by *Glorious* (in fact the two tracks were not far apart), the difference in fuel consumption is still only about 100 tons. Curiously, when asked to comment on all this in 1997, the MOD's Naval Historical Branch replied that it had 'not done that particular sum'.

So, the late introduction by the MOD of that 33 per cent 'requirement' – it was not mentioned for the first fifty-seven years of the controversy – is a red herring in the sense that *Glorious* would have been dipping into that reserve by about the same amount *whichever* way she had returned to base. Likewise, in 1999, officialdom introduced further irrelevancies by invoking the shape of *Glorious*'s fuel tanks and the unusable oil sludge at the bottom of those tanks as factors which would have reduced the amount of usable fuel oil.[15] Lastly, aspects of the ship's design and stability – metacentric height and deck loading – have lately been pulled out of the official hat to suggest that *Glorious* (a shallow draught ship) would have been unstable if the ballasting effect of her fuel 'cargo' had been diminished too far. Maybe she would have rolled unduly, but, like all the other 'factors' just listed, it is irrelevant – because her stability (or instability) would have been much the same whether she had returned home with the convoy or independently. In short, the pundits in Whitehall seem never to have cottoned on to some basic arithmetic.

Three further points. First, and most important, if she had returned with the main group, *Glorious* would have provided a second flight deck. In naval aviation, then as now, this is always considered an invaluable asset against the possibility that, with aircraft already aloft, one flight deck is damaged in action or becomes temporarily unserviceable. Second, *Glorious* would have been able to add her own handful of aircraft to those of *Ark Royal* for patrol duties over and ahead of the convoy. Third, if she had returned with the convoy, the two destroyers she took with her on her independent return would have augmented the six already allocated as convoy escorts.

15. In a letter to the author, Vice Admiral Sir Louis Le Bailly points out that at that stage in the war the Navy was probably using relatively sludge-free fuel oil from the Middle East. Later, it had to rely on American and Venezuelan oil.

The more one examines the decision for *Glorious* to proceed independently, the more difficult it becomes to understand.

Before leaving the fuel 'argument', it must be acknowledged that there had been occasions when both *Glorious* and *Ark Royal* had made individual passages to and from Norway – though always escorted by at least three destroyers, with air patrols out ahead, and crew at 'Defence Stations'. But the debate here centres on why *Glorious* found it necessary to travel independently on this occasion – when, in terms of the fuel 'sums' and the tactical merits of travelling with the nearby convoy, there seems to have been no overwhelming need to do so. Indeed, there were several good reasons *not* to do so. Also, this time she was escorted by only two destroyers; she was flying no air patrols, and neither her crew nor aircraft were in any state of readiness.

So, if not fuel, what? And why?

Various possibilities have been put forward: a pressing need for the ship's company to take leave – the ship had been away from her home port of Plymouth since the end of 1937 and some of her crew had not seen their families for two-and-a-half years. Then there was the undoubted need to ferry back the RAF fighters as quickly as possible. Captain Roskill, the man who had much earlier written the Navy's official history, was disinclined to accept either of these possibilities. Even in combination with *Glorious*'s fuel state, these were not strong enough reasons to risk a carrier. Nothing fitted with what he knew of naval doctrine as it applied to carriers. There was also the puzzle as to why *Glorious* had not been flying air patrols. Where, if anywhere, did the tensions hinted at in those letters from Lieutenant Commander Slessor fit?

In 1973, in a file only released to the Public Records Office a few months earlier, Roskill struck two small nuggets of gold. In an Admiralty memo from the Vice Chief of Naval Staff, handwritten just two weeks after the sinkings, is this question: 'Why did she [*Glorious*] part company with *Ark Royal*?'[16] The fact that the VCNS, of all people, found it necessary to ask such a basic question is revealing.[17] If a fuel shortage had

16. ADM199/478.
17. The VCNS was Vice Admiral Tom Phillips – who was later to go down off Malaya in command of HMS *Prince of Wales* and *Repulse*.

really been the reason, one would surely have expected him to have heard of it. The second, and more significant, nugget revealed itself when Roskill turned the page. On the blank reverse of the VCNS's 1940 memo was a spidery note by a man who had commanded a destroyer, HMS *Diana*, that had been in close company with *Ark Royal* and *Glorious* immediately prior to the latter's departure. In 1968, responding to the VCNS's still-unanswered question of more than a quarter of a century earlier ('Why did she part company . . .?), Commander Le Geyt, now long retired but for some reason given access to the file, wrote that he had seen a signal flashed from *Glorious* to Vice Admiral Wells in *Ark Royal*.[18] It requested permission to depart immediately for Scapa Flow 'for the purpose of making preparations for impending courts martial'. Commander Le Geyt further recorded, 'The request was approved'. *Glorious* left with two destroyers shortly afterwards.

Roskill tracked down Le Geyt. He was clear in his memory; he could even recall that it was a Leading Signalman Harris who had actually taken down the signal that night.[19] Roskill dug deeper and found confirmation of the circumstances that lay behind those impending courts martial. In interviews and letters from a number of senior retired officers who knew most of the personalities involved, he was able to confirm what he had strongly suspected: *Glorious* was a deeply troubled ship.

Roskill found that problems had been brewing for nearly a year – since Captain D'Oyly Hughes had been appointed to the command of *Glorious* while she was based in Malta the previous summer. Now, off Norway, relations between the Captain and the ship's Air Staff had broken down so badly that the Captain was about to court-martial his senior FAA officer, Commander Heath. And who knew who else besides? Which explains that signal to *Ark Royal*.

18. The file was not released to the PRO until 1973, so there is a mystery about how/why Cdr Le Geyt had access to it. It has been suggested that, in retirement, he may have been sometimes employed by Whitehall as a part-timer to check files prior to specially authorized researchers being given privileged access. But no one seems to know for certain.
19. In 1998, with the help of the HMS *Diana* Association, the author traced a Cdr Badger Smith, who in 1940 had been a Signalman in the destroyer. He remembered and corroborated these details.

When the author wrote to the MOD's Naval Historical Branch suggesting that the signal flashed from *Glorious*, as reported by Commander Le Geyt, almost certainly pointed away from the long-promulgated thesis of a 'fuel shortage', the NHB evidently found itself in a quandary. It could hardly accuse Le Geyt of inventing his account. Why should he come up with a story that, unbeknown to him, would then fit with so much else that Roskill was to find years later? Instead, in his reply, the Head of the NHB took a different tack:

> The late Commander Le Geyt defaced a file by a totally unauthorized notation, unsupported by any evidence other than his recollection after 38 years [actually 28 years]. That he should have acted so irresponsibly says much for Le Geyt's mental state . . . I hope you will understand that there is no way that I can officially condone publicly such behaviour even if it had been accompanied by some form of documentary proof . . .

Coming from a professional historian, this was strange indeed. It seemed to derive from a concern with procedure and protocol rather than with history. The reply neatly points to a muddled brief: the MOD's in-house historians are required to be impartial while, at the same time, they must also guard the reputation (as they define it) of the Navy. Evidently, this sometimes leads to a conflict of interests. But it is not clear that the organization even recognizes the problem, let alone its consequences.

Yes, Commander Le Geyt had certainly defaced that file – though, given that he had done so on a blank page and was a uniquely placed eyewitness, perhaps it was not quite the heinous crime that was officially suggested. He almost certainly knew what he was doing, but presumably felt that for future researchers his overriding priority must be to answer that question ('Why did she part company . . .?') put by the VCNS all those years before. One supposes that, in his view, the question had lain inaccurately resolved for twenty-eight years and that he should now make a belated contribution towards its correction.

The MOD had presumably been no better pleased back in June 1980 when, just forty years on from the sinkings, Captain Roskill published a long article in the *Sunday Times*. It was the result of detailed research, and, given the man's loyalty to his service, the reluctant product of much thought and soul searching. But he could see no alternative to reversing the earlier conclusions in his 1954 official *History of the War at Sea.* His conclusion was damning:

> The Admiralty has tried to suppress the truth for 40 years, but it looks as though 1,515 [*sic*] men were killed partly as a result of a whole chain of Admiralty errors but also because the captain of *Glorious*, Guy D'Oyly Hughes, was so disturbed in his judgement that, in his hurry to return to Britain to court martial an officer he did not like, he ignored normal battle precautions.

Elsewhere, he wrote, 'The fuel theory is bunkum.'

Returning once more to 1940, *Glorious*, the Courts Martial and All That, Captain D'Oyly Hughes had been in command for just a year. A submarine hero of World War I with a DSC and two DSOs (one of which must have been a near miss for a VC), he was now reckoned by many to be an absolutely outstanding naval officer – destined, some predicted, to go right to the top. In fact, he was the most decorated officer of his generation – a winner. But even great men can sometimes have flaws. Captain D'Oyly Hughes seems to have had two: a level of courage which verged on unthinking bravado, and an ill-tempered impatience with anyone who did not immediately see things his way. And there was a compounding problem. Having earlier learnt to fly in a low-powered civilian Moth and having served for nine months in another carrier, HMS *Courageous* (though not on the flying side), he evidently saw no need to listen to the counsel of his senior Fleet Air Arm staff. He already knew it all better than they did. In fact, like too many senior officers of those times, he showed a surprising misunderstanding of the FAA's training, tactics and aircraft. That, at any rate, was the opinion of some of the FAA officers who had served with him. Their letters, responding to enquiries from Captain Roskill some thirty years later, are filed at the Churchill Archive Centre (Roskill, who died in 1982, was one of the Centre's founders).

One of *Glorious*'s FAA officers writes how, shortly after taking command in the Mediterranean, Captain D'Oyly Hughes watched some torpedo training attacks and then ordered that the range at which the torpedoes were to be dropped was to be shortened to 200 yards. As the officer dryly records, 'This, *inter alia*, would have required modifying the Navy's 18" torpedoes.'[20] It would also have meant – if not shot down first – the possibility of crashing, kamikaze-like, into the target. That kind of thinking did not generate confidence among the ship's aircrew.

Another officer remembered how disappointed he was when the new Captain first addressed his assembled officers:

> He said that he disagreed with all the doctrine about training in the FAA, particularly on the amount of time spent in reconnaissance training, and that as far as anti-submarine operations were concerned, no aircraft had ever sunk a submarine, nor ever would.[21] I remember thinking that if ever I became a senior officer, I would remember this talk as a classic example of how not to speak to one's officers. He showed contempt for the Fleet Air Arm. He turned down proposals made by Willoughby [the senior FAA officer aboard at the time] and Slessor for future programmes, and would brook no discussion. In a few days the morale of the ship reduced to a level I had never known when serving under her three previous captains.

By the time he wrote that nearly thirty years later, Lieutenant Bolt was the 'senior officer' he had hoped he might one day become. He wrote it as a retired Rear Admiral who had himself commanded a carrier in the Korean War. Another flag officer, Rear Admiral Willoughby, who had been *Glorious*'s Commander (Air) for the first six months of the new Captain's command, wrote in a similar vein. He rated the Captain's ideas on aircrew training as 'mostly rubbish'. Willoughby later commanded a wartime carrier.

Lieutenant Commander Slessor, of course, was not around to reply to Roskill's enquiries. But it was his letters, written at the time, which had partly triggered Roskill to dig further in the first place. Those letters are also in the Churchill Archive Centre.

Surprisingly, none of the MOD's in-house historians had ever looked through the '*Glorious* papers' accumulated by Roskill. When it

20. Lt David Buchanan-Dunlop writing many years later, as a Captain.
21. At the time Captain D'Oyly Hughes was right in the first contention, wrong in the second. Of course, during the twenty-one years of peace that followed from 1918, there had been no opportunity for aircraft to sink submarines.

was suggested that someone might take an away-day to Cambridge, the reply came back that it would serve no useful purpose because the Roskill Papers were 'anecdotal' and 'irrelevant' to the circumstances surrounding the loss of *Glorious.*[22] How the relevance of papers could be determined without reading them was not explained.

There was one particular habit of the captain of *Glorious* that features in those Cambridge files but not in any official records. Admiralty operational files hardly ever include comments about people in terms of their personalities, strengths, weaknesses and tactical habits. It is a drawback of the genre (personal files which do cover such details of character are never disclosed). Yet some knowledge of these things, even if only derived from the unofficial diaries and letters of contemporary witnesses, is vital to any thorough analysis. The habit of Captain D'Oyly Hughes that particularly worried his officers revealed itself soon after the outbreak of war when *Glorious* was sent east through the Suez Canal. Once in the Indian Ocean, she joined a small task force looking for a German surface raider – perhaps the pocket battleship *Graf Spee.* On several occasions D'Oyly Hughes separated *Glorious* from the other ships and steamed off to look for the German ship accompanied only by a destroyer. This was contrary to naval and Fleet Air Arm doctrine; a carrier without an adequate escort is one of the most vulnerable ships afloat. This is even more the case if the carrier is not flying all-round air reconnaissance. 'He thinks we are a battleship,' wrote one officer. 'He wants to win the VC.' Another reported, 'If we meet the whole German Navy, we'll go straight at them with all our guns firing – 4.7" anti-aircraft guns and some 20mm Oerlikons.'[23] To some this might be courage in the Nelson tradition. But, if their comments are to be believed, some of his officers thought it bordered on suicidal folly. Perhaps if D'Oyly Hughes had been posted to command a battleship or a flotilla of destroyers, he might have emerged as one of the outstanding officers of the war. As it was, posting someone to the command of

22. Author's correspondence with the NHB, particularly an NHB letter of 16 June 1998.
23. These comments by Lt Scarlett and Ldg T.A.G. Jolliffe are taken from John Winton's book *Carrier Glorious.*

a carrier who was so impatiently driven towards direct action was surely a misjudgement within the Admiralty.

D'Oyly Hughes's concern to find and engage the enemy at almost any cost almost certainly owed much to his outstanding success as a submariner more than twenty years earlier. But the tactical handling of a submarine and a carrier could not be more different. Submarine commanders are, by training and temperament, accustomed to working independently. Furthermore, because only one person can see through a periscope at a time – and that man is invariably the commanding officer – there has long been an almost joking acknowledgement in the rest of the Navy that submarine commanders are not disposed to take advice. D'Oyly Hughes seems to have taken this trait to an extreme. Indeed, in case anyone questioned any of his decisions too vigorously, he kept a loaded revolver on the bridge. When, according to another of those letters in the Roskill Papers, the Captain was asked what the revolver was for, he said that it was to shoot any officer who failed to do his duty in action. If he was joking, his officers did not get the joke. They were appalled.

In December 1939 after three hard but fruitless months, *Glorious* was recalled from the Indian Ocean to Malta for dry-docking and a hurried refit. In early April 1940 she and *Ark Royal* were ordered back to home waters to take part in the Norwegian campaign. A new Commander (Air) had taken over from Willoughby. Although, by all accounts, Commander Heath was a quiet and modest man, he was also one of the most practised and knowledgeable airmen in the Navy. He had spent the previous two years working on FAA problems and solutions at the Admiralty, so he was very up-to-date on tactics and practice. This was almost certainly part of the problem. Almost from the day he joined the ship (in Aden, on her way back from the Indian Ocean) his captain went out of his way to countermand and belittle him, often in front of his aircrew and, sometimes, in front of the 'lower deck'. By the time the ship got back to the Clyde, immediately before Norway, if the anecdotal evidence in the Roskill Papers is believed, the tension between the Captain and his senior FAA officers was considerable.

Glorious and *Ark Royal* sailed for Norway on 23 April; they were escorted by two cruisers and six destroyers; they flew reconnaissance aircraft out ahead. The next six weeks were very busy indeed. With a variety of aircraft – Swordfish, Sea Gladiators, Skuas and even a monstrosity called a Roc – the two carriers flew anti-submarine patrols for the rest of the fleet, provided air cover against enemy bombers and shadowing aircraft, and supported the army ashore with attacks on the advancing Germans. A number of aircraft were lost – some to the enemy, some to the terrain.

Refuelling was always a problem. Endurance had never been a priority in the design of British warships – we had coaling and oiling depots almost everywhere. Consequently, unlike the Germans, we had neglected to develop the skills and equipment needed to refuel at sea. So every eight or nine days *Glorious* had to make the 2000-mile round trip back to Scapa Flow to replenish her tanks. She used nearly a third of her capacity just getting to and fro. The much more modern *Ark Royal* had far greater endurance. Destroyers and cruisers in those waters were deemed sufficiently expendable that they could risk the German mines which might be laid (from the air) on the approaches to the tankers stationed in the Norwegian fjords. But that was not a risk to be taken with the two carriers – a very practical demonstration of the importance accorded to those two ships.

On one of these returns to Scapa Flow, *Glorious* had to leave some of her own aircraft behind to make room for a squadron of RAF Gladiators which were to be taken north. Indeed, with a much-reduced number of her own aircraft (her full complement was between thirty-eight and forty-two), she was increasingly used as an aircraft ferry.

In mid-May she was back in the Clyde. This time she had been ordered to disembark all her aircraft except for five Swordfish and nine Sea Gladiators. The space was needed for a squadron of RAF Hurricanes which were to be ferried to Bardufoss in northern Norway. There was no question of the Hurricanes attempting a deck landing – they would have run out of deck. So getting them aboard was a minor epic in its own right. Flying north from their base in Lincolnshire, they landed just outside Glasgow at Abbotsinch – the site of today's Glasgow Airport. Then they were taxied through the fields to the Clyde, where they were lifted aboard lighters. These were towed 20 miles down river before their cargoes were craned up onto *Glorious*'s flight deck and then stowed in the hangar below. *Glorious* was chosen for this ferrying duty because her flight-deck lifts were wide enough to take the fixed-wing Hurricanes. Those lifts, unlike the narrower ones in *Ark Royal*, dated from the days before all naval aircraft had folding wings.

The choice of *Glorious* made sense. But to a man of her Captain's temperament and ambition, this relegation to mere ferrying duties – while *Ark Royal* got on with offensive operations – must surely have been deeply frustrating, even humiliating.

It was during *Glorious*'s penultimate 'visit' to Norway, still with only those five Swordfish and nine Gladiators aboard, that she received a signal from the shore-based Admiral Lord Cork, the man in overall command of all operations, naval and military, in the Norwegian theatre. He suggested that *Glorious* might 'consider' the possibility of mounting an air attack on German forces advancing in the area of Mosjoen away to the south. It is almost certain that the shore-based Admiral did not realize that *Glorious* only had a skeleton complement of aircraft embarked; it also seems likely that he thought *Glorious* had some Skua dive-bombers aboard – as she had had a few weeks earlier, and as *Ark Royal* still had. The Skua was an inadequate aircraft, but, compared with the Swordfish, it might as well have been supersonic.

Captain D'Oyly Hughes obviously took the Admiral's suggestion as an opportunity, at last, for offensive action. He sent for his two senior FAA officers, Heath and Slessor. After examining the proposition, they were not enthusiastic. They pointed out that the ship carried no maps of the suggested target area, which was, in any case, away to the south and well out of Swordfish range – unless extra tanks were fitted (a twenty-four-hour task) or the carrier closed the coast to reduce the flying time. Additionally, there was no intelligence available as to the likely disposition of the enemy in that area or, for that matter, whether enemy fighters were likely to be encountered; if they were, it was a fair bet that few of the Swordfish would return. Furthermore, the Swordfish, with a top speed of about 130 knots, was notoriously vulnerable to small-arms fire when used in a low-level role in broad daylight – and at that time of year in those latitudes the sun hardly sets. Lastly, the ship's five remaining Swordfish were specifically for her own defence (for flying safe-circle patrols when at sea between Scapa Flow and Norway) and communications duties. When asked for instructions as to the object of the operation, the Captain is reported to have replied, 'They are to bomb anything they can find – roads, aerodromes, bridges, anything they can find.'

The two FAA officers felt compelled to advise that the operation was likely to be one of almost suicidal risk for very dubious returns. 'We held the view,' Commander Heath later wrote, 'that an air operation without an objective clearly defined and accurately located is fundamentally unsound for low-performance aircraft.' For all that, on the Captain's insistence they went away and drew up orders for the operation as best they could. When the Squadron Commander who would lead the sortie learnt what the Captain planned, he had such strong concerns that, unusually, he asked to be allowed to express them directly to the Captain.

A little later the three officers reported back to D'Oyly Hughes with a completed, but in their view inadequate, operation order. Their concerns provoked a most violent reaction. It was as if a fuse of pent-up impatience and frustration had finally burnt through to the detonator. There was an explosion of rage. Their advice that the project was half-baked (though they would have put it more tactfully than that) was seen as gross disloyalty or cowardice or mutiny, or all three. Commander Heath took the brunt of the blast. He was relieved of his duties and sent below to his cabin. But the proposed sortie was never flown.

When the ship returned to Scapa a few days later to refuel, Commander Heath was put ashore 'pending court martial'. Slessor was retained aboard. Whether he, too, would have been court-martialled is not known. But if not, he would certainly have been the leading defence witness – which might have come to much the same thing.

A detailed 'log' of the crisis exists. It was written by Heath and Slessor in the few hours just before the former left the ship in Scapa. While it is set down in the dry tones of an official report, it is obviously written from the perspective of the two officers. To that extent it could be said to be one-sided. Nevertheless, it reads convincingly. It is in the Roskill Papers in Cambridge.

Glorious was only in Scapa for a few hours, just long enough to put Commander Heath ashore, fill her fuel tanks and take on vital stores. Then, early on 31 May, in company with *Ark Royal* and five screening destroyers, she headed north again – primarily to ferry back the remnants of the RAF Gladiator squadron she had delivered some weeks earlier.[24]

The Norwegian campaign was in its last few days. But the RAF fighters were needed until the very last day to cover the evacuation. So on her arrival back in Norwegian waters, Vice Admiral Wells directed *Glorious* and a destroyer to a safer area 60 or 70 miles to the north. There, just beyond the range of marauding German aircraft, she could 'loiter' to save fuel. Once again, this enforced idleness – while *Ark Royal*'s squadrons of Skuas carried out a hectic series of sorties against the Germans – must have been more than D'Oyly Hughes could bear. At last, on the night of 7 June, the RAF was ready and *Glorious* rejoined *Ark Royal.* Ten Gladiators landed without a hitch. Then, something quite unprecedented was attempted . . .

With *Glorious* charging upwind at over 30 knots and 'with steam coming out of every rivet hole', a flight of those Hurricanes started coming in. The experts back at Farnborough had said that it could not be done – *Glorious*'s flight deck was not long enough. So the order from London was that the Hurricanes should be destroyed on their Norwegian airfield – scuttled. But according to the squadron CO (Air Marshall Sir Kenneth Cross, interviewed in 1997), 'That stuff from

24. What happened to Commander Heath? With *Glorious* gone he was in limbo – there were no charges and no witnesses. The Admiralty solved this awkward problem by posting him to the relative backwater of Sierra Leone. Later he was sent even further afield – to Java, as naval liaison officer with the Dutch forces. With the coming of the Japanese, he escaped to Australia, where, by extraordinary chance, he met Mrs Slessor, who had now returned with her small son (the author) to her birthplace. There, in Melbourne, she was working in naval intelligence. Heath told her all that had happened. She persuaded him, before he began the long journey back to the UK, to let her copy the report he and her husband had written nearly two years earlier. Heath still carried it with him pending the eventual resolution of his case. She recognized its wider significance and was concerned lest the original might be lost. It was her copy that, twenty years later, was passed to Roskill and thence to the Churchill Archive Centre. Over two-and-a-half years after *Glorious* was lost, the Admiralty eventually 'cleared' Heath; his honour was restored. Post-war, he finished his career as Captain of HMS *Heron*, the RNAS at Yeovilton. There he was a founder of the Fleet Air Arm Museum, which ironically, years after his death, refused to accept a copy of his report.

the boffins back home made us all the more determined – what did they know?' The Hurricanes had no arrester hooks, but, with a 25-pound sandbag stowed in each tail and partially deflated tyres, they became the first high-performance fighters ever to attempt a carrier landing.

In the twilight, from far across the water in *Ark Royal*, they watched through their binoculars. The first of three Hurricanes banked and lined up. Too fast? Maybe too slow. Would she stall? No. She had made it. The flight deck was more than long enough. If one Hurricane could do it, perhaps they all could. The other two came in. A signal was sent to the remaining seven Hurricanes waiting on shore 80 miles away. Presently, guided by a Swordfish, they arrived. One by one they lined up. One by one they landed. It was an unprecedented achievement. Even today, more than sixty years on, the memory of one of those who watched from five or six miles away in *Ark Royal* is crystal-clear. He reckons it was one of the bravest feats of flying he ever saw: 'And so consistent too – those RAF chaps really knew what they were doing.'[25]

Even though *Ark Royal*'s flight deck was longer than that of *Glorious*, the Hurricane pilots had chosen *Glorious* because with her larger lifts, their precious aircraft could be stowed down in the hangar without first having their wings sawn off. It was a choice that was to cost all but two of 'those RAF chaps' their lives within less then twenty-four hours.

When Squadron Leader Cross reported to the bridge to thank the Captain, he recalls that D'Oyly Hughes asked him rather irritably why his squadron had taken so long. The question is something that Air Marshall Sir Kenneth Cross always remembered. Perhaps the Captain was anxious to flash a signal across to Vice Admiral Wells in *Ark Royal* so that, without further delay, he could be on his way.

Officialdom has always had the greatest difficulty with the possibility that D'Oyly Hughes's temperament, particularly his impatience – a characteristic identified by almost everyone who ever wrote about the man – may have been the underlying reason for *Glorious*'s independent

25. This was the 1999 recollection of Commander John Casson OBE, who as a senior Lieutenant had been a Skua Squadron Commander in *Ark Royal*.

departure. To risk three ships and over 1500 men to pursue a court martial is, it is claimed, 'too trivial a reason to be credible'. Yes, indeed. But might that not be the very reason why Whitehall has always found the possibility so difficult to accept? To that end there is the inescapable fact that Roskill corresponded with a number of by-then senior (retired) naval officers who had served under the Captain of *Glorious.* They read and commented on the draft of his article. None of them tried to dissuade him from his conclusion that 'the fuel story is bunkum . . . The problem was the Captain's impatience for a court martial.' Such a verdict was, it seems, compatible with what they remembered.

Nevertheless, there *is* a difficulty with the conclusion of Captain Roskill and others: it does not take account of the fact that it was not the Captain of *Glorious* who was ultimately responsible for his ship's early departure. It was Vice Admiral Wells in *Ark Royal*; he was in command of both carriers. Why did he agree to *Glorious*'s request to depart in order to make 'preparations for . . . courts martial'? Given that the Admiralty never asked him, we can only guess.

By definition, a guess is speculative. But that does not mean that it is necessarily without some foundation or evidence. In this case, there is clear evidence in one of those Cambridge letters (written while *Glorious* and *Ark Royal* were at anchor in the Clyde preparatory to their first journey to Norway) that Wells knew of problems in *Glorious.* Given that he was one of the relatively few senior officers who understood the proper use of carriers and their aircraft, and that *Glorious* was now under his command, he would have been worried by the knowledge that the Captain and his air staff had lost faith in each other. In short, he had a deeply dysfunctional ship on his hands.

Briefly, the story is that when both ships were lying in the Clyde before their first departure for the north, he sent for Lt Cdr Slessor. He knew him from their days in *Eagle* out in the Far East only a few years before (they had sometimes played piano duets at ship's concerts). As Slessor's letter tells it, he went across to *Ark Royal* and, after dinner in the Admiral's quarters, the Admiral drew him aside from the other guests and raised the subject of what was going on in *Glorious.* This put Slessor in some difficulty: how could he be reasonably frank without at the same time being disloyal to his Captain? A day or two later he wrote to his wife:

> I wouldn't open my mouth until he [Wells] promised to forget what we had on our respective sleeves, and also that he would keep everything under his hat. I can't tell you the whole story. But he was most sympathetic and reassuring – 'One of my old officers . . . etc'. His last words, seizing me by the arm, were 'Don't worry, old Paul.'

Of course, that single reported snatch is insufficient to indicate that the Admiral's sympathies lay more with *Glorious*'s FAA officers than with her Captain. Anyway, 'sympathies' are irrelevant. What matters is the strong possibility (and Roskill touched on it in the draft of his 1980 article, though it was not part of the article as published) that the Admiral had concluded Captain D'Oyly Hughes was not the best man to command a carrier. Possibly, over the next few weeks of action off Norway, the Admiral became impatient for the problem to be sorted out. A court martial would almost certainly have had that result – whatever the verdict. Despite the doctrine of 'a Captain is always right', it must be far from certain that the Captain's charges against Commander Heath would have held. The night Heath was put ashore at Scapa Flow, he received any number of assurances from men of all ranks that they were willing to stand as witnesses on his behalf. That, in any navy, is not something anyone does lightly who has even half an eye on his future. It would certainly have been noted at the court martial – whatever (again) the verdict. Maybe Wells had a wish to clear the professional air as quickly as possible. Perhaps this, allied with the knowledge that *Glorious* was no longer of much use to him as an offensive weapon, meant that he saw no point in hanging on to her. So he let her go. Maybe his own impatience clouded his judgement. Perhaps and maybe. We will never know because he was never asked.

But of one thing we can be certain. The Admiral would have expected *Glorious* to take the same precautions that had been taken when, eight days earlier, she and *Ark Royal* had come north in company from Scapa Flow. On that occasion, when still well short of Norwegian waters, in addition to a screen of five destroyers, the hour-by-hour log of *Ark Royal* shows that the two carriers had Swordfish constantly flying what were called 'safe-circle patrols'. Now, just eight days later and in the same waters, with only two escorting destroyers, *Glorious* did not even have an aircraft held in readiness on her flight deck. Such an omission was contrary to all carrier and FAA doctrine. Furthermore, according to several survivors, *Glorious* did not have lookouts in her crow's nest. For these crucial omissions no one but the Captain was responsible.

The official explanation for the lack of air patrols is that the Captain would not have wanted to waste time and fuel by turning upwind every two or three hours to operate aircraft. It is further suggested that with tired aircrew (the last few days off Norway had been very wearing) and only five Swordfish, *Glorious* would have found it difficult to sustain a round-the-clock air patrol. If indeed these were factors – and the weariness of the aircrew may have been one – they are surely all the more reason why the ship should have waited to come back with the convoy the next day. As for the other 'explanation' that time and fuel would have been wasted by having to turn upwind, the fact is – given the reported strength and direction of the wind on that day – *Glorious* would have needed to turn through much less than 90 degrees and then for only a few minutes every two or three hours. To operate Swordfish in the reconnaissance role the carrier would not have needed to increase speed beyond the 18 knots she was already doing; the 'extra' fuel expended would hardly have been measurable. The official reason for the lack of air patrols has a distinct whiff of post-hoc invention.

Given that the Captain had not even ordered an aircraft to be held on stand-by, a far more likely reason for the absence of an air patrol seems to have been identified in a comment made much later by Commander Heath – he who had been put ashore:

> *Glorious*' end was a direct result of failing to put a ring round her. The aircrew were pretty well-worn I'm told, but the Captain always maintained that the aircraft were for attack and that he could look after the ship.

Commander Heath might also have commented about the level of mutual distrust that already existed. The Captain – dismissive of advice even at the best of times – was now even less likely to accept the counsel of his Air Staff still aboard. They must have found it deeply frustrating to see their ship being so unnecessarily endangered. It was a concern that had been with them since the days, eight months earlier, when they had been in the Indian Ocean.

And what of the fact, according to survivors, that *Glorious* had no lookouts in her crow's nest? Here again, the official reason seems too easy. It is claimed that the two destroyers, on station between 400 and 800 yards ahead on *Glorious*'s port and starboard bow, would have had lookouts posted in *their* crow's nests instead. Maybe they did, but their horizon would have been closer, by several miles, than that visible from *Glorious*'s much higher lookout position.

Lastly, a brief return to the crux of the debate: in the war diary of the Commander-in-Chief of the Home Fleet, now in the Public Records Office, there are two entries which may be relevant. The first records a signal received by the Commander-in-Chief (based in Scotland) from the Admiralty in London. It is dated 5 June – three days before *Glorious* left Norwegian waters for home:

> Received Admiralty's 09.43 proposing *Glorious* on completion of present duty to proceed to Devonport [Plymouth] and give 7 days leave to each watch, maximum number going on first leave.

The next day, there appears the Commander-in-Chief's reply in which he 'countermands' the previous day's signal from the Admiralty:

> Informed Admiralty: concur AT 09.43, but *Glorious* must first proceed to Scapa to enable a court martial to be held.

No, this is not proof that *Glorious* detached from Norway for the sole purpose of the court martial, but, taken with all the other evidence, it is persuasive that the court martial was likely to have been the overriding motive. The precise timing of the ship's departure would have been left to the two men on the spot: her Captain and her Admiral. And that is where her Captain's legendary impatience may have come in.

IN ADDITION TO THE CONTROVERSY surrounding the claim that a shortage of fuel was the reason for *Glorious*'s 'early' return, there are several other chapters in the official account which diverge sharply from other narratives – not least from *The Official History of British Intelligence* (see below). This 'intelligence' debate centres around whether *Glorious*, among other ships, was denied information that German 'main units' might soon be on the loose in Norwegian waters.

In a paper published by the MOD in 1997, prompted by public interest following a Channel 4 documentary about *Glorious*, there appears this unequivocal statement:

> There was no indication from any source that a powerful German squadron was preparing for a sortie, let alone that one had been at sea since 4 June.

So the MOD account has it that no one was denied information about a possible German incursion because there was no such information to deny. This assertion is too simple by far.

In the autumn of 1939 a twenty-year-old Cambridge third-year undergraduate in medieval history was recruited to work at the recently enlarged intelligence centre at Bletchley Park. Harry Hinsley quickly found that he had a particular aptitude for the business of wireless traffic analysis – a black art whereby intelligence, in the form of hints and inferences, could be drawn from eavesdropping on the frequencies, patterns, Morse 'signatures', call signs, sources and destinations of the enemy's encoded wireless traffic (even if the coded messages themselves could not be broken). But in the years before the war, because most German warships were clustered tightly together in their home ports, there was not enough inter-ship radio traffic on which the British might practice their detective work. So, with little accumulated experience at a national level, it is not surprising that – once the Germans *did* start signalling – Harry Hinsley, despite his extreme youth, had as much chance as anyone else of learning what was involved. He quickly became one of the experts. But there was a problem: being a civilian and no older than many sub lieutenants, his expertise was distrusted within the Admiralty. Indeed, contemporary records (as we shall see) suggest that he was deliberately pushed aside.

Nearly forty years on, in the late 1970s, Sir Harry, now Master of St John's College and soon to become Vice Chancellor of Cambridge University, co-wrote *The Official History of British Intelligence in*

WW2.[26] He readily acknowledges that analysis of German W/T traffic was a relatively new technique and therefore not trusted by the Admiralty – though the Navy in Malta had successfully tried it in a small way 'against' the Italian fleet in the late 1930s. Nevertheless, Sir Harry relates how, from mid-May 1940, based on the analysis of a stream of German naval W/T traffic passing to and fro between Kiel and western Norway, he and others at Bletchley Park judged that something serious was afoot. In early June over a period of several days they passed repeated warnings to the Navy's Operational Intelligence Centre (the Admiralty nerve centre). In their view, German 'main units' were now likely to move out from Kiel into the North Sea and, perhaps, beyond. With increasing frustration, Bletchley Park realized that they were being ignored. Echoes of that frustration can still be heard in a sentence from Sir Harry's official account, written thirty-seven years later:

> The OIC had no good reason for resisting GC & CS's [Bletchley Park] suggestion that it should at least issue a qualified warning to the fleet . . .

This is a long way from the MOD's current assertion that there was no intelligence available 'from any source'. The fact is that the two accounts – Sir Harry's and the MOD's – about what intelligence might have been available could not be more different. If the MOD has a case, it is severely damaged by the frequency with which Sir Harry is selectively quoted in some places and misquoted in others.

A good first place to look at this argument (and the misquotes) is in an interview that Sir Harry gave to the makers of the 1997 Channel 4 documentary about *Glorious*. It parallels his account in the official history, albeit in a more personal and anecdotal form:[27]

> I had a direct line to the Admiralty from Hut 4 at Bletchley and I remember during that period from about a fortnight before those [German] ships moved I pretty much rang the Operational Intelligence

26. This was the last of the WW2 official histories to be published (cf. RN, RAF, Army) because, until thirty-three years after the end of the war, there was an embargo on disclosing details about the breaking of the German Enigma codes.
27. The quoted extracts throughout this section are included at some length because it seems important to give the fullest reasonable context and, thereby, not to commit the same 'selective' errors as the MOD.

> Centre in the Admiralty once or twice a day. And I said, 'Look, you ought to pass a signal out.' But he said he couldn't persuade the boss higher up to pass the signal out. On that day [7 June, the day before *Glorious* and the destroyers were sunk] I was saying, 'For goodness sake, can't you persuade them to send an alert – even if it only says, "It may be the case that . . ."'. He said, 'I can't – first of all my traffic analysts don't agree with your interpretation – they don't see the point. Secondly, my boss – the chief of the OIC – will not go to the operational chaps and send this kind of signal out on your kind of information.'

In answering Sir Harry's charge that the Admiralty ignored his warnings, the MOD (in the NHB paper 'HMS *Glorious* – Points of Controversy', put out to answer questions raised by the TV programme and subsequently placed in the Commons Library) made the following rebuttal:

> The personal recollections of the former member of the signals intelligence community who stated on television that he had personally given repeated urgent warnings to the Admiralty are at variance with the same individual's written account of intelligence circumstances at the time of the loss of *Glorious*. According to the latter account, which appeared in *The Official History of British Intelligence in WW2* (HMSO 1979), there had been no more than a vague warning via GC & CS [Bletchley Park] summarized for the Admiralty on 7 June as 'German naval units may in future be associated in an offensive action taken by German units in the North Sea' [*sic*].

Three points arise. First, the NHB seriously misquotes *The Official History of British Intelligence*; Sir Harry does not write 'there had been no more than a vague warning' from Bletchley Park. On the contrary, the relevant passage (see below) talks about 'persistent warnings' – in the plural. Second, when told of the MOD's rebuttal, Sir Harry claimed that the summary referred to by the MOD ('German naval units may in future . . .') was not, as is implied, made by Bletchley Park for the Admiralty. It was almost certainly a summary made *by* the Admiralty for itself. In all probability it was derived from its own in-house signals intelligence unit (ID8G). Third, Sir Harry wrote that the summary referred to was 'not only almost meaningless, but it wasn't passed to ships at sea'. Indeed, he was rather miffed that such an ill-phrased summary – he called it 'Admiralty talk' – could be attributed to him or to any of his colleagues at Bletchley Park.

The MOD's 1998 rebuttal continues as follows:

> It is not wholly surprising that such a vague and diffuse assessment [i.e. the summary], based on the untried technique of 'traffic analysis' which attempted to derive a pattern of ship activity from a sequence of signals activity, may not have been perceived as firm advice of impending or current operations in northern Norwegian waters – a point Professor Hinsley concedes in his book.

At this point, it is interesting to see exactly what Sir Harry does 'concede'. In *The Official History of British Intelligence*, he writes as follows:

> A fortnight before the German battle cruisers [*Scharnhorst* and *Gneisenau*] made their sortie, Bletchley Park began to report to the OIC that this behaviour [i.e. the pattern of W/T traffic] indicated that German main units were preparing to move from the Baltic northwards up the Norwegian coast. In time, GC & CS's persistent warnings found their way into the OIC daily reports. But the OIC was far from convinced by such evidence, and not even a qualified warning was issued by the Admiralty to the Home Fleet. It is not difficult to understand the OIC's scepticism. Traffic analysis was an untested technique, and one that yielded only broad hints and inferential clues. [The MOD ends its quote of Sir Harry at this point. But what he goes on to say makes all the difference.] The Admiralty, like other service departments, firmly insisted that its own intelligence branch must be solely responsible for the interpretation that was put on any intelligence material within its sphere – indeed it still retained in the OIC the staff it had taken back from GC & CS [Bletchley Park] at the outbreak of war. But although this staff itself was sceptical about GC & CS's claims for traffic analysis, the OIC had no good reason for resisting GC & CS's suggestion that it should at least issue a qualified warning to the Fleet. To make things more difficult, the fact that the evacuation of Narvik was in progress was kept extremely secret. Not only was GC & CS, then and for a long time later, uninformed of British movements, Coastal Command had not been alerted and did not in consequence carry out reconnaissance of the area through which the evacuation convoys and the *Glorious* were to pass.

So, however one views it, there is no foundation for the official assertion that 'There was no indication from any source that a powerful German squadron was preparing for a sortie'. The Admiralty may have distrusted the 'indications' coming in from Bletchley Park, but there is no justification for denying that it was receiving them – trusted or not.

When confronted with the almost total difference between their version of events and Sir Harry's, the MOD's senior naval historian asked the author why, in Sir Harry's TV interview, 'he should have waited nineteen years after publication of his intelligence history before stating that his warnings were stronger and more frequent than page 141 of his history suggests'? It is doubtful, on any objective analysis, that Sir Harry's spoken comments on TV *are* notably stronger than his written ones in the earlier official history. Once one recognizes that Sir Harry's 1978 official account is impersonal and rather formal in tone, whereas his 1997 TV interview is personal and anecdotal, the only difference is in style, not content. But readers can re-read the 'contrasting' quotes above to judge for themselves whether Sir Harry was saying one thing on TV and something markedly different in his official history.

One cannot help wondering why officialdom did not long ago make the best of a bad job. It could have acknowledged that the information almost certainly *was* passed from Bletchley Park to the Admiralty, but, because of the untried and 'boffinish' nature of its main source (a mere twenty-one-year-old), someone obviously decided not to pass the warnings to a more senior level, let alone to ships at sea. The MOD might add, in further mitigation, that an alarm (but not one originating from Bletchley Park) about a possible German invasion of Iceland had caused a good deal of consternation only a few days before. Battle cruisers and destroyers had been hurriedly despatched from Scapa Flow to investigate. The alarm proved to be entirely false. But it may have increased – quite reasonably – the scepticism of the OIC. A straightforward acknowledgement that this could be why no intelligence (just another false alarm?) was passed to ships at sea would be much more persuasive than the current flat denial.

However, there may be more to the Iceland 'alarm' than there appears to be.

The prospector at the Public Records Office never knows what, if anything, he will find – until he has panned through the gravel. Often he is disappointed. But sometimes he finds a small nugget – and curses that he did not bother to research that particular patch before. In the file containing the Home Fleet War Diary (Despatch) for 8 June 1940 – the day *Glorious* was sunk but before the news was known in the UK – the author found this small but glistening entry:

> A busy day for the northern convoys as reports of a German invasion of Iceland are still hanging about. Is it possible that this was done purposely to get our battle cruiser force [*Renown* and *Repulse*] out of the way so that the German ships will have a free hand to operate off Norway?

The officer who wrote that entry refers to *the* German ships? What German ships? After all, there was meant to be 'no indication from any source' that any such ships were on the loose 'off Norway'. So where did that officer get his information about *the* (definite article) German ships from? Could it be that Bletchley Park's warnings *were* passed to the Admiralty and then on to Home Fleet HQ – but no further? Real or fool's gold? Maybe one should not read too much into the nuances of grammar. But one cannot help but be intrigued.

Sir Harry Hinsley, shortly before he died early in 1998, made some interesting observations about tensions between Bletchley Park and the Admiralty in the early days of the war. 'In those days they regarded us as interfering young sprogs who didn't know what we were talking about – civvy boffins. And their own signals intelligence people [ID8G] insisted on checking all our stuff.'[28] From records now in the PRO, it is apparent that the staff of the Admiralty's own intelligence cell (ID8G) were not merely distrustful of their apparent rivals (and usurpers?) from the Buckinghamshire countryside; they were positively resentful. One of Hinsley's colleagues from the famous Hut 4 was sent on an extended liaison visit to ID8G. Parts of Alec Dakin's eleven-page report show that he was not impressed:[29]

28. The author corresponded and had several long phone conversations with Sir Harry.
29. PRO file HW14/7

> [Concerning] ID8G, its relations with us and its attitudes to our staff. Here the prime test is Hinsley and his dope; practically we stand or fall with him. I believe that anyone who reads one or two of Hinsley's Y serials[30] (especially the *Glorious* one, of course) . . . must conclude that there is something in it, that Hinsley's linkages do give him 'indications' of future activity [. . .] But ID8G seem never to have studied a Y serial. In their present state of ignorance, these people are not able to interpret and pass on any information they receive from Hinsley or the watch. That they should be jealous of his success is understandable, and that they should dislike him personally is a small matter, but that they should be so obstructive is ruinous.

It was clearly a personal and subjective reaction, but its general tenor is supported by several other accounts of the early days of Bletchley Park. Harry Hinsley also spent a week on attachment to the Admiralty's ID8G. His report showed that he was no more impressed than Alec Dakin had been:

> It surprised me that after all the work we have put at the disposal of ID8G and after all the work to obtain their co-operation . . . most of our effort has been in vain [. . .] There appeared to be a competitive spirit, which instead of being of a healthy type is obviously personal and couched itself in a show of independence and an air of obstruction.

Reading those two extracts, one cannot help wondering if ID8G's attitude towards Hinsley in 1940 is not paralleled by that of today's MOD, including its Naval Historical Branch, when approached by civilian outsiders who have the nerve to suggest that it might not always be right.

Interestingly, Sir Harry fully credits the Admiralty, in the months following the *Glorious* debacle, with realizing that a serious mistake had been made. He tells (though not in the official history) how, not long afterwards, he was sent north to Scapa Flow to explain the strengths and weaknesses of W/T traffic analysis to Admiral Tovey and senior officers of the Home Fleet. They came to know this rather untidy young man, clad against the Orkney winds in a long black overcoat, as The Cardinal.

30. A 'Y serial' was the designation given to information derived from the type of W/T analysis as described in the main text.

Even though he was young, they were not inclined to dismiss what he had to tell them. He learnt from them, too. All this was some time before the breaking of the German Enigma codes – in which Hinsley also played an important part. After that, the co-operation between the Admiralty and Bletchley Park became extremely close. Indeed, naval historians agree that it was a key factor in eventual victory.

THERE IS ONE REMAINING chapter of the *Glorious* story in which the authorized account must be challenged. It concerns the action taken, or, more accurately, not taken on receipt of *Glorious*'s urgent (some might say desperate) signals as she was being shelled that afternoon. The official narrative has always claimed that the only signal ever heard from *Glorious* was such a 'garbled' fragment that it was 'almost unintelligible'. Therefore, given that the signal was virtually unreadable, no action was taken by the cruiser HMS *Devonshire*, the only British ship to hear it. However, that alleged 'almost unintelligible' is at distinct odds with the recollections of a number of people who were serving in *Devonshire* at the time.

The 'witnesses' include, first, Telegraphist Stanley Rogers and his overseeing Petty Officer, Trevor Jenkins. They were both on W/T listening watch in *Devonshire*. Their claim has always been that the signal they heard was neither a fragment nor unintelligible; they insist that they received and understood it in almost every significant detail – 'in excellent morse and in no way garbled'.[31] Second, and also in *Devonshire*, a midshipman (now a retired Commander) recalls the effect that the signal had on senior officers when it was brought through to the plot and they realized its significance. Third, from *Glorious* (i.e. at the transmitting end) there is an account from the Warrant Officer in immediate charge of sending that signal – an Enemy Sighting Report. WO Blackwell wrote his report when he returned from being a POW five years later. Fourth, and in further divergence from the official narrative, there is an account compiled by a special signals interception unit (Beobachtungs-Dienst) in

31. The signal was heard and taken down in *Devonshire*'s so-called Remote Control Office – a W/T office conveniently sited near the bridge and the ship's plot. The main W/T office would have been several decks down.

Gneisenau. The Germans may have been the enemy, but they were meticulous and had no motive to 'bend' the record of what they heard. Moreover, their account is not dependent in any way on memory. It was written within a very short time of the events it describes. In essence, the German account of the last signal from *Glorious* (shortly before she sank) is different, in the only detail that really matters, from the version of that same signal as later reported by *Devonshire*. Yet the British and the Germans were listening to the same signal – on the same frequency and at the same time.

So, there is something very fishy about the official claim that the only signal heard was 'almost unintelligible'. It does not tally with the claim of the two men who were in *Devonshire*'s W/T office, or with that of the midshipman in the plot. Additionally, there were at least two other witnesses who talk of the anxious reactions caused by the signal as received in *Devonshire* that day. We will come to them. Intriguingly, other than the two telegraphists (who had been out of touch since 1940), none of these people even knew of each other's existence until they watched the TV documentary in the summer of 1997. While their stories varied in some details, they all agreed on one fundamental: *Devonshire* heard more that afternoon than has ever been officially acknowledged.

It will already be apparent that the matter of *Glorious*'s signals is deeply controversial. Who heard what? And when? And does it matter?

It matters because if any ship receives another ship's Enemy Sighting Report (ESR), the implications are so obvious and urgent that, if she does not then hear the signal being promptly acknowledged by the shore station (or ship) to which it is primarily directed, she is obliged, with very few exceptions, to acknowledge and then relay it herself. Clearly it is vital that all ships in a given theatre should know if enemy warships have been sighted. And where. And when. The information will immediately affect their movements. Aircraft may be flown to find and track the enemy – prior to a strike by other aircraft or by warships. And vulnerable convoys may have to be diverted. In this particular case, less than 200 miles behind *Devonshire* there was an evacuating convoy of 12,000 troops setting off from northern Norway. Given that *Devonshire* had left that same coast only the previous night, it seems most unlikely that she would not have known about the convoy. Lastly, if a ship is being attacked, she may need help. There may even be survivors in the sea. It is this last aspect that has always worried the relatives of those who were lost.

There are very few exceptions to the rule that an ESR should always be acted on. The most obvious applies if a ship hearing an unacknowledged ESR thinks that it is bogus – an enemy trick to cause her to disclose her position to his radio direction finders. Another exception is when a ship is under an order of radio silence – though even then, depending on the circumstances, her captain may still feel that relaying the signal must have priority over all other factors.

Devonshire was under an order of radio silence – some say from Winston Churchill himself. She was carrying a special cargo: the King and Crown Prince of Norway, most of their government and several units of both the British and the Norwegian army – over 400 people. She had scooped them up the evening before from the far northern port of Tromsø; she was now evacuating them in a high-speed solo run back to the Clyde. By mid-afternoon on 8 June, her track placed her very close to *Glorious*. She may have been only 40 miles to the west.

Just before 16.15 the destroyer *Ardent* had flashed back to *Glorious* that the two ships on the horizon had failed to answer her coded challenge. It probably took another two or three minutes before she identified them as two pocket battleships. Captain D'Oyly Hughes in *Glorious* would have immediately drafted an ESR. So urgent is an ESR that it is not even put into cipher. We have the Warrant Officer's handwritten report that the Captain ordered him to make the signal. He immediately oversaw its transmission:

> To the best of my knowledge we proceeded without our usual air-cover that day . . . I spent the afternoon in the D/F [Direction Finding] Office situate at the after end of the Flag Deck. Passing the Chart House on my way to tea, at about 16.15, the Captain stopped me and asked, 'On which wave do we make an Enemy Report, Mr Blackwell?' The Captain often asked such questions and I had no idea of the real situation, as I replied, '253 Kc/s Sir, but knowing this area would suggest H/F [High Frequency] as well'. (*Glorious* had left Narvik Zone and had shifted to Home Waves at 1300.) As I finished speaking, Action Stations sounded, and the Captain thrust a message

into my hand saying, 'Then make this quickly, both waves.' The message was self-evident reporting two Deutschland class battleships.

From this report by WO Blackwell we learn three important facts. First, we know the time that *Glorious*'s ESR would have been transmitted – very shortly after 16.15. Second, we know that it was sent on two frequencies: 253 Kc/s and on either 4740 or 8290 Kc/s – these being the appropriate 'Home Waves' referred to by WO Blackwell. Third, we know that the enemy was wrongly identified as two Deutschland class battleships; these were always referred to by the British as 'pocket' battleships. So the signal would have identified them in the Navy's self-evident code as '2PB'.

Strangely, the Germans, though only about 16 or 17 miles away and poised to jam that signal, never heard it. The reason is simple: *Glorious* was transmitting on the wrong frequency. The Germans could not know this and were listening on the right frequency (3700 Kc/s). *Glorious* had shifted (see WO Blackwell above) from the frequencies used by ships in the Narvik Zone to those used in the Home Zone far too soon. The 'change-over' was not meant to happen until a ship crossed Latitude 65° N; *Glorious* was more than 250 miles short (to the north) of that line. How and why the mistake occurred has never been explained. But that it did occur there is no doubt. First, we have WO Blackwell's word for it. Second, we have the Germans' confirmation of it – if *Glorious* had been on the right frequency, *Gneisenau* would surely have heard her. Third, we have the firm opinion of Petty Officer Trevor Jenkins, in charge of *Devonshire*'s W/T watch that afternoon, that the signal he and his operators heard at about 16.20 was on 4740 Kc/s – a Home frequency. *Devonshire*, because of her special mission, must have been 'guarding' both Narvik *and* Home frequencies.[32]

The official account has always claimed that *Devonshire* did not hear that first ESR. The claim is that she *only* heard *Glorious*'s final signal

32. For some reason the official account has long insisted that *Glorious* transmitted her signals throughout the engagement on the Narvik frequency of 3700 Kc/s. This is despite the written reports of both WO Blackwell and the Germans to the contrary, plus the testimony of the W/T staff in *Devonshire* who actually heard the signal. Only towards the end of the action does it seem that *Glorious* switched to 3700 Kc/s.

toward the end of the action an hour later – at 17.20. But it was so 'garbled' as to be meaningless. Naturally, therefore, she did nothing about it. But, against this, there is the testimony of Petty Officer Jenkins and Telegraphist Rogers that they heard *Glorious*'s very first signal – at about 16.20. This is an hour earlier than the allegedly garbled signal. Mr Rogers, who was sitting next to the operator assigned to 'guard' 4740 Kc/s, told the author, with excusable hyperbole, 'The signal I heard was so loud that you could have heard it on the fo'c'sle. And it wasn't garbled.'[33] In 1997, after the TV programme in which the Head of the NHB denied that any understandable signal had ever been received by *Devonshire*, Mr Rogers wrote to put him right:

> During the TV broadcast you requested a witness to confirm that an Enemy Report had been made by *Glorious*. I am that witness.
>
> When the Enemy Report started from *Glorious* it was at strength 9 and sounded very near to *Devonshire*. I read the signal without any trouble and what was sent was in excellent morse and in no way was it garbled. The Enemy Report consisted of the addressee, from what ship, the priority 'O' meaning 'Emergency' or 'O-U' meaning 'Most Immediate', the number and type of enemy, the distance, course and bearing, then 'my' position (e.g. ABCD2143). The position of *Glorious* was never completed but only partly given and no Time of Origin given. Regarding the '2PB' part of the signal, some person came into the W/T Office and queried whether the 'PB' could have been misread to read 'FB', which would have meant 'flying boats'. But there was no doubt that it was 'PB'. This episode was not taken lightly aboard Devonshire . . . On arriving at Greenock, I believe the operator's log and signal pad were despatched in great haste to London.

The other witness in the W/T office, Petty Officer Jenkins (who died in 1998), claimed for over fifty years that he took the pencilled signal through to *Devonshire*'s CO, Captain Mansfield, in the ship's plot. He was always sure about the time – within a minute or two of 16.20. The third person, then a midshipman, now Commander Corkhill DSC

33. The author has talked and corresponded at length with Telegraphist Rogers and Petty Officer Jenkins. Both were unshakeable in their contention about what they heard and that the official record is wrong.

(retired), was on duty in the plot that afternoon. He is unsure about the timing but is adamant that he saw what he assumed was an ESR being brought through to the Captain. Even more relevantly, he recalls the 'considerable consternation' the signal caused when *Glorious*'s position was worked out and it was seen just how close she was. He remembers someone saying, 'But that's almost where we are,' or words very close to that effect. By now, Vice Admiral John Cunningham, who was 'flying his flag' in *Devonshire*, had been called to the plot. The Admiral's personal runner and signalman, Mr Slocombe, recalls, 'We went to some kind of alert.'[34] He also remembers being asked by the Flag Lieutenant if the term '2PB', as just reported, could have any meaning other than two pocket battleships. There was some discussion as to whether the telegraphists might have got it wrong. Could it be '2FB' – i.e. two flying boats? In Morse an 'F' (dot dot dash dot) is very similar to a 'P' (dot dash dot). But both PO Jenkins and Telegraphist Rogers were sure (and still are) that there was no mistake. Anyway, why should *Glorious* be sending a signal (with a 'most urgent' prefix) about enemy flying boats when they were a fairly common sight in those waters? It has also been pointed out that 'FB' was not on the Navy's list of self-evident codes, for the good reason that it would have been too easily confused with 'PB'. The correct group would have been 'PL' for planes.

Scharnhorst and *Gneisenau* were battle cruisers (BCs), much more powerful than the pocket battleships *Glorious* first thought they were. The misidentification is understandable: the enemy ships, though closing, were still distant and not in side-on silhouette. But this misidentification is important, because by the time the Germans had eventually picked up *Glorious*'s later signals at 16.52 and 17.19 (presumably the B-Dienst unit searched all the possible frequencies until it 'found' *Glorious*), she had, according to the very specific German record, now *correctly* identified them as two battle cruisers – '2BC'.

Thus a real problem for the official account, based on Vice Admiral Cunningham's version of events as he reported them from *Devonshire* to the Admiralty the next day, is that it claims that almost the only 'legible'

34. The author has talked and corresponded at length with Signalman Slocombe and Commander Corkhill.

part of the only signal heard was, at 17.20 (over an hour after the action began), still misidentifying the Germans as two pocket battleships – '2PB'. But this is absolutely not what the Germans say of that same signal (same time, same frequency). Indeed, the Germans report that the British carrier had *correctly* identified them as 2BCs almost half an hour earlier, at 16.52. It is almost unbelievable that *Glorious*, having got the identification right at 16.52 (according to the Germans), should then revert to getting it wrong again (according to the British) nearly thirty minutes later. But that is what the official account maintains.[35]

In short, *Gneisenau* and *Devonshire* report hearing a different signal at virtually the same moment (one reports 17.19, the other 17.20) and on the same frequency. The British report hearing '2PB', the Germans report '2BC'. They cannot both be right. There seems to be only one explanation: *Devonshire* must have heard both the first signal ('in excellent morse') *and* the last 'garbled' signal an hour later – 'garbled' because the Germans were jamming it. The next day, when *Devonshire* reported what she had heard, it seems she 'muddled' the times and transposed the '2PB' from the first signal to the last. Subsequent indications (see later) suggest that this transposition may not have been entirely accidental.

Anyway, whatever they heard, and whenever they heard it, those in command of *Devonshire* evidently decided to maintain radio silence. The official account has it that, with only a meaningless fragment to go on, there was nothing to relay. Critics of this reasoning point to the fact that even the official version acknowledges that the signal was not *that* meaningless; if nothing else, it contained the group 2PB. This could mean only one thing: enemy. Surely, they argue, this alone should have prompted *Devonshire* to pass on such important information. And

35. The German B-Dienst log very specifically reports *Glorious*'s transmission at 16.52 as follows: 'Time: 1652. From Glorious to Scapa Flow. Most Immediate. Two Battle cruisers bearing 308. Distance 15 miles. My position 154GQOX11.' The German report goes on with this very revealing entry about *Glorious*'s later and last signal at 17.19. 'Glorious tried at 17.19 hours to transmit the same message [as she had at 16.52] on the Northern Zone wave 81.08m [i.e. 3700Kc/s]. But when they tried to call the Admiral on board Ark Royal it was jammed so effectively that the message did not go through.' The original German runs as follows: '*Glorious versuchte dann um 1819 Uhr denselben Fuinkspruch auf der Bereiuchswelle des Nordge bietes (81,08m) abzusetzen.*'

surely this alone should have set alarm bells ringing. In fact, *Devonshire*'s log shows that alarms bells did indeed ring, but in response to the *first* and still officially denied ESR at 16.20 – the one that according to Commander Corkhill caused 'considerable consternation'. In her log there appears this short but significant entry: '16.25 – Exercised main armament'.

Presumably this means that at that particular moment, all four of her 8-inch turrets were manned and 'exercised' together. But why? A number of naval officers and historians suggest that it must have been because *Devonshire* had heard *Glorious*'s ESR quite clearly enough to take her own precautionary step against a possible threat. If so, why an 'exercise'? Why not 'Action Stations'? Could the answer be that such a call might have alarmed, maybe to the point of panic, some of the more than 400 nervous Norwegians and other non-naval personnel crammed below? With no enemy actually in sight but perhaps presumed to be not far over the horizon, better the less urgent tannoy call, 'For exercise only, for exercise only. Close up turrets ABX and Y. I say again . . .'

When the log entry '16.25 – Exercised main armament' was pointed out to the MOD's in-house historians, they had a problem. After all, it has always been officially argued that *Devonshire* never heard any signal at all at 16.20. Nor, it is claimed, did *Devonshire* know that *Glorious* was even in the vicinity, let alone that she was in contact with the enemy. In which case, one asks, why should *Devonshire* have chosen *that* particular moment (only a very few minutes after we know *Glorious* sent her first ESR signal) to make sure that her four 8-inch turrets were manned and ready? The official explanation is that the timing was just a coincidence; it had nothing to do with the receipt of any signal from *Glorious* at 16.20 – because no signal had been heard at that time. 'The Navy,' rationalized the MOD's Minister John Spellar, briefed for that 1999 Commons debate, 'traditionally uses the period between 1600 and 1800 for Evening Quarters to exercise gun crews.' Well, yes and no. If one is going to invoke tradition, it is worth pointing out that the Navy, even in wartime, usually tries to make an hour or two on Saturday afternoons available for 'make and mend' – a time when anyone who is not actually on duty is allowed a little time for personal maintenance. To call for a mere practice 'exercise' of a ship's main armament during this time, while very far from impossible, would have been rather unlikely. In any case, the *Devonshire*'s log shows that this was the first time in over a month she had 'exercised' all main armament simultaneously – though she had certainly exercised her 8-inch turrets individually during that time. Furthermore, it was the first time in four months she had exercised all four turrets simultaneously in the First Dog Watch. And never in the First Dog Watch on a Saturday. Perhaps she was an even more traditional ship than has been officially suggested.

The authorized account reinforces its denial that the 8-inch turrets were manned in response to a perceived surface danger by suggesting that 'in the presumed absence of enemy surface ships, German long-range aircraft were an expected threat'. So it was allegedly against this aerial possibility that the 8-inch turrets (in their rarely used high-angle AA role – which would also have required special AA ammunition) were being manned. Perhaps. Who knows? But once again, *Devonshire*'s log is interesting: at 05.30 the very next morning, a shadowing Heinkel bomber was spotted, yet the log contains no mention of the ship's 'main armament' being 'exercised' in response. The entry simply reads: 'Port AA defence closed up. 05.46 opened fire.' And *Devonshire*'s log also shows that she had been over-flown by German aircraft several times during the preceding month, but not once is there any indication that her 8-inch turrets were manned in response. So why on this occasion?

It has to be emphasized that the official version of events insists that *Devonshire* did not know *Glorious* was in the vicinity, let alone that she had sighted two enemy warships. Further, until it was drawn to their attention, the MOD's in-house historians did not appear to know of an entry in an Admiralty file (now in the PRO), which seems to have a direct bearing on what *Devonshire* really heard and when. In the diary of the Admiralty's Operational Intelligence Centre (OIC) for 10 June is this entry: 'At 16.15, 8 June, an intercepted message from HMS *Glorious* indicated that she was in contact with an enemy naval force.' That information can only have originated from *Devonshire*. If the entry means what it says (and why not?), it seems to confirm that the British cruiser *did* hear the 16.15 signal – something the official account has always denied. And that, of course, might further confirm that she was 'exercising' her 8-inch turrets almost simultaneously with the moment we are told by her W/T operators that they heard that first signal.

The problem with so much of this episode is that we will never know for sure because, extraordinarily, except for that OIC entry just quoted, the official records are almost non-existent. The MOD (in the Commons debate) confirms that Vice Admiral Cunningham 'reported in some detail on the intercepted signal, but there is no surviving copy in the archives'. Why not? And if there is no surviving copy, how does anyone know that the Admiral 'reported in some detail'? A week after *Glorious* and the destroyers were lost, the Director of Signals at the Admiralty asked all stations ashore and afloat if they had heard 'any signal or fragment of the message which might have been made by the ships concerned'. As the MOD now puts it: 'Nil returns were received from all authorities except Vice Admiral Cunningham whose reply is not preserved.' It is very difficult to believe that, with a carrier and two destroyers on the bottom, the imperative of guarding those last signals (against, for example, a Board of Inquiry) would not have been immediately recognized at the time. Consequently, the 'not preserved' is strange. And the 'no surviving copy'? What happened to it?

There is one more 'witness' to the events in *Devonshire*. The only one not interviewed for this book was a cadet who found himself drafted to help with Admiral Cunningham's burgeoning signals and cipher traffic. In a letter now among the Roskill Papers at the Churchill Archive Centre, Commander Dean (long deceased) remembers how later (the next day?) Vice Admiral Cunningham seemed distraught that he had not taken positive action on *Glorious*'s signal, or signals. Commander Dean writes:

> I recall him [Cunningham] slumped in the corner of the bridge, chain smoking and convinced that he would be condemned for turning his back on *Glorious*, an action so contrary to all the traditions of his service. Knowledge of the intercepted signal was ordered to be restricted as far as possible to avoid ill-feeling among the ship's company. Nevertheless there were mutterings. For what it is worth, we did break silence to relay the enemy report as soon as we cleared Cape Wrath and entered the Minch [presumably this is how that entry in

> the OIC diary above came about]. The Admiral's relief was plain when, on arrival at Tail o' the Bank [the Clyde], he received a personal message from Churchill entirely approving his action and indicating that there were times when a mission transcended in importance even the most noble tradition. After all, for a thin-skinned 8" cruiser to engage two German battle ships/battle cruisers was suicidal. We could not have helped *Glorious* and her heroic escorts.[36]

Those last two sentences go to the heart of this whole signals controversy: if *Devonshire* had heard enough of *Glorious*'s signals to strongly suspect (a) the carrier might be under attack, (b) she was not far away ('But that is almost where we are' and 'Exercise main armament'), and (c) her signals were not being acknowledged by any other station, what action should she have taken? Given that she was under orders of radio silence and had the King and his large entourage aboard, opinion varies. Some hold that, alerted by the group '2PB' (or '2BC') in the signal, she should, at the very least, have broken silence to warn other ships of the possibility (if no more) that two powerful German warships were at large. She would almost certainly have known there was a very large troop convoy less than 200 miles to the north-east; this was the convoy escorted by *Ark Royal*, two cruisers and six destroyers. What if the Germans had found that convoy? It was, after all, what they were looking for. Where then would have been the mitigation of 'radio silence'? True, the Germans might (just) have been 'seen off', but at what price? Other commentators think that, given the importance of the royal 'evacuees' in terms of boosting the morale of Norwegian forces then reforming in Britain, *Devonshire* was justified in steaming on and maintaining silence. This is what she seems to have decided to do. One notes Commander Dean's comment of 'knowledge of the intercepted signal was ordered to be restricted as far as possible'. Could that be why no record of the first signal – the ESR 'in excellent

36. When this letter was brought to the attention of the MOD's historians, they were 'reluctant to accept Commander Dean's testimony' on the apparent grounds that, as a mere cadet, he would not have been privy to an Admiral's thinking. Probably not. But he may have overheard a conversation or learnt something from a third party.

morse and in no way garbled' – has ever featured in any official account? Maybe. Maybe not. We will never know.[37]

Lastly, there are some who think that, having first alerted other ships, *Devonshire* should have turned towards the action and attempted to find and shadow the enemy – communicating with the rest of the fleet as she did so. She might have come upon some survivors and then, at least, have alerted others to their presence. But without radar and given the well-known precision of German gunnery, any attempt to shadow the enemy would have been a risky undertaking. Nevertheless, shadowing was a role for which the 32-knot cruisers of *Devonshire*'s class were partly designed. There is some irony in wondering what Captain D'Oyly Hughes would have done if he had been in command of *Devonshire*.

Of course, it is easy enough to debate these dilemmas over a distance of more than sixty years and without the responsibility of having to Get It Right. But almost every one agrees, with the exception of the MOD (which does not even acknowledge a problem in the first place), that any decision would have been very difficult. Many think Vice Admiral Cunningham – it would ultimately have been his judgement – did the right thing in regarding his passengers as his first responsibility, even at the expense of the troop convoy to the north and *Glorious* to the east. But were the details of the signal deliberately muddled 'to avoid ill-feeling among the ship's company' and, subsequently, elsewhere across the Navy? It is a pity all the contemporary records have been lost – 'not been preserved'. They would almost certainly have pointed to the truth of what really happened.

So, in conclusion, given the strength of evidence from a variety of sources, including the German B-Dienst reports, it seems probable that *Devonshire* heard *two* signals that afternoon. The first, at about 16.20, was clear enough ('strength 9 . . . excellent morse') to know that *Glorious*, if

37. One of the mysteries of the signals story is why no other ships ever heard any of *Glorious*'s transmissions. Quite apart from the fact that she was transmitting on the wrong frequency for much of the time, another likely reason seems to be that in the spring of 1940 there was an unusual amount of sunspot activity. The resulting interference is always more pronounced in the high latitudes. It is known, for example, that W/T communications between the Admiralty and ships in the waters of northern Norway were frequently unreliable and spasmodic.

not under actual attack, was, at the least, in contact with the enemy. And her position. The second, at about 17.20, was most likely rendered 'almost unintelligible' by German jamming. If that hypothesis holds, it might explain why that second signal is the only one which, then and ever since, has found a place in the official narrative.

IN CONVERSATION and correspondence with Admiral Sir John (Sandy) Woodward about the chapter in this book examining aspects of the *Belgrano* controversy, it was natural that the subject of *Glorious* should come up. Sir John, having read the account above, had this interesting comment:

> If one accepts that *Devonshire* heard enough (and that 'exercised main armament' would seem to be a pointer) to know that *Glorious* and the Germans were not far away, then Admiral Cunningham was on the horns of a very nasty dilemma. All his naval training would have told him to head for the enemy and for *Glorious* – and quite possibly a posthumous VC. But his existing orders, no doubt, told him to avoid action and get the Norwegian Royals and co. back to the UK safely regardless. And that is quite apart from the unreadiness of his ship for action with all those hundreds of passengers. A very difficult decision for him and quite likely (as Dean's letter implies) to leave him feeling that he'd blown it – and that he might be accused of cowardice. Churchill's reassurance (if Dean's memory is correct) when *Devonshire* arrived in the Clyde was probably the best thing to happen to him for weeks. But it is not too surprising that the records of exactly what *Devonshire* heard that day have long since disappeared.

And what about *Glorious*, *Ardent* and *Acasta*? From the moment the enemy were correctly identified as battle cruisers, it must have been obvious that there was no hope of escape. Had *Glorious* been able to accelerate quickly to her full 31 knots, she might, screened by smoke from the two destroyers, have just got away. It was not to be. Curiously – and the enemy remarked on it – she did not immediately turn away, but remained on a broadly convergent course with *Scharnhorst* and *Gneisenau* until well into the action. They slowly overhauled her from her starboard quarter. So unexpected was it that *Glorious* did not bear away, some German reports contain suspicions she might have been trying to draw them towards a lurking submarine.

At 16.32 *Scharnhorst* opened fire with her two forward 11-inch turrets; *Glorious* was over 14 miles away. The shots fell short. A few minutes later, at a range of 26,465 yards (over 13 miles) and aided by radar and the

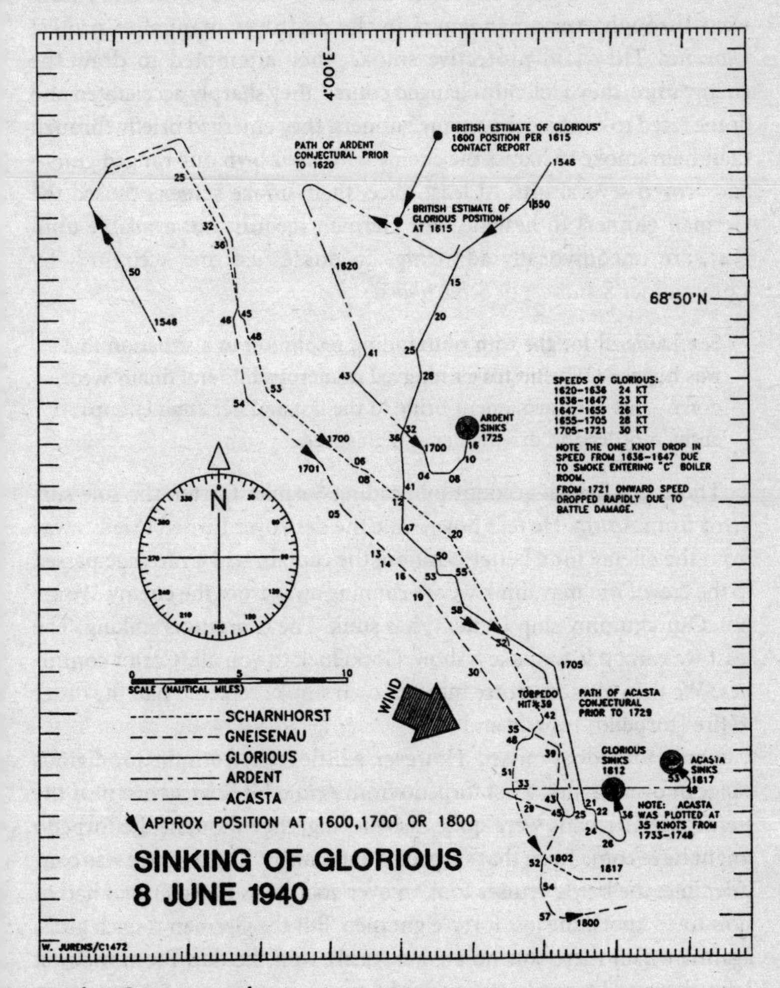

Based on German records.

best optical range-finders in the world, she found her target. It may well have been the longest direct hit in the history of naval gunnery. The shells would have been in the air for over a minute. Shortly afterwards, *Gneisenau* began firing too.

The two destroyers did their best, and evidently it was a very brave best indeed. With no thought for their own safety, *Ardent* and *Acasta* went through every manoeuvre in the destroyer manual to protect *Glorious*. They laid protective smoke, they attempted to draw the enemy's fire, they violently changed course, they sharply accelerated and decelerated to confuse the enemy gunners, they emerged briefly through their own smoke to harass the enemy with their own out-ranged guns – and scored several hits. At least once, their smoke screens caused the German gunners to hesitate. The German records, not available until 1945, are unequivocally admiring. To quote just one account – by Commander Schubert of *Scharnhorst*:

> She [*Ardent*] fought with outstanding resolution in a situation that was hopeless. The destroyer received numerous hits and finally went down – her bow armament firing to the last and her engines apparently in order and driving her at high speed.

There is a British account by Leading Seaman Carter, the sole survivor from *Acasta*. He tells how, while the destroyer turned briefly away from the enemy for a better position, the captain had a message passed to the crew: 'You may think we are running away from the enemy. We are not. Our chummy ship [*Ardent*] has sunk. The *Glorious* is sinking. The least we can do is to make a show. Good luck to you all.' Carter continues, 'We then altered course into our own smoke screen. I had the order to fire [torpedo] tubes 6 and 7 . . .'

Those torpedoes missed. However, a little later, from the prodigious range of over 5 miles, a last torpedo from *Acasta* hit *Scharnhorst* near the stern. The Germans were quite disbelieving; they thought the torpedo might have come from that suspected submarine. The damage was considerable: the battle cruiser took in over 2000 tons of water and had to slow to 20 knots; she lost forty-eight men. But the German 11-inch guns, against which there was no answer, easily won the day. From the first salvo there had never been any doubt.

One of those German shells hit the stern of the already sinking *Acasta*. Leading Seaman Carter again:

> It seemed to lift the ship out of the water. At last the Captain gave the order to abandon ship. I will always remember the Surgeon Lieutenant [H.J. Stammers], his first ship, his first action. Before I jumped over the side, I saw him still attending to the wounded, a hopeless task. And when I was in the water I saw the Captain leaning over the bridge, take a cigarette from a case and light it. We shouted to him to come on our raft. He waved 'Goodbye and good luck.' A ridiculous end to a gallant man.

Carter was the only survivor from *Acasta*.

No one knows how many went down trapped or wounded in the three ships, but from the estimates of the few survivors there may have been as many as 1000 men in the sea. Some were in Carley floats, some were clinging to the floats, some were struggling to get to the floats. It was cold. A Carley float was nothing more than a large oval-shaped buoyancy device which would float either way up; its floor was a lattice of wooden slats open to the sea; anyone in or on it sat with their feet in the water. None of the rafts carried any food, water or signalling flares. The survivors assumed that *Glorious*'s signals would have been heard. So those who could find a raft were hopeful of rescue. The sea was not rough but there was a long swell.

By the next morning, it seems that there were only a hundred or so left alive. The cold was the killer. On one float ten out of twenty-five came through the night; by that evening only five were left. On another float just two survived out of twenty-three. Later that day some of them saw a Swordfish and a Walrus. But the aircraft did not see them. In fact, the aircraft, from *Ark Royal*, were not looking for them; they did not even know that *Glorious* and her escorts were gone. They were flying patrols ahead of the convoy.

Normally, German radio announcements about their naval 'triumphs' were treated with some scepticism (in the first eighteen months of the war, Lord Haw Haw was to 'sink' *Ark Royal* at least three times). But on this occasion there were no doubts. To add to the anger, especially in the Fleet Air Arm, it was only six months since *Glorious*'s sister ship

Courageous had been lost in the Western Approaches. She, too, had been escorted by just two destroyers – while trying to find U-boats. But a U-boat found her first. The questions asked then about the proper deployment and handling of aircraft carriers were now asked again with even more vigour.

What the Germans did not tell the world was that *Scharnhorst* and *Gneisenau* had been forced to put back to Trondheim. *Acasta*'s torpedo prevented the battle cruisers from continuing to the north where they would probably have intercepted their target – the troop convoy. So maybe *Glorious*, or more specifically that torpedo launched by *Acasta* in her final throes, played a vital part in the safe passage of the convoy and the lives of those troops.

But while the Germans were congratulating themselves, there were men struggling to stay alive on those rafts. By the third day, when they were found by a small Norwegian coaster evacuating herself to the Faeroes, there were just forty left. The Carley floats were spread over many miles; most contained only corpses. The little *Borgund* pulled aboard all those she could find who were still alive. Most were too weak to help themselves. The coaster had no radio, so she could not alert anyone to what she had found. With no resources other than a few blankets, she did her best:

> No one could have done more for us than those Norwegians – their kindness was beyond praise. They gave up their bunks for the worst cases. They gave us cigarettes, shared their only half bottle of whiskey and made tea and coffee for us. Then they pointed out the warmest places to sleep . . .

By the time the *Borgund* reached the Faeroes two days later, one of the survivors was dead; two more died in hospital.

Meanwhile, another Norwegian ship, also on her way to the Faeroes, had found four other survivors. Unfortunately, shortly after picking them up she was harassed by German aircraft and forced to return to Norway. Two of those four died, but WO Blackwell and Joiner Joe Brown (one of the only two survivors still alive in 2001) spent the rest of the war as POWs.

A destroyer, under Commander Broome (later of Convoy PQ17 fame), brought the survivors home from the Faeroes to Rosyth. It was many months before they recovered from their ordeal; a few never really did. Most of them (curiously, not all) were questioned by that Board of Inquiry. As we know, the minutes and the findings (such as they were) of the Inquiry were initially embargoed for 101 years.

There is one more note to this part of the narrative – though it comes much higher than a mere footnote. It goes back to *Ardent* and *Acasta*. German reports of the action were deeply admiring. The following comment comes from *Gneisenau*'s account, as written by her Captain:

> The conduct of *Ardent* was particularly spirited and clever. She outmanoeuvred [our] fall of shot very capably, laid smoke and used it with great skill, and varied her speed from 10 to 35 knots. In this way she made the task of our guns very difficult.

That and other German narratives were, of course, not available until after the war. But there was one exception. Some days after the encounter – one can hardly call it a battle – the official German news agency, which normally was only concerned with Nazi propaganda, carried an admiring account of the way the destroyers had tried to shield their charge: 'But the destroyers did not give up . . . these brave opponents.' The full report, which made some use of the Captain's comments above, was reprinted in *The Times*. From that account, and from what could be learnt from the few survivors who had been in a position to see *Ardent* and *Acasta* (from the two destroyers there were only three survivors), the Rear Admiral in charge of destroyers recommended that Lieutenant Commander Barker and Commander Glasford – in command of *Ardent* and *Acasta* respectively – should be considered for posthumous Victoria Crosses. This was turned down on the grounds, it is said, that there were no witnesses of sufficient rank to verify the courage of those concerned. According to some, there may have been another reason: why draw attention to something the Navy's hierarchy would rather forget? Perhaps this is why, even after the war, when other admiring accounts written by the German Admiral and others came to light, a renewed recommendation for VCs was still rejected.

Instead, back in 1940, the Admiralty settled on a Mentioned-in-Despatches apiece, plus specially inscribed letters of condolence. The families still have them. And at the PRO the calligrapher's invoice rests modestly in the same Admiralty file as a host of official comments, questions and criticisms: 'For two letters written on vellum in black and red, ribboned and cased . . . £6'.

Perhaps the greatest tribute to the crews of those two destroyers came forty-six years later, at a German naval reunion in 1996. Among many others, there was a sprinkling of old men who had served in *Scharnhorst* and *Gneisenau*. One of them told Ben Barker, the grandson of Lieutenant Commander Barker of *Ardent*, and the producer of the Channel 4 documentary, about it: 'As we left and headed back to Trondheim, both our ships flew their ensigns at half mast – as much for your people as for ours. Those destroyers – that was one of the bravest things we ever saw.'

IT IS A LONG STORY from a long time ago. And some will be asking, 'Why bother? After all this time, what are you trying to prove?' I can see why the questions are asked, but I think they miss the point. Of course, I am interested in researching the misjudgements I believe surround this rather obscure piece of naval history in which over 1500 men were killed. But the men who made those mistakes are as long gone as the people who suffered them. There is no point in directing one's questions, let alone one's ire, at them. Anyway, perhaps tired and distracted by other priorities, they did the best they knew. One hopes so.

What interests me far more, and is now much more important, is the way Whitehall officialdom has always dissembled and, even now, continues to explain away all the mistakes to the point where they are hardly even minor errors. To read the Minister's reply in the House of Common in 1999 (just as in 1946), or the MOD's account recently lately placed in the Commons Library, or any of the letters sent by the Naval Historical Branch to MPs and others, one might suppose – so confident are the answers – that there have never been real uncertainties about what happened. I, of course, think that very considerable doubts surround the official version of events. And I think, together with the evidence behind those doubts, that they should be recorded. Which is what, I hope, this chapter has done.

So that is one answer to the question 'Why bother?' But there is another, perhaps more important one. The men who were killed in

Glorious, though much less so in *Ardent* and *Acasta*, did not go down in any memorable way. They never had that chance. If they had to go, they would surely have preferred to have made some more useful contribution to the fight against the tyranny of their time than to be the sitting ducks, the non-contributors, they actually were. Their lives were utterly wasted. Their ship, too. The least they deserve is an attempt to get nearer the truth than the narrative of the long-standing, official account – with its mistakes, half-truths and opinions elevated to certainties. The reader, having got this far, can judge if that view is too harsh.

The fact that 'it is all so long ago' makes the endeavour more urgent, not less. In another few years all the 'witnesses' who served in Norwegian waters, or, for that matter, who saw service through the war, will be gone. Lastly, while we still have a Navy, there may even be some lessons to be learnt. Who knows?

AFTER THAT 'Debate on the Adjournment' in January 1999, Alan Beith MP privately suggested to John Spellar, the Minister who had batted for the MOD, that if the officials drafting the paper (an expanded version of the Minister's speech) being prepared for the Commons Library could be persuaded to include a note that some other naval historians and researchers held 'alternative' views to their own, then the debate which had lasted for nearly sixty years would quietly go away. That was all the 'opposition' had ever hoped for. A few weeks later the Minister wrote to Alan Beith:

> On my instructions, the paper has been revised following the Adjournment Debate to make it plain that the MOD, while explaining how it derived its own conclusions from the available contemporary evidence, acknowledged that there were contrary opinions.

After several years of debate with the MOD, those last six words were progress indeed – though it was a pity the Minister did not make it plain that those 'contrary opinions' had belonged to a range of respected naval historians and retired naval officers, not just a few amateur malcontents. In the event, when the paper came out, both the professionals and the amateurs were to be disappointed. The Minister's instructions were evidently too much for the relevant personnel at the

MOD to swallow. Maybe pride got in the way. In a document of 4000 words, the best that the Naval Historical Branch could manage was as follows:

> Contrary views on certain aspects, particularly the *Glorious*' fuel state, have appeared in Captain Roskill's commercially published 'Churchill and the Admirals' having been previously suggested, without reasoned argument, by Mr Churchill himself. John Winton, a former naval officer, has written a balanced account for which he was granted privileged access to most of the records which remained closed between about 1972 and 1973.

When told of this, Alan Beith commented: 'The MOD seem to have done as little as they could get away with, and to have qualified it in a deliberately unhelpful way.' In fact, even at that grudging level – 'commercially published', 'without reasoned argument', 'privileged access' – the MOD could not get it right, as John Winton pointed out in a letter:

> I was granted no 'privileged access'. When I wrote 'Carrier Glorious' in 1984/85, all the records I consulted were in the public domain. Other sources were obtained by me by private research. Further, the NHB may describe my book as 'a balanced account' but that does not mean that I go along with their arguments.

Lastly, in rejecting any and all hypotheses other than its own, the MOD does not hesitate to 'rubbish' those who disagree with it. Typically, in a letter to the author the NHB claims that its shortage-of-fuel certainty 'has only been discredited by those who do not understand the fuel management practices of the day'. This category would have to include, among others, a number of officers who served through the war. They would include Captain Roskill; he had been in the Navy for twenty-five years before the war even started; he is no longer with us to dispute the proposition that he did not know what he was writing about. But one wonders about Vice Admiral Sir Louis Le Bailly. Here is a man who served throughout the war as an engineer officer, who sat on various committees concerned with naval fuel oil, who wrote a history of fuel and fuelling practices in the Navy, and who finished a forty-three-year service career as the Director General of Intelligence at the MOD.

He is probably the most respected naval officer of 'the old school' alive. He is entirely supportive of the thesis that fuel had little, if anything, to do with the *Glorious* debacle. In 1998 I wrote a detailed research paper on the whole *Glorious* debate, including, of course, an analysis of the arithmetic surrounding the fuel argument. I sent a copy to Sir Louis asking for his reactions and advice. This, with his permission, is his reply:

> I am very grateful to you for keeping me in touch with your fight to expose what really happened in the *Glorious* disaster. What a convincing paper; it must be preserved. If your figures are right (and they make sense to me) I cannot understand how the MOD can be so sure that *Glorious* returned ahead of the main force because of a fuel shortage. The loss of *Glorious* and her destroyers is one of the three great RN tragedies of the War (Convoy PQ17, *Prince of Wales* and *Repulse* are the others) which were due to incompetence and misjudgement. And it is the one which has been the least explained, though Roskill had a go before he died. And Winton certainly expresses his doubts.

That endorsement from one of the Royal Navy's elder statesmen was obviously a great encouragement and, even though quoting it points to an unbecoming level of self-satisfaction, it seems a good place to end this story.

A SOLDIER'S STORY

'There appears to be a conspiracy'

There appears to be a conspiracy to hold my constituent completely incommunicado and deprive him of evidence for his defence.

Virginia Bottomley MP, in the House of Commons

I have an obligation to be mindful of the security and defence of the nation. It is not my obligation to intervene on investigations undertaken by the Ministry of Defence Police.

Doug Henderson, Minister for the Armed Forces,
in the House of Commons

I have no doubts whatsoever. In Bosnia, he played an absolute blinder.

General Sir Michael Jackson KCB, CB

AS SOON AS HE OPENED his front door it was obvious that they had really worked the place over. It was a mess. He was surprised it had taken them so long – nearly seven hours. After all, it was only a small terrace cottage: two-up, two-down and a kitchen out the back. A couple of competent burglars would have been through the place in minutes. But then they had not been looking for 'valuables' – at least not in the sense that burglars would have been. Seven hours? Then he realized that they had almost certainly been through his room over at the Staff College as well; they would have scooped up his computer, his notes and all those floppy disks. Even so, they seemed to have taken their time. Maybe they had stopped for lunch at some pub along the way. He went through to the back room where he kept most of his books, papers and letters. There they had been even busier; they had pretty well stripped the place. Upstairs, too, no doubt.

His address book, diary, scribble pad, folder of bills and receipts – gone. Even though it made him hot with anger, he was not too surprised.

Given the bizarre logic of the whole business in the first place, he could see why they would want to have a good trawl. But why those magazines? Why one picture but not another? Why those novels but not the other books? Why the old family photographs? It all seemed so indiscriminate. They had even taken some sheets of sandpaper and the take-away pizza menu kept by the phone. And his blood donor's card. And a bunch of old Christmas cards. Then he saw that they had taken his father's medals. What possible use could an old man's medals be? These people were just not thinking. Or were they trying to tell him something? Upstairs it was no different. True, there was less to take away. They had left his clothes but had obviously been through all the pockets and checked the linings. And probably looked under the mattress. Madness.

On the table they had left a copy of the search warrant signed by the stipendiary magistrate at Bow Street two days before. And there were some seizure-of-property forms. Presumably they wanted him to know that all was proper and above board.

It had all happened so quickly. There had been no warning. Someone, and it would have been a 'sixth floor' civil servant working in the very highest echelons of the MOD, must have authorized the whole thing. And the topmost brass in the Army had evidently not had the guts to ask any questions or to do any checking. They must have just stood aside and let it happen. Yet they would have known that, innocent or guilty, it would most probably wreck his career. Considering the events of the previous eleven hours, it was no wonder that Major Milos Stankovic MBE of the Parachute Regiment was still in some shock. Why had someone done this to him? Or, at the least, why had the people at the top allowed this to be done to him? He felt betrayed.

It was now nearly 8 p.m.

Just twelve hours earlier, the day had begun like any other. He had closed the door on his cottage in Farnham and wheeled out the big Suzuki. It was the same journey every morning. Threading through the rush-hour traffic he could make it to the Joint Services Staff College over in Bracknell in about thirty minutes. That gave him time to change into uniform and maybe have a cup of coffee before the day's studies and lectures began. On that particular morning he knew the syndicate discussion was to centre on the pros and cons of women serving in frontline units. He half wondered if he would suggest that they might start them off in the Paras and the Commandos, then see how it went from there. Would that be politically incorrect? He never got the chance to find out. Just as people were beginning to go into the lecture hall, one of his instructors, a Brigadier, came across, held him back and then rather apologetically led him off towards a side room 'for a quiet word'.

The Brigadier opened the door. Wrong room – there were two men already there. The Brigadier ushered him forward. The men at the other end stood up and produced warrant badges from their suit pockets. They were MOD policemen. Both were rather overweight. After formally asking if he was, indeed, Major Milos Stankovic, one of them cleared his throat and read from a piece of paper. It was an arrest warrant: 'Section 2.2b of the Official Secrets Act, 1989 . . . passing information which might endanger the lives of British soldiers . . . embarrassing the British government . . . maintaining contact with the Bosnian Serb leadership.' It was as simple – and as deeply complicated – as that. Then there was the closing ritual: 'You have the right to remain silent, but anything you say may be taken down and used in evidence against you. Do you understand?' He was very tempted to say that, no, he did not even begin to 'understand'. But he did not think they would have got the point. Anyway, he was stunned. What was this all about? Why?

One of the men then produced a search warrant for his house. He had to hand over the keys. He noticed they had his address wrong: they would be wasting their time if they went looking for his cottage in Farnham in Hampshire, as he lived in the other Farnham, the one in Surrey. It seemed careless. If they could get that wrong, what about other more important things? It would have been easy enough to let them go off on a wild goose chase, but he put them right. He did not want to give them any grounds for saying later that he had been unco-operative. Next they demanded the key to the Suzuki. What had that got to do with it? He evidently had no choice. He was taken to his room to change out of uniform, then escorted outside – into the back seat of an unmarked MOD car.

Forty minutes later they drove into Guildford Police Station. The desk sergeant was not expecting them. Indeed, no one was. They had not called ahead. Once the sergeant had got over the shock, the usual rites were followed. The charge was read out by the taller MOD man – at dictation speed so that it could be two-fingered into the station computer by a young and pop-eyed constable. But the charge had changed; now it involved the Prevention of Terrorism Act. A mistake? Next, while a young drunk hiccuped in a corner, Major Stankovic was told to take off his tie and belt, and surrender everything in his pockets. He could keep his cigarettes but not the lighter. Before he was led to a cell, the MOD men told the sergeant that while they were away searching his house, he was not to be allowed any phone calls – 'because of the seriousness of the charge'.

The cell was much as he expected; he had seen them on TV – a heavy wooden door with a small sliding hatch, and a loo with no seat. But TV does not tell you about the smell – a mixture of disinfectant, pee and puke. There was a bench to sit on. Sometime after the MOD men had gone, the young constable unlocked the door to say that he and the sergeant had checked 'higher up'. An inspector had confirmed that, in denying the Major a phone call even to a solicitor, the MOD was breaching 'your rights'. (Good for the Surrey Constabulary. Bad for the MOD Police, who should surely have known better.)

The Major did not know any lawyers. So the PC phoned a duty solicitor from 'the list'. Presently she turned up. She had been here before – many times. But she quickly realized that this was different. Totally. This was serious stuff. Within a few minutes her businesslike brusqueness changed to incredulity. This was not like anything she had come across before.

The MOD men eventually returned after nearly eight hours. Allowing for driving time, that meant they had spent upwards of seven hours on their search. One could call them thorough. Or maybe they could not find what they were looking for. Now came 'the interview' – an interrogation. It was all taped. The Major answered the questions as straightforwardly as he could. But the problem was that the MOD men were obviously out of their depth on almost anything to do with Bosnia, let alone with the Major's service there – which, after all, was what it was really all about. The giveaway lay in their questions; they just were not the right ones. They hardly seemed to know where Bosnia was, let alone what elements of the British Army had been doing there for the last four years.

Their ignorance, though worrying, was not their fault; political analysts who have spent years studying the labyrinthine chaos that is the Balkans still get it wrong. Indeed, it was (and is) sometimes said that the only people who are confident that they know what is going on are those who have been inadequately briefed. The Major had seen the symptoms in some of the Whitehall warriors who used to buzz in to Bosnia for a quick look-see.

To be ignorant is one thing, but not to recognize it in oneself is something else. This 'innocence' was exemplified when the senior MOD man confidently announced towards the end of the interview that they would 'get this thing wrapped up by Christmas' – not much more than two months later. To the Major this was further confirmation that they did not know what they were getting into. A year would probably be insufficient. But, as far as this interview was concerned, the MOD men thought that they had 'got enough for the time being'. He got the feeling that the interview had mostly been a cover; the real objective had been to get him out of the way while they searched his house.

He was now on bail – until he had to report back to Guildford in mid-December, in two months' time. Meanwhile, he could go home. But he was warned that he must not contact any of his army friends; he was incommunicado. And, if that were not enough, he realized that until he could prove his innocence, he had obviously lost his place at Staff College. By the time this was all cleared up (and who was to know when that might be), he might even be beyond the age limit. It would almost certainly cost him promotion. He had gone from bright future to bleak present in less than twelve hours.

On his way home he tried to think things through. What had happened? And why? He already had some ideas. He remembered the articles in those smudgy Sarajevo papers, *Vecernje Novine* and *Ljiljan*. Surely the MOD had not fallen for that stuff? But what about those pieces in the *New York Times*? Who had prompted them? And why? Now *that* could be more serious.

MILOS STANKOVIC'S FATHER was a Royalist Serb who fought the Germans as a guerrilla from 1940 to 1945. For much of the war the Royalists and Communist partisans spent almost as much time fighting each other as they did the Germans and their local allies, the Croats. But in 1945, with Stalin's help, Tito and his Communists prevailed. Radomir Stankovic was forced to flee Yugoslavia – the country he felt he had helped to liberate. There followed two years being shunted from camp to camp in Italy and Germany. Then he landed in England with, as he would say in later years, 'No socks, no money, and no English.' But one does not need much of any language to hump bricks in a Bedfordshire brickworks – which is what he did for the next three years. Afterwards he found himself a job as a cleaner at Rank Bush Murphy's TV factory in Chiswick. And, more important, he found digs with an English family while he set about getting a proper grip on the language. When he had accumulated enough vocabulary, he took evening classes in electronics. By day he swept and polished; by night he studied. Twelve years after coming down the gangway at Southampton, he got a degree in electronics – and became a TV design engineer in the same factory where he had been a cleaner.

In 1960 Rank sent him to Southern Rhodesia to help set up a TV network. There he met his wife – half-Scot, half-Serb. During the war she had driven an ambulance in the Western Desert for the 8th Army. Their son, Milos, was born in Salisbury in 1962, a British citizen. In 1965 the family returned to England, back to Rank in Chiswick. Then to another factory in Plymouth. In time, Milos wound up at Plymouth College – head boy and head of the school cadet force. His father wanted him to be a lawyer. But the day he finished his A-Level papers – Greek, Latin and Ancient History – he walked into the local Army recruiting office. He said that he wanted to join the Parachute Regiment. His father only forgave him towards the end of his life.

After a year in the ranks, Milos Stankovic was selected for a commission. On passing out of Sandhurst he was sent on a four-year course to learn Russian, first at Manchester University, then in Minsk. At last he was back in the Parachute Regiment. As a Lieutenant he quickly became a platoon commander. He was a thoroughly competent young officer. True, he had an impatience with almost any kind of administrative job – but if that had been his 'thing', he would never have joined the Paras in the first place. By 1992, he was a Captain and had served in Northern Ireland, Belize and Mozambique.

After the Gulf War, in which to Milos Stankovic's disappointment he was not involved, the Army quickly went back to peacetime routine: training, exercises and courses. Then more training, exercises and courses. There were few places where there was any 'action'. One was Northern Ireland. Captain Stankovic had already served in Northern Ireland three times, besides which, none of the Parachute Regiment's battalions was in the province at the time. As it was, he managed to bypass routine with a posting to the UN team patrolling the demilitarized zone between Kuwait and Iraq. But the novelty of the desert soon wore off. Where would they post him next? What about Bosnia? Surely the British units that were part of the UN peacekeeping force would have use for someone with a working knowledge of the language. And over the years, listening to his parents, he had absorbed something of the history of the place.

Once the centrist grip of Tito had gone, Yugoslavia began to splinter apart. Each ethnic, religious or nationalist group, of which – according to one definition – there were at least six, sought to set up its own quasi-state. Or was fighting to do so, as in Bosnia-Hercegovina. Here the high-octane mix of Serb, Croat and Muslim meant the conflict was bitter and almost inevitable.

Each ethnic group had its own army and its own warlords. Each group fought to defend what territory it already held, and to terrorize and thereby drive out anyone of different 'origins'. In cunning and brutality there was not much to choose between them. But, perhaps because they had more military muscle, the Bosnian Serbs – backed by Belgrade – were the most effective in the whole terrible business of 'ethnic cleansing'.

It was tribal warfare – as it had been off and on for at least 1000 years. Yet now the murders, with civilians as the main targets, were carried out with sniper rifles, mortars, machine guns, long-range artillery, tanks, even helicopters and gunships. The Serbs would attack a Muslim village, kill or drive out the locals and dynamite the mosque. Somewhere else the Muslims would retaliate by murdering some Serbs and then, for good measure, putting a bulldozer through the cemetery to scatter the bones. The Croats, the smallest group, were not much better, and if they were not pitchforking some Muslim farmers, they looked on with thinly disguised pleasure to see their two enemies beating the hell out of each other. It was medieval.

The UN had got involved with several objectives. The first was to try to impose a kind of peace while Western politicians attempted to pressure some sense into the heads of the belligerents. To this end, the 'international community' in the shape of the UN imposed an arms embargo on the three warring parties. Unfortunately, it was a lopsided prohibition. It barred the Muslims and the Croats from arms supplies but had little effect on the Bosnian Serbs. The latter could pull all of the weapons they needed from their allies in Belgrade. This imbalance worried the Americans much more than it did the British. Indeed, in American eyes, the British seemed increasingly blinkered to the Serb advantage.

The UN's second task was directly humanitarian: the distribution of thousands of tons of 'aid' to the tens of thousands of unarmed civilians who were trapped in enclaves surrounded by 'the other side'. This was the job of UNHCR – the UN High Commissioner for Refugees. The UN's third task was the protection of the aid distribution centres and escorting the convoys as they made their way cross-country to the enclaves. This was the job of the UN Protection Force. UNPROFOR, in blue berets and white armoured personnel carriers (APCs), was made up of soldiers from ten or more different nations. Some were better at the job than others. But even if it had been part of the UN mandate (which it was not), the variegated battalions of UNPROFOR were never in sufficient strength to enforce any kind of military solution. They were meant to be a peace*keeping* force; they were not there in enough numbers to be a peace*making* one.

Captain Stankovic had never been to the Balkans. However, since he had been a small boy, he had spoken and read enough Serbo-Croat to more than 'get by'. The British battalions with the UN would need interpreters. So it would only be a matter of time before he was summoned. Also, it was where the 'action' was. While still in the Gulf, he put in an application – several times. He waited on the call. It never came. Typical.

So at the end of the UN assignment in the Gulf, it was home again. And another course – six months of it. Surprisingly, at the end of the course someone in the MOD must have seen sense. And Captain Mike

Stanley was in an RAF Hercules on the way to Split. The Army gave him that new name because, with a name like Stankovic, his Serb ancestry would be too easily recognized by the Croats and the Muslims.

At the time there were nearly 2500 'Brits' in Bosnia. And there were ships of the Royal Navy, including a carrier with Sea Harriers, patrolling the Adriatic to prevent any seaborne import of arms. Elsewhere in Croatia and Bosnia, at one time or another, there were battalions or sub-units from Pakistan, Bangladesh, Jordan, Canada, Denmark, Norway, Spain, France, Holland, Sweden, Russia, the Ukraine and New Zealand. It was the biggest multinational operation since Korea forty years earlier. And that had been a UN operation in name only.

So where was NATO in all this? It was with the Americans at Aviano and Vicenza air bases in northern Italy. The Americans chose to operate under their own flag – with, for form's sake, a nod to the emblems of NATO – rather than that of the UN. They have always been sceptical about the efficacy, let alone the politics, of the UN. Furthermore, since the American public had not long seen the corpses of their servicemen dragged naked and bleeding through the streets of Mogadishu, Washington had shuddered at the idea of 'putting ground troops into a hostile environment'. No more body bags. So the American input was airborne. In Italy they based several squadrons of fighter-bombers. And they flew an almost continuous high-altitude patrol of surveillance aircraft. In theory, these made sure that no aircraft were used to smuggle arms and ammunition through the UN embargo.

Almost from the start there were Americans who were impatient with what they saw as the UN's soft-on-the-Serbs approach. Many of them were vocal in saying that by not calling for punitive air strikes on the Serbs, the UN was endorsing ethnic cleansing. In time their frustration was to be particularly directed at the British.

But in the early days of his posting Captain Stanley was not much concerned or involved with the high politics of what was going on. His job was at the sharp end, working alongside the Commander of BRITFOR, Brigadier Cumming.

Sometimes he was translating for eleven or twelve hours a day. Together with a driver, the three of them were constantly on the move. When things got too hot – shelling or snipers – they would 'cross load' from the Brigadier's white Land Rover to whatever armoured vehicle was available. If he was not with the Brigadier, he was working with Lieutenant Colonel Bob Stewart, the flamboyant CO of the Cheshires. Most of the job was crisis management in a flak jacket, often in deep snow and freezing temperatures. Not easy.

Keeping the convoy routes open was what much of it was about. Someone had blown up a bridge. How best to get it repaired? And how to prevent it being blown up again? Somewhere else, the Serbs had moved artillery overnight to cover a vital stretch of road running through an area controlled by the Muslims; they had put down a few threatening rounds to let the UN, and the Muslims, know that they could put more down any time they felt like it. How to persuade them to see sense? Then there was a local Serb commander working over a UN convoy bound for a Muslim enclave; he was pulling it apart on the grounds that it might be carrying hidden arms. He knew that was not the case, but he was doing it anyway. Maybe he had just lost his wife and children to the Muslims. Somehow, he had to be hauled off.

One day it was a bunch of mad Serb women squatting on the road. No aid convoys in, no empties out. How do soldiers move fifty determined women and children? It is not in the manual. In fact, they were not mad; they were desperate. They wanted somebody – the UN, the Red Cross, anybody – to find out if their husbands and sons were still alive. The men had been captured and taken away by the Muslims some weeks before. Since then, not a word. Captain Stanley earned his pay. 'A load of play acting, nodding, and grovelling. But we did it.' The Red Cross would make immediate inquiries about the men – a promise.

In Captain Stanley the people who ran BRITFOR got more than an interpreter. They got someone who, besides the language, understood the minds of the people they were dealing with. He surprised even himself. There were many times when he hated all their guts. But one does not have to like someone to understand them.

Yet there were some things that were beyond all comprehension. Why did they have to shoot Corporal Edwards? Through the head? He was driving a Warrior – escorting an ambulance full of wounded civilians. The driver of a Warrior needs to see where he is going, so, unless it is a full battle situation, he usually drives with his hatch open. Even so, the

Corporal would have had only a small part of his head exposed. To hit the top of a man's head in a moving vehicle, the shot must be very carefully aimed. Half in resignation, half in anger, Captain Stanley wrote in his diary, 'The only thing worse than being shot at by the enemy is being shot at by the people you are trying to help. He was doing his humanitarian duty and some bastard killed him.' That was Bosnia.

In the three-and-a-half years that the Bosnia war lasted, more than 300 UN soldiers and civilians lost their lives. Over 1000 were wounded.

IN THE WORLD BEYOND the Balkans, via television, radio and the press, the Bosnian Serbs were seen as the thugs. Perhaps deservedly. Their leaders, Ratko Mladic and Radovan Karadzic, were later to be listed as war criminals. They did not invent 'ethnic cleansing', which, after all, is only a new name for a very old human trait, but they were among its most cruel and efficient practitioners. The army of the Republika Srpska was also by far the best armed – supplied through Belgrade with Russian T55 tanks, helicopters and modern artillery. There was very little the UN could do about it. The embargo was leaky in other directions, too. Iran made no special secret of supplying the Muslims. And Americans were involved in the shadowy business of gunrunning to the Croats and the Muslims – to 'balance' things. Nevertheless, both Croats and Muslims were, with some justification, able to persuade the world that the UN arms prohibition meant they were fighting with one arm tied. Indeed, to them, the UN – and particularly the British element – was known as 'Serbprofor'. They wanted the embargo lifted – so that they could get hold of even more arms to redress the balance. There were Americans in Washington and NATO who agreed with them. However, that was something for the UN and the politicians to decide, not BRITFOR.

By the spring, though he was still working for Brigadier Cumming, Captain Stanley found he was being used more and more by the Brigadier and his immediate command as a one-man fire brigade – negotiating a local cease-fire here, unblocking a convoy there, twisting the arm of some local warlord somewhere else. Then the very next day he would be guiding and translating for some visiting VIP. They all came to have a look: the Prime Minister, American Senators, bigwigs from the UN, top brass from the MOD and the Foreign Office, generals and admirals from NATO, even Bianca Jagger doing her humanitarian 'thing'.

It was a job with no set routine. On one occasion, Brigadier Cumming, just back from a quick trip home to attend a what-do-we-do-about-Bosnia session at Number 10, returned with a small package. Somewhere in the MOD it had been given to him by Major General Michael Jackson (another Para), who asked if he could get it to a middle-aged Muslim couple marooned in Sarajevo. The parcel was from their daughter; she was the Jackson family's 'au pair'; she had been unable to contact her parents for many months. Captain Stanley got the delivery job.

Sarajevo, the old capital of Bosnia, was a mostly Muslim enclave 'guaranteed' by the UN. The guarantee did not mean that it was saved from shelling and sniper fire by the Serbs, who had long lived in (and now occupied) the southern suburbs. But at least the presence of the UN had slowed the rate of killing; hundreds had been killed by Serb shelling before the UN got a grip. But the Muslims had sometimes deliberately 'invited' such shelling. To start things off, they would fire some mortar rounds at extreme range out into the Serb-held countryside beyond the suburbs. This would, by design, provoke heavy retaliatory shelling into the closely populated city. Muslim civilians, sometimes children, would be killed. The world's media, and not just its more gullible elements, would get the message and the all-important video footage: Serb thugs, Muslim victims. In reality, in terms of callousness there was not much to choose between them. Maybe the Serbs were ahead because they were better armed and had more opportunities.

On one of his assignments into Sarajevo, Captain Stanley took time off to deliver the Jackson parcel. He was appalled at the cold and hunger in which the old couple was living. They were pathetically grateful. It was only much later that he recognized the effect that the 'errand' was to have on him and his attitudes. It was not the only 'postman' job he did. A few months later General Jackson sent his thanks to Captain Stanley. And another parcel to deliver. That one weighed over 50 pounds.

There was sometimes a much more terrible side to his job: watching a man digging to bury his son – a quick, night-time, shallow-grave burial so that the sniper out there did not get the father and brother as well. Or being thrown around in the back of an APC (which was being used as an ambulance) while someone tried to find an old woman's vein for a saline drip. But her veins had collapsed – she was in deep shock. A sniper had shot her in the chest. That was peacekeeping.

Captain Stanley tried to keep a diary. After one particularly difficult day, he wrote, 'At home they think that all we do is escort convoys. We are piggy in the middle of a vicious, chaotic and bloody civil war. Most of the corpses we see are those of old men, women and children, rarely the actual combatants. All around us people are dropping like flies and we are able to do almost nothing about it. What do they think that does to one? Drip, drip, drip, every day drip-fed stress. I am not at all sure that we really know where we are going . . .'

For nearly a year, he was a mobile troubleshooter and fixer. He was very good at it – good enough, when he got back to Britain at the end of a tour of nearly a year, to be awarded an MBE. Once home, he could drop the 'disguise' of Mike Stanley.

Not only was eleven months much longer than most people served in Bosnia, but Captain Stankovic had been stressed beyond any usual limits. His 'return to normal' was not helped by the speed with which the adrenalin of tension was so suddenly withdrawn. Just three hours in a Hercules and then he was back on the M4 – RAF Lyneham behind, Farnham cottage ahead. Cold turkey. So it was not surprising that the Army found him 'a soft number' – a staff job in a Territorial HQ in Nottingham. It would give him time and space to recover.

Of course, it did nothing of the kind. There was no way he could settle to such an anti-climactic and, as he saw it, pointless job. Counting paper clips would have been more interesting. His attitude did not go down well. On Friday evenings he could not wait to get the Suzuki onto the motorway and away from the place. He recognized that, once home in Farnham, he was drinking too much and becoming increasingly bad-tempered.

He watched the television and read the papers; almost every day there was something about Bosnia. Frustration. There was a new man out there. General Rose, ex-Coldstream Guards, ex-SAS, was evidently nobody's fool. He had taken over from a Belgian General who had resigned in protest at the conflicting political orders he was being given. So Rose now had day-to-day charge of the whole of the military end of the UN mission throughout Bosnia, not just the British element. Major Stankovic itched to get back – although he was worried about what another tour might do to him.

Once again his chance came without warning. General Rose had asked for him. He needed someone who knew his way around.

A few days later, he was Captain Stanley again. In the six months he had been away there had been some changes. General Rose was running things from the UN's 'forward' HQ in Muslim Sarajevo – to which the Captain now reported. Once it had been a handsome city with its own symphony, opera and ballet; ten years earlier it had hosted the Winter Olympics. Now, although the main weight of Serb artillery had withdrawn, it was a half-derelict city filled with refugees. It was also the 'seat' of the Bosnian-Muslim government. In the UN HQ there were new faces to 'learn'. Out in the rest of Bosnia there were new battalions, too. But the biggest change was that the Croats and the Muslims had joined together in an uneasy federation. There was little trust between them – too many throats had been cut for that. At least they were no longer fighting each other. The agreement had been thrashed out in Washington, but the incentive lay much closer – the ever-growing threat from their old and common enemy, the Serbs.

Once more, Captain Stanley was in at the deep end. One of his first assignments was across on the Serb side of 'the conflict line' – he called it 'The Dark Side' – checking that the UNHCR food aid was not being 'appropriated' by the Serb army. This meant that he had almost daily negotiations with a small posse of middle-rank Serb officers. Over endless coffee, cigarettes and Slivo brandy, he got to know them. And they him. They were not long fooled by his name; they had worked out his background. But that same background meant he was not fooled by them. They understood each other.

He was used more and more by General Rose as his go-between to the Serbian top brass – people like General Ratko Mladic and Doctor Radovan Karadzic, the self-styled President of Republika Srpska. Much of the time they were to be found at their HQ in the small 'winter resort' town of Pale. Although it was only about 12 miles east of Sarajevo, the journey up through the mountains could take over an hour. During the next few months, Captain Stanley got to know every bend in that twisting road.

His initial contact up there was often Radovan Karadzic's spokesman, Dr Jovan Zametica. He had a Cambridge PhD, spoke perfect English and had written pamphlets for the Institute for Strategic Studies in London. He asked Captain Stanley if he could get him a regular copy of *Yachting Monthly*. Doing these people the occasional favour was a way of getting to know them. Vital. Sometimes he would pick up a useful snippet; other times he knew he was being fed a line. But the line-feeding could be useful – if he could work out why they were feeding it to him in the first place. Putting two and two together, detecting an indiscretion here, an inference there – that was what the job was all about. Because he understood the language and its subtleties, plus the dark corners of the Serb soul, he was able to catch clues that would otherwise have been lost.

It could be quite a circus. His success depended on knowing, for any given problem, 'whose button to push'. Sometimes, to achieve what General Rose back in Sarajevo wanted, he would have to play on the rivalry that existed between Mladic and Karadzic – and hope the penny dropped with neither. The job was part manipulation, part intelligence-gathering. It involved understanding the nuances within the Serb leadership. It involved getting close to them. It was a rather dangerous game. Perhaps more so than he knew at the time.

As General Rose's fixer, he would sometimes be sent up to Pale with a single and specific task. 'Mike, go and wave your magic wand' was the usual preliminary. 'Sort the buggers out.' There were occasions when he knew he was acting far above the normal responsibilities for a captain. He also knew he was now regarded with deep suspicion by both the Muslims and the Croats in Bosnia. Their reasoning was simple: they had worked out that his name was not Stanley and, anyway, anyone who spent *that* amount of time with the Serbs and spoke their language was obviously deeply partisan to their cause. At the same time, he knew some of the Serbs thought he was spying not for them, but on them – for the benefit of General Rose and the UN. In a way, he was. But to anyone who thought about it, there was nothing particularly covert about what he was doing up in Pale.

Sarajevo was where he was most at risk. The Muslims and their new allies, the Croats, were now playing a very serious game in which they were denigrating the UN at every opportunity. Because General Rose would not order air strikes against the Serbs, they saw him as the villain, and Captain

Stanley as his spy and right-hand man. The Muslim government encouraged a local paper to run attacking articles. In one, the Captain was called 'The Trusted Mole' – trusted by the Serb enemy. This was dangerous because it gave licence to any Muslim hothead to take a pot shot at the person they called 'the spy in our midst'. Beyond Sarajevo, the Muslims had hired a firm of Washington lobbyists at a reputed cost of nearly $1 million. The message being put across was that as the UN arms embargo made them vulnerable to the bullyboy Serbs, they were the victims of UN and, in particular, British policy. It was not an entirely unjustified charge. They wanted the embargo lifted and their Serb enemy struck with the full weight of those US fighter-bombers lined up in Italy. 'Lift and Strike' was the slogan. The possibility that this might lead to an all-out war in the Balkans – with possible Russian involvement – was not a concern. Nor was the problem of 'evacuating' all the UN forces before the bombing began; they were simply not equipped to take their chances in full-scale hostilities. As General Rose's bodyguard once observed, 'You don't get into a shooting war if all your armour is painted bloody white.'

But 'Lift and Strike' made good copy in US newspapers and persuasive footage on the evening news. To the Americans, the 'Brits' and the rest of UNPROFOR with their careful impartiality were almost as much a part of the Bosnian problem as the Serbs. The division between the Americans and the British on the business of 'Lift and Strike' brought about the most serious foreign-policy rift between the two countries since Suez. The British case was certainly weakened by the way Douglas Hurd and Malcolm Rifkind (Foreign Secretary and Defence Secretary respectively) characterized the American thinking as naïve; the American case was weakened by the fact that they were unwilling to put any troops on the ground. It was the 'bodybag' problem.

Anyway, the Americans worked secretly to adjust the balance. To this day they deny it. But then no one would have admitted to the arms-to-Iran affair either – until Colonel North was 'caught'. But in Bosnia there were too many eyes not to notice that unmarked American (or American-sponsored) C-130 aircraft were making low-level night flights into Bosnian Muslim territory. They were not carrying blankets.

What was more surprising was the way the Americans bugged the UN HQ in Sarajevo, including General Rose's office. The NATO 'liaison' unit in Sarajevo, manned by Americans, was housed in a building close alongside the one occupied by the UN. It bristled with aerials, dishes and antennae. UN communication experts had no difficulty in identifying the equipment; it was capable of eavesdropping on 'every bleep and fart' for many miles in every direction.

The Bosnian Muslims knew what was going on too. There were no doubts about how they were getting the information – from their own bugs and, second-hand, from the Americans. There were occasions when transcripts of phone conversations between General Rose and the Serbs would be handed out at the UN in New York the next day by that PR firm. The Serbs, too, were not apprentices in the skills of electronic hoovering. Everybody, except for the UN, was bugging everybody else.

Towards the end of General Rose's tour, the now promoted Major Stanley became a key player in the most difficult of all the UN's endeavours: negotiating a cease-fire. Because the Serb leadership would not be persuaded to come down to Sarajevo, Stanley (and a colleague) were stationed with Mladic, Karadzic and co. in Pale – on the end of a satellite link (bugged?) on which he could talk to General Rose. The only place they could rely on an effective signal was in an unheated attic, with the antenna held out through a skylight. So one moment Stanley was telling Rose of Serb reactions as they quarrelled among themselves about each successive clause of the agreement; the next moment he would be dashing down three flights of stairs and running up the road to the Serbs to 'interpret' Rose's own reaction to their latest counter-proposal. A mad hatter's tea party. In the end they got some sort of consensus. When signed, it became known as 'The Cessation of Hostilities Agreement'. It held for four months. It would have held longer if the West, in the shape of the UN, had shown more resolve. But that is another story – best described in Milos Stankovic's own unparalleled book, *Trusted Mole.*

In January 1995 General Rose was relieved by General Rupert Smith, another ex-Para. However, for the remaining two months until the end of his own tour, despite the uneasy truce between the combatants, Captain Stanley's role was not much changed. More bad tempers and rancid coffee up in Pale. More waving of the magic wand. More VIPs with their solutions. More eavesdropping by the Americans. More reading about himself in an ever more hostile Sarajevo press. The gist of the latest article was that even though General Rose had left, his mole had stayed on to continue spying for the Serbs.

Well, they could stuff it. He was going home.

THE ENVELOPE WAS ADDRESSED to Mr M. Stankovic. It was from the MOD Police and told him that their inquiries were taking longer than they had anticipated. They would therefore be extending his bail for a further three months. He should not surrender himself at Guildford on 11 December, but on 11 March. He was not surprised the envelope addressed him as a civilian; that had been MOD practice ever since the IRA began targeting serving officers. But the letter inside would normally have carried his rank; he was now a Major. And what about his MBE? Were they trying to tell him something? Guilty already? Or were they just being careless – again? He could have told them that their inquiries would take them much longer than the two months they had originally estimated. Indeed, he had told them. The letter was enough to set him ticking once more. But in the two months since that day in Guildford Police Station, he had learnt to redirect his anger and his hurt into determination. 'Don't get mad, get even' was, under the circumstances, not a bad motto.

Two months earlier, the day after that first 'visit' to Guildford, a Colonel had come in an Army car to take him back to Staff College to clear his room. As he had guessed, the MOD Police had already done the job. They had taken almost everything, even his three medals and the MBE. Why? Later he was driven back to the Parachute Regiment in Aldershot where, after he had come back from Bosnia and before going to Staff College, he had been a company commander. His Colonel was clearly flummoxed and indicated, by looks rather than words, that he found the whole thing unbelievable. 'Mr' Stankovic was told, apologetically, that a long signal had just come in from the MOD detailing precisely what he could and could not do. It formally repeated what the MOD policeman had said the day before: he was forbidden from contacting anyone in any of the services. The signal ended by saying that he was free to organize his defence. That was big of them.

Over Christmas and through January and February, while waiting for his delayed appointment to return to Guildford, he had plenty of time to think. A number of colleagues who had served with him in Bosnia quietly got in touch. It had to be 'quietly' because it seemed likely that his phone was tapped. His friends were deeply suspicious of the motives that lay behind what was happening. Their distrust (and his own) pointed at the Bosnian Muslims, in collaboration, perhaps, with some elements of the US State Department. Or, possibly, 'persons unknown' within US military intelligence or even the CIA. Maybe it was one of those 'non-existent' cells like the one set up by Colonel North. But no one seemed to be in much doubt that, one way or another, the Americans were involved somewhere. All intelligence services are into 'dirty tricks'. There was the thought that someone might be trying to settle scores with General Rose. Maybe it was part of the Muslims' 'We, the victims' game again. Perhaps they wanted to imply that, through a spy, the cards had been stacked against them. They would have had nothing to lose.

Among Milos Stankovic's colleagues there was concern that the investigation was in the hands of the MOD Police. They were not equipped to understand, let alone to handle, the shadowy yet complicated issues involved. Their normal role was looking after the security of MOD establishments and investigating theft, leaks and similar crimes inside those establishments. Examining NAAFI break-ins and 'disappeared' computers was said, by their detractors, to be their forte. That was probably unfair. But to give them the job of probing an alleged case of treason of Balkan complexity – for that is what any investigation would inevitably become – was reckoned to be as appropriate as asking British Transport Police to investigate a case of international fraud. By rights, if Major Stankovic's alleged crime was even half as serious as was implied, it should have been a job for Special Branch or MI6. Why one or the other was not given the job is one of the lasting mysteries of the whole affair. The decision by the high command within the MOD to keep the job 'in house' was a thoroughly bad one.

The inexperience of the MOD Police in Bosnian politics was compounded by the fact that they were themselves under some scrutiny in terms of value for money. This meant they would have been unusually anxious to justify their existence. Having won the 'contract', they would subsequently be unlikely to be dissuaded by anything as simple as a lack of hard evidence. A number of his friends urged Major Stankovic to get himself as good a lawyer as he could find. He had already come to that conclusion. Ten days before he was due to reappear at Guildford, contacts led him to Desmond de Silva QC and Steven Barker. The choice was fortunate. The first was a renowned barrister, and in the second he had a solicitor who combined energy and experience. Mr Barker recognized that the situation Major Stankovic was in was anything but routine. They hit it off straightaway.

Then another letter to Mr M. Stankovic arrived. They needed still more time. Bail was again extended – until September. So it would be eleven months since his arrest. Could it be they were having trouble finding anything against him that 'stood up'? If so, it would not be for lack of trying. It seemed they were interviewing anybody and everybody who had ever had anything to do with him – over a hundred so far. Apparently, they liked always to emphasize that they were 'operating at the very highest level'. What was that meant to mean? He also learnt they had been to the United States. He still had no specific details of what it was he was alleged to have done. There was an article in the *New York Times*; it did not tell him anything that he did not know. All the same, it was interesting.

BRITISH OFFICER SAID TO GIVE NATO PLANS TO BOSNIAN SERBS

> The British Government is expected to charge an army major next month with providing classified NATO information and documents to the Bosnian Serb leadership during the last two years of the Balkan war, according to senior Western diplomats.
>
> In a case compiled in part by American intelligence officials, the major, Milos Stankovic, 35, is alleged to have seriously undermined the effectiveness of the UN peacekeeping effort in Bosnia, the diplomats said. He is said to have kept the Bosnian Serb military commander, Gen. Ratko Mladic, who has been indicted on two counts of genocide by the international war crimes tribunal in The Hague, abreast of top-secret NATO plans and procedures and of bickering within NATO during the 1992–95 war.

The article went on for over 1000 words. Its reference to 'senior Western diplomats' was almost certainly code for the Bosnian-Muslim Embassy in London. It seemed most probable that, with backstairs American support, the Ambassador had made accusations about Major Stankovic to the Foreign Office. The dossier would have been discussed with the

MOD and then passed to them for action. In addition to 'the General Rose factor', the Bosnian motive may have been to send a message to the British government that they expected, in all respects, to be taken seriously. To explain the American agenda, one can spin all kinds of theories. One such theory centres on a need to discredit Major Stankovic. What had he done that some Americans might want to 'rubbish' him? Almost certainly he knew more than they wanted him to know about their disregard for the UN arms embargo.

Interestingly for a newspaper that, editorially, had often been sceptical about the British role in Bosnia, the latter part of the *New York Times* article gave prominence to the views of the independent MP Martin Bell. As the main BBC correspondent in Bosnia through most of the conflict, he had known and respected Major Stankovic. His quoted comment about the MOD Police was uncompromising: 'They are completely out of their depth.' Elsewhere, he was more reflective:

> This could be another Dreyfus case . . . He was ordered to win the trust of the top Serbs – Mladic and Karadzic. He did win their trust. Everything that his superiors used him for, valued him for and asked him to do, which was to connect with the Serbs, is now what he is being punished for, under an Official Secrets Act which had to do with regular conventional warfare – spying and so on. It is not appropriate to the much greyer world of peacekeeping and peace enforcement.

In fact, Martin Bell had already raised the whole affair in the House of Commons. Again, he drew on lengthy first-hand experience of Bosnia – an advantage not shared by anyone else in the House:

> Major Stankovic's job was to deal with the Serbs – the most difficult of the three ethnic groups – and he did so. His job was to get to know them, and he did so. In the Bihac crisis he was personally responsible for freeing fifty Canadian UN hostages held by the Serbs and unblocking convoys and the airport. He did that alone. He saved the life of a Muslim woman wounded by sniper fire in the town of Vitez. He scooped her up and took her to hospital and saved her life. He was awarded the MBE. He received his medal from the Queen. Beyond the line of duty, Major Stankovic took part in humanitarian endeavours. I cannot specify exactly what he did, though if charges

> are laid against him I may have to do so because they bear on his courage and his character.[1]

Martin Bell made a number of other points, including the fact that the Major had been deprived of the Army's customary procedures: notably, he had no 'Soldier's Friend'. He was severely critical of the MOD Police. Gerald Howarth, MP for Aldershot, and Virginia Bottomley, the Major's constituency MP, also spoke:

> There appears to be a conspiracy to hold my constituent completely incommunicado and deprive him of essential evidence for his defence . . .

Replying for the MOD, the Minister for the Armed Forces, Dr John Reid, felt restrained to 'the answer expected':

> I would not wish to make any comment that might in any way influence the investigation that is under way . . . The Chief Constable [of the MOD Police] is responsible for the conduct of the investigation and he is independent of the Government under law.

Dr Reid's reply was a sophistry because, of course, while the Chief Constable was indeed responsible for the conduct of the investigation, he was certainly not a prime mover in the decision to mount the investigation in the first place. That was a policy decision and would have been made at the very highest level within the MOD itself – by a civil servant who would then have 'advised' the Chief of Defence Staff and the Minister. So, both in constitutional theory (a minister is accountable for everything done by his ministry) and in practical fact (the Minister would have had some responsibility for the decision to proceed with this

1. *Hansard*, 13 December 1997. Martin Bell's mention of 'humanitarian endeavours' was a reference to an unofficial and clandestine 'organization' in which Milos Stankovic played a leading role. Quietly known as Schindler's List, it smuggled people out of Sarajevo. If, for example, the children of an old Muslim couple had long since made their lives in the West – UK, Canada, the US, wherever – the couple were spirited away. The next night it might be a Serb widow desperate to join her married daughters in Belgrade, Bolton or Baltimore. Or a Croat orphan going to the care of an uncle. It was dangerous work. But in nearly a year Captain Stanley and the other Scarlet Pimpernels did not lose one of their several hundred 'evacuees'.

particular investigation) Dr Reid had inescapable responsibilities in the matter. In the Commons he could take cover behind the 'I can't interfere' shield. But on returning to his office that same evening he could have checked to make sure the investigation had not become a fishing expedition. And curtailed it if that looked likely. However, like all ministers, he would have been dependent on the advice and truthfulness of his civil servants. As they would have been the very people who had advised him in the first place, they were hardly likely to now admit that they might have been wrong. It was the Whitehall Loop.

So what *was* the early role of the MOD? One does not know the level at which the Stankovic dossier (or that part of it which originated with the Bosnians) crossed from the Foreign Office on the north side of Whitehall to the MOD on the south. But one can be sure, given the very serious nature of the allegations (treason), that the file made its way up to the sixth floor and landed on the desk of one or more of the three senior MOD civil servants. From that moment the mistakes accumulated.

Just possibly, the Bosnian side of the accusation might have been shuffled into someone's 'permanently pending' tray and allowed to stagnate. But the Americans would have been taken more seriously. The MOD (indeed, the nation) is too dependent on the Americans to do otherwise – on their goodwill, their satellites, their military and political intelligence, their weaponry. It would not have been possible to brush aside an American 'complaint', from whatever quarter, as a matter of no consequence. But, first, if there really did have to be a full-blown investigation, there are (as has already been observed) more sophisticated tools at the disposal of MOD mandarins than the blunt instrument of their own in-house police. Second, one wonders if any of the senior officers for whom the Major had worked in Bosnia, particularly Generals Rose and Smith, were informed of the allegation about to be laid against him. In light of what followed, it seems unlikely. Third, one wonders about the quality of advice given to the Chief of Defence Staff, Field Marshal Sir Peter Inge (or to his immediate deputies) by the civil servants. Or was it expedient for him just to 'sign off' the file and acquiesce – allowing things to go through to the Minister without question? Fourth, as the investigations grew more and more protracted – presumably because there were real difficulties in finding evidence that 'fitted' – why didn't someone at the top call a halt? It is just not true to say, as officials like to claim and the Minister had insisted in the Commons, that once an investigation has commenced, it is 'all in the hands of the police' and cannot be stopped. The MOD Police are not wholly stupid, and even if they are, they can be given advice – with varying degrees of firmness. In fact, many police investigations are abandoned when it becomes apparent that further enquiries are unlikely to garner enough evidence to sustain any sort of prosecution – let alone a successful one. The need of the MOD police to justify their existence in what they obviously saw as their Big Chance may have blinded them to that simple wisdom. But that does not excuse the senior functionaries to whom the force ultimately reported and who had started the ball rolling in the first place. They are paid to know better.

So what was going on? We are unlikely to find out the details for at least another thirty years. And, even then, the files may well have been 'disappeared' – along with any associated embarrassment. It has happened before. So speculation is inevitable. It may be right. Or wrong.

As soon as he was familiar with the situation, the Major's solicitor, Steven Barker, advised that they should run a proactive defence. Initially, this took the form of contacting a range of army officers, some senior, some middle-ranking, some recently retired, whom they reckoned would be willing defence witnesses. Mr Barker is necessarily cagey about names, although one can guess. Some of these potential witnesses told him that the Head of the Security and Policy Unit at the MOD had advised them that they were not obliged to co-operate with the defence. The same official did not suggest that a parallel option would apply when it came to co-operating with the MOD Police. Second, Mr Barker requested that the MOD Police allow him to inspect the many papers and other items they had seized from the Major's home during their search. This request, though standard under the 1984 Police & Criminal Evidence Act, was refused on the rarely invoked grounds that it would 'prejudice the inquiry'. Given that the MOD Police had been sitting on the material for nearly six months when the request was made, Mr Barker thought this refusal was unreasonable. He threatened legal proceedings. The Chief Constable of the MOD Police had to agree – but said that there would be a six-week delay. In writing to arrange Mr Barker's appointment the Detective Chief Inspector actually 'running' the case employed as high-flown a piece of MOD-speak as one is ever likely to encounter: 'I have re-set my operational investigative schedule in order to accommodate your attendance.'

It was a close colleague of this same officer who habitually referred to what he called 'Bosnia's warring fractions'. Anyway, Mr Barker 'attended' the Braintree HQ of the MOD Police; he had set aside two full twelve-hour days for the task. But the Detective Chief Inspector explained that office hours were from 9 a.m. to 5 p.m. with time out for lunch. They sat him at a table in a large and draughty hall. They brought him the papers, item by item. Among other things, they handed him a London *A–Z*, several blank sheets of paper, some Christmas cards and a Suzuki owners' manual. It was all irrelevant. When he complained, he was informed that they intended to hold back 40 per cent of the material. While the visit had told him a good deal about the MOD Police, it was otherwise a wasted journey. Maybe it was meant to be. He was back in his West End office by teatime on the first day. He applied to the High Court for a judicial review on the Chief Constable's refusal to give access to the material still being withheld. In due course – these things move slowly – the High Court ordered the Chief Constable to justify his continued refusal. More backing and filling from Braintree. But less than twenty-four hours before the High Court's final deadline, the MOD capitulated. Access was given to all but about 1 per cent of the papers. And the Treasury Solicitor's Department, which was acting for the MOD Police, had to agree to pay towards the costs incurred in seeking the judicial review – a five-figure sum.

So far, so good.

By this point in the narrative, a question is overdue. What about those several senior officers for whom Major Stankovic had worked and who had, presumably, put him up for his MBE? Where were they in all this? Had they collectively or individually asked for a meeting with Field Marshal Sir Peter Inge? Or with one of his immediate assistants? Or, for that matter, had anyone at the top of the MOD asked them for their comments? One wonders if they had explained that their regard for Major Stankovic could mean – if they were called as character witnesses – that the MOD was embarking on what might ultimately be an embarrassing undertaking. Perhaps they did not think the authorities could be that stupid. If so, they were surely overestimating the sagacity of the MOD.

Major Stankovic is loyal to those with whom he served and rejects any implied criticism – of naïvety, if nothing else. He is not forthcoming about why they held their peace during the ongoing investigation. So one must guess. They may have thought the idea of his being a spy was so outrageous that they reckoned the investigation would quickly come to the same conclusion. Therefore, there was no reason to 'interfere'. Indeed, better not to do so. The very fact that the MOD Police had been put on to the job may have further persuaded them that nobody in the MOD was taking the allegation seriously. And, of course, by the time it became apparent that the MOD Police were engaged on a protracted trawl, it may not have been possible for a 'collective' of mere serving officers, even senior ones, to start blowing whistles. After all, even the Minister had claimed he could do nothing. Lastly, once they learnt that matters were not going to be simply resolved, each of those officers had given Steven Barker a firm statement of support, in writing, for the Major. They would also have testified in court. Maybe they thought it would turn out All Right in the End – even if things were sometimes 'going to be a little unhappy for Milos along the way'.

Both the Major and his solicitor were half expecting bail to be postponed a third time. They were not disappointed. He was now told to delay presenting himself at Guildford until 28 October 1998 – more than a year after he had been arrested. During that year, in what must have been an ever more desperate attempt to find something, anything, to pin on the Major, the agents of the MOD had conducted over 200 interviews.

As part of the proactive, rather than merely reactive, strategy, Steven Barker, Desmond de Silva QC and the Major started to put together a detailed document. It almost certainly leaned on information from those army officers who knew Milos Stankovic and, even more relevantly, knew what he had done in Bosnia. When finished, the file would be delivered to the Director of Public Prosecutions (DPP) and the Attorney General – so that those two Crown authorities could see the strength of the defence. And, presumably, weigh it against the relative weakness of the MOD case. At the same time Barker was repeatedly asking the MOD Police for information regarding who had made the original allegations about Major Stankovic and what, in reasonably specific terms, those allegations were. He never got any reply that made sense. To Dreyfus one could now add Kafka. It was a fair bet that the MOD policemen were appreciative of neither. Maybe they thought they were Muslim enclaves somewhere in Bosnia.

Before the Guildford appearance, de Silva, Barker and the Major carefully went through their tactics. On the appointed day it was down to Surrey and the police station. When the MOD Police turned up, there were four of them. It seemed they intended to operate in two shifts over the next two days. They told the Guildford Custody Sergeant that, as yet, they had insufficient evidence to lay any charges against the Major. This was after two years of inquiries (they had spent a year on a covert investigation before the arrest). Now, they wished him to be held in custody while they questioned him in order to get the evidence – so that they could lay specific charges. They were fishing.

Everyone sat down. The senior of the four policemen slid a multi-page list of questions out of a file and looked round the room to check that everyone was ready. The two tape recorders were switched on. He was about to lead off with his first question when Major Stankovic got in first. It had been planned the night before. Quickly identifying himself, and speaking with a deliberation that made sure the tapes would not miss a syllable, he began:

> I would like to address your Detective Chief Superintendent, as I recognize him to be the senior investigating officer in this case. I heard your Detective Sergeant here tell the Custody Sergeant that he does not have sufficient evidence to charge me. That does not surprise me. It doesn't surprise me as I know you don't have it. I know you don't have it because I have done nothing wrong. I can tell you another thing – you can investigate this case for the next two years and all you are going to come up with is a box of contradictions.
>
> I am not going to sit here and have my life – my professional life and my private life – dissected when you have had two years to investigate me. Two years! One year of which was after my arrest, during which time you have pored over every single scrap of paper that you could find in my house or in my room at Bracknell. During which time you have interviewed close to 300 people, and during the course of that you have tried to debunk me and tarnish my name and blacken me with some of the witnesses.

And what have I had to do in the meantime? I have had to fight for my right to get access to this documentation – which you seized over a year ago. And you, at every twist and turn, you have tried to deny me this. Then in a letter you tell me that you are prepared to give us the statements of eighty-two witnesses. Then you change your mind and give us a synopsis. Then you give us a second synopsis – because the first has mistakes in it. Then at the eleventh hour and fifty-ninth minute you toss us four statements. I haven't had time to deal with these statements because you did it at such a late hour. It is symptomatic of everything that has gone on this last year. It's a cheap and dirty trick.

I tell you, two days is not enough time to discuss Bosnia. I could sit here for two weeks, two months even, trying to build the sort of picture to place all of this stuff in context. And in so doing I would have to tell you things that would make your eyeballs pop out. Things that even the Generals don't know about.

I'll tell you another thing. The British Army was my life, and not only was it my life, it was my soul. I gave everything to that Army – everything. I committed myself wholly to it and you have destroyed that. You and your Chief Constable have taken that away from me. Your Chief Constable insisted that I was removed from Staff College. And you have destroyed my career – along with these other people and their shadowy allegations that you won't even tell me about.

And not only have you destroyed my career, you have also destroyed what is left of my family. My father died because of the pressure and strain that I put him under simply because I was out there in Bosnia. He died a bitter old man who should be alive today. And I have the burden of that. No one else. And you have come close to destroying me as well.

I can tell you now, you have done nothing this past year to convince me that this is a fair investigation. I am sorry – I do not trust you and I do not trust the motives in this investigation. You have to take what I am going to say seriously. I am not going to say anything to you. I am now going to sit here and this is the very last thing that you are going to hear me say to you in this police station.

Milos Stankovic had not raised his voice. In the long silence that followed, the only sound was that of deep breathing. Then the interviewing officer said he was going to ask his questions anyway. He had a job to do. He put in a new tape. He began. He had a list which ran to several pages. After reading out each one, he would glance up in the vague hope of an answer. None. Then on to the next question. Five times he interrupted himself to give what is known as a 'Code C warning'. This means that, if it can later be shown that information has been deliberately withheld, it may be used as a weapon in court by the prosecution. The process took over an hour. There were a lot of questions.

Steven Barker informed the MOD team that the Major's defence and many of the answers to the questions just asked were contained in two files which he now put on the table – thereby conforming with Code C. One file contained a 216-page defence paper, the other supporting annexes and 'witness' statements. No, the MOD Police team could not read them. They were going, the very next morning, straight to the DPP. But first the MOD team would witness them being sealed in two large envelopes. The seals would then be signed by Steven Barker and countersigned, please, by the interviewing officer. Thus the MOD Police could not subsequently claim that the files had been put together after hearing the questions just asked. Even more important, the sheer bulk of the files would silently demonstrate that the Major and his solicitor were now seriously on the attack. The Detective Chief Superintendent had no choice but to sign. He also had no choice but to unconditionally release the Major from bail. He and his team had failed – in two years of investigation and in the 'interview' just finished – to gather enough evidence to do otherwise. The MOD Police had been drilling a dry hole.

Anyway, with a coolness that, presumably, was meant to disguise their embarrassment, the MOD team gathered up their papers and left the room. What they had scheduled to take two days had taken a couple of hours. The Custody Sergeant, with what Steven Barker thought might have been just the hint of a wink, directed him and his assistant and the Major to a nearby pub, which, it was said, always kept a bottle or two of champagne in the chiller cabinet.

The next morning the two sealed envelopes were delivered to the DPP and the Attorney General. A month later, at the end of November 1998, the MOD Police submitted their own report. Steven Barker hoped that, given the apparent lack of police evidence and the obvious need for

Major Stankovic to rejoin his regiment as quickly as possible, the DPP's staff might now be able to expedite their review. In fact, perhaps because of the 'security' nature of the case, the DPP took five months to grind through the details. The MOD Police must have known that their own case was almost worthless because, shortly before the DPP's office was due to announce its decision, they asked Major Stankovic's permission to examine the contents of those two 'sealed' files. Presumably, they wanted to be able to rejig their own submission in light of what they found inside. The Major refused permission – the more firmly in light of the MOD's own steadfast refusal to tell him anything useful about the charges they had been seeking to pin on him.

At last, a letter from the DPP was delivered to Steven Barker's office. It stated that the Chief Constable of the MOD Police was being informed that, after careful consideration, the DPP had concluded there was 'insufficient evidence' to bring any charges. In lay terms, there was no chance of a jury convicting. When first told, Major Stankovic's relief was tinged with anger. What did they mean, 'insufficient evidence'? There was no bloody evidence at all. Steven Barker explained that the DPP always uses the same equivocal formula because to use one which was any stronger would open the way for too many 'ex-defendants' to sue the police – for malevolently continuing inquiries long past the point where they knew them to be unwarranted. In legal terms, this is known as 'malicious process'. It was a course of action Steven Barker was considering . . .

So the MOD Police had lost. But that conclusion is altogether too straightforward. It underestimates both the Police and, more particularly, their masters in the MOD. If they could not 'get' Major Stankovic one way, they would try another. Why not use the 'no-smoke-without-fire' gambit? In any case, the Chief Constable and his MOD bosses were not about to acknowledge that the investigation had been a major waste of time and money – two years and something like £1 million.

The Major was anxious to resume his career as quickly as possible. Within twenty-four hours of the DPP dismissing the case against him, he was back in uniform reporting to his commanding officer on Salisbury Plain. But instead of a 'Welcome home' and a drink in the mess, he was told that there was one remaining problem. With some embarrassment, the CO said that before reinstatement was possible, he had been instructed by the MOD that the Army was required to conduct its own inquiry. Apparently, the MOD Police had lately reported that, in searching the Major's house over eighteen months earlier, they had found evidence that some regulations in the manual of military law had been broken. They would be forwarding the evidence shortly. In other words, though 'cleared' by the DPP, he had not been cleared under military law. Therefore he could not yet rejoin his regiment.

His regiment told the Major that in recognition of the two years of his life that had already been wasted, the Army and its Legal Service would make every effort to complete the investigation within two weeks. Of course, that timetable had assumed the MOD Police would promptly hand over the so-called evidence. This it now refused to do. Nor, amazingly, was there any mechanism whereby it could be compelled to do so. During the next six months, the Army Legal Service requested sight of the 'evidence' three times. It was always refused. The MOD would not have been ignorant of this refusal by its own police force; indeed, if it did not actually authorize the refusal, it did nothing to expedite matters.

It is known that, in its frustration, the Army Legal Service considered applying to the High Court for a judicial review to compel the MOD Police to hand over the 'evidence'. But it was advised that this was not possible because the Treasury Solicitor's Department – the organization handling all government legal business – would have found itself in the 'impossible' position of representing both sides in the dispute. Further, in constitutional terms the Crown finds it difficult to seek a legal remedy against the Crown. Impasse. Or, translated, this was yet another variation of the Whitehall Loop.

In an attempt to breach this manifestation of the Loop, Steven Barker once again enlisted Martin Bell. The MP had taken a sharp interest in the case since the beginning. He had been keeping his powder dry against the day when he might be called on again. In fact, it was nineteen months since he had first raised the problems of Major Stankovic in the House of Commons – and the then Minister had invoked the 'I can't interfere' cover. Now, in a brief Adjournment Debate, Martin Bell tried for justice once more. For the benefit of those MPs who were unfamiliar with the background, he first outlined the Major's service in Bosnia and his subsequent arrest. He touched on what he called the 'ransacking' of his house, the long delays in the whole investigative process and the way the MOD Police had even made inquiries to see if the Major was really entitled to his MBE. Then he got to the nub:[2]

> The injustices multiplied. We discovered that the MOD Police were trying to turn neutral witnesses into hostile witnesses. A distinguished former soldier, who knew Stankovic well, had recently left the service and set up a private business. He was threatened with damage to that business if he did not co-operate with the MOD Police in the way they wanted. We have documentary proof of that.
>
> Another distinguished ex-soldier who had held command testified to the MOD that, to his certain knowledge, Stankovic had acted in Bosnia with loyalty and propriety at all times. The investigators told him that, in that case, he might be interested to know what Stankovic had written about him in his diary. Stankovic's diary contained the kind of personal assessment that any man might make in his diary of another. I [Martin Bell] have protested personally about that to the Chief Constable of the MOD Police, Mr Walter Boreham, and pointed out that it was a flagrant attempt to turn a friendly witness into a hostile one. The Chief Constable could not even see the point.
>
> There was another strange gap in the evidence. A key witness was Lieutenant-General Sir Michael Jackson – a true British hero who now leads the NATO force in Kosovo and is Colonel Commandant of the Parachute Regiment. He submitted written evidence to the MOD Police stating what he knew about Major Stankovic. However, when we saw the list of witnesses provided by the MOD Police, there was a declaration on the front cover that General Jackson had refused to give any evidence. That was a demonstrable lie. The MOD Police proceeded with their case on the basis of that kind of mendacity, half-truth and lying . . .
>
> The spotlight must now turn on the MOD itself. There are questions that the Ministry and its advisors must now answer. Why was Major Stankovic taken out of Staff College, thereby ruining his career? Where was the presumption of innocence? It could not possibly have been on security grounds, because officers from foreign armies, who have no British security clearance, study at the College . . . What about the rest of the Major's career? Where is the apology? Where is the reinstatement?

2. *Hansard*, 14 July 1999.

> Where is the sense that the duty of care has not been exercised? He is entitled to answers on all these points . . .

Martin Bell raised other issues. He asked who within the MOD had decided to give the MOD Police their heads. He asked to whom the MOD Police were accountable. He asked who, now that Major Stankovic had been totally cleared, was going to pay his very considerable costs. He asked why the MOD investigations had been so protracted. And lastly, he asked when the evidence that the Major had transgressed army regulations would be revealed.

Virginia Bottomley also spoke. She asked how the MOD intended to 'regain respect and confidence in the accountability, management and supervision of the MOD Police'?

Mr Bell and Mrs Bottomley might as well have been whistling against the wind. *Hansard* shows that the Minister for Armed Forces, Doug Henderson, had been carefully briefed by his civil servants – the same ones who must have set the MOD Police onto Major Stankovic in the first place. They, through the Minister, were not going to answer any of the questions that mattered. They, through the Minister, could hide behind one of the oldest dodges in the 'How-to-handle-difficult-questions' chapter of the Whitehall Handbook. First, plead the paramount importance of 'the security and defence of the nation'. Then explain that one cannot interfere with any police investigations or statutory procedures. The Minister had been primed to employ both manoeuvres. Of the nineteen questions Martin Bell and Virginia Bottomley had asked between them, none concerned national security. But, because it was already in his script, it did not stop the Minister from invoking that particular defence anyway – at the top of his reply:

> I want briefly to explain my obligations in this matter. First, I have an obligation to be mindful of the public interest and the security and defence of the nation. I have to be mindful also of the strict application of the Official Secrets Act. I take that obligation extremely seriously. It is not my obligation to intervene on investigations undertaken by the Ministry of Defence Police . . .
>
> In relation to Major Stankovic's current situation, it is not my responsibility to decide whether further action should be taken

> against him. It is a matter for the Army chain of command to decide whether there was a breach of Army regulations or whether it could lead to further administrative action.

Elsewhere, Mr Henderson said that he had 'every confidence in the MOD Police'; if there were complaints, they should be referred to the Police Complaints Authority. This was presumably meant to take care of the lie about General Jackson – among other easily checked transgressions. In any case, the Minister would have known that going to the PCA is an eight- to twelve-month process – at best. He went on to justify the many months the police had taken in their investigation:

> Hon. Members will be aware that in most democratic countries legal processes are often slow acting because balances are built in and there is an obligation on those investigating to make sure that they get to the bottom of the evidence. In this case eighty-eight witnesses were interviewed, some on two and three occasions; 107 statements were recorded and tens of thousands of documents had to be examined, many of which had to be translated into English. I hope these figures give a flavour of the complexity of the investigation that was undertaken by the MOD Police.

Apart from answering Mr Bell's question about the protracted investigation, Mr Henderson avoided all but one of the other questions. What about the crucial refusal by the MOD Police to disclose the 'evidence' they claimed to have that Major Stankovic had, in some way, broken army regulations? Until that evidence was handed over to the Army Legal Service and then to the CO of the Parachute Regiment, the Major could not be reinstated. So why the refusal? The Minister claimed that it was all the fault of the Major's solicitor, who, he said, had 'objected to the release of some of the documents'. He would have been repeating the MOD 'advice' he had been given. The truth was very different.

Because the Major was desperately anxious to resume his career, Steven Barker had repeatedly asked the MOD Police to send the relevant 'evidence' to the Army. At the same time, since the DPP had decided months earlier that there was no criminal case to answer, Barker had asked that all the *other* material still held at Braintree should be released directly to him rather than the Army. This was now conveniently misinterpreted by the

MOD Police as an 'objection' to *any* of the documents being released to the Army. Proof that this was the purest MOD invention lies in the fact that even when its 'mistake' was pointed out, it still refused to release the 'evidence' to the Army Legal Service. The MOD knew full well that as long as it denied access to the 'evidence', it was denying the Major any chance of reinstatement in his regiment.

This official manoeuvre made it clearer than ever that within the MOD there was a resolve to force Major Stankovic to give up the fight, to resign his commission. It was a way out of a deeply embarrassing debacle because, even though no charges could now be brought against him, his 'voluntary' resignation would be seen by some as confirmation that the MOD had been right all along, and that 'Stankovic knew the game was up'. By this means, the MOD and its Police evidently thought they would be vindicated. Indeed, one could almost hear the MOD quietly briefing the more trusted of the media's defence correspondents and, for that matter, senior officers in the Parachute Regiment. 'Couldn't pin a criminal charge on the fellow – not quite enough hard evidence. Don't ask us for details – Official Secrets Act and all that. But we all know, don't we, that there's no smoke without fire.'

Maybe that thesis is wrong. But, in the most unlikely event that it is, the MOD can only blame itself for being seen in such a poor and dishonourable light. The problem is that, in its arrogance, it seems not to care how it is regarded.

Through all this time the MOD Police had still not handed over their 'evidence'. Six months had passed since the first request. A posse of colonels and brigadiers, meeting at Bulford Camp for a second time, told the Major and Steven Barker that they were powerless to compel the MOD Police to co-operate. The Police were, in any case, being directed by the MOD itself. Steven Barker predicted that none of them would see any of the 'evidence' until the Major resigned from the Army. In other words, the evidence was being withheld with the express purpose of forcing his resignation. And that is exactly the way it turned out. A few days after the Major sent in his official request to leave the Army, the 'evidence' was released. A Colonel in the Royal Military Police was despatched from Bulford to the Braintree HQ of the MOD Police to collect it.

The evidence came from the search of his house over two years before. The first exhibit was one round of 9-millimetre pistol ammunition. It is, of course, contrary to Army regulations to 'appropriate' any ammunition. But it is easily done. Somewhere on active service one is loading the magazine of a pistol. One legitimately puts some spare rounds in one's pocket. At the end of the day, or the week, one genuinely misses a round when clearing that pocket. When one eventually finds the round, it would be sensible to throw it into the nearest long grass. The Major had not done so. It had been in a drawer with his socks.

The second item was the diary he had kept in Bosnia. It is against regulations to keep a personal diary while on operational service. Which must mean that in almost every conflict in which the British Army has ever fought there have been senior officers in breach of that regulation. At a more immediate level, a reading of General Rose's book about his year in Bosnia, *Fighting for Peace*, openly shows that it was partly based on a diary. In Major Stankovic's diary he had occasionally written about the problems of 'fighting for peace' in the mayhem that was Bosnia. Sometimes he had doubts: 'I am not at all sure that we know where we are going.' This and some other similar comments were held to indicate 'disaffection', which, of course, is a latent offence in itself.

The third offence was his acceptance of an award from the Bosnian Serbs without prior Army Board permission. It was called 'The Humanitarian Cross'. There was no actual medal, just a piece of A4 paper on which was inscribed in Cyrillic script: 'To Major Mike Stanley (Milos Stankovic) for extraordinary efforts in reducing the suffering of the civilian population in Bosnia-Hercegovina'. When Radovan Karadzic, who had played a full part in causing much of that suffering, presented it to him in Pale a few days before he left Bosnia, the Major had been told, 'We worded it that way because we know that you have helped Muslims, Serbs and Croats alike.' It was certainly an offence to have accepted the thing, but it was a sin replicated in one way or another by several much more senior officers who had had contact with the Serbs. Indeed, they later gave the same decoration to Tony Blair; he would not have needed permission from the Army Board, just the Queen. It seems doubtful that the subject came up at one of those routine audiences at Buckingham Palace.

The Major and his solicitor were called down to Bulford Camp once more. Steven Barker was asked to wait in the anteroom while the Major was 'interviewed' by his CO. In less than three minutes the CO told the Major that he and other senior officers had reviewed the 'evidence' and dismissed it all. So that was the end of that – three minutes at the end of three years.

The MOD has never made any attempt to explain why it persisted in withholding those three items until after Major Stankovic had resigned.

In the weeks that followed there were attempts by officers who knew him well to get him to change his mind about leaving the Army. It was too late. He had lost faith. Anyway, he concluded that in years to come, in the minds of some there would always be that 'no smoke' question mark over him. He feared that, had he insisted on reinstatement, the MOD would have made sure he found himself serving in backwater administrative posts with no chance of promotion or ever rising to worthwhile command within the Parachute Regiment. He was almost certainly right. The Army had been his life, but he preferred to resign while he was still young enough to find another career, rather than to retire in five or ten years' time as a 'passed over' Major. Almost certainly the Army did not try hard enough to persuade him otherwise. Perhaps the Army appreciated his reasoning. Perhaps it was afraid of the civil servants at the MOD.

Milos Stankovic is ambivalent about what 'might have been'. He does not like to hear it suggested that the Army, which in one sense means the Parachute Regiment, might have stood by him more vigorously. Yet one can hear a change of key in his replies when he is pressed closely about whether the Army could have done more. Is it anger that the question is put? Or disappointment that it needs to be put? He is ambivalent about that, too.

When asked how he explains the campaign mounted by the Paras in defence of Corporal Clegg while he himself lacked similar support, he points out that he was an officer – 'and officers are meant to have broad shoulders'. He does not add that no one was taking any career risks in backing Corporal Clegg. But the offence of treason for which Milos Stankovic was under investigation for over eighteen months is, apart, possibly, from outright cowardice, as serious as any a soldier can face. So perhaps the officers at the top of the Parachute Regiment, with their own careers to consider, can be forgiven for not standing too closely by their man. But what of the Army Board? Why did this small group of the most senior officers in the Army, who, given that they would all be retiring within a very few years and therefore had nothing to risk or lose, not stand up to the civil servants? If they could not stand up before the DPP's 'no-case-to-answer' decision, then why not after it? The reply usually given is that by the time an officer reaches the level of the Army Board, he has become a very political animal. Indeed, political sensitivity is a prerequisite for high military office. And political sensitivity means a well-developed sense of what is expedient. One doubts the Army Board would see it that way. However they see it, the fact remains that collectively and individually they let down an officer who had a right to expect better. They banged no tables. They shrugged their shoulders. They looked the other way. They chickened out. If those conclusions are mistaken, it would help to see the evidence.

WHO WERE THE Major's original accusers? What were the specifics of their accusations? We are unlikely to find out in any detail for at least another thirty years – when the files are released to the Public Records Office. Even then, if the absence of some key documents in other compromising MOD episodes is any indication, the papers that matter may well be missing. So speculation is inevitable. It may be right; it may be wrong.

The Americans were certainly involved. One can assume that the *New York Times* was well informed when on 1 March 1998 it said that the case against the Major had been 'compiled in part by American intelligence officials'. Perhaps they formed one of those clandestine cells that are sometimes put together which, like Colonel North's Iran-Contra outfit, can be disowned if anything goes wrong. But what was the motive? Could it have had to do with their view that General Rose had been too partisan towards the Serbs? But one assumes that the Americans would surely have had more sense: any attempt to 'neutralize' the General by blackening one of his aides would have been so late as to be pointless. There had to be more (or less?) to it than that. Was it simply an attempt to discredit Major Stankovic? Why bother? Because by suggesting to the MOD that the Major's secret allegiance was to the Serbs, immediate doubt would be raised about the veracity of almost anything he might have reported – about, for example, the clandestine help the Americans were giving to the Croats and the Muslims. That 'help' certainly included those covert flights which broke the UN arms embargo. If news of that Black Op got out, who knew where the embarrassment might end? In a different direction, and while Captain Stanley was in Nottingham, there was suspicion about an infamous 'mortar bomb' which had exploded in Sarajevo's market place. It killed sixty-eight people. Military engineers were mystified by the trajectory. They were unable to work out from where the thing had been fired and, consequently, by whom. There was a suspicion that it had been detonated 'in situ'. By the Bosnian Muslims? By the Bosnian Serbs? Could it have been part of a Black Op that got out of hand? Who knows? There were other shadowy possibilities. In the case of those secret arms flights, a Norwegian Major had seen the planes come in and had subsequently asked some direct questions of NATO's Americans in Italy. Too many questions? Too embarrassing? He was promptly recalled to Oslo. He was given a backwater job. He was led to understand that 'complaints had been laid'. He could see that he was unlikely to go much further in his career. So he resigned. The parallels with Major Stankovic are obvious.

Then there were the Bosnian Muslims. There was no love lost between the Bosnian government in Sarajevo and General Rose. The General took a particular dislike to Ejup Ganic, the Bosnian Vice President. In a *Sunday Times* article (which closely parallels *Fighting for Peace*) he pulls no punches:

> Ganic was the leader of an extreme political element within the ruling Muslim Party for Democratic Action. I came to regard him as ruthless, without a shred of human decency. He was also in charge of military operations and was responsible for implementing strategy to drag the US and NATO into the war. He seemed to be interested neither in peace nor in the continued suffering of the Bosnian people. Instead, he fed the media the concept of the 'victim State'. I regarded him as a contemptible individual.

There is more in the same vein. Milos Stankovic sees these criticisms of Ganic as too harsh. But his own more charitable thoughts about the man have not done him any good. Ganic would have been well aware of General Rose's views; the intense dislike was mutual. Ganic would also have seen the General as a major obstacle to his key strategy of getting the Americans to 'Lift and Strike' – to lift the arms embargo and to attack the Serbs.

Moreover, he would have regarded Milos Stankovic as the General's pro-Serb disciple. Laying charges, through the London Embassy, was a way of discrediting both men. If successful, the media publicity would boost the perception of Bosnia as the 'victim'. If unsuccessful, no harm would be done. In short, in making accusations, the Bosnians had nothing to lose except the 'human decency' that General Rose found so absent in Ejup Ganic in the first place. But why should the Bosnians have waited until well after both men had left Bosnia? Indeed, was it the Bosnians at all?

So many questions. So few answers.

MAJOR STANKOVIC COULD be forgiven for a degree of paranoia. A few months before he formally left the Army, he was on his way to his solicitor when he took a call on his mobile phone from the Metropolitan Police. They had already been to his cottage in Farnham. They wanted to ask him some questions. What about? They would prefer to leave that until they were face to face. So the interview was arranged in Steven Barker's office. Presently, the two officers arrived. They came quickly to the point: could the Major account for his movements on the previous 26 April? Why? Because that was the day Jill Dando had been shot – nearly a year earlier. The Major stared at both of them in near shock. He did not believe what he was hearing.

The murder had had no apparent motive. There were all kinds of theories. She had fronted a television appeal for a Kosovo refugee charity, so there was an idea floating among some journalists that the Serbs could have wanted to get rid of her. There was an alternative thesis derived from the bombing of the TV station in Belgrade a few days before her death; the Serbs wanted revenge and therefore had targeted a prominent TV personality. Both 'stories' seemed most unlikely. Anyway, what had prompted the Met to ask the Major to account for *his* movements? How did he come into these or other theories? The detectives explained, 'We're not at liberty to divulge that information. But you're a Serb, aren't you, sir.' It was a statement rather than a question. The Major did not know whether to laugh or explode. He did neither; he coldly explained that no, he was not a Serb. Never had been. He was an officer in the British Army. And it so happened that he knew exactly where he had been eleven months earlier. He had had an appointment with the Colonel of his regiment at 2 o'clock that afternoon. One of the detectives thought for a moment and then pointed out that 'Miss Dando had been shot at 11 o'clock that morning'. And three hours was time enough to drive from Fulham to Aldershot. 'You see, sir, we need to eliminate you from our inquiries.' Well, it so happened that, preparatory to the interview with his Colonel, he had ironed his uniform at his home in Farnham and then, because it was raining, he had borrowed a friend's car – rather than mess up his uniform on the motorbike. The friend would remember. The detectives asked for an address. Their interview had taken an hour. As they left, the Major was reminded of the line: 'I may be paranoid, but that doesn't mean that someone isn't out to get me.'

So how had this extraordinary situation come about? Who had ensured this one last harassment? We will probably never know. But a possible explanation must be that it was someone either in or close to the MOD or its Police. When, after two years' work, their investigation came to nothing, was there still the hope that, at the least, the Army would court-martial the Major for those minor misdemeanours centred on that 9-millimetre round and the diary? And when even that assault failed (because the Paras refused to play the MOD's game), did someone decide to have one last go at him? 'Put the wind up Stankovic, even though he is about to leave the Army.' Far-fetched? Given other aspects of official behaviour in the Stankovic story, nothing can be as improbable as it sounds.

IN JANUARY 2001, over three years since he was taken to Guildford Police Station, Milos Stankovic issued a writ against the MOD Police for what, in legal language, is called malicious process. He and his lawyers will seek to show that the disruption of his life, to which he was subjected for two years, went far beyond any reasonable bounds. The writ alleges a number of specifics: false imprisonment, making scandalous allegations, inducing mental anguish in both Milos Stankovic and his father, 'misfeasance in public office', and, not least, 'causing the loss of career opportunities'. Why did the investigation take so long? Why were there so many last-minute delays and procrastinations? Why was he never given any proper understanding of the charges against him? Above all, once it became apparent that the case against him was a non-starter, why did the authorities continue to pursue him? His lawyers will argue that the MOD and its agents were motivated by factors which lay well outside the conduct of a proper investigation – that there was a degree of malice in the process. Why, for example, even at the end, should there have been such an unnecessary delay in handing over those three small items of 'evidence' to the Army?

In legal actions against the Crown, things move very slowly. By May 2002, after nearly eighteen months, the Treasury Solicitor's Department had still to make a substantive reply.

The writ is formally issued against the Chief Constable of the MOD Police. However, by implication it is also clearly aimed at those senior personnel working within the MOD to whom the Chief Constable and his force are accountable. If precedents are an indication, one can guess that Whitehall will give an absolute priority to avoiding embarrassment. It will be no great surprise if the MOD persuades itself to smoke-screen parts of the evidence by invoking a Public Interest Immunity Certificate on the grounds of the national interest. Who knows but there may even be some genuine reason for it to do so on some particular aspect. But one can be fairly sure that if a PIIC *is* conjured up (if Matrix Churchill is anything to go by), its net will be cast wider than necessary – to include elements well beyond the reasonable imperatives of security. Furthermore, if the jury eventually decide against the MOD, one can be certain that no heads will roll within the MOD or its police force. The press office will have been primed with the standard answer to media questions: 'The transcripts, including the judge's summing up to the jury, must be carefully studied before any reasoned reply can be made.' The responsible minister will say much the same thing in the Commons and, if he is asked, on radio and television. Then, no doubt, officialdom will hope that media interest will move on.

Of course, things may never get that far. The MOD and its Police, knowing the weakness of their case, and the strength of some of the senior witnesses who may be called against them, may prefer to avoid the public comment and criticism which will surely follow their cross-examination in open court. They may try to avoid such discomfort by offering a cash sum and thereby attempting to settle 'out of court', with a 'gagging' clause under which Milos Stankovic will have to agree never to reveal any details of the settlement or the size of the compensation – the size being a ready measure of officialdom's culpability in the whole affair. Of course, he may decide that the compensation on offer is inadequate. In any case, he may still want to have his day in open court. That will be his right. One imagines that he might prefer to see the MOD trying to explain itself in public. That way, too, would be the clearest demonstration of his innocence. But if that is the route he chooses, he runs some risks. If the jury decides that he is only deserving of a sum lower than that already offered by the MOD (and the jury will not be informed of the MOD offer), he will, in effect, have lost the case – and all compensation.

For these and other reasons, neither Milos Stankovic nor his lawyers are willing even to hint at the amount at which they might settle. But there is nothing to stop a layman making a few calculations. Of the various elements in the equation, the one arising out of 'the loss of career opportunities' is the most susceptible to an outsider's arithmetic. The civilian analogy would be 'constructive dismissal' – the process by which an employer, unable to find any legal basis for sacking an employee he wants to get rid of, seeks instead to make life so uncomfortable and unrewarding for that person that, in the end, they quit anyway. A jury might see a close parallel in certain activities of the MOD and its Police, not least in the way – even after the DPP had judged a 'spying' prosecution was never going to stick – they 'played' that 9-millimetre round, the diary and the Humanitarian Cross. After that, plus all that had gone before, it was surely reasonable for the Major to conclude that, if he stayed in the Army, the authorities would steer him into a series of dead-end postings with no hope of further promotion. So he saw no alternative but to resign. This scenario would seem neatly to fit the definition of a 'constructive dismissal'.

The compensation arithmetic starts with two 'givens'. First, here was a very promising officer who had devoted himself to the Army; it was his whole life. His ambitions have been completely denied. Second, only about 10 per cent of officers get recommended for Staff College; they are not put forward unless it is thought that they have the potential to reach the rank of colonel, probably brigadier. One remembers that the Major was at Staff College when arrested. Thus it is reasonable to assume that from the age of thirty-seven he would have had a minimum of fifteen years' more service ahead of him and have reached the rank of colonel, if not higher. So, allowing for tax (but not for inflation) over that period, he might reasonably have expected to 'take home' a total of at least £500,000 by the year 2013. On retirement in his early fifties he would have been entitled to a tax-free 'lump' equivalent to his final annual salary which, at today's rates, would be between £60,000 and £70,000. Thereafter, he would have had a yearly pension of about half that final salary. Set against all that, one would have to subtract a fair proportion of the income he might reasonably be expected to earn as a civilian during that period, plus the small major's pension that he is already drawing. But these 'deductions' might be more or less equalled by compensation for the other parts of the legal action, namely the false imprisonment, the scandalous allegations, the misfeasance and all the rest of it. Of course there would have to be an allowance for inflation. Even at a mere 2 or 3 per cent a year (compounded), over fifteen years the 'lift' becomes very considerable, perhaps more than 35 per cent. So, without going into further specifics, one can begin to judge the financial bracket within which the Major's expectations may lie . . .

The MOD, via the Treasury Solicitor's Department, will almost certainly go through a protracted ritual of making a series of out-of-court offers, each one a little higher than the last. Because, above all else, Whitehall will want to avoid publicity, each offer will be conditional on a gagging agreement. This aversion to embarrassment will mean that the final offer may be forced, unusually, to bear some loose relationship to the arithmetic just outlined. But if past Whitehall performance is any guide, the offers will start at a very low level indeed.

We will just have to wait and see. However, it seems unlikely that Milos Stankovic will be either forgiving or particularly understanding of the MOD's problems. Why should he be?

AN INTERESTING POSTSCRIPT: a few days before Major Stankovic's formal resignation from the Army, he received a letter from the Military Secretary's office:

> 27 July 2000
>
> Dear Major Stankovic
>
> On the occasion of your retirement from the Army, I am directed by the Army Board to thank you most sincerely for the loyal service you have given since you were commissioned. The Army Board recognises

that, in carrying out your duties as an officer, you will have had to make many sacrifices, putting the interests of your country, the Army and your soldiers before your own. This is very much appreciated and the Army wishes formally to express its gratitude for the service you have given and for the excellent contribution you have made.

I wish you all the very best for the future and every happiness in the years to come.

Good luck and thank you.

Yours sincerely,

Alistair Irvine
Major General, Military Secretary

As Milos Stankovic comments, 'I'm grateful. But, after all that went before, it really doesn't make much sense, does it.'

IN THE EIGHTEEN MONTHS that have elapsed since this chapter was finished, not much has changed on the surface. But underneath, the MOD has been made very aware – though, from the beginning, it has never had any grounds for doubt – that Milos Stankovic and his legal team are determined to go the whole distance.

The prediction made a few paragraphs ago has proved wholly accurate: 'the Treasury Solicitor's Department will almost certainly go through a protracted ritual of making a series of out-of-court offers, each one a little higher than the last'. This is exactly what has happened. And each time, Milos Stankovic and his team have told the other side to go back and think again – to be more realistic. The government can procrastinate only so long. It knows that, in the end, unless a wholly appropriate offer is made, the case must come to court – probably within the next eighteen months. It knows, too, that in open court, the potential embarrassment for the MOD is huge. Other aspects of the case are also likely to be significant . . .

In another context, one might be saying: 'Watch this space.'

A MARINE'S STORY

'An inevitable dichotomy'

Her Majesty does not give reasons for Her decisions and it would be wrong to speculate on Her thought processes that caused Her to arrive at Her decisions.

From a letter from the MOD's Naval Secretariat

I fear that no amount of correspondence between us seems likely to resolve the essential differences between yourself and the Department on this key issue.

From another letter from the MOD's Naval Secretariat

In my view, proper procedures have not been followed.

Lt General Sir Robert Ross KCB, OBE,
Commandant General, Royal Marines

SOME WOULD SAY THAT it was a cast-iron basis for a cock-up. Placing one officer over another when the second is markedly more senior and more experienced puts both men in a very difficult position. Unless they are extraordinarily forbearing, problems are inevitable. As it was, things started to go wrong before they even knew each other.

The new Naval Attaché had arrived in Peking a few days earlier. Now he and his wife were at a small drinks party to which twenty or so other service attachés and their wives had been invited. It was an opportunity for the new man to meet these attachés – American, Australian, Dutch, German, Russian, Israeli, Thai and others – with whom he would almost certainly be in liaison over the next two-and-a-half years. So it was a part social, part professional occasion.

The host was Acting Colonel Winfield; he was the only other British service attaché. He had already been in Peking for six months. Presently, the talk turned – as it sometimes does when service people get together – to the Falklands campaign. Colonel Carter, the new man, had not been in the South Atlantic, but having served in the Royal Marines for over thirty years, he knew plenty of people who had. Thus it was with some surprise that he listened to his host voicing the view that the Falklands War had been a big mistake and certainly not worth the lives it had cost. The American attaché took particular, but polite, issue with Colonel Winfield. Later, he privately commented that he thought it an odd view to advance on that occasion. Although Carter thought it better to hold off, he, too, felt that his colleague's remarks were rather inappropriate in front of foreign guests. Such doubts are better kept 'in the family'. But presently, as the discussion continued, Carter let his embarrassment get the better of him. Instead of trying to move the conversation on, he interrupted with the comment that given Winfield's staff background in the Royal Army Education Corps, his views might be misunderstood by the comrades of those who had been killed. For someone who had seen active service in the RM Commandos in several theatres, and who knew some of those lost at San Carlos and beyond, it may be that it was an understandable, even if rather tactless, reaction. It might have been better left unsaid. Carter realized this and a little later, as the party wound down and people moved to get their coats, he waited until almost everybody had gone, then tried to make some amends with his host.

Given that the two men were going to be working out of the same office in the coming months, it was not an ideal start. Although Colonel Carter could see his mistake, he felt that he was not solely to blame. The seed of discord sown that evening, before it reached full flower, would have consequences which went far beyond any imaginings at the time. Besides providing a classic example of the working of the Whitehall Loop, those consequences would include a change in policy on the appointment of service attachés to British Embassies around the world. And they would eventually involve the constitutional role of the Queen herself, even dragging her, or at least her name, into the Loop. From such very small beginnings . . .

COLONEL CARTER HAD already served as the Military Attaché in Norway for three years in the mid-1980s. His success certainly had a good deal to do with his ability to speak the language and that he was married to a Norwegian. But it seems also to have been due to the fact that he was a very good attaché – as his Ambassador pointed out in writing when recommending him for an OBE: 'One of the best attachés I have known.' Perhaps Royal Marine officers have an advantage: they are familiar with both Naval and Army practice and, further, their Commando background gives them experience of 'sharp end' soldiering. They are highly professional (and know it), and are well respected by those with whom they work – their immediate colleagues, attachés in other embassies and the armed services of the host country.

Carter was good at the job and he liked the diplomatic life. Naturally, then, when he was approached some years later, in 1991, about the possibility of becoming the next naval attaché in China, he jumped at it. 'Of course, I had to check with Eva – but she was almost as keen as I was.' First, he would have to learn Mandarin – a task that would take nearly two years. But, to someone who had always been 'quite good at languages', this was more of a challenge than a problem. As the time drew near for the actual posting, there was a sequence of briefings within the MOD and the Foreign Office. It is no secret that one of the roles of any service attaché is the gathering of intelligence about the training, equipment, morale and, above all, the capabilities of the armed services of the host country. Preparing for this takes time – meetings, reading assessments from one's predecessors, finding out what London wants to know, ascertaining where best to find it. Then there are administrative details to be sorted out. It was one of these that, rather late in the day, needed to be checked; it concerned the working arrangements within the Defence Section of the Embassy in Peking.

Embassies are hierarchical places. At the top is Her Majesty's Ambassador, or HMA. Below the HMA in descending rank is the Minister, then Counsellors, First Secretaries, Second Secretaries, and so on down the line. There is a Political Section, a Commercial Section and a Consular Section. One of the few places where a fixed pecking order does not apply is the Defence Section – the 'home' of the service attachés. Here, because each of the attachés – Army, Navy and Air Force – is usually of broadly similar rank and because each has his own areas of interest on which he reports directly to his service heads in

London, there is more often an air of comradely respect rather than one of observing the nuances of seniority. Nevertheless, there is always one member of the Defence Section who is *the* Defence Attaché. In a way, it is a headquarters role and is usually more concerned with interpreting the host nation's general defence policy than with the specifics of its operational units in the field. Sometimes the appointment goes to the attaché who is the least busy, or it may simply be the turn of the Army (or Navy or Air Force) to fill the post.[1] So, although for formal purposes the Defence Attaché is *primus inter pares*, he has no practical authority over his colleagues. This is as well, because there are occasions when he may be the junior officer in the Section.[2] It was apparent that this was going to be the case in Peking; indeed, Colonel Carter would outrank Acting Colonel Winfield by nearly eight years. And that, in service terms, is a very considerable gap.

Carter had been in a similarly anomalous situation when serving in Oslo. There, the RAF officer who had been the Defence Attaché was not the senior officer; he owed his appointment to the fact that, as Norway has only had a small air force, he had more time to give to the broadly political demands of the job than his Army and Navy colleagues. The arrangement had worked without any problems. But now, within the MOD, it was recognized that Colonel Winfield, because he was currently the only attaché in the Peking Embassy, saw himself as the head of the Defence Section. Indeed, he *was* the Defence Section. However, the Royal Marine was assured in London that his appointment was seen as especially appropriate; his 'land and sea experience' would make up for any deficiencies in Colonel Winfield's armoury. The Army man had fluent Mandarin – which was one of the reasons he had been appointed to Peking while still only an Acting Colonel. While he had

1. In a few embassies, the Defence Attaché regularly comes from the service that has the greatest involvement with the host nation. So, for example, given the number of British Army units stationed in Germany during the Cold War, the DA was invariably a senior Army officer.
2. Because the Defence Attaché is sometimes the junior attaché (as in China at that time) the relevant MOD/FO protocol recognizes the potential problem and specifically states, 'The DA is not formally in command.' Embassies in Washington and Moscow are exceptions to this rule.

shown himself adept at interpreting the political dimensions of Chinese defence thinking and strategy, he would obviously wish to avail himself of Colonel Carter's operational experience. In short, the qualifications of the two officers were different but complementary. It would be a useful combination.

It was not to work out that way.

A day or two after the 'Falklands incident' and on his first full day at work, the new arrival was told by Winfield that he, as the Defence Attaché, would expect to be consulted about any non-routine activities or field trips Carter intended to make. He also mentioned that he, Winfield, was ranked as a Counsellor within the Embassy hierarchy, whereas Carter would be one rung lower down, as a First Secretary. To Carter this seemed a rather unnecessary putdown. It was also untrue – a fact confirmed a day or two later by the Embassy's administrative people. At the same time the Ambassador let it be known that he was 'entirely happy that a *primus inter pares* system should operate'. But perhaps that message was not conveyed to Colonel Winfield, or maybe he felt that the Latin was ambiguous. He did not know that there already existed an 'advice' contained in an MOD memorandum, 'Instructions to Service Attachés and Advisors' (INSAA 1/17). It reads: 'The Defence Attaché is not formally in command.'

As it was, in Peking both men were in a difficult position. One was likely to be sensitive about his comparative lack of 'soldiering' experience. The other, who came from a frontline Corps and who had already served as an attaché, knew that the present situation was not the customary way of doing things within an embassy's Defence Section. Further, given the large seniority gap – and at that time a colonel in the Royal Marines equated to a brigadier in the Army – it was not the normal way of doing things anywhere. But he did not want to be seen as the 'new boy' who, perhaps over-concerned with status, immediately started to rock the boat. He thought the best thing to do was just to get on with his own job.

Over the ensuing months things did not get much better. But they did not – as far as Colonel Carter could judge – get much worse. His masters in London seemed well satisfied with his work and signalled their approval on several occasions. That was the main thing. Nevertheless, at the local level Colonel Winfield, by now promoted up from his earlier acting rank, seemed to take the view that his senior colleague was too independent and unco-operative when it came to taking his guidance.

There was an occasion when Carter went with the American Assistant Naval Attaché on a week-long trip to 'have a look' at various civil and other facilities of interest to London and Washington. There were some risks – there always are – but they were overcome, and the trip yielded worthwhile results. London was pleased and Washington took the trouble to send a signal thanking Colonel Carter for his co-operation. Yet the Defence Attaché viewed the sortie as one that could have compromised some of his own work – which, if things had gone wrong, it probably would have done. In this reservation he had an ally in a member of the Embassy's Political Section. Within most embassies such occasional tension between the caution of the 'politicos' and the more go-getting stance of the 'soldiers' is not unknown. Just occasionally things can come unstuck – with embarrassing results. But if the more cautious 'politicos' always had their way, very little useful intelligence work 'in the field' would ever be accomplished. It is a problem . . .

Some time after this sortie, Carter saw a signal logged in from London. It was from the Naval Captain who was the head of the MOD's Attachés and Advisors Liaison Section (HAAL), suggesting that Winfield should stop worrying about Carter's activities: 'Carter is an experienced officer and knows what he is doing' – or words very close to that effect. Carter was annoyed that his colleague had evidently questioned his activities with HAAL without telling him first.

In fact, Winfield's theory that he was the man to whom Carter should report now received a boost. A new Ambassador had arrived; he took the view that the Defence Section should be run in a more hierarchical way than his predecessor had required. That was all very well, but it ignored custom and practice in British embassies around the world. It also ignored the unambiguous INSAA 'rule' – which, curiously, no one in Peking seemed to know existed in formal and written terms.

As time went on, the Royal Marine was finding it increasingly irksome to be continuously nannied by someone whom he felt often knew rather less about his job than he did – even though Colonel Winfield was now acting with the delegated authority of the Ambassador.

The crunch was almost bound to come. It occurred as a result of a letter Colonel Carter wrote to the Chinese Foreign Affairs Bureau. It was, as he later acknowledged, an 'own goal'. He had heard that the Chinese were being asked to change the way all the service attachés in Peking (more than eighty of them) were officially listed in terms of precedence. The international convention has long had it that precedence is solely dependent on the length of time a given attaché has been in the host country (the convention is also confirmed in that INSAA memorandum). Thus in China the senior attaché – the Dean of the Attaché Corps – was a Colonel Makuta from Zaire; it was just that he had been there longer than anyone else. Indeed, it was Colonel Makuta who had written to the Chinese authorities suggesting that the traditional protocol should be replaced by a system whereby Defence Attachés would be ranked on their own list – separate and senior to a secondary list of army, navy and air force attachés. As the West European representative on the Dean's steering committee, Carter phoned Makuta and asked him to rethink his suggestion. He doubted that Makuta would do anything, so he felt he had some cause to write a parallel letter direct to the Chinese Foreign Affairs Bureau pointing out that such a change would break a long-standing convention. He drew attention to the fact that the incoming Japanese Air Attaché was senior in rank to the Japanese Defence Attaché. But he made the mistake of also citing the anomaly of his own position vis-à-vis Colonel Winfield. He compounded the error by not telling Winfield – who he thought had played a part in prompting Makuta's suggestion. Nor did he tell Colonel Makuta.

The 'affair of the letter' came to a head a few weeks later when Colonel Makuta learnt from the Chinese that he had been 'corrected' by the British Naval Attaché. He was considerably miffed. He brought the matter to the attention of Colonel Winfield, who in turn told the Ambassador's deputy, Minister Hodge – who had only just arrived in Peking. It was concluded that the Chinese would now deduce (via the sentence in Carter's letter where he explained that he was senior to Winfield) that there were tensions – 'disaffection' is the preferred term – within the ranks of the British attaché section. And who knew what mischief the Chinese might make of that? This is just the kind of small problem that intrigues the finely tuned minds of HM Diplomatic Service.

It happened that while all this was going on, Carter was back in UK on a debriefing and liaison session at the MOD. On returning to Peking, pleased with the praise he had received in London, he was met with the news that Minister Hodge wanted to see him immediately.

During the four weeks that Minister Hodge had been in Peking, Carter had been away in London for two. Consequently, they hardly knew each other. But it quickly became apparent that Minister Hodge had been briefed on the Naval Attaché's shortcomings. He came quickly to the point. From what he had been told, he judged that the disharmony within the Defence Section could not continue; the 'unauthorized' letter was the last straw. He was recommending to the Ambassador (when he got back a day or two later from an out-of-Peking tour) that Carter should be relieved of his post and sent home. Carter was stunned at what he saw as a quite considerable over-reaction to what, yes, he acknowledged had been a mistake – even though he had written the letter as a member of Makuta's committee. But he seemed to be faced with a decision already taken – before he had had any chance to explain himself. In disbelief, he asked to see the Ambassador immediately on his return.

It was several days before the Ambassador, Sir Leonard Appleyard KCMG, could see Carter. This delay may have been caused by the Ambassador's need to communicate with London. For example, because the Colonel was employed by the Navy, not by the Foreign Office, it had to be the First Sea Lord (1SL) who formally recalled him. However, given the difficulties of discussing the rights and wrongs of the situation via a series of diplomatic telegrams or even long-distance phone calls, the 1SL's approval could only ever have been a forgone conclusion. Almost certainly he would have been forced to accept, without real question, civil service advice (relayed from the Foreign Office) that Carter no longer had his Ambassador's confidence. So the question of whether the Ambassador was reacting to the results of a proper investigation or just to second-hand allegations was not one that seems to have been raised.

The Ambassador eventually met Carter in the embassy's 'secure speech room'. Sir Leonard began by saying how sorry he was to have to do what he was doing. It was the recommendation of both Winfield and Minister Hodge that the Colonel should go. Thus a decision to that end had been made. Evidently, it was all a 'fait accompli'. The Ambassador pointed out that the letter had been a notable mistake, but, as Carter would be aware, there were other matters; he talked of 'a pattern of behaviour'. It was all most regrettable. When it came to his turn, Carter pointed out that it seemed inconsistent that he should have fallen from grace so quickly – largely on something as vague as 'a pattern of behaviour', which must, by definition, imply a degree of unsatisfactory conduct over a period of time. Yet only the previous month the Ambassador had, in writing, complimented Carter on his work. Surely this alleged behaviour pattern, now under such severe review, must have long pre-dated that report. Yes, there was the letter. He regretted it. But that was a relatively minor mistake and, anyway, he had apologized to Makuta – who now was not nearly as upset as was being reported. Given the severity of the 'sentence', could he know the specifics of the charge as it related to 'a pattern of behaviour'? The accusation must surely derive from more than the fact that he and the Defence Attaché had their differences. To this the Ambassador replied (and he was later to repeat in writing) that, because the Colonel was not employed by the Foreign Office, he did not feel able to respond in specific terms to the question. The MOD, and the Admiralty Board, would have to provide the answers. The Colonel reflected – but forbore from commenting – that there was something very odd in a situation where the Ambassador did not feel obliged to justify the sacking, but nevertheless felt that he had the authority to recommend it.

Although the die was now cast, the Ambassador may have had some unofficial sympathy for the Colonel and his wife. On the eve of their departure for London a few weeks later, he gave the Colonel a farewell lunch to which a number of official guests from the Chinese defence establishment were invited. And he spoke of the contribution, social and professional, the Colonel had made over the previous ten months.

Some other members of the Embassy felt strongly that an injustice had been done – not least because, after his departure, it was (they said) put about that Carter had been a thoroughly squeaky wheel in the smooth running of the Embassy. The Americans, with whom Carter had worked closely, were especially puzzled by the curious ways of the British. Lastly, in later letters to Colonel Carter's Portsmouth home, one member of Embassy staff thought the tag '*nec illegitimi carborundum*' was apposite. Another hoped he would pursue his case 'until you get some justice'. That was now the problem – first, what *was* justice in this case, and second, how best to pursue it?

COLONEL CARTER COMES FROM a family whose military and naval roots go back many generations; to such people, there is nothing old-fashioned about personal 'honour'. To be put ashore from one's ship – and that is what had just happened in Peking – is seen as a disgrace; it implies either gross incompetence or some kind of scandalous behaviour. But, at the least, the person so humiliated is usually given his day (or longer) in court to defend himself and, hopefully, to clear his name – through a court martial or a Board of Inquiry. Once back in England, Colonel Carter would have been delighted to have been given either option. Sadly, it quickly became apparent that neither the Foreign Office nor the Army were willing (then or subsequently) to allow the Ambassador, Minister Hodge and Colonel Winfeld to be questioned in any way about the events in Peking. Given that there was no mechanism that could compel their participation in some kind of investigative forum, justice (or at least a hearing) would have to be sought by other means.

First, it was necessary for Colonel Carter to find out the exact nature of the indictment against him. The charge sheet – even if it only existed in a figurative sense – had been (still was) Kafka-like in its lack of specifics. He had asked the Ambassador about this on the day he was sacked – without success. From his perspective it seemed he had been accused and found guilty almost entirely on the evidence of the Defence Attaché, who, while no doubt a thoroughly honourable man, was obviously not a disinterested party. The same might even be said of the Ambassador and the Minister. Certainly, the complaint laid against Carter had never been subjected to any kind of thorough, let alone impartial, review. That might not have worried the MOD, but it worried Carter.

Carter accepted that, in the armed services, there is sometimes a need for a rougher form of justice than might be the case in civilian life. But this was very rough justice indeed. Without any formal and/or written warning or, indeed, any real chance to defend himself before a sentence that had already been decided, he had seen an unblemished and successful career, spanning thirty-three years, peremptorily terminated. He took legal advice. The professional conclusion was that yes, the whole affair had been very badly handled.

So, how to proceed?

One cannot just write a letter enquiring: 'Dear First Sea Lord, Why was I sacked?' The First Sea Lord, in the sort of quasi-legal situation the Carter 'affair' might become, was dependent on the advice of his advisors within the MOD's Naval Secretariat. In questioning executive decisions, there are procedures that must be followed; those procedures are in the hands of the civil servants. One has to play the game at their pace and according to their rules. Some of the rules have solid justification, others are merely bureaucratically convenient. Besides, one confronts the Whitehall Loop – wherein the people who give the advice are almost invariably the same people who decide what evidence will be heard (or passed upwards) in support of that advice. Thus they quickly become the gate-keepers and the arbiters of their own cause.

Colonel Carter decided he should try to get, at the least, a written apology for wrongful dismissal. Apart from the matter of honour, he would need something official once he looked for civilian employment on retirement. But there was no chance of an apology from the Foreign Office – because, in theory, he had not been sacked by the Foreign Office. This was an expedient fiction – a characteristic of both the Loop and of the bureaucratic mindset of Whitehall. After all, there was no realistic way the First Sea Lord could have avoided complying with the recommendation of an Ambassador thousands of miles away who, he would assume, had based that recommendation on a very thorough investigation of all the evidence. And the Naval Secretariat would have done nothing to disabuse the First Sea Lord of that assumption. And the Foreign Office had already pointed out that the sacking of Colonel Carter was no business of theirs. Hands had been thoroughly washed.

So the Colonel had to try for an apology from the Navy. He needed to get specific statements from, among others, the Ambassador, Minister Hodge and Colonel Winfield. He obviously could not approach them directly. The chain was a long one: Carter to MOD to Foreign Office to Peking, then back to MOD to HQ Royal Marines to Carter. The process took four months.

When it eventually arrived, the Ambassador's account contained a number of interesting comments. First, he said the initial mistake lay with the MOD in sending too senior an officer to Peking. If there was truth in that, there was even more in the idea that the mistake had been in sending too junior an officer – when it was already known that his senior would follow a few months later. Either way, the man on the spot, the Ambassador, could surely have resolved or, at the least, ameliorated the error within five minutes – by reining in the more junior Defence Attaché to a role where, as in other embassies, he acted merely as *primus inter pares*. It was Colonel Carter who was now paying the price for other people's mistakes.

At another point the Ambassador wrote that Colonel Carter 'considered himself senior to the Defence Attaché'. This reveals a significant level of misunderstanding. It is the same as saying that a Sergeant considers himself to be senior to a Corporal. 'Considers' has nothing to do with it. A Sergeant just *is* senior to a Corporal – always has been. To require the junior of any two officers to exercise significant authority over one who is markedly the more senior, and not to anticipate a problem – as the Ambassador and the Minister evidently did – amounts, in man-management terms, to a surprising lack of forethought. They might as well have expected a Minister to defer to a First Secretary. Again, it was Colonel Carter who paid the price.

There is some irony in the thought that the whole situation might have been anticipated and, thereby, quietly solved by a touch or two of common or garden diplomacy. Or was that too much to expect from two senior diplomats?

Minister Hodge's narrative parallels the Ambassador's in most respects. When it comes to Colonel Winfield's account, one has to make a choice: Winfield's word against Carter's. According to Winfield, Carter managed to get most things wrong. But there seems, at times, to be a certain gloss on the narrative. For example, in claiming that Carter publicly insulted him at that first cocktail party by saying that he did not have frontline experience, the fact that the comment was made in response to his own (inappropriate?) comments about the Falklands campaign is not mentioned. And there were other witnesses to that besides Carter. Clearly both men had been at fault. Winfield ends his report by saying that, in the work of an attaché section, 'There is no scope for sensitive ego and personal aggrandisement.' A very fair point. And one that might have been made just as reasonably by Carter. You pays your money.

Returning to a particularly significant part of the Ambassador's report, at one point he writes, 'It was clear to me that this [the Makuta letter] was not an isolated incident, but part of a pattern of behaviour which had continued for some time.' Elsewhere he refers to 'various warnings' Carter had been given. This is odd. If things had become so serious that Carter had to be sacked, one might have thought the Ambassador would have put at least one of those warnings (certainly the final one) in writing. Indeed, he would have been obliged to do so. One might have thought Carter would have been given a copy; one might have thought there would be another copy in the Ambassador's files, which he would now have forwarded to London by way of corroboration.

Further, in light of all these alleged warnings, it seems strangely inconsistent that less than three weeks before Carter was sacked, the Ambassador should have written a complimentary report on him for his RM superiors. This was a point taken up by Lieutenant General Sir Robert Ross KCB, OBE, Commandant General of the Royal Marines. Sir Robert knew Carter well enough to be very doubtful, disbelieving even, about the allegations that had been made. It is worth quoting part of a long memorandum that he wrote to the Second Sea Lord (2SL) and Permanent Under Secretary (at the MOD) in support of what had now become an official complaint by Carter. It goes to the heart of the matter:

> There is an inevitable dichotomy between the version of events related by Carter and that recalled by some of the others involved in the case. I find Carter's identification of discrepancies in the Ambassador's account persuasive. For example, the Ambassador formally stated as late as 3 February 1995 that Carter 'had the necessary combat and policy making experience, and personal qualities to go further in the Service' and referred to 'his very considerable abilities'. [Carter was dismissed just two weeks later, on 17 February]. I have difficulty equating this with the 'pattern of behaviour' and apparent

continuous disregard of warnings alleged in the Ambassador's account. By all accounts Carter was clearly doing a thoroughly professional job. Furthermore, I note that the decision to remove Carter was effectively taken after one meeting between the Defence Attaché and Minister, at the DA's request, on 9 February when Carter was away on duty in the UK. This does appear to be something less than the 'full consultation' which the Ambassador claims to have taken place.

In my view, proper procedures were not followed in that:
(a) MOD was not involved at any stage. If the Defence Attaché felt as strongly as he did, HAAL [Head of Attachés and Advisors Liaison at the MOD] should have been informed and given the opportunity to investigate the problem before unilateral action was contemplated.
(b) Carter was never formally warned and, according to statements he made shortly after the incident (and not nine months later in the case of most of the contrary statements) he was never warned at all. He admits that there had been occasional differences, but this hardly justifies the subsequent statements made by the DA. A proper warning process should have been initiated if there was serious concern about Carter's conduct or the performance of his duties.

I am uneasy about the role of the DA in this case. At least some of the blame for the clash of personality between him and Carter must rest with him. Furthermore, there is evidence to suggest that his lack of experience caused him to resent Carter. Whatever the rights and wrongs of the situation, there can be little doubt that the DA handled the whole affair clumsily and unprofessionally.

I do not subscribe to the Ambassador's view that the problem 'stemmed from the MOD's initial decision to send Carter'. Carter's reputation as an attaché was extremely good. He had worked happily and most effectively in the Oslo Embassy in which – as in Peking – single service attachés were senior to the Defence Attaché. Indeed his performance in Oslo led to the award of an OBE. His credentials could hardly have been better, and I am inclined to the view that the source of the problem was the choice of the Defence Attaché rather than the Naval Attaché.

In his final paragraphs the Commandant General wrote that in over thirty years he had never had the slightest doubt about Carter's integrity.

Lastly, he underlined the potential effect that the affair – if unresolved – might have on Carter's chance of civilian employment when he retired from the Royal Marines later that year.

The top civil servants of the Naval Secretariat at the MOD would have gone into a huddle – almost literally – when the Commandant General's missive arrived. He was saying, quite unequivocally, that Carter was due an apology for some very bad mistakes. But apologies do not come easily from Whitehall. The problem here would have been that one could not ask the First Sea Lord to apologize for mistakes made by Foreign Office staff – who refused to acknowledge that any apology on their part was called for. Foreign Office staff do not make mistakes. Yet, at the same time, the Navy did not think the debacle had really been any fault of theirs. True, it was the First Sea Lord who had recalled Carter, but on the strongest possible recommendation of the Ambassador.

It was a typical Whitehall impasse.

Nearly a year had now passed since the sacking. Then someone in that figurative MOD huddle seems to have thought of a solution. All senior RN and RM officers receive a testimonial signed by the First Sea Lord on retirement, but, in this case, perhaps the text could refer in a little extra detail to the splendid service the Colonel had given over three decades; it would avoid all mention of any unpleasantness in Peking. Moreover, why not offer Carter a six-month extension of service beyond the date at which he would have normally retired? This would go some way in compensating him for the considerable financial loss he and his family had suffered by their premature return from Peking. A condition of acceptance of this 'full and final settlement' would have to be that Carter should then shut up – though it would be put more eloquently than that.

At first sight this seemed a solution. But at second sight it was recognizable for what it was: an attempt to sweep the whole affair under the carpet. It would not be a full-blown cover-up, but it would certainly qualify as a hush-up. Nevertheless, Colonel Carter would almost certainly have accepted the proposal – it had very obvious merits – had it not been for an unfortunate phrase in the letter from the senior civil servant who put it forward:

> Colonel Carter's complaint has been very carefully considered below Board level [i.e. among top civil servants but just below Navy Board level – the 1SL and his immediate colleagues] and it is apparent that there are wide discrepancies between the versions of events portrayed by Colonel Carter on the one hand and by members of the Diplomatic Service on the other. Colonel Carter's version of events would mean that there were significant shortcomings in the procedures that led to his reappointment [*sic*] from Peking to the UK.

Colonel Carter's response pointed to the sentence that began, 'Colonel Carter's version of events would mean that . . .'. To him, the phrase 'version of events would mean' implied a considerable level of official doubt about his assertion that he had been wrongly sacked. This was precisely what his complaint had been about since the very start. If anything, this attempt to find a way out – or, more precisely, its careless and equivocal phrasing – made the Colonel more determined than ever. It would now take more than a testimonial letter and six months' gardening leave to assuage what he keenly felt to be a further slur on his integrity.

Sir Robert Ross had now retired; the new Commandant General RM was Major General David Pennefather CB. He was no less supportive than his predecessor. He wrote to the senior civil servant who was clearly 'running' the case on behalf of the MOD, saying that as the other parties in the dispute would not take part in a Board of Inquiry or, indeed, answer any questions, it was imperative that the whole affair be referred to the very top: to the Navy Board.

Other than an acknowledgement that the Commandant General's memorandum had been received, nothing happened for four months.

Then, not quite out of the blue, there arrived a glowing testimonial signed by Admiral Sir Jock Slater GCB LVO, the new First Sea Lord. Was this a last and hopeful attempt by the MOD's Naval Secretariat to get rid of the problem? It seems unlikely that Sir Jock knew any of the details. He had only recently taken office and, in any case, 'the problem' was left over from his predecessor's regime. There is something intriguing about the way, after three paragraphs of compliments, the letter slides around the events in Peking:

On promotion to Colonel, you remained on the staff of the Commandant General as the Director of Personnel before again demonstrating your flair for languages by learning Chinese and moving to Peking as the Naval Attaché. Here, you were successful in expanding contacts with the Chinese in difficult circumstances with commendable imagination and energy. You took up your final appointment as the Director of Royal Marine Reserves at a time of considerable turbulence and uncertainty for the Reserve Forces.

Does the phrase 'in difficult circumstances' refer to the problems of working with the Chinese? Or with Colonel Winfield? Perhaps the ambiguity is deliberate. Perhaps, who knows, there is a nice touch of irony here. Anyway, it was obviously hoped that the whole affair might now be persuaded to go away without becoming one of those inconveniences of bureaucratic life: a Fuss. Nevertheless, with the Commandant General's direct backing, the case did eventually reach the Admiralty Board. It had to. The Board's finding – and one can bet that the civil servants rather than the Admirals had the most to do with it – is a fine example of The Fudge, or the use of language which allows the practitioners to have it all ways at once. It is a well-developed Whitehall skill. Consider the following:

> It is our opinion that, when it had been decided to recommend Colonel Carter's withdrawal, he was denied natural justice by not being given a proper opportunity to state his case to his superior military authority and to influence events. We find no evidence that he was removed for reasons of misconduct or professional inadequacy. [So far, so very good. But . . .] However, we judge that the Ambassador's recommendation to have Colonel Carter removed was justified in the light of the way in which his behaviour affected the morale and cohesion of the Embassy.
>
> As for redress, we offer Colonel Carter our apologies for the procedural shortcomings we have identified. We note that Colonel Carter refused the offer of a six month extension of service by saying that the matter was first and foremost one of honour.

So now one had a situation where the 'court' not only finds that the defendant had been unjustly treated, but that there has been no 'misconduct or professional inadequacy'. Yet it then immediately says his removal was justified in the light of his behaviour. Question: how can anyone be innocent of inadequacy in their professional role, but at the same time be guilty of such seriously disruptive behaviour – in that very same professional role – that the only solution lies in their being sacked? One wonders at the intellects that fail to see such an obvious contradiction in their own argument. Clearly, the problem had been how to cope with the *amour propre* of the Ambassador and the Foreign Office in the face of the obvious (and now admitted) legitimacy of the Colonel's claim. Answer: Fudge. And hope nobody notices. What had obviously to be avoided at all costs was giving offence to the Foreign Office. Of course, the FO has always thought of itself as the intellectual elite of Whitehall, but there seems to be no good reason why the MOD should have been so ready to roll over.

There followed a long exchange of letters. Unfortunately, given the nature of the Whitehall Loop, nothing was actually moving. In frustration, the Colonel considered his chances in civil law. He was warned the MOD would use its lawyers to make the case as hard, expensive and protracted as possible. If he could last the course, he would probably win, but he would still be severely out of pocket. It was not an option. Besides, he had to get on with the rest of his life.

It was now two years since the Carters had left Peking. For all his efforts, all he had squeezed from the system was a qualified apology for the fact that the correct formula had not been followed in his dismissal. In other words, 'We're sorry that the proper procedures came rather unstuck, but we find that the sacking was justified.' The Colonel was not giving up. From private letters he knew he had allies back in Peking – those who thought the Ambassador had dismissed him on an improperly investigated charge. 'I am glad,' wrote one, 'that you are still fighting for justice.' Because they had their careers to think of, he had always been reluctant to ask them to state that support in any official way. But now, given that he was still guilty of 'a pattern of behaviour' which had allegedly damaged 'the cohesion and morale of the Embassy', he took the risk of asking two of his more senior ex-colleagues for their written backing. One wrote back almost immediately:

> I am happy to support you and can categorically state that your behaviour did not affect the morale and cohesion of the Embassy. Indeed, the decision to withdraw you had a negative effect; colleagues were alarmed that the Ambassador and his Deputy could arrange the removal of a senior career officer without any apparent grounds that merited such an action.

That was written by a First Secretary who was not long from retirement, so he could write without the need to look over his shoulder. Others wrote equally critically of what one called 'the unwarranted and precipitate nature of your departure'. Carter forwarded the most persuasive letters to the civil servants handling his case. He asked, in the light of this new evidence (and the earlier contradiction), that the Admiralty Board take another formal look at its earlier 'innocent but still guilty' finding. He added that, if now found innocent of all charges, he hoped he might be compensated in part for the quite considerable costs (to say nothing of the concern) he had incurred. He had not accepted the earlier offer of six months' pay because it was conditional on his abandoning his first priority – the attempt to clear his name.

It took six slow months before the Navy Board eventually concluded it had been wrong in its earlier verdict that it had been Colonel Carter's 'pattern of behaviour' which had brought about his sacking. The Board even apologized for its earlier mistake. That made two apologies. But the Board was not about to give tangible expression to this acknowledgement of its errors – it found 'no validity in Colonel Carter's claim for financial compensation'. Apologies, of course, do not cost anything and, when made collectively by a group such as the Navy Board, they don't cost any individual his pride. In fact, it is doubtful that the Navy Board (i.e. the First Sea Lord and co.) had anything much to do with it; they would have been acting on the advice of their permanent civil service advisors. Still, one is surprised that this group of very senior naval officers should have lent their names to such an obvious travesty.

As Carter said, 'After nearly three years, I had been cleared of all charges, but had been left with considerable financial "damage" – caused by the mistakes of others.' Quite apart from the legal advice he had received (from a lawyer who felt so strongly that he had cut his fees to the bone), his premature return from Peking had denied him six months of service pay, eighteen months' income on the rental of his house, his wife's job teaching English in Peking had been suddenly cut short, and there were other charges. At the least, one might have expected a token and ex gratia payment of, say, £1000 – 'without prejudice', of course. Honour might have been satisfied – just.

Armed as he now was – and it was no less than his due – with a clean bill, the Colonel thought to appeal for these 'out of pocket' costs. For a service officer, the final 'court' of appeal takes the form of a Petition to the Sovereign. Although the ritual goes back to the time when the monarch really did have a hand in these things, it has long become a wonderfully British (and rarely used) fiction – admirable, arcane and laughable at one and the same time. One is meant to suppose that, with the advice of the relevant minister at her elbow, the Queen really does examine the pertinent papers and come to a decision. The Colonel made a formal application in February 1998, three years to the month since his sacking. He had now been a civilian for nearly two years.

After seven months he had not heard anything useful. His enquiries every five or six weeks indicated that his Petition was still with the MOD's Naval Secretariat, 'pending clarification on certain issues'. What issues? They could not be revealed. Such obfuscation and delay is a Standard Operating Procedure (SOP) in Whitehall – hardly surprising where the very functionaries whose decisions are the subject of an appeal are the same people who decide the priority and timing they will give to the processing of that appeal.

At last, in late October, word came that 'the Petition had been forwarded to Her Majesty, The Queen'. Three months later – nearly twelve months after it had been first submitted – it was admitted that regretfully, the Petition had not been passed to the Queen after all; it was still at the MOD – with George Robertson, the Minister for Defence. It then got stuck for a further eight months in the Minister's pending tray – which, as anyone who has worked in an office will know, is the place where most low-priority, 'What do we do with this?' problems wind up. By September 1999, more than eighteen months after submitting his Petition, the Colonel was getting impatient. He saw no point in more letters to the civil servants in the Naval Secretariat with whom he had been in continuous correspondence for three-and-a-half years. Instead, he wrote directly to George Robertson – to catch him before he moved on to become Secretary General of NATO.

Of course, in any normal appeal both sides of a dispute submit their 'arguments' to the appeal authority, which, in time, makes a judgement that, together with the reasoning behind the judgement, is communicated back to the interested parties. In the case of Colonel Carter's appeal, the civil servants in the Naval Secretariat through whose hands it passed would, before sending it upwards, have appended their own counter-arguments and comments – without informing Carter of what they were. With such a hammerlock on the process, it is hardly surprising that almost every such appeal is doomed before it begins. Such was the fate of Colonel Carter's Petition. In February 2000, two years after he had submitted it and just over five years since he had been closeted in the 'secure speech room' with the Ambassador in Peking, he was told: 'No validity was found in any of your claims.'

It will be apparent by now that Colonel Carter does not give up easily. He wrote asking for a copy of his Petition as it had actually been sent forward by the civil servants to the Minister of Defence and thence, in theory, to the Queen. He wanted to see how far his Petition had been edited – filleted – along the way. Even more important, how fair and how accurate had the MOD's attached memorandum been? After all, significant errors and contradictions had occurred in the past. And what was the reasoning behind the rejection of his Petition? But the MOD functionaries were giving nothing away. In their reply, with its clear inference that it is not they who make such decisions but the Minister and the monarch, they provide as polished an example of the Whitehall Loop as one is ever likely to find:

> You requested a copy of the Report submitted to Her Majesty. I am afraid that such correspondence between the Secretary of State and Her Majesty is confidential and, as such, it is not possible to disclose the Report to you. Moreover, Her Majesty does not give reasons for Her decisions and it would be wrong to speculate on Her thought processes that caused Her to arrive at Her decision.

It is worth noting that it is not the Crown, in the broadly constitutional sense, that is being invoked, but Her Majesty in a rather more personal sense. On the evidence above, one can apparently be as opaque (pompous even) as you like – if you invoke the Queen. 'Don't look to *us* for answers,' say the civil servants, 'we are mere cogs in a machine.' One might think that the Queen actually sat down and had, on this and other matters, 'thought processes that caused Her to arrive at Her decision' without following precisely – as she is constitutionally bound to do – the advice of her Minister, who, in turn, would have been closely advised by his staff. In fact, the Queen had, and has, nothing to do with it. She has much less input than she has in the Queen's Speech at the State Opening of Parliament – on that occasion she at least puts on her spectacles and reads the thing. But there is no pretence that she has a hand in mapping out the government's intentions. The truth is that all the 'thought processes' in Colonel Carter's case were generated within the same coterie of civil servants in the Naval Secretariat that had been making the key decisions since the beginning. That is how the Loop works. There was not the remotest chance that they would now, after careful reflection, have found themselves to have been wrong in their earlier judgements. That is *not* how the Loop works. It is doubtful if even the Minister himself had any input; he almost certainly ruled as he was advised to rule – but in the name of the Queen. Of course, all executive acts of government are undertaken in the name of the Queen. Most of her subjects are quite happy with the general arrangement – it works better than most others. But the over-the-top charade contained in the passage above is enough to give constitutional monarchy a bad name.

Colonel Carter has been retired for several years; he works for a shipping company. Although he prefers to be called Mr Carter now that he is a civilian, he remains indelibly a Royal Marine. He is proud of his Corps and the thirty-three years he spent in its service. He is not so sure about the Corps' governing body, the Navy Board. It let him down.[3] It too easily bowed to the Foreign Office in accepting the fiction that it was the Navy and not the FO's man in Peking, the Ambassador, who had sacked the Colonel. And yet, at the end of the day, the Admirals who constitute the Navy Board have some excuse: once they get away from

3. Comparisons with the Army Board's role in the story of Major Milos Stankovic are too obvious to need spelling out.

ships and maritime defence policy, they are not well equipped to get involved in the inter-departmental politics of affairs such as that of Colonel Carter. They must rely on their civil servant advisors, their Secretariat.

The fact is that, from Whitehall to Peking and back to Whitehall, people made serious mistakes of judgement at every point in the Colonel's story. None of those mistakes was inevitable. But, once made, governmental bureaucracy thinks it must defend them at all costs. Ironically, in the end, it was yet further mistakes – those thoughtless contradictions in the official papers – that triggered the long-delayed, even if only partial, correction of a notable injustice. That injustice was averted by one man's persistence; it took over four years and a great personal investment – of time, energy and money. And in his wife's case, her health.

One good thing did emerge: the MOD and the Foreign Office have changed their practice in the appointment of service attachés. Care is now taken to ensure that a senior officer is not placed in a position where he is expected to take orders from a junior.

The Colonel's story may just be one of a considerable storm in a teacup. But from such small examples there are sometimes wider lessons to be learned. In this case, they lie in a pattern of attitude and performance by the professionals within the MOD and the Foreign Office. And it *is* a pattern. It is the Loop. This was not an isolated example. Whether any lessons *will* be learned is another matter.

GROUPTHINK AND THE INFALLIBILITY SYNDROME

'Yours not to reason why'

The relentless growth in size and functions of the Departments of State and the relatively high level in calibre of those who staff them, coupled with the steady decline in importance and function of MPs, has led to a gradual transfer of power and influence from the floor of the House of Commons to the private rooms of permanent civil servants.

Professor G.W. Keeton, *The Passing of Parliament*

PERHAPS PROFESSOR KEETON attributed 'the passing of Parliament' rather too exclusively to the equal and opposite 'rising' of the civil servants. Politicians in office, centred on Number 10 under both Margaret Thatcher and now Tony Blair, have also had a good deal to do with it. So have Brussels, creative lawyers, the media and a hugely increased load of administration coupled with a volume of so-called 'secondary' legislation which never goes anywhere near Parliament. Nevertheless, given that the Professor was writing over fifty years ago about the growing power of Whitehall officialdom, his crystal ball was more prescient than he ever knew. One wonders what he would be saying about the dominance of civil servants if he were alive today.

IF YOU MAKE A BIG enough nuisance of yourself – because you distrust some of the answers they are giving you – the people in Whitehall are likely to label you 'a conspiracy theorist'. It is a catch-all term meant to imply that you are off balance and pathologically suspicious. There is certainly no need for anyone to take you seriously: 'After all, the fellow is a bit of a nutter.' It is a convenient way to write off the sceptic. That way, everyone (except the sceptic) goes home with an easy mind.

So what constitutes a 'conspiracy' and what is merely 'prudent contingency planning'? It probably depends on one's point of view and the honesty of the answers being worked out. If the answers are co-ordinated to mislead, one might reasonably apply the pejorative term. Where should one place, for example, the thinking of those civil servants who, once upon a time, worked out a plan to disguise the expulsion of the Ilois? 'These steps should be ordered and timed to attract the least attention and should have a logical cover worked out in advance.' Mere contingency planning? Where does one put the assertion that the MOD never sued Textron-Lycoming for faulty Fadec software? What about the plan to get rid of Milos Stankovic?

The fact is that for a co-ordinating conclave there is seldom much need to pull down the blinds and pull up the chairs. As often as not, the groupthink of Whitehall is enough to ensure that everyone working on a problem is more or less 'on message' anyway. So perhaps it is a case of 'not so much a conspiracy, more a shared way of thinking'.

Chief among Whitehall's ways of thinking, learnt from the day a recruit joins, is that one should 'never let the side down'. This means that once an official decision has been made on 'the line to take', be it on BSE, Foot and Mouth, the safety of depleted uranium, the reliability of the Challenger tank (in all but unchallenging conditions), or any of the other 101 'controversies', big and small, involving Whitehall, it is imperative to hold a solid and united front. Nothing must ever be said which might remotely suggest that anyone has even the slightest doubt about any aspect of the authorized version of events. (Just think of WMD ready in forty-five minutes.) As already implied, this commandment hardly ever needs formal promulgation because, through intellectual osmosis, Whitehall minds learn to think alike. And if a choice *must* be made, departmental loyalty will win over objective truth. If that last sentence is thought to be too sweeping, consider any of the charades in this book.

Yet the reality is that there *are* civil servants (there must be) who have consciences. After all, these people are not fools. Indeed, at home in Bromley or Surbiton they are thoroughly decent citizens – even if inclined to some minor pomposities. They are good neighbours who serve on the PTA, who fill in their tax returns with meticulous honesty, and who would chase after you if you dropped a £5 note. Nevertheless, at work, if any one of them harboured doubts and suggested that, as a consequence of an agreed 'line to take', they might collectively be working themselves into a morally untenable position, it would be seen – by most of those other thoroughly decent citizens – as subversive and rocking the boat. That is a powerful disincentive to the questioning of received wisdoms, big or small. So, for example, among the several MOD audiences summoned to listen to the Chinook 'presentations' given by the Air Marshals, it is a fair bet that no one took the risk of asking why some of those illustrative slides were so misleading. Yet to suppose that no one noticed the inaccuracy is to presume a very low level of intelligence among those audiences.

Thus while the policy of 'collective responsibility' is usually thought of as applying to decisions taken at cabinet level, it is also an imperative up and down the bureaucracies of Whitehall. Clive Ponting's real sin was less to do with telling the truth than with the fact that he let the side down. In blowing his whistle he had broken the rules; he had not identified tightly enough with the interests of his ministers and his colleagues. Loyalty (or its variant, 'collective responsibility') is an admirable quality – until it blocks the uncovering of an injustice or an untruth. One man's concerned whistle-blower is another man's dishonourable grass. *Problème.*

In a parallel dilemma, where should one place Colette Bowe in what the *Sun* called 'The Chopper Whopper'? During the infamous Westland Affair in 1986, this well-regarded press officer of the DTI was ordered to leak a copy of a letter that the Solicitor-General had just sent to Michael Heseltine, the Minister of Defence. The letter suggested Heseltine had been too optimistic, inaccurate even, in some parts of his 'prospectus' of a European future for Westland, the only British helicopter manufacturer. Who ordered the leak is still debated. But Number 10, who favoured an American connection for Westland, was not going to stand in the way of Heseltine getting his comeuppance – via a leak. And Leon Brittan, the Minister at the DTI (whose copy of the letter was leaked) would have thoroughly appreciated that point. However, secretly releasing a confidential paper to the press, even when ordered to do so, was against all Bowe's instincts and training. She sought advice but she could not find any of her bosses (where had they gone?). So in the end, and with great reluctance, she did as she was told. The row was immediate. The Solicitor-General Sir Patrick Mayhew was furious and pointed at a clear breach of the Official Secrets Act. Sir Robert Armstrong, the Cabinet Secretary, was instructed to get to the bottom of the tangle. Bowe insisted on immunity before she would answer his questions. But the questions that really mattered were ones that were never really asked. First, who had let whose side down? And second, when is a leak not a leak? The answer to the latter seems to be that a leak is not a leak when it is a ministerial expediency. In which case, it becomes 'an unattributable release'. Or a 'designer divulgence'? They happen all the time. And hang the Official Secrets Act. The inconsistency is not atypical.

Collective allegiance to an 'agreed line' is a Whitehall necessity. Indeed, it is an imperative so strong that it can reach back far into the past – well beyond the point where one might think even Whitehall could suppose there was still any need for it. It is this that makes the ancient history of HMS *Glorious* relevant. One might think that something that happened so long ago could be viewed by the present-day authorities with complete objectivity. After all, this long afterwards there can be no issues of policy still to be defended. All the participants are long gone, so reputations or embarrassments hardly enter into it. To all but a very few, the subject is not even of academic interest. In short, there seem to be none of the factors that can sometimes get in the way of admitting, at the least, a few uncertainties.

Why so stubborn, then? Part of the reason must be 'collective allegiance' again – a perceived need to maintain an unbroken continuity between then and now, no matter how long ago 'then' was. Again, it seems to be the case that any deviation, no matter how slight, from a long-standing and authorized account is seen as betraying the 'line long-taken', and thereby erosive of the credibility of everyone involved – including those previous generations who, after all, may have worked in that same office and hung their hats on the same hooks. To suggest that anyone might have got any part of the story wrong would not only be disloyal to those who went before (mostly dead anyway), but also to another core Whitehall principle: never, unless caught red-handed, admit to doubt. Even then, rationalize and make smoke. Anyway, and this is really the point, if a line can be held so firmly on a matter of such long-past history, how much more firmly is it going to be held on contemporary controversies – 'histories' which still matter?

At the very heart of the problem is the difficulty that any institution has in changing any part of a decision (whether made days, weeks or decades before) without thereby admitting an earlier mistake. Not only is 'face' involved, but, within Whitehall's groupthink, second thoughts are too often held to demonstrate a weakening of resolve rather than a reappraisal of the facts. Again, once a 'line to take' has been cemented into place, any rethink is held to be letting the side down. These must be some of the answers to the question 'Why so stubborn?'

Obviously, it would be unfair to claim that Whitehall in general, or the MOD or the FO in particular, are uniquely governed by these tenets. All tribes – the Metropolitan Police, the BBC, Chelsea fans, Marks & Spencer, the Paras – develop their own groupthink and loyalties. It is why history – whether of a football match, a sales campaign, or a battle – is not what happened, but what people *think* happened. The particular problem with Whitehall is that, aided by the Loop, interpretations made by civil servants are especially powerful; their analyses are the authorized ones; their thinking is official, their pronouncements become encyclicals. Furthermore, there is the compounding factor of secrecy. It is often said that in very few of the world's democracies is official secrecy – far beyond any reasonable security needs – as ingrained as it is in Britain. Why?

Could the answer be that secrecy is very close to power? It is a desirable adjuvant in that it increases the potency of power by allowing it to operate with little or no braking interference from outside. Additionally, the possession of information denied to others is, in itself, a boost to a feeling of authority. And there does not seem much doubt that power and authority are seen by some people as desirable ends in themselves. So they probably play a part in the mental make-up of at least some of those who seek careers in the upper levels of the civil service.

Anyway, it is not surprising that in Whitehall there is general agreement that effective government is, almost by definition, closed government. The populace 'out there' need only know what Whitehall decides it needs to know – which is not much. Give them any more and they will want to set up public inquiries, or, at the least, they will expect answers to their questions. And then, before one can spell 'confidential', the dreaded media will be meddling and setting the agenda – which it is always trying to do anyway. That way lie all kinds of problems. So, revealing any official information (which can mean almost anything that those in command decide it means) without authority can lead to a damaged career. Or the sack. Or even the Old Bailey.

Of course, lip service is paid by almost all politicians to the idea of increasing the transparency of government – until they find themselves in office. At which point, nobbled by their senior staff – 'Oh, Minister, if only it were that easy' – they tend to go native.

This respect for closed doors runs deep in Whitehall. Any social psychologist will confirm that knowing that one is 'on the inside', and party to the confidences of a closed society, is a powerful glue. One is privy to information not available to ordinary civilians. Moreover, as a young civil servant, having yourself been through the initiation rite of signing the Official Secrets Act, you are now charged with keeping things that way. And, even further, you will have been subject to a security vetting and not found wanting. All this confirms what you thought about yourself when, in the first place, you passed the very difficult selection process to join the fast-stream of the executive grades. You are confirmed as one of the very brightest and best. You are trusted with information denied even to the House of Commons. No wonder you feel you are part of a sanctified elite, far more involved in the real governing of the nation than anyone, except, just maybe, a few ministers. And even ministers are only 'here today and gone tomorrow'. No wonder the sense of Us and Them is reinforced. No wonder there is a tendency towards arrogance – both personal and institutional.

The trouble with arrogance, even a whiff of it, is that it makes the acknowledgement of a mistake very difficult. Clever people know that they do not make mistakes. If they did, they would not be clever. Ergo: the idea that anyone in Whitehall might be wrong and that the ordinary citizen might be right is absurd.

So an early reaction to any public scepticism directed at official orthodoxies tends to be denial. Such is the confidence with which these denials are made, one is often persuaded that, though wrong-headed, they are nevertheless sincerely advanced; the civil servant really does believe what he is saying or writing. Or causing his minister to say or write. If he is capable of so deceiving himself, is it any surprise that he is quite put out when he fails to convince the public?

These sincere denials can result in some laughable situations. One such small but typical example arose recently when, more than forty years after the British nuclear tests in the Australian desert, a researcher from Dundee University was working through some old files in the National Archives in Canberra. Inside a 1956 file were papers marked 'Secret – Guard'. This was serious stuff. The papers concerned a group of about eighty servicemen – British, Australian and New Zealanders – who had been guinea-pigged onto the edge of the fallout zone of a nuclear device a few days after the explosion. Subsequent measurements evidently showed that a squad of Australians had received more than 'the maximum permissible radiation exposure'. It is claimed that some of them never really recovered. An Australian Army memo of the time explains the purpose of the test: 'The object was to discover what types of clothing would give best protection against radioactive contamination in conditions of warfare.' Evidently the Australians had been wearing a type of uniform that gave inadequate protection. Which, presumably, made the tests a success; after all, it was what they had been set up to find out. When in May 2001 the author suggested to the MOD that it might have been safer to have draped the clothing over coat hangers (with test patches or even Geiger counters hung inside), the answer was that 'soldiers were necessary because they sweat and move about. And that can make a difference.' Fair enough. But the MOD went on to say that the troops had not been subject to any unnecessary risk. 'We were testing the effects of very low level radiation fallout on clothing, not personnel.' Come again?

Obviously, no error of judgement was recognized – either in setting the parameters of the 1956 test or in the 2001 defence of it. It is this bombproof self-confidence in the face of logic that is both hair-raising and risible. One might call it the Infallibility Syndrome.

Infallibility characterizes a great many of Whitehall's answers to questions it does not think should be asked. The attitude works in close harness with another belief: the 'integrity of command'. This is really a military concept, but it seems to spill over into the senior grades of Whitehall. It would be easy to dismiss it as being in the same general area as the Divine Right of Kings or Papal Infallibility. But at the right time and place it has a much better rationale than either. In its simplest form, when military action is joined (or about to be joined), it allows a senior officer to give orders without having to justify himself. If time is pressing, he just has to be trusted. Besides which, justification (or lack of it) will come soon enough – in success or failure, victory or defeat. At its crudest the concept has a strong element of 'Yours not to reason why . . .'. It is when this thinking is transferred to less urgent times that problems accumulate (in its Whitehall guise, it might be called the 'omniscience of office'). The consequence is seen on those occasions when officials become thoroughly irritable and seek to get shot of inconvenient inquiries by seeming to say, 'By virtue of the authority vested in us, we're right and you're wrong. Now shut up.' The preceding pages have contained several examples of the attitude – not least in the Chinook saga.

Whitehall resents having to explain itself. The reasons merge with each other. But, surely, one explanation stands above most others: the admission of error is thought to diminish the authority of the organization (or the person) making that admission; it dents the integrity of command. The consequence is that the organization, particularly if it is an organization of government for which 'authority' (or power) is all important, will go to almost any lengths to rubbish anything that might erode what it sees as its credibility and effectiveness. This in turn means that it will resort to all kinds of stratagems (SODEMs) to deny or disguise a mistake. Not least among them is the cover-up.

Lastly, anyone who has 'debated' an issue with Whitehall will recognize one recurring tactic. When one quotes from an article in, say, a scientific journal or cites expert evidence that casts doubt on a Whitehall fact or, indeed, a whole narrative, one will be told that the author of the article or the evidence has a hidden motive – they have their 'own agenda'. The implication seems to be that their motive is entirely self-serving, and therefore their conclusions should be ignored. Yes, of course there are people 'out there' who have motives that do not always meet the eye. But it is the almost automatic suggestion that *anyone* who questions official conclusions is propelled by questionable motives that is improper. The obvious fact is that we all have our 'own agendas'. And that includes, most obviously of all, ministers, civil servants and ministerial press officers. Indeed, one might claim that they are actually paid to have their own agendas. For any of them to pretend that they alone are solely fuelled by wholly disinterested objectives is absurd.

No doubt any Whitehall worker who has reached this far in this book (a doubtful proposition) will point to it, in part or in whole, as clear evidence that the author has his own agenda and that he is, to boot, a conspiracy theorist. He can, therefore, be disregarded. Which, in a way, is where I came in.

ACKNOWLEDGEMENTS

The word 'acknowledgements' sounds rather formal and unappreciative. 'Gratitudes' would be better. I must thank so many people who gave me so many hours of their time. And then, very often, the next day, or the next week, they patiently welcomed me back for more. They allowed me to pick their brains on everything from the mores of Whitehall to the aerodynamics of helicopters, from parliamentary procedures to naval fuelling practices in World War II. They let me use *their* research, to look through *their* files and to tap into *their* direct and first-hand experiences. In short, they lent me their expertise. Furthermore, and just as valuable, by their interest and support they encouraged me to think that I was not wasting my time. Or theirs. But for all that, when they now read what I have written, I do not know if they will approve. I hope they do.

In the names that follow, I have left out decorations and honours – to keep the list rolling. And, to be honest, because I am frightened of missing something out. All the servicemen are now retired: Admiral Sir Louis Le Bailly, Olivier Bancoult, Ben Barker, Captain Nick Barker, Steven Barker, Dave Bartlett, Rt Hon. Alan Beith MP, Martin Bell, Malcolm Brown, Frederick Butcher, Sqn Ldr Robert Burke, Larry Cammock, Colonel Brian Carter, Commander John Casson, Lord Chalfont, Captain John Cook, Commander David Corkhill, Geoffrey Cox, Air Marshal Sir Kenneth Cross, Tam Dalyell MP, Sally Francis, Richard Gifford, Sqn Ldr Charles Gillow, Sir Harry Hinsley, Professor Malcolm Hooper, Captain Vernon Howland, Trevor Jenkins, William Jurens, Captain Barry Kent, Quaiser Khanzada, Dr Tom Koeze, Captain Ralph Kohn, Ulf Larsstuvold, Dr Simon Lennane, Commander Robert McBride, Rolf Monteith, Flt Lt John Nichol, Matthew Parris, Malcolm Perks, Clive Ponting, Mike Ramsden, Stanley Rogers, Dr Douglas Rokke, Nicholas Roskill, Shaun and Maria Rusling, Captain Michael Russell, Michael Shaw, Ralph Slocombe, Commander Badger Smith, Major Milos Stankovic, Michael Tapper, General Julian Thompson, Georgie Vestey, John Winton, Daniel Wolf and Admiral Sir John Woodward.

In a slightly different direction, I must thank five friends: David Harrison, David Heycock, Edward Mirzoeff, Nick Ross and Anthony Smith. They read much of what I had written and allowed me to bounce ideas at and off them. Their advice was often trenchant; it was always useful.

I must also thank the staffs of Southfields Public Library, the Public Records Office, the Churchill Archive Centre, the Imperial War Museum Library, the Fleet Air Arm Officers' Association, the BBC's News Information Centre, the Copyright Department of HMSO and *Private Eye.* Further, it would be churlish not to acknowledge a debt to D.B. and C.P. – two inhabitants of Whitehall who, quite unwittingly, provided much of the start-up stimulus for this book.

There are two other people to whom I owe a particular debt. The first is Hannah Tausz of Aurum Press, who, on the strength of a synopsis and a chapter that I sent her unannounced and 'un-agented', then phoned back and asked to see 'the rest'. What she does not know (until she reads this) is that several other publishers had already turned me away – 'too contentious' or just 'not commercial'. But now I can look back on those rejections as honourable, even meritorious citations. I hope that I have not let her down.

Lastly, there is my wife, Janet. It can't have been much fun to have me disappear up to the back room for (seemingly) days on end. On second thoughts, it may have been the very abatement she needed. Anyway, the only occasions when she became just a little short were when my word-processor misbehaved and the surrounding air then became both loud and expletive. At all other times she was extraordinarily patient, supportive and encouraging.

What neither of us could know when that last paragraph was written was that she would die just a few weeks after the original hardback was published. The book and the work that went into it are dedicated to her.

BIBLIOGRAPHY

The Whitehall Loop

This chapter is, as the preceding Preface implies, the distillation of research into the stories that follow. After a while, a pattern emerges of both the style and techniques employed by Whitehall to rebut criticism. Beyond that, confirmation of the pattern can be found in a variety of books on recent or contemporary political history. The list that follows is in no way systematic.

Alder, J., *Constitutional and Administrative Law*, Macmillan, 1994.

Barker, A., *Practising to Deceive: Whitehall, Arms Export and the Scott Inquiry*, Political Quarterly, 1997.

Bell, M., *An Accidental MP*, Viking, 2000.

Campbell, J., *The Liar's Tale*, W.W. Norton, 2001.

Cliffe, Ramsay and Bartlett, *The Politics of Lying*, Macmillan, 2000.

Curtiss, L., *Ireland: The Propaganda War*, Pluto, 1984.

Elliot, M., *Mad Cows and Englishmen*, BBC2, February and March 1998.

Geraghty, T., *The Irish War*, HarperCollins, 1998.

Gavshon and Rice, *The Sinking of the Belgrano*, Secker & Warburg, 1984.

Harden and Lewis, *The Noble Lie: The Constitution and the Rule of Law*, Hutchinson, 1986.

Hooper, D., *Official Secrets: The Use and Abuse of the Act*, Secker & Warburg, 1987.

Ingham, B., *Kill the Messenger*, Fontana, 1991.

Leigh, D., *Betrayed: The Real Story of the Matrix Churchill Trial*, Bloomsbury, 1993.

Michael, J., *The Politics of Secrecy and the Public Right to Know*, Penguin, 1982.

Nolan, Lord, *Report of the Committee on Standards in Public Life*, HMSO, 1995.

Ponting, C., *The Right to Know: The Inside Story of the Belgrano Affair*, Sphere Books, 1985.

Pyper, R., *The British Civil Service*, Prentice-Hall, 1995.

Rawnsley, A., *Servants of the People*, Hamish Hamilton, 2000; Penguin paperback edition published 2001.

Rogers, A., *Secrecy and Power in the British State*, Pluto, 1997.

Scott, R., *Report of the Inquiry into the Export of Defence Equipment to Iraq*, HMSO, 1996.

Staler, J., *Stalker*, Harrap, 1988.

Stanley, M., *How to be a Civil Servant*, Politicos, 2000.

Hutton, Kelly, Gilligan and All That

The material for this chapter was primarily found in the daily transcripts of the proceedings of the Hutton Inquiry. Beyond that, there was a vast amount of contemporary (and useful) media comment. A very useful collection of Hutton Inquiry transcripts can be found in *The Hutton Inquiry* by Tim Coates, a self-published book available from Littlehampton Book Services.

The Ilois

The research for this chapter derives from a number of interviews, books and articles; to that extent, as elsewhere in this book, I have had to rely on other people for much of the raw data. Some letters and papers are unpublished. Particularly valuable (and revealing) have been the 1967–72 BIOT files of the Foreign and Commonwealth Office. These were 'released' in response to the legal process which eventually led to a High Court hearing of the Ilois' action again the FO before Lord Justice Laws in the summer of 2000. Copies of those files were made available to me by (and at) Sheridans solicitors. I must thank Richard Gifford, the solicitor who, over the years, must have spent hundreds of hours working on behalf of the Ilois. Gratitude is also due to Tam Dalyell for his advice; he first raised the issues back in 1968 and has been pursuing them in Parliament and beyond ever since. And I also owe my thanks to Olivier Bancoult, around whom the Ilois' action against the FO in 2000 was centred.

Edis, Richard, *The Peaks of Limuria*.
Hansard, 9 January 2001.
Madely, John, *Diego Garcia – a contrast to the Falklands*, The Minority Rights Group, 1985.
Scott, Sir Robert, *Limuria*, OUP, 1961.
Sylva, Herve, *The Sylva Report – the condition of those displaced from the Chagos*, Port Louis, Mauritius, 1981.
Winchester, Simon, *Outposts*, Hodder & Stoughton, 1985.

Besides a seminal article by David Ottaway in the *Washington Post* of 9 September 1975, there were several newspaper articles in British broadsheets during the third week of July 2000, when the Ilois' legal action came to court and, again, in early November when Lord Justice Laws found for the Ilois.

The *Belgrano*

There are, of course, no significant files about the Falklands conflict yet released. This chapter is therefore drawn in part from a number of accounts in books and articles. Additional information has been gathered from *Hansard* for various relevant dates. But other than these sources, the author has discussed and been in correspondence with a number of participants in the conflict, including Admiral Sir John (Sandy) Woodward, Major General Julian Thompson RM, and, before he died, Captain Nick Barker RN. On the civilian side, I have also had discussions with Clive Ponting, Tam Dalyell and several others, who for various reasons prefer to remain anonymous. I am very grateful to them all for their help, but I have no idea whether any of them agree or disagree with my various interpretations or conclusions.

A number of books cover aspects of the *Belgrano* affair and/or its aftermath. They include the following:

Dalyell, Tam, *One Man's Falklands*, Cecil Woolf, 1982.
Dalyell, Tam, *Thatcher's Torpedo*, Cecil Woolf, 1982.
Hansard, particularly for 3 and 29 April 1982; 4, 5 and 13 May 1982, 12 and 18 February 1985.
Hastings, Max and Jenkins, Simon, *The Battle for the Falklands*, Michael Joseph, 1993.
Heseltine, Michael, *Life in the Jungle*, Hodder & Stoughton, 2000.
Middlebrook, Martin, *The Falklands War*, revised edition, Penguin, 2001.
Nott, John, *Here Today, Gone Tomorrow*, Politicos, 2002.
Ponting, Clive, *The Right to Know*, Sphere, 1985.
Rice, Desmond and Gavshon, Arthur, *The Sinking of Belgrano*, Secker & Warburg, 1984.
Thatcher, Margaret, *The Downing Street Years*, HarperCollins, 1993.
The *Sunday Times* Insight team, *The Falklands War*, André Deutsch, 1982.
Woodward, Admiral 'Sandy', *One Hundred Days*, HarperCollins, 1992.

Chinook – Zulu Delta 576

The contents of this chapter are derived from many sources. In addition to a wealth of documents, reports, papers and letters, some going back to the time of the crash, some even earlier, there are a large number of experts in aviation, avionics and, of course, helicopters who have allowed me to take up their time, and who have frequently followed through with subsequent letters and advice. Many of these people are featured in the text. Without their help, I could not have begun. I thank them. Others, perhaps still serving, have advised me as far as they have felt able. I thank them, too. To one person I owe a particular debt; over the years, David Harrison has assembled a library on almost everything that has been written, official and unofficial, about ZD576. He has given me complete access. He has also given me many hours of his time. Written sources, official and unofficial, include the following:

Aerospace International (The Royal Aeronautical Society, particularly the correspondence columns for the issues of April and July 1998; December 2000; August, September, and October 2000).
Collins, Tony, 'RAF Justice', *Computer Weekly*, May 1999.
Hansard, Commons Debate, 19 March 2002.
Mull of Kintyre Group, *A Review of the Chinook Accident*, August 2000.
A reply to the above by the MOD.
Ramsden, J.M., *Chinook Doubts – a Plain Person's Guide*, 20 Townsend Drive, St Albans, Hertfordshire.
Russell, Captain Michael, *A Professional Pilot's Assessment* (published privately).
Tench, W.H., *A Study of Aircraft Accident Procedures in the Armed Forces*, January 1987.
The Report of the Air Accident Investigation Board (AAIB).
The Report of the RAF Board of Inquiry (BOI).
The Transcript of the Scottish Fatal Accident Inquiry (FAI).
The Determination of the FAI by Sheriff Sir Stephen Young.
The MacDonald, Kohn and Hadlow Paper on Chinook ZD576 (published privately).
Proceedings of House of Commons Select Committee on Defence, 4 March 1998.
Proceedings of House of Commons Select Committee on Public Accounts, 8 March 2000.
Proceedings of House of Lords Select Committee on Chinook ZD576, Autumn 2001 (8 November 2001 and 31 January 2002).
Final Report of House of Lords Select Committee on Chinook ZD576, 31 January 2002.
National Audit Office, Controller General's Report, 11 February 2000.
Claimant's Post-hearing Brief American Commercial Arbitration Tribunal, 1 June 1995.

Gulf War Syndrome

While there are not many books about Gulf War Illnesses, there are several hundred reports, pamphlets and papers on every aspect of the subject. Among the wealth of official and semi-official documents are the press releases, statements and rebuttals put out by the MOD and the US DOD, the minutes of evidence gathered by Parliamentary and Congressional Committees, memoranda originating from various military arms, submissions authored by numerous veterans' groups and their advisors, and, above all, a seemingly endless number of investigative papers by medical research teams and individuals all over the world. At the unofficial end of the spectrum there have been a vast number of journalistic endeavours; some are more rigorous than others, some are stronger on human interest than they are on science. But all (well, nearly all) make interesting reading. Lastly, there are the unpublished comments (in letters and in conversation) of servicemen and women (including doctors) 'who were there'. I thank everyone for their advice. Particularly, I thank Professor Malcolm Hooper who has helped me (very much a non-scientist) to understand some of the more difficult issues.

I readily admit that I have been able to read (let alone absorb) only a minute proportion of the many millions of words which seem to be available. Most of the sources of specific information quoted in the chapter are indicated in the text. What follows here is a rather arbitrary selection of information that seems to have a prime bearing on this difficult and contentious subject. As implied, it is absolutely not exhaustive.

Coker, Wing Cdr *et al.*, 'Clinical findings for first 1000 Gulf Veterans in the MOD assessment programme', *British Medical Journal*, 1999.

Eddington, Pat, *Gassed in the Gulf*, Insignia Publishing, 1997.

Golomb, Prof. B., *Pyridostigmine Bromide and Gulf Veterans*, Rand Corp., October 1999.

Gulf War Veterans' Association, 'Depleted Uranium', a paper by Prof. M. Hooper. October 1999.

Gulf War Veterans' Association, *A Help Guide*, 1998.

Haley, Prof. R.W., *et al.*, 'Is there a Gulf War Syndrome?', *Journal of American Medical Association*, 1997.

House of Commons Defence Committee: scientific submissions by the two main UK Veterans' Groups (December 1999). Includes a detailed submission by Prof. M. Hooper, scientific advisor to Gulf Veterans' Association.

Institute of Naval Medicine, Radiological Protection Service, *DU, Personal Protection* (undated).

Jamal, Prof., *et al.*, 'Dysfunction in the Nervous System', *Journal of Neurology*, 1996.

Korenyi-Both, Col. (Surgeon), *Eskan Disease, an explanation of Gulf Syndrome*, Gulf War Research Center, Washington, September 2000.

McManners, Hugh, *The Scars of War*, HarperCollins, 1993.

MOD, *Policy on Gulf Veterans' Illnesses* (a succession of bulletins on www.mod.uk/gulfwar).

MOD, *Gulf Veterans' Illnesses: Information Pack* (primarily designed for GPs), January 2001.

MOD, *Report on The Al Jubayl incident of 19 January 1991* (published 20 January 2000).

House of Commons Defence Committee – evidence to and recommendations by the Committee, November 1995.

MOD, the Government's reply to the above, 30 January 1996.

MOD, numerous answers (twenty-five-plus) to Parliamentary Questions put by the Countess of Mar from 1991 to 1996.

Nicolson, Prof. Garth, 'Gulf War Illnesses – Causes and Treatments', Institute for Molecular Medicine (Huntington Beach, California).
Rook, G. and Zumala, A., 'Gulf War Syndrome, is it due to a systemic shift in cytokine balance?', *Lancet*, 1997.
Schwartz, Prof., 'Health among Gulf War Veterans', *Journal of American Medical Association*, 1997.
Stead, C.F., *Oil Fires, Petroleum and Gulf War Illness* (paper), Putney, Vermont, February 1999.
Thomas, William, *Bringing the War Home*, Earthpulse Press, 1998.
UK Army, *Depleted Uranium, expended rounds, decontamination procedures.*
Unwin, C. *et al.*, 'Health of UK servicemen who served in Gulf War', *Lancet*, 1999.
US Army, *Depleted Uranium, expended rounds, health concerns* (an internal memo), 8 March 1991.
US Institute of Medicine, *Gulf War and Health: DU, Sarin, PB, Vaccines*, September 2000.
Various directives and signals issued by Director Land Service Ammunition in early 1991.

HMS *Glorious, Ardent* and *Acasta*

The contents of this chapter are drawn from many sources – books, official and unofficial files and reports, interviews and correspondence. The relevant Admiralty files are now all available at the PRO; the last ones were 'released' in 1993. The more directly relevant include:

ADM1/19984 – Report on the loss of HMS *Glorious*
ADM1/21251 – Board of Inquiry minutes
ADM1/19910 – Official translations of German documents
ADM53/112339 – *Glorious*'s log for March 1940
ADM53/111433/34 – *Ark Royal*'s logs for May/June 1940
ADM53/112009 – *Devonshire*'s log for June 1940
ADM199/361 – Home Fleet War Diary (Chronology)
ADM199/393 – Home Fleet War Diary (Despatch)
ADM199/478 – Includes reports on *Glorious*'s survivors
ADM199/2205/6 – Admiralty War Diaries for May/June 1940
HW14/7 – GS & CS (Bletchley Park)

A very useful file is that put together by Captain Stephen Roskill DSC, the Navy's one-time official war historian, during the course of his research in the 1970s into the circumstances surrounding the loss of *Glorious*, *Ardent* and *Acasta*. The file contains letters and comments from a number of (by then) senior officers who had served alongside those involved. The file is part of the Roskill Papers in the Churchill Archive Centre at Churchill College in Cambridge. This file has recently been augmented by papers, tapes and notes collected by John Winton (see below) following his death in early 2001.

The only book which deals with the *Glorious* affair at length is John Winton's *Carrier Glorious* (Leo Cooper/Secker & Warburg 1986). However, because the book was written before all the Admiralty (ADM) files were released to the PRO, there are some omissions – particularly in the contentious areas of signals sent and received, and of intelligence about German warship movements.

A host of other publications touch to a greater or lesser degree on the events under discussion. The most interesting include:

Austin, John and Carter, Nick, *The Man Who Hit Scharnhorst*, Seeley Service, 1973.
Broome, Capt. Jack, *Make a Signal!*, Putnam, 1955.
Brown, David (ed.), *Naval Operations of the Campaign in Norway*, Frank Cass, 2000 (originally printed as an Admiralty confidential book in 1951).
Churchill, Sir Winston, *The Gathering Storm*, Cassell & Co., 1948.
Cross, Air Chief Marshal Sir Kenneth and Orange, Vincent, *Straight and Level*, Grub Street, 1993.
Garrett, Richard, *Scharnhorst and Gneisenau*, David & Charles, 1978.
Healiss, Ronald, *Adventure Glorious*, Muller, 1955.
Hinsley, Sir Harry, *The Official History of British Intelligence in WW2*, HMSO, 1979.
Hinsley, Sir Harry and Stripp, Alan (eds), *Codebreakers*, OUP, 1993.
MacIntyre, Capt. Donald, *Narvik*, Evans Bros, 1959.
Parkes, Oscar, *Ships of the Royal Navies*, Sampson Low, Marston, 1936.
Roskill, Capt. Stephen, *The War at Sea 1939–45. Vol 1* [the official history], HMSO, 1954.
Roskill, Capt. Stephen, *Churchill and the Admirals*, Collins, 1977.
Roskill, Capt. Stephen, 'The Cantankerous Captain', *Sunday Times*, 15 June 1980.
Thompson, Major General Julian, *The War at Sea*, Sidgwick & Jackson, 1996.
Sebag-Montefiore, Hugh, *Enigma*, Weidenfeld & Nicolson, 2000.
Winton, John, *Find, Fix and Strike*, Batsford, 1980.
Winton, John, *Carrier Glorious*, Leo Cooper/Secker & Warburg, 1986.
Butcher, Fred, *An analysis of Glorious' WT signals*, 10 Harbourside, Tewkesbury, GL20 5DT.
Hansard contains relevant references (parliamentary questions and answers, debates, etc.) on the following dates: 31 July, 21 August, 24 October and 7 November 1940; 8 May 1946; 19 March 1947; 28 January 1999 – the latter is the Adjournment Debate referred to at the beginning of the chapter.
The latest MOD account is lodged in the House of Commons Library under the title *The Loss of HMS Glorious, Ardent and Acasta – Points of Controversy*, dated August 1997, amended February 1999.

A Soldier's Story

This chapter is primarily based on conversations with Milos Stankovic and his lawyers, Steven Barker and Quaiser Khanzada. And, of course, an essential source has been Milos Stankovic's own book about his service in Bosnia, *Trusted Mole*. Indeed, where Bosnia is concerned, the contents of this chapter are only a washed-out version of the real thing as recounted in that book. Other books that have added to my understanding (and sometimes to my confusion) are listed below.

I have been asked if I have sought the views of the MOD or their Police – 'the other side'. The short answer is that I have not, because there seemed no point in it. Martin Bell recounts in a chapter of his book, *An Accidental MP*, how he visited the Chief Constable of the force – to no avail whatsoever. As for the MOD itself, they would be no more forthcoming in reply to a letter of enquiry than their various ministers have been to a number of Parliamentary Questions.

Bell, Martin, *An Accidental MP*, Viking, 2000.
Bell, Martin, *In Harm's Way*, Hamish Hamilton, 1995.
Glenny, Mischa, *The Balkans 1804–1999*, Granta, 1999.
Magas, Branka, *The Destruction of Jugoslavia*, Verso, 1993.
Owen, Lord (David), *Balkan Odyssey*, Gollancz, 1995.
Panorama, BBC TV, 23 January 1995, 'General Rose's War', reporter: John Simpson.
Rose, General Sir Michael, *Fighting for Peace*, Harvill Press, 1998.
Simms, Brendan, *Unfinest Hour – Britain and the Destruction of Bosnia*, Allen Lane, 2001.
Stankovic, Milos, *Trusted Mole*, HarperCollins, 2000.

A Marine's Story

This chapter is based on several long interviews with Colonel Carter. Additionally, I have had access to his and his solicitor's files on the affair; the files contained statements and letters from all the main players – including the statements from the Defence Attaché, the Minister, the Ambassador and other FO personnel. Letters of enquiry were subsequently written to the three main 'Peking players'. If I had thought it might have been fruitful, I would have been in direct touch with the Foreign Office. But, given that the FO had preferred to look the other way from the beginning (and one well knew the answer one would be given), there seemed to be no point in going in that direction.

INDEX